The Magnetic Labyrinth

John Baldan

Copyright © 2021 by John Baldan
Second Edition
ISBN 978-0-578-57933-7

All rights reserved. No part of this book may be reproduced or transmitted in any form or by any means, electronic or mechanical, including photocopying, recording, or by any information storage and retrieval system, without permission in writing from the publisher.

Published by Upper Right-Hand Corner LLC
Cover photography by Carol Baldan

Contact the author at thegoingplacesclub@gmail.com
Additional information at www.thegoingplacesclub.com

Dedication

I dedicate this book to the composers of the soundtrack of my life. I have quoted many of their lyrics in these pages. It would be impossible to name them all, but any hall of fame would have to include:

Laurie Anderson, Billy Bragg, Peter Blegvad, Chris Butler, David Byrne, Elvis Costello, Jonathan Coulton, Chris Difford, Thomas Dolby, Stephen Duffy, Donald Fagen, Neil Finn, John Flansburgh, Roddy Frame, Graham Gouldman, Neil Hannon, Sara Hickman, Robyn Hitchcock, Peter Holsapple, Joe Jackson, John Lennon, John Linnell, David Lowery, Kirsty MacColl, Paddy McAloon, Paul McCartney, David Mead, Scott Miller, Joni Mitchell, Martin Newell, Gilbert O'Sullivan, Andy Partridge, Brian Protheroe, Kimberley Rew, Amy Rigby, Adam Schlesinger, Michael Shelley, Jill Sobule, Wesley Stace, Michael Stipe, James Taylor, Glenn Tilbrook, Suzanne Vega, Loudon Wainwright III, James Warren, Jimmy Webb, Susan Werner, Brian Wilson, Brian Woodbury, "Weird Al" Yankovic

And not forgetting the one-hit wonders, the ones who had one great song in them, who by sharing it made the world a richer place.

This book is also dedicated to everyone for whom I have ever made a mix tape. I must have wanted to impress you.

I especially dedicate this book to Carol, my wife. I knew that one day I would win the heart of a good woman with music.

Finally, I dedicate this book to the people who started it all: Dad, who introduced me to melody through the medium of eight-track tape; and Mom, who bought me my first record albums.

Side A (Penny Lane)

1. Whatever It's Called 1
2. The Life Force 5
3. Viva Las Vegas! 15
4. Irony/Virtualization 25
5. Right Field 37
6. Dream One 44
7. Sonata for Jukebox 46
8. Sing We Now of Christmas! 61
9. Magic Realism 73
10. Dream Two 96
11. Monsieur Proust 98
12. Labyrinth 111
13. The Lost Art of Wasting Time 116
14. Stars and Stripes 138
15. Dream Three 142
16. Inventory 145
17. Wheatland County 159
18. Roman Numerals 168
19. Alone Again (Untruthfully) 184
20. Game Six 189

Side B (Strawberry Fields Forever)

1. How to Play Guitar 203
2. Radio Days 212
3. Rhiannon 223
4. Dream Four 231
5. The West Village 233
6. My New England 256
7. Searching for Dolphins 263
8. Colleen 268
9. Dream Five 281
10. Flatland 283
11. My Body 286
12. The Class of '81 300
13. Communications Breakdown 311
14. Dream Six 321
15. Great Results of Mathematics 324
16. Correlation and Causation 358
17. Still on the Line 374
18. Dream Seven 384
19. (Bonus Tracks) 388

In "Beautiful Boy," John Lennon sang:

Life is what happens to you while you're busy making other plans.

For me, it would be more accurate to sing:

Life is what happens when you aren't paying attention, because you have something else, possibly a John Lennon song, stuck in your head.

Side A (Penny Lane)

Whatever It's Called

I love naming things.

I'm no virtuoso on guitar, but I'm prolific at naming rock bands. I've named my own a thousand times – and I'm sure that one of those names will come in handy on the day my band exists.

Ever since that pivotal moment of youth when I realized that musicians, unlike most of us, can call themselves whatever they like, I've been looking for the perfect band name. Every time I take a walk I think of two or three more. Unfortunately, I forget them before I get home.

Similarly, I've named this book a dozen times. Here at least, there is a paper trail. I first thought of calling it *Me*, to distinguish it from my first memoir, which was not about me; but that title felt like it belonged to Shirley MacLaine. At other times, I contemplated *The Corners of My Mind* (a nod to Michel Legrand, who recently departed this world to sing with angels even more celestial than the Swingle Singers) or *The Mind's Workshop*, or *Ideas for Living.* That last title, inspired by Georges Perec's remarkable novel *Life: A User's Manual*, sounded too much like a Martha Stewart magazine.

For a while, I went with *Preoccupations*. The epigraph hints at why. We spend too much time thinking about everything except what's right in front of us.

Then it was *The Mix Tape.* The book's "hook" would be my life-long mania for making impressions through music. *The Mix Tape*, mind you, not *Mix Tape* – the initial "the" makes a difference. As Paul McCartney once told Yoko Ono, who habitually called her husband's band "Beatles": "It's *The* Beatles, luv." This title made sense because I found that, as I collated chapters, I was unconsciously following time-tested mix tape principles which had become second nature: put the hit song right up front, modulate between fast and slow, and so on.

Finally, after I'd had my fun, my wife Carol stepped in, read the book, and came up with the perfect title for it, just as she'd done for my first book, *The Going Places Club*. Once again, she identified the chapter title ("Labyrinth") that should lend its name to the book. Then she made a connection: what, after all, is a cassette tape than a *magnetic labyrinth* – a path in Side A and out Side B, with enlightenment (hopefully) along the way? I bow to Carol's judgment. And I'm sure that when it comes time to name my band, she will do that, too.

The scope of this book also changed with time. I originally intended it to be strictly about music, with each chapter describing a memory triggered by a particular song. That was too limiting. If I'd followed through with that idea, though, I could have called it *Fakebook*, running the risk that musicians would get the reference and everyone else would just assume it was about social media, something I know nothing about.

This book is not exclusively about music, though there's much of that here. Actually, it's about anything or anyone I've ever fancied, provided they could be shoehorned into essays. Ah, essays – the unloved stepchild of literature which many of us were introduced to in high school, though admittedly in a straitjacketed version that could not accommodate our anarchic, adolescent thoughts. It didn't have to be that way.

In college, I took "Foundations of Western Thought," a survey of literature from antiquity to modernity. That's where I met Montaigne, the man who "invented" the essay in the sixteenth century. His *Collected Essays* was one of the few college texts that I did not sell to my hometown bookstore when I left school, because in Montaigne's hands the essay is weird and wonderful. If, in high school, I had submitted any one of his essays as my own work, I'm sure my grade would have been docked – not for plagiarism, but for disorderly thought.

For someone five hundred years old, Montaigne writes crisply and breezily on anything that strikes his fancy – drunkenness, vanity, thumbs – sometimes on a single page. His essays not only discourse and illustrate, but they argue, digress, ramble, and contradict themselves. I marveled, in my 1980s classroom, at how they had outlasted the centuries to come into my own hands. Each is larded with quotations, one or more to the page, many by authors of antiquity. You might think Montaigne summons such august ghosts to bolster a thorny argument, but you'd be wrong. The quotations, as often as not, add little to his line of reasoning.

I wondered if I might try something similar. But rather than quote antiquity, I'd stick to the scripture I most like to cite – song lyrics. To a large extent, they have formed my worldview. Carol, my partner in

Scrabble as well as life, will attest that almost all my vocabulary comes from pop music.

Montaigne, who assumed that we have more commonalities than differences, believed that by writing about himself, he could illuminate the human condition. His motto might have been, "Look within." When I do, I see that I have defined myself through hobbies, not jobs; through trivia, not politics or religion; and through books, films, and music, not society. The so-called unimportant stuff.

***

Before six a.m., the last scene of a dream wakes me, rescuing me from Carol's alarm clock.

Carol bought her infernal P'Jammer at the age of thirteen from a Bluefield, West Virginia Kmart. It sits smugly on the end table at her side of the bed, stolid, square, and secure in the knowledge that it has known her longer than I have, so I can't touch it. Once white, now off-white, its knobs still sport flecks of splashy 1980s colors: teal, lavender, raspberry creme. It still works, though the tuner is stuck on a frequency which, where we live, is occupied by an awful modern pop station. Before it blasts at six, I free myself of the bedcovers and stagger downstairs, hardly more functional than the P'Jammer, to begin my morning round.

I load the coffee grinder with beans. I fill the cats' saucers with kibble. I make sure I haven't reversed them. The kettle warms, and I rehearse each detail of my still vivid dream, fixing it before it fades. This is important, because our lives follow our dreams more closely than we know. That is why, at six o'clock, I am willing to lean over the kitchen counter and examine each facet of my dream like a jeweler at his bench, my reading glasses my loupe, my pen my tweezers. But first I need paper. I search the kitchen for something, anything, on which to write: a shopping pad, the back of a receipt, a sheet of stationery from a B&B where we once stayed – The Golden Plough Inn, The Inn at the Alameda, The Spruce Point Inn, some place where I failed to send a letter. I quickly jot down keywords that will enable me, later, to reconstruct the dream, as it came to me, by aligning them on a page like stepping stones across Lethe's river, like the dark supermarket floor tiles I once skipped across with my siblings Frankie and Robbie in an attempt to avoid being swept away by "white hot lava."

In my first book, *The Going Places Club*, I quoted my father, an eminent philosopher and man-about-town. Twenty-five years ago, he and I were dining at the Warszawa, an elegant Polish restaurant in Santa Monica. I poked at my beef aspic – something I have not ordered since – and Dad said:

"When you talk with someone, keep the conversation focused on them. They'll think you're more interesting if you do."

He added:

"Besides, you already know about yourself."

I wonder. I'd like to think that in fifty-plus years, I have a little self-knowledge. It's been over a thousand years since the invention of the venerable beef aspic, and over two thousand since a philosopher chiseled, in a cavern in the Temple of Apollo atop Mount Parnassus, the words: "Know thyself," in time for Socrates to elaborate, "The unexamined life is not worth living."

Sorry, Dad. Despite your well-meaning advice, I *will* monopolize the conversation here. This book is about me, and all the disorder that entails. Most chapters are set in the past – some long past, others more recent. Some chapters discuss art, others mathematics. Some describe people, others dreams. They can be read independently, though I've arranged them, like songs on a mix tape, in what I hope is an illuminating order. Together, they offer a tour of the labyrinth (landscape, workshop, forge, windmill) of my mind.

The point being, when I'm gone, someone should be able to pick up this book and say:

"So, that's what he was like!"

The Life Force

She said sex is the opposite of death
It's alright child, it's natural, it's wild
It's just the life force
      - The Roches, "Maid of the Seas"

For five years, Carol and I lived near the vital core of Manhattan, when it had one. Before and after, we lived across the glassy Hudson in Hoboken, New Jersey, the fourth most densely populated town in America, even more thickly inhabited than New York City.

We lived on West Thirteenth Street in the newly chic Meatpacking District. Its cobblestones were hosed to a luster not by the blood-stained, aproned butcher boys of yore but by lackeys of developers who swanned in with the High Line, the defunct elevated railroad spur that had been refurbished into a lushly landscaped pedestrian mall.

Our apartment building faced historic Gansevoort Street, named after a grandfather of Herman Melville. At its foot, by the docks, Melville had worked in a customs office, a has-been. Now it was *primo* hipster territory. Our first year there, if we happened to get out early, we might see some ladies of the night, buxom women in tight-fitting, neon-colored, spandex dresses, at the corner bodega for a pick-me-up (coffee). A year later they'd been replaced by willowy, underdressed young things teetering on heels, negotiating not only the cobblestones but the lingering effects of the cosmopolitans they'd consumed the night before.

Our bedroom faced the rear of our apartment building, which meant that the living room, though quiet, lacked interesting views. At the top of one window we could see a sliver of the disembodied needle of the Empire State Building rising above a jumble of walls, windows, and weeds littered with drywall buckets and abandoned construction supplies. To see more required a trip to the lobby and the sidewalk beyond, where one turn in any direction put you in the mix.

In contrast, our Hoboken apartment surveyed, from the height of a dozen floors, a maze of alleys like those of an excavated city, like Pompeii. To walk past the old shopfronts lining those canals where sunlight penetrated with difficulty was to wonder if their owners were being punished by the gods. For Hoboken, too, had a long history: it was the birthplace of Frank Sinatra (who left as a young man, never to look back), Maxwell House coffee, and baseball (though Cooperstown, New York got the credit). And for years it was home to a thriving music scene: many record albums in my collection had been recorded by bands who had at one time either lived in town, performed at its famous club, Maxwell's, or cut records there.

> *Man on the phone says, I ain't jokin*
> *Would youse ever come and play for us out in Hoboken?*
> - Black 47, "Green Suede Shoes"

Hoboken hummed day and night, except weekend mornings when residents – mostly young professionals - slept off hangovers they'd contracted on its bar-and-restaurant strip, Washington Street. Its sidewalks thronged with commuters going to and from the train station. And late at night, if I focused on exactly the right point of the bedroom window from an aerie of propped-up bed pillows, I could admire a pointillist image of taillights belonging to a frozen line of cars a mile away, on the helix of the Lincoln Tunnel. I watched their glacial advance with *schadenfreude*. It was better than the local traffic channel on Friday afternoons, when everyone tried to simultaneously leave town, and even better than a sudden downpour, when I would assume my post at the living room windows to see kids half my age, too cool for umbrellas, run like lemmings as fast as their gym-toned legs could carry them.

But people watching was better in Manhattan. It was a play with a more varied cast. Look at them all! The pizza guy in his charcoal-stained apron stepping out from his tiny joint beloved of Julianne Moore (if one was to believe the cheaply-framed, yellowing newspaper clipping on the wall) for a drag; the delivery guy unchaining his bicycle; the shoulder-strapped courier stopping short in the bike lane for a housewife lifting a double-width stroller over the curb. Here, a twenty-something gal with spiky hair, nose ring, and yoga mat; there, a button-down businessman broadcasting his side of a Bluetooth-enabled phone call to the world; everywhere, livery drivers impatiently nudging my thighs with their front bumpers as I crossed gridlocked intersections.

When Carol and I lived in the West Village, I would take late afternoon strolls in the West Forties, along Ninth Avenue. Hell's Kitchen had just been rediscovered by developers, so construction was rampant. At one job site, a group of picketers protesting labor injustice had dwindled over time until they were down to one sad-looking man offering leaflets that no one wanted.

But then he got a comrade, a twenty-foot inflatable gray rat. Rats are Manhattan icons, long-standing union symbols for picket-crossing "scabs." The rat squatted on a parking space, its tail wrapped around its legs like a Christmas tree skirt. For maximum impact it faced the street, where drivers could behold its sulfurous, bloodshot eyes, maw of yellow teeth, and forepaws aloft in the air.

The next day, counterprotesters had marshaled their own rat, maneuvering it across the street to face the first like an opposing piece on a chessboard.

A day later, rats and protesters had vanished, leaving everyone none the wiser.

Are we ever, I wondered?

What motivates us? Why do I go for walks? Why do protesters protest? Why, for that matter, do companies rent giant inflatable rats?

Real rats need no *raison d'être*. They focus on the here and now, the gnawing belly, the immediate threat. Are we better off for our ability to plan? As animals, we are animated by vital forces, but ours are not all physiological. Some are psychological, unique to each individual.

A young New Yorker in jeans and concert T-shirt crosses against traffic, totally in the moment. He revels in sensation, thinking no further than the next meal, game, or date. But he has a goal: to get a job. To get *that* job. To work in Silicon Valley. To make a million by age thirty. To get that girl. To marry his childhood sweetheart. To sign a music contract, tour the world, and become famous. Or perhaps he's not so self-centered – he'd rather save the Amazon.

James Taylor, on his latest album, sings in "Angels of Fenway" of his Nanna, a life-long Red Sox fan who longed to see her team win the World Series. It had been eighty-six years since they had, the year she was born. When it happened again in 2004, she saw it on a television set by her hospital bed. She passed away with a smile on her face.

December of 1996, my Nana was in a similar place. On Sundays, Mom and I would visit her Montclair hospital room. I didn't think Nana had anything left on her bucket list – nothing sports-related, certainly – but I couldn't be sure. Asking her was not an option because her stroke of two years previous had deprived her not only of speech, but possibly reason.

My inner curmudgeon tells me that "bucket lists" have been done to death. What is the point of *1001 Books to Read Before You Die* (does it include itself?) except as a checklist of inadequacy? Yet each of us has something that keeps us alive. As Emily Dickinson wrote, "Hope is the thing with feathers / That perches in the soul / And sings the tune without the words / And never stops at all."

One Sunday, Mom and I met Aunt Ro and cousin Lynn at the hospital. Nana had a double room to herself, so we spread out, making ourselves comfortable and talking a long while. Occasionally, Aunt Ro would try to bring Nana into the conversation by saying:

"Isn't that right, Mom?"

If Nana made a sign, however faint, we would laugh. But today she was quiet. Once in a while I glanced at the mute TV in the corner of the room to check on the football action – there were playoff spots in the balance. Then Lynn suggested a trip to the cafeteria: she wanted a bite, and we could carry something back for the others.

That's when Nana passed away, while we were out. She had held on until surrounded by family; then, exercising her usual delicacy, she had let go while her grandchildren were out of the room.

***

Why are we here? I think of the guy hawking tour bus tickets on Columbus Circle, or the guy living in the car plastered with graffiti and parking tickets that hasn't moved in months, or the person dressed as Snow White posing for photographs with Times Square tourists.

Consider the young woman eating lunch on the dark green park bench. Her headphones are on; she eats from a Bento box. She sees the Manhattan I do, but her choice of sound – indie rock, Don Ho, ambient chill – colors it in a way I can only guess at. Or maybe she hears only the sound of noise cancellation, the world on mute. Or she listens to music, but hasn't chosen a soundtrack, living aleatorically, player on shuffle, music colored by what she sees, what she sees colored by music, an endless feedback loop. She may as well be from another universe. I cannot see what she sees, because that depends on her state of mind, her deepest motives, which she may not know herself. She couldn't explain them to me, even had I the nerve to ask.

Manhattan streets are still crowded but, in suburbia, weeds grow through sidewalk cracks and no one sees. People live indoors, tethered to computers, dependent on virtual reality. "Friends" are capitalized: if we believe Facebook's claims, it has a 25% share of the global population. In one way, people are more connected than ever: fewer degrees of separation exist between any two people chosen at random. The mathematical formula for this is:

$$\text{Average degrees of separation} = (\ln P) / (\ln K) - 1$$

where P is population size and K is the average number of connections per person. Grab your calculator and we'll run through some examples.

Suppose you have 250 classmates and that, on average, a classmate has twelve friends within the class. Then, the average number of classmates needed to connect two randomly selected classmates is:

$$\ln(250) / \ln(12) - 1 = 5.52/2.48 - 1 = 1.22$$

That is, two classmates can typically be connected through one common friend. (1.22 is just larger than 1.)

Moving to Facebook, where the number of active users is P = 1,940,000,000 (one quarter of the Earth's population) and the average number of Friends is K = 338, we have:

$$\ln(1{,}940{,}000{,}000) / \ln(338) - 1 = 2.67.$$

So, two random Facebook users can be connected on average by a chain of approximately three other Facebook users. That is a remarkable level of worldwide connection.

Those are averages, but there will always be folks like J.D. Salinger who are harder to know. The parlor game Six Degrees of Kevin Bacon asks you to link any actor to Kevin Bacon using only feature film roles. I'm intrigued by actors with high "Bacon numbers," the actors who require the most movies to reach Bacon. Since actors, particularly Bacon, are notoriously promiscuous (in terms of roles), it's difficult to find anyone not easily connectible to him. In fact, ninety-eight percent of actors can be linked to him through four feature films or fewer.

I don't know if anyone has applied these ideas to Facebook and defined a "Bacon number" for social networks. But my point is that though the *online* world is one of unprecedented connection, the real world is still a forum where each of us is unreachable in a unique way. Our worldviews differ. Some of us are disposed toward social activism, others toward fundamentalism, and on issues such as abortion never the twain shall meet. Or to take a more frivolous example, Yankee fans and Met fans will forever be divided into those who like the status quo and "root for U.S. Steel," and those who like anarchy with a bit of Dada. Some of these differences may originate in DNA and others in childhood memories, but they are virtually intractable.

As for me, I like listening to my favorite songs again and again. When I was young, I believed that by sharing recordings, I could make a listener hear what I did; that my appreciation of a bass line or key change would travel, unimpeded, from my mind to theirs. The song was a go-between, a way to inject my essence – my wit, humor, and caprice – into another. Depending on the ears I hoped to penetrate, this could be an intimate act. So, for years, I wooed with carefully selected collections of songs that were once called "mix tapes" after the medium on which they were recorded. It took me quite a while to realize that the recipients of my mixes weren't hearing what I was. How else to explain their propensity to misplace them or return them to me without comment?

***

What is reality?
    - Firesign Theatre, "High School Madness!"

I've been dreaming, and remembering dreams. It's increasingly difficult to tell apart dreams and reality in my fifties, because the world has changed far beyond anything the absurdist comedy troupe Firesign Theatre imagined in 1970. That was the year they released *Don't Crush That Dwarf, Hand Me the Pliers*, the album on which they anticipated a highly individualized experience of reality: "U-TV, for *you*, the viewer." I own machines that speak, listen, play any song in the world, and not only correct my spelling but anticipate my words. In my pocket I carry a modern Library of Alexandria, an encyclopedia of world knowledge that sticks its tongue out at Douglas Adams' old *Hitchhiker's Guide to the Galaxy*. Humanity is realizing its age-old dream of subjugating the natural world; happiness, the equilibrium of desire, lies within our grasp.

But are we not like Proust's Aunt Léonie, the eternally bedridden invalid who never stops dreaming of the day that a conflagration will engulf her home, killing her family while granting her time to effect a leisurely escape? She astonishes her hometown by appearing at her loved ones' funeral, then pays a visit to the ancestral estate that she has longed to see for years. Like her, do we not unconsciously hope for a maelstrom to destroy our inertia, so we may finally act? Climate change is too slow – we need war, cataclysm, Revelation! It is not enough to possess the world; we want to entomb it with us, like a pet in a pyramid.

There is a school of thought in quantum physics that we live in a multiverse. Each instant, the universe in which we find ourselves branches into two universes, distinguishable only by the fact that something happened in one but not the other. If that's the case, then we have every right to be optimistic about the future: we will always be pulled into the universe where we survive! Perhaps each morning we wake to a universe different than yesterday's in some infinitesimal way that makes all the difference.

Or is reality like it was explained to me once on the radio, by Alan Watts, the Zen popularizer from Northern California? I listened to his lectures on WFMU, decades after a student recorded them in the 1970s. In one that stuck with me, Watts explained that each of us is a different manifestation of the universe, and that life is a game – you are the universe playing you; I am the universe playing me. And though life is just a game, that doesn't make it any less important for each of us to completely be ourselves.

Or maybe this is already the afterlife. If the modern world feels like Limbo, maybe it is. Perhaps we're in a way station to Heaven, like Albert Brooks in *Defending Your Life* or Warren Beatty in *Heaven Can Wait*. To advance, we must accomplish a meaningful or beautiful task.

***

When life is confusing, I remind myself why we're here. To be happy, and to help others be happy. That's it.

Many satisfy these needs by procreating. Parenthood may offer many joys – class trips, Little League games, scout jamborees, parent-teacher conferences, did I miss anything? – but for me they never added up. I'm not cut out for the institution.

What I most envy about parenthood is how it breaks the ice at neighborhood parties. Parents, like dog walkers, have a ready-made topic when they meet. Carol and I know the drill – having just four felines to discuss, we keep quiet and listen to mildly boring tales of childrearing. We are destined to forever remain outside the pale of polite society. Our lack of investment in the next generation must smack of atheism! The unasked question, of course, is:

"Exactly how do you spend your time again?"

But there's more than one way to spread your seed. There's the messy, age-old method with gametes, and there's that more recent evolutionary wrinkle, art. Meet Art! (I shop for music on a website which, when it is unable to display a record album's cover art, shows the picture of a sad-looking Paul Simon next to the words, "Art Not Available.")

One day when I was ten, Mom and I walked out to the car to run errands. On the way, I noticed something in the brilliance of the sky, or the scent of the air, that reminded me of a similar, recent morning, and I mentioned it to Mom. She said I must have an artistic sensibility. I believe she was right. I never feel more alive than when confronted with resonant representations of life, and never more fulfilled than when I share them with others. That is how I get and give pleasure.

And around that age, I discovered that pop music could not only be enjoyed at home, but serve as a conduit to schoolboy dialogue.

On Peck School's playground, my buddy Mac would climb the jungle gym and sing with gusto, if a bit off-key, the hit songs of the day with the kind of humor (I'd yet to learn its name, satire) that I already knew from the faux advertising trading cards known as Wacky Packs. One day, he sang a jingle from a TV commercial advertising the new Paul McCartney live album:

"Let us… entertain you… with *Wings Over America*!"

Mac was zany, a foil to his best friend Chad, who was sensible, thick-lipped, and phlegmatic. Chad kicked at the dirt while he watched Mac hang from the monkey bars. Mac was short and dark-haired, with a cubic head, a bit like a Rock 'Em Sock 'Em Robot, with bushy black eyebrows that arched over Marty Feldman eyes. His loud, raucous laugh signaled that he was an absurdist – long before the rest of us knew there was an absurd.

Weeknights after school, Mac drew comics. That blew my mind. I bought *Archie* from grocery store checkout racks on summer vacation, but he *wrote* them, the whole shebang: strips, stories, gags, ads, captions, art. He even bound them in books, a fact I learned the Saturday I visited his house, when Mom dropped me off for what would today be called a "play date." In his bedroom, Mac pointed to a tall bookshelf: the bottom shelves were stacked high with hand-drawn comics. I leafed through them, marveling at drawings and jokes like those in *Mad* magazine.

Unfortunately, that was my one chance to see them because my old childhood curse – to never see the interior of a friend's home more than once - struck again. I was not invited back after Mac's mother discovered that we'd binged on peanut butter Oompa Loompas (a then-popular candy like Reese's Pieces) that I'd purchased at the supermarket where Mac's mother had taken us to do some shopping. She got upset when her son admitted to eating some of my candy – apparently, sugary candy made him sick. I had indeed noticed that he was more manic than usual that day, but Mac hadn't said anything about his condition.

The album of which Mac sang, *Wings Over America,* featured a version of Paul McCartney's "Silly Love Songs," a song I knew from the radio. It had evidently lodged itself in Mac's mind as well. When he sang it on the jungle gym, it validated my own love of the song, creating a bond between us. But did the way he sing it mean he was parodying the song, or just the advertising campaign? Either was a possibility given Mac's comic sensibility.

Much later, I learned that I wasn't the only one who wondered about "Silly Love Songs." Many of McCartney's critics wrote that the ex-Beatle had gone soft since his band's demise. And yet, on this song, Paul had the final word:

> *Some people want to fill the world with silly love songs*
> *What's wrong with that?*
> *I'd like to know, 'cause here I go again....*
> - Paul McCartney, "Silly Love Songs"

That song had the life force. How else to explain its conquest of the Western hemisphere? It scaled the toppermost of the poppermost in dozens of countries, including our own *Billboard Hot 100*, where it sat at number one for five weeks. Mac knew that song had life; that's why he sang it. And when I heard him sing it, its force was transferred to me.

From that moment, a new fantasy supplanted the one in which I walked hand-in-hand on Peck's grounds with my secret crush, Elizabeth. In this new daydream, I was a pop star. But, having no older brothers to explain what pop stardom entailed (perhaps by making me stay up late to watch *Don Kirshner's Rock Concert*), I had to invent it.

I imagined the boys and girls (especially the girls) of my fourth-grade class gathered around me. I'd open my mouth, and out would come the songs I loved! But not like karaoke. (The karaoke machine, a recent Japanese invention, had yet to reach America.) What issued forth was the song in all its accompaniment: guitars, keyboards, drums, horns, and so forth. It was as though, when I opened my mouth, a tape recorder had been activated in my larynx. Was that so misguided? I'd yet to learn the difference between deejays and pop stars; I only knew that I wanted to share music.

First, a prayer for Mac. I hope he became the artist he was meant to be, and didn't fritter away his life at a succession of unloved jobs.

As for me, I've been fortunate to realize my dream in many ways. Home taping soon evolved to the point where I could make mix tapes. Later, as a disc jockey, I had another means of sharing my favorite songs. Who knows? Maybe one day I'll learn to play them on guitar.

Viva Las Vegas!

I first heard this story the day I turned twenty-one. My parents and I were dining at L'Allegria, a fancy Madison ristorante. Since I had picked the place, Mom and Dad provided the entertainment. They regaled me with their origin story, something I'd never thought to ask about.

To avoid sowing dangerous ideas, they had hidden this story from their children until then. But it had leaked. The previous Thanksgiving, my brother Frank had driven from college in Seattle to join my Uncle Mike and Aunt Margo in Eastern Washington for a home-cooked meal. At dinner, my aunt and uncle told part of this story, assuming that Frank already knew it. After listening in silence, he finally said, "You're kidding, right?" They turned to each other and said, "Uh-oh." Later that evening, Uncle Mike called Mom to break the news.

The morning of February 9, 1965, a Tuesday. Frank Baldanza, owner of the Springfield House, was at his restaurant. Business was good due to his recent appearance on *The Joe Franklin Show*, during which the legendary New York City television personality interviewed him for a few minutes. (Under the glare of the studio lights, Frank's performance was stiff but genuine.) Other promotions were going well: Dom's Auto Sales, Route 22, North Plainfield, was running a deal where purchasers of current model year cars could win steak dinners for two. And the Springfield House had recently hosted a women's fashion show, run by the Fanwood Junior Women's Club, in which debutantes modeled the latest fashions, followed by dessert and bridge.

On any given day, there were many attractive women at the Springfield House, and some were not averse at making a play for the attractive bachelor owner. Frank's mother, Helen, who managed the front of house and locally famous salad bar, kept an eye. She knew how to put the more brazen ones in their place – she had gone to a woman's apartment once to tell her to leave her son alone – but she knew that her thirty-two-year-old son was too wide-eyed for his own good.

Jack Maloney, the golf pro at Spring Brook Country Club in Morris Township, stopped by. His golf visor sported the club logo, a ball on a tee.

"Want to fly to Vegas? We can play some poker and get in a few rounds of golf. I'm going today."

"You've got to be kidding! I'm too busy. I don't even have time to pack."

"I made the reservations. Just bring your clubs – that's all anyone needs! You can buy anything else you need when we get there."

Frank considered. He hadn't taken a vacation in a while. Getting his first sole proprietorship on a solid footing had been a job and a half. But winter was getting old, and this might be his best chance to get away.

"Okay, I'll go."

He called Helen. She wasn't happy to hear about this junket that smacked of carefree youth, not something a serious businessman should be up to. But she conceded, and promised to look after the restaurant.

The young lions boarded the flight in their golfing outfits. They touched down in Las Vegas and took a cab to the Desert Inn, where Jack's secretary had made a reservation. (This was the same Desert Inn that would become famous after Howard Hughes moved into a top-floor suite on Thanksgiving Day, then refused to move out. Rather than leave, he bought the hotel and stayed for four years.)

Inexplicably, the hotel had no record of Jack's reservation, and was completely booked. A bit disoriented in the unaccustomed midday heat, the pair hailed a taxi and asked to be taken to a hotel with a room. The driver knew to take them to the Stardust, just a half-mile south on the Strip, where they arrived five minutes later.

After they fetched their clubs from the trunk and tossed them on the hotel beds, they stopped at the casino to cool off. They took a seat at the bar and bought keno tickets from the girl with the early shift, who was about to go off-duty. Frank saw her replacement from across the room – blond, taller than average, her height enhanced by her updo, Doris Day to Frank's Cary Grant. He turned to Jack and said:

"I'm going to marry that girl."

Jack glanced across the room, then back at Frank, and grinned:

"Fine, go ahead and marry her."

Seen from outside, Betti Hines' path through life looked like willful disobedience, but she knew better. She was selling keno tickets, cigarettes, and gum at the Stardust because, quite simply, she needed to save up for her next move. Raised in sleepy Pasco, Washington, where she was high school valedictorian and Most Likely to Succeed, Betti had driven two hours up Route 395 to Gonzaga University, where she got her Bachelor of Science in Chemistry. She returned to Pasco and landed a job at General Electric, then moved on to the Atomic Energy Commission, an employer that loomed large in Eastern Washington due to its Hanford plant, the site of early atomic bomb research. But small-town Washington didn't offer much excitement, so Betti headed for the bright lights of Los Angeles.

It was easy then for a newly-minted college graduate to find an apartment and a job. Betti got a pad in Santa Monica and a well-paying gig at UCLA. Unfortunately, the job required little brainpower: if she worked slowly enough, she could stretch the work to half of an eight-hour day. To avoid going crazy, she took a job at GMAC, where she tracked automobile loan payments. The pay was lower and the work still not challenging, but it kept her busy and it paid well enough for her to enjoy her evenings and weekends.

When GMAC opened a Las Vegas office, where Betti sensed the lights might be brighter yet, she put in for a transfer. The new job was not enjoyable, and it did not cover rent. To make ends meet, she took a job selling keno tickets at the Stardust Hotel and Casino. Her plan was to save money for a month, then move to either Denver, San Francisco, or Honolulu. Though a free spirit, she was organized enough to short list cities.

So, when Frank walked up to her in the casino lobby and asked:
"Will you marry me?"

She ignored him. He looked like he *was* married, though she couldn't say why. At the least, he was crazy or drunk. She continued her rounds.

But he approached again:
"I'm not kidding. Will you marry me?"

He seemed nice enough. Betti assured him that in Las Vegas he wouldn't have trouble finding company, though she didn't do that sort of thing. He walked off a second time.

And then something strange happened. One of his keno tickets came up a winner. In Betti's experience, no one ever won at keno, but this guy did. She counted out his winnings and brought them to the bar, but he wasn't there. Jack collected for him.

A little later, they met again. This time Frank said:
"All right. May I take you to dinner?"

Finally, an acceptable proposition! Betti said yes, because in the mid-1960s, men paid for dinner; it would never have occurred to her to "go Dutch." Besides, she needed to save. So why not?

In college and afterward, Betti had made friends easily. She dated. She had even gotten engaged, but broke it off because it didn't feel right. That rupture dismayed her mother (who liked the boy) and devastated her grandmother, who wrote her off as an old maid. To a woman from southern Italy, single women going on twenty-five had missed the boat. And yet here was Betti, preparing to meet a stranger for dinner, more excited about a date than she'd been in quite some time.

They met in the Stardust's showroom, famed for its Lido de Paris Review, an extravagant burlesque, touted in capital letters on the immense marquee outside the casino as the "World's Greatest Floor Show – 70 Stars – Adults Only!" In this grand space with long tables arranged perpendicularly to the stage, couples sat opposite one another, keeping one eye on their partner, the other on the show. Betti and Frank trained all four eyes on each other and fell into a long, easy conversation about their lives: their upbringings, their families, their experiences, their likes and dislikes, even their beliefs. As they talked, platters of food arrived, dancers high kicked, and the crowd murmured. What they didn't realize was that their neighbors on either side were listening to their every word:

"I'm serious. Will you marry me?" Frank asked.

Betti thought a moment, and said:

"I must be crazy, but yes."

At that moment, the show ended, the stage lights dimmed, and the table broke into spontaneous applause and congratulations for the lovestruck couple. The exception was a short man with a big cigar in his mouth who said:

"Don't do it."

His wife, who was a foot taller than he was, jabbed him in the ribs with her elbow:

"You shut up! I think it's wonderful!"

The newly pledged pair levitated to the casino to meet with Jack and some friends that he and Frank had made. (One person who didn't show was the stewardess from their inbound flight, with whom Frank had broken a date.) They uncorked a bottle of champagne, and everyone gathered for a toast. Frank slipped the cork into his pocket. That was the cork which, on their tenth anniversary, Frank would present to Betti in a block of Lucite bearing a brass plaque that read:

"Thanks for saying yes. February 9, 1965."

(That memento sat for years in our living room. One day, my brother asked Dad why the date on the plaque was just six days before our parents' wedding anniversary. Dad hastily improvised, "Oh, they got the date wrong!")

Frank wanted to get married there and then, that night in Vegas. But though Betti was surer of this man than anyone whom she had ever known, she knew that that would crush her mother. The wedding would have to take place in the family church, in Pasco.

Now realizing what lay ahead, Frank escorted Betti to his hotel room. Leaving the door ajar for propriety's sake, he got on the phone to arrange for her car and belongings to be shipped to New Jersey – a place further east than she had ever been, which she knew nothing about, other than that it bordered New York. Frank then booked a flight to Pasco for the next day. His work done, it was Betti's turn, and Frank returned to the casino.

Betti picked up the phone to make the call she was dreading. She and her mother Edythe were very close. They never lied to one another, so Betti's wording would have to be precise.

"Mom, I'm coming home!"

But she had just been home for Christmas.

"What's wrong?"

"Nothing. I'm getting married!"

"Who to?" Edythe knew Betti wasn't in a serious relationship.

Suddenly Betti realized she didn't know Frank's last name! She hesitated, then said:

"To a wonderful man named Frank."

"How long have you known him?"

"For a short while."

"How short?"

"Well, I met him yesterday." Technically true, since it was just past midnight.

A long pause followed. Betti thought the connection was lost.

"Mom?"

"I'm here."

The daughter brought the call to a close only after agreeing to her mother's suggestion to see a doctor in Pasco. A psychiatrist.

"Mom, you'll like Frank when you meet him!"

Her mother didn't believe that, but managed to say good night before hanging up. Then she stayed awake all night, never going to bed. When her husband Les asked her the next morning what was wrong, she shouted:

"Betti's getting married!"

At the casino, Frank and Betti found a place to sit and talk at a blackjack table. They were so rapt in conversation that they hardly paid attention to the dealer who for some reason kept asking them, "Do you want a hit?" When they finally rose from the table, they discovered that they had won over a thousand dollars, not a bad sum for 1965. To celebrate (as if they needed another reason), they went to the cocktail lounge for a nightcap. Betti joined Frank in a brandy milk punch, a drink she had never tried. That night she consumed more liquor than she was accustomed to, yet by evening's end she didn't feel it at all.

Finally, it was time for her to return to her apartment and gather her things. Frank walked her to her car. They stood there a moment to say their goodbyes; then Frank extended his arm and they shook good night.

At the apartment, Betti identified the few things she couldn't do without, carried them to her car, and consigned the rest to history's dustbin. At four o'clock in the morning, she finally drifted off.

And woke up late! She briefly panicked, since there was little time to get to the casino, pick up Frank, drive to the gas station from which Frank had arranged for her car's cross-country transport, and then to the airport.

Frank, when he woke, realized he had only two golf outfits to get married in. Fortunately, Las Vegas was not lacking in haberdasheries. With a new suit and old golf clubs, he waited for Betti at the valet station outside the Stardust. He waited quite a while. Finally, he said to himself:

"I can't believe this! I'm getting married – and I'm getting stood up!"

But Betti arrived, and Frank threw his things in her car. They raced to the gas station. As they got in a cab for the airport, Betti looked once more at her car, and it crossed her mind that she might never see it again.

On the plane, Frank and Betti got the last two seats. Of course, they weren't adjacent.

"Would you mind switching?" Frank asked the guy next to Betti.

The guy took a look at Betti.

"I'm not switching."

So, on the first leg of the flight, they sat apart. The route from Las Vegas to Pasco, known colloquially as the "milk run," had so many stops along the way – Salt Lake City, Boise, Walla Walla – that it was past ten p.m. by the time they arrived at tiny Tri-Cities Airport.

Edythe was at the gate. Though she'd seen her daughter only six weeks earlier, she hugged her as though they'd been separated for ages. Then she turned to Frank, whom Betti introduced while crossing her fingers behind her back in the hope that she was correctly saying her future last name.

Frank craned his neck and gave the airport a once-over. He'd grown up in Paterson, New Jersey, a town with a hundred thousand residents but just a bus stop to its name. He was impressed.

"This is a nice airport for a town this size."

Edythe, in a huff:

"Well, we *are* civilized out here."

Frank decided to visit a nearby cigarette machine.

"Where's Dad?" Betti asked.

"He's in the car. He wouldn't come in."

At the car, Les offered Frank a purposely limp handshake, one befitting an Eastern playboy. He looked at the luggage, then at Frank:

"Where do you want your golf clubs?"

Frank wasn't tone deaf. He could hear the sarcasm. And so he tried to save himself:

"I don't want to cause trouble. Perhaps you could drop me off at one of these motels." Les answered:

"Well, maybe our home is not what you're used to, but we think it's comfortable."

The whole way home, there was silence.

Frank carried his clubs across the threshold, and Betti followed. Once everyone was inside, Betti's twelve-year-old brother Mike padded into the hall to visit the bathroom. He strained his head around the corner to get a gander at the goose to be cooked, then was shooed off to bed.

They sat down to talk. In the West, it was customary to offer coffee, not cocktails, to visitors, so Betti got up to make a pot. She knew her parents liked their coffee black, which was also her preference, but she had no clue how the love of her life liked his. She rifled through the kitchen cabinets to look for sugar, which she placed on the tray next to the milk. She then carried it to the dining room table, an entirely new procedure for her.

The conversation began innocently enough and expanded to fill the time. By three a.m., politics, sports, and weather had been covered much more thoroughly than on the evening news. In fact, the four had discussed everything but the one thing they were there to discuss.

Finally, Les pushed back his chair.

"Well, do you want to talk about it?"

Frank cleared his throat.

"We want to get married. We want your blessing, but we're going to get married."

With the impasse on the table, all parties agreed they were too tired to discuss further. Talks were suspended for the night.

The next morning, Mike asked his mother:

"How is he?"

"Well, he's not as bad as I thought."

"He couldn't have been much worse."

That day, Les got off early at the automobile lot that he managed, and drove Frank to a cocktail lounge. For the first time since his arrival in the Olympic State, Frank felt he was on home ground, among regulars at a drinking hole. He loosened up, no longer sounding like he was on *The Joe Franklin Show*, and managed to win over his prospective father-in-law; by the end of the afternoon, they were old pals. When they walked in cheerfully through the front door, Edythe was not pleased.

The next day, it was Betti's turn to feel better. She took Frank to see "Uncle Ed," a family friend who was her trusted confidant whenever she needed one. The couple knocked at his front door, which opened instantly. Beaming, Ed grabbed Frank by the arm, pulling him inside:

"Boy, am I glad to meet you! What did the grizzly bear say?" Frank and Betti had another ally.

That week, they were under surveillance. Mornings, Edythe chaperoned, taking time from her bookkeeping job at St. Patrick's Roman Catholic Church; Les took the afternoons. These arrangements amused the young couple, who had not found an opportunity to kiss. That didn't happen until the day before their wedding, when they stole a quick one in the kitchen.

Frank, having a restaurant to run, needed to return soon, so the wedding date could not be delayed. But in the 1960s, it was not simple for Catholics to marry on short notice! There were rites and rituals to observe, in particular the banns of marriage, which were usually posted three weeks in advance of the wedding date. Enter Edythe. The Church did not want to lose their dependable volunteer bookkeeper, so they bent the rules for her. Frank, for his part, produced a letter stating that he was "free to marry," signed by his priest, who also happened to be his regular golf partner.

T-minus two days: Edythe insisted on talking separately with Betti and Frank. She impressed upon each of them that it was not too late to change their minds. Betti, as she listened, thought with wonder:

"People don't do things like this. *I* don't do things like this!"

But she did.

The couple were relieved that the wedding date was so near, as neither liked big weddings. Despite this, Edythe pulled out all the stops. To Betti's amazement, many of her friends made it to Pasco for the ceremony, as did many relatives, including the entire Montana side of the family, in an age when long-distance travel was not simple.

Walking down the aisle, Betti felt one final butterfly. But when she saw the altar boys' sneakers peeking out from under their cassocks, she realized that even if she did have feet of clay, she could make it through whatever lay ahead.

The flight to New Jersey was a red-eye – some wedding night! The next day, the newlyweds checked in to a fancy Manhattan hotel and finally got a day and night to themselves. It all seemed like a dream to the woman who didn't know Broadway from the Bowery.

The next day, Frank drove his new bride to Essex Fells, a posh suburb of golf courses and hydrangeas, to meet his sister's family.

The crew there waited on tenterhooks. Besides Helen, there was Frank's sister Ro, her husband George, and Frank's three young nieces, Donna, Karen, and Lynnie. The anticipation was intense. The girls, who idolized Uncle Frank, could hardly wait to meet the glamorous starlet he'd brought home, while Helen and Ro did their best to dismiss nagging fears that Frank had been ensnared by a "showgirl," as the Springfield House wags were calling her.

There was nothing to fear. Helen knew it as soon as Betti walked in the door. Helen's intuition, so strong in many ways – politics, sports, people – told her so. With the introductions barely over, she took Betti aside, placed her hand on her shoulder, and said:

"If you have any trouble with my son, just see me. Because you'll be right."

Helen had foreseen it all. For the next thirty years, it was always Betti who was right.

Irony/Virtualization

Round, like a circle in a spiral
Like a wheel within a wheel
Never ending or beginning
On an ever-spinning reel
        - Michel Legrand, "The Windmills of Your Mind"

Yesterday, at the supermarket, I was shopping for ingredients for a new pasta recipe. Our Acme, which serves crowds of summer tourists and considerably fewer off-season locals like us, doesn't typically stock the sort of specialty foods desired by neither. They didn't have the type of olive I needed, so I examined the small olive bar to see what they had.

Without warning, I was floored by the whoosh of a synthesizer. It ushered in a simple melody, leading it like a parent takes a child by the hand. I instantly forgot my errand, stunned by what I was hearing.

"It can't be," I murmured.

It was. For the next three minutes, I was transfixed by "Love Will Tear Us Apart."

When released forty years ago, this song did not approach commercial success, at least not in the United States. It was a dirge, albeit a catchy one, by Joy Division, a resolutely independent band from Manchester, England named after the sexual slavery wings of Nazi concentration camps. Only after this song's release, which was inspired by lead singer Ian Curtis' marital troubles and suicidal tendencies, did the band gain notoriety. The song nibbled at the British top twenty, but this side of the pond it only got an airing in New York City danceterias. The record sleeve photo didn't help – the song title etched on gray metal, acid-aged to resemble a stone slab, like a gravestone.

Joy Division's record label, surprised by the song's British chart success, rushed to release a video. Then, three weeks later, Ian Curtis killed himself. His wife commissioned a tombstone with the epitaph: "Love Will Tear Us Apart."

Why was I hearing this song in the supermarket?

Abandoning my cart near the olives, I distractedly searched for ditalini. I warily regarded the patrons, each oblivious to the music. I couldn't read the package labels; I couldn't focus. Though not a Joy

Division fan, I could not help but feel that a travesty was being perpetrated, against whom I could not say. But it was clearly inappropriate for this song to be playing here, on a Monday afternoon.

I was turning into my father.

When I was young, one day Dad and I were listening to the car radio. He scanned the left end of the FM band, pausing briefly at a non-commercial radio station. After the music stopped, the deejay proceeded to employ some colorful words I'd never heard. Dad was angry, as he told me so years later. I don't remember if he called the radio station, but it wouldn't surprise me; he had, after all, called the studios of WABC-TV during halftime of *Monday Night Football* when he was sure Howard Cosell was drunk. (Cosell didn't return for the second half.)

In retrospect, I attribute Dad's anger to a fundamental need to protect his children from the world's darkness. For someone born in the era that Nana called the "height of the depression" (an awkward phrase that unfortunately made me laugh), the 1960s and early 1970s must have seemed like the end of the safe, stable world in which he'd grown up, what with the Kennedy and King assassinations and protests over Vietnam, Kent State and Watergate. At least Dad could curate the music that his children heard - unless of course he slipped up, like that night in the car.

When I was older, Dad and I tended to avoid weighty topics like society's unraveling; we were more likely to talk baseball. And as pop music changed, and with it his children's tastes, Dad refrained from commenting on the sounds emanating from our transistor radios. Once in a while, though, he let his guard slip and I'd catch a glimpse of his confusion at how the world had changed.

On one car trip, "Life in the Fast Lane" came on. I wasn't crazy about the Eagles, but the song was catchy, so I let it play. As a newly fledged teen, I heard only the music, not the lyric about two sex-crazed, coke-addled socialites. (Looking back, it *is* shocking that it was a big hit.) But Dad had heard enough – perhaps just the prominent "goddamn" in the chorus – to know he didn't like it. He wondered at a band that would record such trash. Well, he was right that it wasn't family listening.

About the same time, I happened to be listening to a John Lennon song when Dad informed me of a several-hour movie that John and Yoko had once made of a fly walking on a naked body. His scorn was audible; his unspoken question, "These are your role models?"

Another time, I repeatedly played Bob Seger's "Shame on the Moon" on his bedroom stereo, which before I had my own, was the best one in the house. In response to the line "blame it on the moonlight," he asked:

"Blame *what* on the moonlight?"

I suppose he thought that folks should be responsible for their own actions, not blame them on the moon.

Dad's criticism wasn't restricted to music. Two moments from junior high school come to mind. The first involves one of Dad's "bathroom books," which sat for a long time on the small, marble-topped stand in my parents' bathroom. *The People's Almanac*, by David Wallechinsky and his father, Irving Wallace, was a surprise 1975 best-seller, a huge paperback packed with all sorts of bizarre facts and lists. One list enumerated the shortest-lived network television shows of all time; at number one was *Turn-On*, a Laugh-In-like counterculture revue that aired exactly once. Its entry mentioned one joke: a beautiful woman stands before a firing squad, and the squad leader, after offering her a cigarette, says:

"I know this is unusual, but in this case *we* have a final request."

I asked Dad about this joke when he and I were driving along Kings Road, near Samson Avenue. I had a suspicion of what it was about, but it was only a guess. Dad did not directly answer my question, but pointedly said the joke wasn't funny.

The other memory was a result of my own poor judgment. My school chum Dave and I had created a mock *TV Guide* full of listings of awful-sounding shows. One was a nightly news report of fake news stories. When I showed him our handiwork, Dad got serious and said:

"John, that's not funny. That sounds like Russia. We depend on the news."

Goodness, gracious. Some things I'm glad Dad didn't live to see.

***

Another memory: on a sunny afternoon the summer after Dad's passing, I'd just cut the front lawn and was standing with Mom on the front drive. We were discussing a yard sale that would rid the basement of many of Dad's possessions. Mom was pointing out where to set up the sale when a car slowly pulled up to the curb.

The man who got out of the car was a few years younger than the age that Dad shall forever remain. Neither Mom nor I knew him. He moved slowly, as though he'd had a couple, walking straight toward us across the freshly cut lawn, raising his hand and uttering a cheerful hello before a sudden cloud darkened his face, and he offered his condolences. I pictured him as a regular at Spag's Cantina, the downtown diner where Dad would have a Taylor Ham and egg sandwich and catch up with the *paisanos*.

Having exhausted his meager store of things to say to Mom, he turned to me and said he'd recently been to Florida during Spring Break, where at one beach the young women were more than happy to let you take their photographs – and for a little money, they'd take off their tops! I had no clue why he directed the conversation that way. Perhaps he only wanted to lift the gloom, and had hit upon this topic in an effort to find something a young man could relate to. Whatever his motivation, I found the comment – especially in Mom's presence – to be somewhat embarrassing and in poor taste, so I let it pass. He soon left.

It dawned on me: with Dad no longer here, I was on my own when it came to judging the world for its occasional lapses of propriety. Nor could Dad counsel me on right and wrong. It would be up to me to make sense of the world while taking care not to yield to my tendency – one Dad had warned me about – to see things in "black and white."

***

Back at Acme, channeling Dad, I wanted to protest the in-store music. But unlike the case with *Monday Night Football* so long ago, there was no one to call. I was a figure in a remake of Bruegel's famous painting of Icarus, *Supermarket with the Fall of Curtis:* the singer crashing to the earth as market shoppers ploughed the aisles with their shopping carts, oblivious to the falling lyrics:

> *As desperation takes hold*
> *Is it something so good*
> *Just can't function no more?*

Today's artists work with a broader palette, one with torments and traumas that Cole Porter would have locked tight in a bedside drawer. If they're lurid enough to attract eyes and ears, they might reach the masses. (Not that anyone will pay heed.)

Some of my earliest lessons in the new promiscuity happened at the Princeton Record Exchange, where I encountered shocking band names and dubious cover art. I couldn't help but wonder, browsing that music, whether my generation was profoundly unhappy. And a few band names I didn't understand, one of which led to humorous consequences. One summer day, my Uncle Mike took me to a Montana bar so we could shoot pool. As we crossed the parking lot, I described what my college roommate James, a deejay at the campus radio station, listened to. I liked some things, but couldn't abide some of the punk bands.

"Yeah, he listens to stuff like the Circle Jerks," I said.

For a second, Uncle Mike's pace slowed, as though he needed to catch his breath. He stifled a guffaw and smiled broadly as we crossed the threshold into a dimly-lit bar of paunchy old farmers. He must have seen from my expression that I had no clue what the phrase meant.

***

Don't get me wrong: I favor artistic expression. What annoys me is its promiscuous *distribution*. Why should "Love Will Tear Us Apart," a suicide note that raging at the lack of justice in a godless universe, be used to sell groceries?

Sometimes I wonder if people still understand irony. One part of me, not the noblest part, savored the irony of hearing "Love Will Tear Us Apart" in a supermarket. Another part wondered whether popular culture is capable of assessing art. We seem to have devolved. The written word, the most precise form of communication ever devised, has been replaced by a hundred forms of static and noise - music algorithms, Siri and Alexa, social networks, bots, smart thermostats, robocalls, clickbait, virtual reality. Have they robbed us of our ability to reason?

If music is now context-free wallpaper for sale to the highest bidder, can we ever hear "Love Will Keep Us Apart" again in the way Ian Curtis intended?

Recommendation to Acme – play light jazz.

***

December of 1989, Macy's at the Short Hills Mall. In every store corner, stacks of boxes wrapped in bright, glossy paper; attached to every supporting column, huge frosted ornaments; in every aisle, tables recently hauled from deep storage that constricted the flow of shoppers, such as me.

These tables were laden with last-minute gifts, and I still had folks to shop for, so I stopped at one to check out its wares. There was a hill of identically-sized cardboard boxes the size of watch cases.

"What have we here?" I wondered.

It was the Berlin Wall.

Well, part of it. A newly-minted Eastern European capitalist had found a market for discredited totalitarianism – Macy's! Each individually-packaged chunk of concrete, roughly the size of a river rock, came with a certificate of authenticity. I bought two, earmarking one for my former high school English teacher and unrepentant liberal, Mr. Russo. The gift's irony would, at least, not be lost on him. As for me, I was dumbfounded by the Wall's final resting place. It was as though the Holy Grail had ended up in Harrod's – a possibility that Monty Python had considered when they scripted an ending for their first film.

To keep my mental equilibrium, I need irony now more than ever.

***

Not all art is created equal. I believed that as an English major and, before that, as a child who read books. I still do, in fact. I can entertain the idea that people are of roughly equal worth, but that's not true of their creations, which span the spectrum from masterpieces to mediocrities to dreck. And I've never shied away from calling out hackwork, regardless of popularity. And though I'd be the first to admit that my judgment isn't infallible, to not exercise it would be an abdication.

I've panned movies my mother liked. Sorry, Mom! When Mom played *Let it Ride*, a horse racing comedy starring Richard Dreyfuss, I took an instant dislike to it; my wisecracks so annoyed her that she turned it off. And in a theater at the Morris County Mall, I stayed to the end of *Dances with Wolves* only because Mom liked it so much. I agreed with her that its panoramic views of Montana's sere and stark plateaus, ravines, and distant hooded mountains, so familiar from our own annual summer visits – was glorious. Not so compelling were the acting and plot. The only scene I still remember is the one in which Kevin Costner, or a body double, stands in long shot regarding the landscape, buttocks to the camera. That scene went on so long that I could no longer look at the scenery; I had to wonder about the provenance of those buttocks. But here's some consolation, Mom – you weren't in my college Introduction to Film course. There, I so disliked Frank Capra's *Mr. Smith Goes to Washington* that I considered writing a polemic against movies like Capra's that try to manipulate viewers into certain viewpoints. (I hate Hitchcock, too.)

Even my wife Carol is not immune, though she knows me well enough to anticipate and parry any rough handling of her film favorites. (Don't get me started about *Titanic*!)

***

Sesame Street taught me circles and squares are all around -- all one has to do is look. I see irony everywhere. A friend from Maine writes that in his supermarket, he heard the Smiths' "Shoplifters of the World Unite." How perfect is that?

On a recent visit to the clinic where I had the pleasure of my first colonoscopy, nervously strapped to a gurney, I was wheeled down an antiseptic white hall to a dark room, where I was tethered to a machine. Two nurses and a doctor were busy with procedure, so I could only assume that the piped-in music from unseen speakers (they were invisible to me because I was prone, a catheter up my wazoo) was for my benefit. When a nurse explained that the sedative she was about to administer would put me to sleep, my attention naturally wandered to the music, where I heard my last ever communication from the living world before going under: the song "Urgent," by Foreigner, and its repeated refrain of "Urgent, urgent, emergency...."

Note to endoscopy clinic – play light jazz.

***

The other day, I considered art's hierarchy while viewing *The Thomas Crown Affair*, the original movie starring Steve McQueen and Faye Dunaway. It's a real head trip, not least because it's an exercise in time travel, full of period detail.

The scene is Boston, the fashions Swinging Sixties, and the theme the breezy, psychedelic "Windmills of Your Mind," written by Michel Legrand. The Ivy League fashions – four-in-hand knotted, double-pleated ties, straight-point collars, mock turtleneck sweaters, and checked cardigans – never looked better than on McQueen; meanwhile, Haskell Wexler's cinematography, including several scenes in split-screen Technicolor (a guilty pleasure of mine), choreographs a bank heist to precision.

Bored playboy and real estate mogul Thomas Crown (McQueen) engineers a burglary that he can watch in real time from the aerie of his executive office high atop a downtown Boston skyscraper, using accomplices who are strangers not only to him but to one another. (Jack Weston sublimely plays a shlub.) Vicki Anderson (Dunaway), an insurance investigator (right!) is called on the case, and suspects Crown almost immediately. The rest of the movie is cat and mouse, the pair dancing around one other (and closer still, if I correctly read the not-so-subtle chess scene) while Vicki attempts to ensnare Thomas.

On the other hand, the movie lacks big ideas. The only one available seems to be existentialism: when Crown's golfing partner tells him on the green that he's made a "sucker's bet," Crown answers:

"What else are we going to do on Sunday?"

And when Crown's fashion model girlfriend asks him what a man in his position has to worry about, he replies:

"Who I want to be tomorrow."

The film is amoral. And so I wonder, *why do I like it so much*? It doesn't even have a tragic ending, like most of my favorite movies. (On second thought, perhaps it does -- a bad man getting away with everything is kind of tragic.)

I love it for its style. Everything is pitch perfect: script, dialogue, acting, characterization, cinematography, costumes, soundtrack. The producer-director, Norman Jewison, wasn't trying to make the movie anything other than what it gloriously was, a triumph of form. Still, the subtext is there, and the film doesn't hide it: these characters are empty.

Though reasonably successful in theaters, the movie was not a blockbuster. I wish Hollywood still cared enough about art to make such films. And Jewison's DVD commentary is amusing because it is so apologetic. He laments the film's lack of depth that characterized his movies *In the Heat of the Night and The Fiddler on the Roof*. At times he sounds downright embarrassed. But whenever he does, I want to reach through the TV screen, shake him, and say, "It's perfect as it is!"

Unlike many patrons of the arts, I enjoy art that calls attention to its artifice. The split screens in *The Thomas Crown Affair* do nothing to advance the plot, and actually detract from its pacing, but they just look so cool. They give the film an art house sheen. (My favorite scenes in just about any movie are the ones that not only fail to advance the plot, but dare you to examine the screen -- the ones that say, "you're missing the details! Look at that chair! Pay attention!")

But whatever it is, *The Thomas Crown Affair* doesn't seem like a Hollywood movie designed to maximize the box office.

As an actuary, I attended insurance ratemaking conferences. (I never met anyone who looked like Faye Dunaway there.) At one, the keynote presentation was given by a pair of analysts who worked for a small firm in Hollywood that made good money selling predictive models to studios who wished to improve their scripts. ("Improve" in the sense of increasing revenue.) Since insuring feature films was such an expensive and uncertain endeavor, wouldn't it be good to maximize the possibility, before production, of eventual payback? They proceeded to tick off the movie variables – cast, plot, even the movie title – with the greatest potential to boost sales.

How ridiculous, I thought. But a look at my local theater's "Now Playing" posters tells me that the algorithms have won.

I grew up in a household that did not discuss art. At dinner, we did not spar over the relative worth of songs, books, or movies, and sometimes it seemed that I alone cared about such things. For others, art was a pastime. To get excited over it would be silly! Today, I find myself in the same position at wine-and-cheese parties with neighbors; though in their case, it might be due not only to diffidence about art, but a reluctance to discuss anything contentious in today's political climate.

***

They took the credit for your second symphony
Rewritten by machines on new technology
   - The Buggles, "Video Killed the Radio Star"

Who killed irony? As in an Agatha Christie story, the suspects are legion: was it Apathy, Political Correctness, a need for Consensus? Or was it that dark horse, Virtualization?

In a plug-and-play world, one in which machines are judged solely by efficiency, art is the spanner in the works. There has been a marked decline in value for antique furniture like dressers, armoires, and rolltop desks: pieces like these, no matter how ornate their scrolling, have no place in a sunlit, open-plan home. Their modern equivalents are much easier to clean and use.

Over a decade I've received no more than a handful of letters, by which I mean handwritten communications of length and depth, in print or cursive, on stationery or writing paper. How I would like to open my mailbox to find an envelope from a friend! Handwriting alone suffices to summon a person's essence. E-mails just can't compare -- not only because they are typewritten, but because linguistic beauty is sacrificed for brevity.

As a former middle manager, I supervised one veteran employee who could not fit his e-mails on three screens, much less one, as is the recommendation. But what a joy to read! A lifetime of scientific enquiry (he was a former physicist) had inculcated in him a predilection for preambles and detailed methodology: hypotheses, plans of attack, even dead ends encountered along the way. Bad journalism, yes – he "buried the lede" – but a great education! I read them many times, making slow sense of them. I never tried curing him of his prolixity.

Conversely, music has been miniaturized, compressed. Literally. An MP3 file is a reduced waveform compared to good old analog -- do you remember analog? When I was young, collections of ten to twelve songs were etched on vinyl albums, physical artifacts, works of art in themselves, from their front and back covers to their inner sleeves, liner notes, and record label stickers. Record companies staffed teams of designers who crafted packaging of a piece with the listening experience, which I studied while I listened. (When I was done listening,

I would file the records in milk crates purloined from Dad's restaurant business.) Most of that paraphernalia has disappeared, and the rest has been virtualized. Today people prefer, it seems, to lease music from conglomerates rather than buy it at record stores.

Money too has been virtualized. As a child, I loved collecting beautiful coins, in particular Morgan silver dollars, those satisfying, heavy disks engraved with matronly visages in long tresses personifying Liberty, and Mercury dimes depicting the same Liberty when she was younger, nimbler, and poorer. (The Mercury name arose from confusion with the winged god.) Cash is now an anachronism, and even credit cards are feeling quaint. Soon all we'll have are cell phone swipes and electronic bank transfers. When aliens rediscover our civilization millennia from now, they'll wonder what happened to our money.

And as a long-time fan, I'd like to mention sports. Baseball and football were once fonts of poetry, inspiration to writers and visual artists. Now, TV presents them as video games and markets them as gambling vehicles. Professional leagues believe that fans are more interested in "fantasy" teams than the actual ones. Does anyone still notice, or describe, the poetry of a centerfielder's gait, or the majesty of a football team's march down the frozen tundra of a playoff game?

To watch baseball on TV today is to see not the time-honored view from the bleachers, but a Bloomberg ticker. It has come to this -- I keep a driftwood plank, rescued from a nearby beach, to place over the continuous scrolling of scores and "breaking news" at the foot of the screen. But the driftwood cannot cover all the logorrhea on my screen: pitch counts, exit velocities, and too many statistics to fathom. Good writing eschews numbers – the mind can assimilate only so many, and not as efficiently as it absorbs descriptive language. Broadcasters should keep that in mind the next time they quote a launch angle. The onscreen superimposed rectangle designed to frame the strike zone just makes the ball harder to see. What happened to the crack of the bat, the cloud of dust, and the smell of the grass? The game's poetry has been put on mute. My advice to old-time fans is to go back to radio and let the game's action unfurl in the theater of your mind.

To virtualize experience – letters, music, money, sports, sex, and more – is to commoditize it. It greases the wheels of the marketplace, but leaves irony in the cold. Irony, by saying *what it does not mean*, demands involvement and an active evaluation of context. But context takes time to parse, and reduces efficiency.

Irony's demise is one step toward the end of opinion. Opinions cause conflict. To coexist in today's complex, interlocked world, people must agree, and quickly, on the value of things. An internet sensation is interesting if it gets views. A politician is respected if he or she receives votes. Non-quantifiable forms of criticism are expendable and beside the point: the Smiths' "Shoplifters of the World Unite" and Joy Division's "Love Will Tear Us Apart," both of which had limited chart success but which can now be had for a song, are suitable for supermarket airplay. "Urgent," an even bigger hit, is suitable for sedation.

Relax, you'll soon be asleep!

Right Field

In January, 1992, I was getting my ears lowered (as Dad once would say) at an Upper Montclair barber shop, down Valley Road from the school where I was pursuing the undergraduate degree that had eluded me for eight years. The rotating barber's pole of red, white and blue advertised to all and sundry that it was a traditional shop. The barbers, all male, wore powder blue work shirts with starched collars; their fussy silvered hair, too short to merit trimming, made them look like singers on *The Lawrence Welk Show*.

There was always enough trade to keep two barbers on duty. One was always quiet, and the other would always talk off your ear. I liked the former, but learned more from the latter: hearing I was from Madison, he told me about a barber from my hometown who had once become celebrated (he didn't use that word) for refusing to serve blacks. He said this in a confidential tone of voice that hinted of admiration, or even envy, for a guy with the balls to do that. I let the subject drop.

One day, waiting my turn, I sat in a hunter green chair with chrome armrests near the wood coat rack that resembled the one in the Princeton barber shop I'd once frequented, also a guild shop. That one stood adjacent to an antique glass entrance door with a bell affixed to a brass handle, and was a piece of college football history - it was literally a piece of the goalpost from an early twentieth century game against Yale.

I'd never realized how the barber shops of my youth were lairs of privilege. That was true of the first one I remember, the barber shop in the men's locker room at Spring Brook Country Club, in Morristown, where Dad took me to have my golden locks of youth shorn; and it was true where I was now. I'd been seduced by the scrape of a straightedge razor, the tingle of talcum, and the warmth of fresh-whipped, aloe-scented shaving cream.

I'd forgotten my textbook, so I absentmindedly read the *New York Daily News*. Like many *Daily News* readers (though not my Nana, who favored its liberal-leaning political pages and celebrity gossip), I began on the last page and thumbed backwards through the best stuff: sports, comics, TV, radio. I worked the Jumble in my head, skipped the annoying Cryptoquote, and then tried something altogether more challenging, the deciphering of the football picks of a prognosticator who knew every synonym ever coined for the word "dollar." He placed sawbucks here and laid simoleons there, and I did my best to keep pace.

I read a short notice. That coming Sunday, Super Bowl Sunday, Jonathan Schwartz would broadcast his annual "Salute to Baseball" on radio station WNYC. It promised to be a "hot stove" romp of conversation, when Jonathan would speak with ex-ballplayers like announcer pal Tim McCarver and showbiz friends who loved the American pastime almost as much as he.

> *Their production will be second to none*
> *And of course Henry the Horse dances the waltz*
> > - The Beatles, "For the Benefit of Mr. Kite"

After the emceeing and banter, Mr. Schwartz would then retreat to the privacy of his microphone and the place in his mind he liked to call "The Make-Believe Ballroom" to play baseball-themed songs. He would reminisce about his highly personal connection to the game, one that began at a tender age. He would tell the story of playing baseball games with dice and rules of his own invention, and broadcasting them via a low-power transmitter that had once served as the baby monitor that his parents used to listen to his nighttime infant snufflings, while they entertained in their grand Manhattan suite. (His father, the famed songwriter Arthur Schwartz, had written Bing Crosby's 1930s hit "Dancing in the Dark" among many other notable songs.) The transmitter, a primitive walkie-talkie, had a signal that carried a full two blocks. Friends of his parents – fathers preparing for Manhattan workdays, mothers doing morning chores – would say:

"Great show, Jonno!"

I made a mental note to listen.

***

At Montclair State, I slept weeknights at my grandmother's home, just fifteen minutes from school. Nana lived on the edge of Essex Fells, an Anglo-Saxon enclave surrounded by working class towns with large Italian populations. Her son-in-law, my Uncle George, had split the cost of her house with my father. Uncle George once was Vice-President of the Essex Fells Country Club, where his daughter, my cousin Lynn, was a champion swimmer. (Her name may still be immortalized there on a gold clubhouse plaque.) Nana lived next to one of the final holes of the course, across a street barely wider than a golf cart path, along which she would take her morning constitutional, harvesting stray golf balls from rhododendrons, gifts of errant golfers that she pocketed without penalty. Later, she would place them in a bucket to give to Dad, even though he no longer played the game.

On weekends, I returned to the childhood Madison bedroom that I had lived in since sixth grade. My programmable stereo was still there; on it I would set the dual-deck tape recorder to capture radio programs of interest. On Super Bowl Sunday, before the Bills and Redskins vied for world supremacy, I captured on two cassettes Jonathan Schwartz's show about a gentler, more venerable sport for later listening.

The following weekend, a pleasantly brisk and overcast Sunday afternoon, I donned my sweats and winter jacket and drove to Jockey Hollow National Historical Park on the far side of Morristown. I parked at the Visitor Center, collected my Walkman and earplugs, and struck out along wooded trails to listen.

Jonathan Schwartz adored baseball. He must have, because it nearly killed him. The 1978 one-game playoff between the Yankees and Red Sox, my highest high as a fan, was his all-time low. (I wrote about it briefly in *The Going Places Club*; Mr. Schwartz sublimated his grief in *A Day of Light and Shadows*.) He described baseball in the fond, hushed, caressing tones that he normally reserved for the Great American Songbook, that compendium of popular song among whose pages lived the immortals: Frank Sinatra, Tony Bennett, Johnny Mercer, Judy Garland, and his father. From it he scripted Sunday devotionals. But on Super Bowl Sunday he saluted baseball – not only would it drum up interest for the coming season and help fans get through the darkest month of the year (in an era before 24/7/365 sports broadcasting), but it would let him thumb his nose at the sport that had supplanted the one and only true national pastime in the hearts and minds of young America.

I, who have always loved baseball, radio, and sylvan walks, was in heaven. Or church: Jockey Hollow, and its slowly dying old-growth overstory, was my cathedral, its oaks my Corinthian columns, adorned with lianas rather than acanthus leaves, its framed naves and transepts marked by gentle descents, carpeted with the litterfall of a hundred soft autumns. It was the closest I could get to boreal woods without a day's drive -- my shortcut to solitude, a retreat to youth one-hundred-and-eighty degrees removed from the paint-by-number, cement block campus of Montclair State. Tracing leaf-strewn paths, I heard Mr. Schwartz's *divertimenti,* which ranged from big band tributes to Joe DiMaggio and Willie Mays, to snippets of old baseball broadcasts, to quirky odes like Dave Frishberg's "Van Lingle Mungo" and Steve Goodman's "A Dying Cub Fan's Last Request."

Some songs were familiar, such as the ballad "Right Field" by Peter, Paul and Mary. Perhaps I'd heard it on Pete Fornatale's Sunday morning WNEW folk show, "Mixed Bag." It charmed me anew as I listened in the woods. A thought – who were Peter, Paul, and Mary?

The benevolent trio had been with us as long, it seems, as their namesake saints. Once upon a time, children's music was composed not by employees of media conglomerates, but by songwriters mining personal memories of childhood. Peter, Paul and Mary wrote many such songs. "Puff the Magic Dragon," which had pride of place in my stack of childhood 45s, was perhaps the best known, but the trio also wrote for adults, whom they accorded the same respect as they did children.

"Right Field" which tells of an inept young baseballer, was from the group's late-career album *No Easy Walk to Freedom*, released twenty-five years after "Puff," in 1986. It sounds older than it is because its details don't mesh with Little League: the players choose up sides, situating the song in an earlier era when kids played on sandlots, called their own shots, and got to games without the help of helicopter parents.

Because the protagonist isn't very good, he is sent to play right field. (A note to baseball novices: right fielders see less action than other fielders in youth baseball because most batters hit right-handed and "pull" slow pitches to left field.)

Right Fielder spends his innings daydreaming:

Right field, it's easy, you know
You can be awkward and you can be slow
That's why I'm here in right field
Just watching the dandelions grow

Right was Dad's position, but he was nothing like this kid. Dad was always chosen first, or more likely the guy doing the choosing. He played right field for Clifton High School (1948-1951), the Orlando Senators (1952), and the Bradford Phillies (1953). His right arm – to take Nana's account at face value, which I have no reason not to – was one of the best in professional baseball. Scouts called it a "cannon" because he could unfurl a "clothesline" from deepest right, nailing runners at third and home. Eventually, runners stopped testing him.

Meanwhile, the kid in the song forgets the score, the number of outs, and the baserunners' positions. Again, nothing like Dad, who would impress upon me the importance of situational thinking. It worked, too! I remember one Little League game that Dad managed in which I played right. With a runner on third and one out, a fly ball came my way; remembering Dad's advice, I caught it while running forward and immediately threw home, uncorking a peg thirty feet up the third base line that hit high off the backstop. The throw was off-line, but the runner did not advance – because I'd been decisive.

In the song, Right Fielder catches a fly by sheer dumb luck after becoming aware that his teammates are pointing to the sky. He looks up, and the ball falls into his glove. The punch line goes:

> *Here in right field, it's important you know*
> *You gotta know to catch, you gotta know how to throw*
> *That's why I'm here in right field*
> *Just watching the dandelions grow*

Is this song for kids? I think not. They'd find its humor frivolous. Kids know proficiency doesn't come through luck; it has to be earned. And the manner in which the song is sung, in a voice that cracks on occasion, with humorous hesitations such as the drawn-out enunciation of "dan-de-li-on," is too cutesy by half. There's too much winking going on. There's even a musical quote of "Take Me Out to the Ball Game" in the song's intro and bridge. The song is probably meant for adults – the ones who grew up with Peter, Paul and Mary, in fact.

My right field play was lackluster, not as bad as Right Fielder's, but nothing like Dad's. Like the kid in the song, I was uncomfortable on the field. When I played in Madison Little League, it was never top of mind for my new coach to pencil me in the lineup. So I can identify with the scene in the 1976 film *The Bad News Bears* when little towheaded right fielder Lupus, after drifting to the fence, catches a fly ball like a scoop of ice cream in the championship game's final inning, as the soundtrack swells to a crescendo – a moment that still induces goosebumps when I see it. That feel-good moment is a glimmer of light among darker shadows in a film that raked the American Dream over the coals.

The Bears, a squad of misfits are, courtesy of a class action lawsuit, enrolled in an uber-competitive Little League in proto-Silicon Valley California. Their fathers, who had the clout to litigate them into the league, are too busy to attend practices or games.

Initially, the team is horrible. (They are, tellingly, the only team not bestowed with a major league moniker; their nemeses are the Yankees.) Their shortstop, Tanner, points out – in a line that would not escape the cutting room today – that they are a team of "Jews, wops, niggers, spics, and even a girl." The kids on opposing teams treat them like shit, but they're just taking cues from their parents and managers, who are appalled that the Bears have been dumped on their doorsteps by a legal remedy. Parallel crises can be inferred: major league baseball's integration crisis of twenty years earlier, and a breaking story when this movie was in the theaters, school busing.

And so we have two depictions of youth baseball: one, a song set in the golden sandlots of youth, the other, a war movie set in Silicon Valley. The former is baseball before the Fall, played by innocents and set to a waltz; the latter, a documentary-like depiction of American Dream strugglers, scored to the rough language that kids my age actually used. Which is closer to the truth?

There were, in my experience, managers who did what managers of Little League teams should do – teach skills and sportsmanship. There were also managers who prioritized victory, encouraging their players to take advantage of weak opponents, such as stealing bases at every opportunity. Similarly, there were parents who encouraged children and parents who cheered opponents' errors; parents who berated coaches, and parents who abused umpires. All for what? No one in my Little League had a chance of making a living at baseball.

When my youngest brother Danny was nine, Dad managed his team, Police Department. I went to his games at the Lucy D. Anthony fields when I was on my *New York Times* kick, reading the paper front to back. My bleacher neighbors must have thought me odd as I carefully paged the broadsheets to avoid invading their space. Anyway, after one particular pitch, I looked up to see Dad yelling at the other manager. The next moment, they were jawing face-to-face near the pitcher's mound, really going at it. I had no clue what triggered the argument, nor why Dad was so angry: perhaps the other manager had said something to rile him. Before they made contact, Dad was restrained by an assistant coach, and the incident was over almost as quickly as it had begun. I could hardly believe my eyes, and neither could Danny's teammates – all along the dugout bench they stared in the wide-eyed, unselfconscious way that only children allow themselves. One young boy in particular looked stunned.

I was too embarrassed to ask Dad about the incident, so I can't shed light on it now, but it was the sort of thing one saw from time to time in youth baseball, human nature shutting out idealism.

> *People work hard to keep a lid on their anger*
> *To see that justice will prevail*
> *To no avail, their efforts fail*
> *Something else is working harder*
>   - The Golden Palominos, "(Something) Else is Working Harder"

Silicon Valley or Eden? In America, baseball is played to win. But despite its darker moments, *The Bad News Bears* has a happy ending. The Bears remain stay in the league that tried to evict them, striking a blow for diversity and upward mobility. They lose the championship game, but save their souls.

Dream One

This is the first of seven dreams I had while writing this book. They likely resulted from excess thinking about the past. I present them in the order that they occurred -- unadorned, unexpurgated, as remembered upon waking.

Dad is in the driver's seat, a cushioned, swiveling captain's chair. His strong forearms, thickly matted with hair, rest on the wheel in the way I remember so well from long-ago motorhome trips. My wife Carol and I sit in the booth by the kitchen galley, on the passenger side of the craft. But when I peer across the aisle, I see a vehicle larger than a motorhome – it's a chartered bus full of high school classmates. We're off to gamble, dine and shop at a Las Vegas casino. First up, dinner at a popular theme restaurant.

Dad looks for a parking space. It isn't easy like in the 1970s, when he'd commandeer several spots at the back of a supermarket lot, parking on the transverse. He carefully navigates a honeycomb of small lots with narrow entrances and exits, like the satellite lots of New Hope's Peddler's Village, which were designed in a time before oversize vehicles. No single space can accommodate the bus, yet Dad manages to ease it gently onto one, with a generous bit of overflow. The parking space bears a word stenciled in yellow paint: "Deptford."

That's our destination, one of a chain of restaurants named after the London neighborhood where Squeeze, the rock band I idolized for years, formed. Glenn Tilbrook, still their lead singer, makes appears there on occasion, when in town to perform at the casino. When he does, he does a photo op and samples the steak and kidney pie, black pudding, and other dubious delicacies craved by Londoners five thousand miles from home. Glenn isn't there today, but at the restaurant entrance, a larger-than-life cardboard cutout of the guitarist-songwriter greets us. It disorients me. Having committed every feature of Glenn's face to memory when he was in his twenties and thirties, I can't get used to him as a sixty-something. His face is red and blotchy, his cheeks inflated like puff pastry, his once gorgeous mane of hair a scraggly, overgrown mess. But under it there is that recognizable smile.

Carol and I meet up with Clay, my best friend at school, and file into a banquet hall with our classmates. We sit at the end of a long bench, near a wall, where we talk between us, ignoring the others. The wait staff, which is exclusively male and black, circulates in bright white dinner jackets. One waiter hands me a book of matches, and I recognize the dark, blocky letters on alternating plum and violet vertical stripes - the logo of Dad's old restaurant, the Widow Brown's. I turn to the waiter and remark at the coincidence. He tells me that he's pleased to serve guests from "Jersey," and that he's originally from Rahway. I'm confused, because Rahway isn't near Madison.

I turn to my left and look down the long banquet hall for a smile, or any sign of recognition. I thought I saw one girl look my way, but each time I try to fix her gaze, she has turned away. A sixth sense tells me I'm being watched. I remember how adolescence is a time of surreptitiously checking out peers and trying to read their minds, measuring ourselves against people who know no better than we do how to behave.

After dinner we're given a few minutes to shop in a nearby mall, which is connected to the restaurant by a breezeway. Carol and I find an outlet of our favorite bookstore, (the fictional) *Berkshire Books*, which is mobbed with holiday shoppers even though December is months away. I see no classmates there, though again I sense them nearby.

Then I awake.

What I find odd is that Glenn Tilbrook, that rock-and-roll manchild (critics of Squeeze held his perpetual adolescence against the band), is the one person who has grown old. His cardboard photo is seedy; he has loaned his name to a restaurant chain in a grab for cash; and he's playing Vegas! But everyone else in the dream looks exactly as they did years ago: Dad is the same as during my childhood summer vacations, my classmates the same as when they dragged my heart around, and Carol the same as on the day we met. The ones we love don't grow old.

Sonata for Jukebox

No scene in *2001: A Space Odyssey* is more moving than the one near the end when David Bowman, the only surviving astronaut (played by the never-smiling Keir Dullea), bent on deactivating HAL, the renegade computer in control of his spacecraft, removes HAL's memory cartridges one by one, in reverse order. The irony is supreme. As HAL regresses to its "childhood" in Urbana, Illinois (or, equivalently, speeds toward senility, where one remembers only youth), every inflection of his electronic voice betrays the pain that is otherwise absent in the film. No wonder Pauline Kael, that overemotional yet intuitive movie critic, hated the movie, calling it a shallow exercise in craft: a computer was its most human character! As Bowman ejects each memory cartridge with a tool curiously like those that come with IKEA furniture, it slides out noiselessly, an incandescent rectangle of memory.

Those racked cartridges remind me of the core of the jukebox that once sat in my family's basement rec room. Each time I unlocked and lifted its glass display panel, I saw the dense, segmented fruit of 45 RPM records slotted in an arrangement of heavy but flexible metal dividers rather like the sections of an orange -- or a cerebral cortex.

For me, singles are memories. An MRI of my brain would mostly reveal the songs I love. I'm not sure life has taught me more than what I learned from FM radio, from platters of polyvinyl chloride, from shiny discs of acrylic, polycarbonate, and aluminum. Carol has played me often enough at Scrabble to know that most of my working vocabulary derives from band names and lyrics.

We learn that HAL's earliest memory is the song "Daisy Bell," also known as "Daisy," or "Bicycle Built for Two." It might be my earliest memory, too, since I sang it with Mom and Dad when I was very young. But did you know it was also the first song sung by a computer? At Bell Labs in 1961, in the first-ever demonstration of artificially synthesized speech, computer music pioneer Max Mathews composed an arrangement to which the IBM 704 "sang" the words to "Daisy Bell." (That day, Arthur C. Clarke, the author of *2001*, happened to be visiting Bell Labs. He was so impressed by this demonstration that he decided to use it in his book's climax.)

When our family sang "Daisy Bell" in the car – just the chorus, not the musty old verses – we were never closer. Families that eat together, they say, stay together; but those that drive and sing together are literally joined at the hip. Physical proximity tethered us three kids on the rear bench seat, me the monkey in the middle, Frankie and Robbie trying to crush me on turns, Dad at the helm, hairy arm draped across the rudder, Mom the co-pilot reading the stars. Like the von Trapps, our repertoire was traditional and varied. It consisted of nursery rhymes, Christmas carols (in season), and lots of *Sesame Street*: "Rubber Duckie," "Who Are the People in Your Neighborhood," and our theme song, "Five People in My Family."

(Quiz: Other than being on *Sesame Street*, what do those last three songs have in common? Answer: they were the brainchildren of Jeff Moss, a Princeton Triangle Club graduate, who wrote for *Sesame Street* during its first season.)

We also dipped into the canon of popular song, mainly oldies like "Daisy Bell" or more modern fare like "The Candy Man," the song from *Willy Wonka and the Chocolate Factory* that Sammy Davis, Jr. had made a hit. Below I'll list some other favorites, but first I'd like to echo Dad, who would introduce his favorites with the words, "And then I wrote...."

"High Hopes," written in 1959 by veteran film songwriter Jimmy Van Heusen and popularized by Frank Sinatra, was another firm family favorite:

> *Just what makes that little old ant*
> *Think he'll move that rubber tree plant?*
> *Anyone knows an ant, can't, move a rubber tree plant....*
> *Oops, there goes another rubber tree plant!*

Our family songs swung with bright melodies, playful lyrics, wit, whimsy, and loads of optimism. No existential, angsty, Brechtian dirges for us! Our songs were suitable for community sings in a day when popular music, like the space program, promised results, and before overeducated youths pioneered tales of psychedelic navel-gazing and journeying to the center of one's soul. True, those vibrations still lingered in pop culture when we kids were young in the 1970s, but thanks to Dad's curatorship of the car radio, the sunny music of earlier decades was what we heard.

By the 1970s, Dad's taste in music had solidified. He kept a fondness for the big bands of his youth, the Dorseys and Artie Shaw, and the mellifluous, throaty jazz crooner Billy Eckstine (when young and still living at home, Dad played "Mr. B." on the phonograph so often that it drove my grandmother crazy). He loved Pavarotti, and Sinatra, particularly with the Nelson Riddle Orchestra. Though he didn't dwell on music's nuts and bolts, Dad took the time to point out to me the elegance of Riddle's arrangements, and Sinatra's behind-the-beat phrasing.

Dad even took his love of music to work. At the Widow Brown's, his Madison restaurant, he set up a Banjo Parlor by the bar, where food was served with a side of bluegrass. The Ragtime Three played Tuesdays through Thursdays, and Mondays belonged to The Wild Colonial Boys, "back by popular demand."

***

This morning I woke to an earworm, a song stuck in my head. (Audiologists and researchers who take professional interest in such matters also call them earworms.) The melody was one I'd sung long ago with my family; for no apparent reason, it had surfaced overnight from my subconscious. I could place neither the artist nor the title, but I remembered its melody and these words:

> *Would you like to swing on a star*
> *Carry moonbeams home in a jar*
> *And be better off than you are*
> *Or would you rather be a mule?*

Online, I learned it was "Swinging on a Star," winner of the 1934 Academy Award for Best Original Song. Interestingly, it was also from the pen of Jimmy Van Heusen. (Van Heusen, one night in 1953, drove Sinatra to the hospital after Ol' Blue Eyes had slit his wrists over Ava Gardner.) The song's genesis dates to a dinner invitation from Bing Crosby, who unlike many famous men of his era, invited guests to family dinners. When one of his children complained about having to go to school the next day, Bing replied, "If you don't go to school, you might grow up to be a mule."

Jimmy ran with it, and the rest was history. His song contrasted the life that one might have with an education with the life one would surely have without:

And all the monkeys aren't in a zoo
Every day you meet quite a few
So you see it's all up to you
You can be better than you are

We kids didn't hear the song as a public service announcement; we just liked its animal imagery and silly lyrics. But Mom and Dad and Jimmy Van Heusen were planting seeds. What better way to transcend this hidebound earth and extend one's orbit than to swing on a star? Just imagine a rope attached to the infinitely sharp point of a crescent moon, and looking down on creation from that illuminated perch. Isn't that what the astronauts did, with the help of scientists and slide rules? In the 1960s and early 1970s, Mom and Dad, like most Americans, didn't consider the cost of the space program: they just wanted their kids to get there, and get there first!

***

Another morning, another earworm. This time I woke to the snippet "Roses and lollipops, lollipops and roses." That's all one needs today -- "Lollipops and Roses" was by Jack Jones, and according to my pop music reference books, it was the first of his more than twenty hits in the 1960s. (Dad played his greatest hits collection on the eight-track player.) It reached only #62 on the Billboard *Hot 100*, but placed higher on the Easy Listening Chart, where it hit number twelve. It begins:

Tell her you care each time you speak
Make it her birthday each day of the week

Perhaps this was the song that inspired the family tradition of dining on ice cream and cake every April second, Dad's birthday. The ice cream was from Baskin-Robbins, and Mom made the cake. Actually, she baked two Betty Crocker mixes, one of which was always Super Moist Spice Cake (as the box said, "There's pudding in the mix!"). This was how Mom showed her love for a birthday-dreading husband who never admitted to his real age. She coddled him like Jack Jones advised husbands treat their wives:

> *Bring her nice things, sugar and spice things,*
> *Roses and lollipops, and lollipops and roses*

***

The portable phonograph that Mom took to college resembled a suitcase when folded. Its beige speakers were mottled with small black pips, like spice cake with miniature chocolate chips, or vanilla ice cream speckled with bean. Mom had driven it one hundred fifty miles from her hometown of Pasco, Washington, to Gonzaga University, where she and her roommate whiled away the hours playing Vince Guaraldi and a whole lot of Edith Piaf.

Later, after Mom and Dad married, graduating to high fidelity, it became their kids' record player. With it we inherited Mom's collection of forty-five rpm singles, our first hit parade. With pink new ears, I heard each song as a one-of-a-kind miracle, its personality deriving from its name, label color, and unique sound. Ignorant that songs were products of songwriting schools, I assumed each had formed fully fledged, with no need of brooding parents.

All our favorites, even if written for teens or adults, sounded like kids' songs:

> *Little Jackie Paper loved that rascal, Puff*
> *And brought him strings and sealing wax*
> *And other fancy stuff*

and

> *There was green alligators and long-necked geese,*
> *Some humpty-backed camels and some chimpanzees*

and

> *Cause she's afraid to come out of the water*
> *And now the poor little girl's turning blue*

and

> *Right from the moment that those lovers start arrivin'*
> *You'll see more kissing in the cars than on the screen*

and

> *I got married to the widow next door*
> *She's been married seven times before*

It was comic book rock and roll by songwriters who came of age before rock dominated the marketplace. The songwriters had probably assumed, like my maternal grandfather, that Elvis and the movement he spawned would never be more than a fad. But we kids didn't care about authenticity, or record sales, or industry trends – we just liked songs that were bright, catchy, and easy to sing.

And Mom, like many mothers, wanted nothing more than for us to be strong, smart, and successful. Intuiting that the way to my mind was through my ears, one day she bought me a gift. She sat me down in a chair by the living room stereo and, one by one, produced a set of record albums. On the cover of each, rendered in primary colors, was a childlike drawing of an object: a magnet, a moon, a moth. The back covers read:

> *Motivation Records proudly introduces its series of SINGING SCIENCE RECORDS. We believe they are a unique landmark in young people's records and in science education. A remarkable combination of charming melodies and delightful lyrics, they contain an amazing amount of scientific information and delight the mind while they enchant the ear and the heart.*

The complete list of Singing Science Records appeared on the albums' back covers. They were a sextet, of which I still have five: *Space Songs, Weather Songs, Nature Songs, Experiment Songs,* and *Energy and Motion Songs*. (I lack only *More Nature Songs*.) The cover text indicates that the lyrics were penned by one Hy Zaret.

Hyman (Harry) Zaritsky was born in 1907 in New York City and became, according to his *New York Times* obituary, "one of the last Tin Pan Alley lyricists." His biggest chart success was the theme to an obscure prison movie called *Unchained*. "Unchained Melody" was not only a gargantuan hit for the Righteous Brothers, but was recorded by so many other artists that Mr. Zaret's financial independence was assured. His obituary notes, though, that he was equally proud of his educational songs.

I had yet to hear "Unchained Melody": that song was for adults. But I wore out the grooves on my five albums, as I can attest by holding them to the light today. My favorite was *Space Songs*, and my favorite song on it, in an early indication of a preference for theory over experiment, was "Why Does the Sun Shine":

The sun is a mass of incandescent gas
A gigantic nuclear furnace
Where hydrogen is built into helium
At a temperature of millions of degrees

Millions of degrees! Mind duly blown: that was way higher than the top of the thermometer outside the kitchen window!

These records had more than liner notes, though. They had lyric *books*. Each song got its own page, and when the lyrics didn't fill it, there was a reminder that "when you see an empty space, put a picture in its place." But I didn't draw pictures – I was content with the lyrics.

***

Years of listening to Dad's music inevitably served to ground my own taste: the light pop and rock of the Carpenters and Neil Diamond, the cosmopolitan country of Glen Campbell, and the light soul of the Fifth Dimension and Gladys Knight and the Pips. The latter ensemble recorded a song Dad particularly admired, which he once dedicated in front of us kids to Mom, saying it described his feelings for her:

If anyone should ever write my life story
For whatever reason there might be

You'll be there between each line of pain and glory
'Cause you're the best thing that ever happened to me
  - Gladys Knight and the Pips,
    "Best Thing That Ever Happened to Me"

These tunes continually loop on the eight-track player of my mind. Dad's had a sizable collection of eight-tracks, due in no small part to Mom's father, Grandpa Hines. Grandpa, a Ford salesman, knew better than anyone that a good stereo is one of a car's strongest selling points, and every month he received from the home office a new collection of popular songs, a proto-mixtape with the title *Ford Motor Company Presents Stereo for Today*.

I recall a day when Grandpa showed off his treasure trove. He motioned Dad and me to the trunk of his car, from which he extracted a faux leather case. He unlatched the case to reveal two dozen "demonstration tapes" in slots within, each containing a light pop-and-rock mix that would put speakers through their paces without abrading the ears. Grandpa had duplicates, which he was happy to give Dad. The two men stood behind the car, going through the tapes, reading the song selections on each. Clearly, someone back in Dearborn knew how to assemble a mix! There were soft hits like Wings' "Uncle Albert" and Hall and Oates "Sara Smile," pop-country from Ronnie Milsap, easy listening like O.C. Smith's "Little Green Apples" (I still catch myself, on occasion, singing the line "God didn't make little green apples, and it don't rain in Indianapolis in the summertime"), "semi-classical" tunes like Walter Wanderley's "Summer Samba," and even sweetened versions of recent pop hits like "Dancing Queen," done by the mysteriously named Living Voices and Living Strings. It was like WPAT, the New York radio station that played "beautiful music," only cooler.

But eight-track was a maddening format. For a start, there was no rewind button -- the only way to replay a song was to switch programs and carefully fast forward. Also, to equalize the lengths of the four stereo "programs," manufacturers sometimes hacked songs in two. Whenever that happened, the song would abruptly halt, and after a long pause, a loud clunk would sound before the music resumed. My ears eventually become accustomed to the clunks, effectively making them part of the songs.

Like us kids, Dad had his own stack of 45 rpm singles. But he didn't play them on the family hi-fi or on Mom's old record player: they stayed in the jukebox. The jukebox – actually, one of many that stood in our basement rec room over many years, with one periodically swapped in for another for no apparent reason – had pride of place on a linoleum floor near the main garage entrance.

The linoleum may once have been meant for dancing. If so, it would have accommodated no more than four legs. It was scuffed not by high heels but by the casters that scraped it whenever the jukebox was repositioned, leaving skid marks like those of a wayward car. (And like a classic car, the jukebox was made from chrome and steel, and seemed to weigh at least a ton.) A tiny brass key, comically disproportionate in size to the jukebox itself, opened its glass-topped panel and exposed coiled plastic entrails linking the rear panel to the spherical core of metal dividers that housed the records.

Today, I have Dad's hall-of-fame 45s in shoeboxes. There's Artie Shaw's "Frenesi," Perez Prado's "Patricia," Tommy Dorsey's "Opus One," Bobby Day's "Rockin' Robin," Bobby Darin's "Mack the Knife," and dozens of others. Honorable mention must go to Seals and Crofts' "Summer Breeze," that rare pop hit about marital bliss, which Dad particularly admired for the line "blowing through the jasmine in my mind." Oddly, "Summer Breeze" is linked in my mind to another hit song about summer romance, this one of an ephemeral kind, which was likely Dad's favorite song ever: Sinatra's "Summer Wind." I'll return to that song later, on Side B.

***

> *I was raised on the Beatles' music,*
> *Sat singing their songs for hours*
> *And I've been known to speak in lyrics*
> *When my own words lack the power*
>   - Addison Love, "Like the Beatles"

My apprenticeship to Dad's taste in music had made me something like a cub pilot. But soon I was flying solo, off his radar. The songs I discovered on these maiden flights weren't novelty tunes or dance crazes, more like poetry. They certainly weren't optimized for jukebox play. What sounded good on the jukebox was what sounded good on AM radio, singles that had been "mastered hot." The jukebox, with rear panel controls that moved mountains of bass and stirred tsunamis of treble, could work with those songs. But it could not simulate nuance, fidelity, or intimacy. (And turning down the volume yielded only crackle, hum, and hiss.)

Thirteen years after conquering America, the Beatles conquered me. I heard their songs on pop radio stations WNBC and WABC, which played a mix of oldies and current hits. But I needed more than chance encounters with my favorite band; I needed to possess them. So, I did what one did in those days – I asked Mom to drive me to Sam Goody.

Capitol Records made my album choices easy. They had recently reissued the Beatles' greatest hits on two double vinyl albums, *The Red Album* (1962-1966) and *The Blue Album* (1967-1970). Their nearly identical cover photographs showed the four lads staring down the camera from a stairwell landing inside the London headquarters of their record label, EMI. The only noticeable difference between the photos – and it was eye-popping – was the length of the band's hair: it had sprawled from a 1962 length that merely called their masculinity into question to a 1969 length that portended the end of Western civilization.

Behind the band, not one molecule of the glass and stainless steel stairwell had changed. The contrast between hair's organic sprawl and the rigidity of architecture symbolized -- if I may stretch the point -- the eternal struggle between change (the imperative of art) and stability (the corporate imprimatur). Or maybe it was just cool shorthand for the Beatles' Side A and Side B – their insouciant and exuberant early songs, and their more mature and complex later ones.

Unlike the early teenyboppers who'd fallen for the band, for me songs took precedence over personalities. At first, I didn't even know if it was John or Paul (or George) singing. I certainly didn't know who'd written what; only later could I distinguish Paul's ebullient compositions from those of moody John.

But following my conversion, I felt a deep need to proselytize. At every opportunity, I played Beatles music for friends and family, a first step toward making mixes. One early, primitive attempt utilized the household intercom: I played Beatles' tunes while the two middle-aged cleaning women worked downstairs. After a couple of songs, I clearly heard one call out to the other, "Hey, that's the Beatles!"

Sharing music made me giddy. But I didn't consider the possibility that those flashes that lit my synaptic pleasure centers like pinball bumpers might not be affecting others similarly. I would sit my younger brother Frankie down at the stereo and play him Beatles songs, asking him to rate each on a ten-point scale. For a while he played along, but when he assigned low ratings to songs that I would have given nines and tens, I had a first inkling of how subjective a taste for music could be. As Bruce Hornsby once said, "music is in the ear of the behearer."

I strove to prove my Fab Four worthiness. I challenged Clay, a classmate, to a Beatles' song-naming contest one day after school. By that point, I knew enough of the Beatles' catalog to rattle off a hundred songs by heart, but I wanted to see if anyone knew more. We met in the parking lot, joined by Mike, who as referee would listen for repetitions as we alternately named titles until someone was stumped. I hadn't told Clay, but Mike had coached me before the competition, compiling a list of lesser-known Beatles songs from his parents' record collection. Still, I lost. Clay had been listening to *his* parents' records since early childhood, which proved more than enough to defeat a novice like me.

But over time, I amassed quite a Beatles collection. Some albums I owned many times over thanks to Nana, who kept buying them -- often, the same ones over and over -- at garage sales. I eventually had all the albums and many of the singles, and still remember where I got most of them. *The Beatles Second Album*, for example, came from a mall record store in Washington State; Uncle Mike said he'd buy an album for me that summer, and I picked that one. And I got the "If I Fell/And I Love Her" single one Sunday at Scotti's, in Summit, where I'd ridden my bike. When I told Aunt Margo about it on the phone later that afternoon, she said I'd picked a "good one."

Soon I could spread out the entire Beatles catalog on my bed in chronological order, which was a revealing way of bringing their achievement into focus. Then I'd spin the records, one by one, on Mom's old phonograph. I'd unlatch the suitcase, drop the turntable heavily into place with the thunk like a pneumatic press, and carefully lower a single over the black-and-white plastic spindle, like a tight-fitting T-shirt over a torso.

Along the way, I had to parry a gross error of my father's: he believed the Beatles didn't write their own songs! He thought their management solicited ghostwriters. That's the way showbiz had always worked, so he reasoned it must be particularly true for the Beatles, who had so many hits. I didn't even try to argue against this crazy notion, but I must say this -- if Dad had been right, he would have had a hell of a scoop over dozens of Beatles' biographers.

Now it was my turn, as it had once been Dad's, to "write" the songs I loved. I'd select a song order – easy for the Beatles, since chronological order provided a ready-made scaffold of unfolding complexity – and reconstruct not only the band's career, but imagine it as belonging to me. I pretended to have written each song, trying to force my brain to hear it from the perspective of someone hearing it for the first time. That isn't easy to do! Familiarity with the songs forced me to play them louder and louder, so I could hear them anew by bringing forward the details buried in the mix. (Mom and Dad, bless them, never complained that I was playing them too loudly.) I imagined my growing fame, and could see my friends and classmates, mouths agape, saying:

"How could you have written 'Penny Lane,' then 'Strawberry Fields Forever'"?

The answer, of course, was that no one could. Those twin odes to lost Liverpudlian innocence were stepchildren of different fathers, McCartney siring the former, Lennon the latter. Both remain favorites of mine to this day. If I were given the cruel choice of bringing only one to a desert island, I would pick "Penny Lane," but it was Lennon's song that more deeply affected me as a teen. In a dreamlike four minutes and seven seconds, it encapsulated the self-absorbed, ambivalent otherworldliness of adolescence:

> *Living is easy with eyes closed*
> *Misunderstanding all you see*
> *It's getting hard to be someone but it all works out*
> *It doesn't matter much to me*

It was as different as could be from the can-do songs that we had once sung together in the car as a family; it would never have found a spot in my parents' record collection. It was somber, inward-looking, and unresolvable, hinting at what felt like deeper truths of life. Some hurdles are insurmountable. Good guys don't always win. Maybe they *shouldn't* even win.

To chase the chill induced by this moral relativism, I stacked another single on the spindle, the beatific "Hey Jude." I had acquired this song, which did not appear on any original Beatles album, at the Rainbow Trading Post in Morristown, a used bookstore on the north side of Morris Street, just down from the Green. It was a ramshackle place staffed by spotty collegians, one of whom had joked about my purchase of Dire Straits' "Sultans of Swing":

"You must really be in those to want that." It took me a beat to get the play on words.

In its day, "Hey Jude" was an unprecedentedly long hit. Seven minutes and eleven seconds long, it unspooled slowly on the turntable, giving my mind time to wander. I brushed aside an annoying thought, something I'd recently read in a library book. *Subliminal Seduction* was Wilson Bryan Key's so-called exposé of hidden advertising in pop culture; in it, the author cited "Hey Jude" as one of many pop songs with hidden drug references. A baseless charge: Paul had written the song to cheer up John's son, Julian, after his parents separated. Still, I must admit the lyric that the author cited, "The movement you need is on your shoulder" is odd. The author then went on to cite Simon and Garfunkel's transcendent "Bridge Over Troubled Water" for its line, "Sail on, silver girl," supposedly about a hypodermic needle. Too much! I mentioned the latter charge one day in high school biology, and my classmate Laura sided with me. As for "Hey Jude," I knew the Beatles had taken drugs in the late 1960s; but that didn't mean that all their lyrics were coded messages.

I watched the slow rotation about its core of the Granny Smith apple, the logo of the Beatles' record company, Apple, before the name was stolen by a tech company. Like a hypnosis wheel, it rid my mind of care in a more salutary way than drugs ever could, reminding me that only music will ever save my soul. I doubt I'll ever get closer to nirvana than in its final four minutes, when the band slowly builds to a crescendo, shamanistically chanting "na na na."

***

Dad died in 1996. Three years later, Mom sold the house in Madison. My sister Robbie couldn't bear to part with the jukebox, so being the only child with a home in which to store it, she had it hauled to Berkeley Heights, where it sat in her basement for years.

When Carol and I bought our place in Madison, it was our turn to house the jukebox. Extricating the jukebox from Robbie's basement may have been the single most foolhardy physical act I have ever attempted. It first required a vinylectomy – the removal of its heart of one hundred singles. I removed them one by one from their sleeves in the metal core, recognizing each one without reading the label due to long familiarity. And unlike Astronaut Bowman, I didn't have to listen to the jukebox complain as I ejected its memories.

Clay and I rented a truck and a furniture dolly. It took us an hour to raise the machine, still several hundred pounds unencumbered, up a narrow flight of stairs to the ground floor. Clay cinched it with a strap and pulled from above as I supported its weight from below with my shoulder, blindly directing my weight like a football player confronting a tackling dummy; then, a few minutes later, we'd awkwardly maneuver around the banister to trade places. At times, the jukebox threatened to crush us or the banister – but we eventually got it to its new home.

Then for two years, Carol and I kept it in our dining room, on the threadbare wall-to-wall carpet that was a step down from linoleum. I fired it up once or twice, but it sounded all wrong in a room where it could not be played loudly enough to make a glorious noise – it really needed a cavern to blast away in. So, when we planned our move to Manhattan, it had to go. I placed an ad in Craigslist and got an immediate bite from a fellow in Long Island, who arrived the following Saturday with a large pickup truck. He was on a mercy mission – two other jukeboxes had already been tied down to the flatbed. He showed me snapshots of still other units in his man cave at home, proving to my satisfaction that ours was going to a caring home where it would be among friends after being restored to full working order.

***

2001: A Space Odyssey ends when Astronaut Bowman traverses a psychedelic portal – part circuit board, part fallopian tube – to find himself dining alone in a residence as elegant as Versailles, a scene of placid domesticity that is utterly disorienting after the preceding vision of deep space and the sound of throbbing electronic music. But in the astronaut's final resting place, the most striking detail is utter silence: the silence of old age, after memories, after music, after "Daisy Bell."

Sing We Now of Christmas!

A gray sky glowers. Planet Earth slows as it approaches the solstice, dipping beneath the ecliptic plane. One beacon illuminates winter's frozen landscape – Christmas!

I flick on the armchair lamp: which liturgy to read? From a shelf weighed down by Charles Dickens' *A Christmas Carol* and Joseph Bottum's *The Christmas Plains* (his collection of essays about a South Dakota Christmas), I extract two pamphlets thin as missalettes – *TV Guides* from December, 1976. Why not? Television taught me some of my earliest lessons about Christmas. In December, each show had a special holiday episode, syrupy with sentimentality, sweet as fruitcake, capped with a moral as cloyingly sweet as a maraschino cherry.

When these *TV Guides* hit the racks of newsstands and supermarket checkout aisles, I was ten. That was the year Mom and Dad finished their holiday shopping on Christmas Eve, and Frankie, Robbie, and I spent the day at our grandparents' in Blairstown. Nana Edie watched over her flock in her warm and comfortable house, but a morning and afternoon of watching TV on her chintz sofa, in the modest living room onto which the front door directly opened, had me feeling penned in.

I had run the Christmas gauntlet and lived to tell the tale: *The Brady Bunch* (*TV Guide*: "Laryngitis may prevent Carol from singing at the Christmas service"), *Bewitched* ("When an orphan who doesn't believe in Santa visits the Stevens' for Christmas, Samantha takes him to the North Pole"), *That Girl* ("Ann tells Donald about a Christmas she spent with a sick boarding school student") and *Family Affair* ("Buffy befriends Eve, a sick girl in her apartment building, and asks Uncle Bill if they can celebrate Christmas early in case Eve is not alive in December.")

I was like the child dosed with too much cherry cough syrup. TV may have helped to pass the time, but Christmas Eve moved slowly without my books and toys at home. And after enough shows and commercials for toys I'd forgotten to add to my Christmas list, I needed a break. Happy that my own shopping was done (washcloths for Uncle Mike and Aunt Margo; costume jewelry for Nana -- "just get the cheapest pair of clip-on pearl earrings they have behind the counter at Macy's" -- and crystal salts that would make the flames in my family's fireplace turn red and green), I zipped up my brown-and-olive sleeveless vest coat that beetled my chest like a flak jacket, and stepped onto my grandparents' frosted front lawn.

The cold evening air was the balm I needed for the month-long fever I'd been running in anticipation of the morrow. My limbs were galvanized; having lain dormant so long, I could feel each muscle twitch. I drank in the air and watched my vaporous exhalations halo the red sun setting in a field of deep indigo. Nana Edie and Grandpa Hines lived in a newish development of uniform split-level homes on lawns that sloped to the street; above me, telephone wires divided the sky into polygons that shapeshifted as I walked, like changing kaleidoscope patterns. Stars appeared; I recognized the Big Dipper. The abiding quiet seemed to hint at an older Christmas story than the ones I'd seen on TV, one that could be sensed only by escaping from noise, bustle, and other people. But soon I was chilly, so I went back in.

Even as a juvenile *TV Guide* reader, I assiduously read the sidebar descriptions of every holiday program. Now, decades later, I reread them from my armchair. Many were for animated children's "specials." One of the best-known premiered the month before I was born.

A Charlie Brown Christmas was the Gospel according to Charles Schulz. As in his iconic comic strip, *Peanuts*, Schulz's ten-year-olds voiced grown-up philosophy: in this case, that Christmas had become too "commercial," its meaning lost in the seasonal shuffle. My epiphany on Nana Edie's front lawn echoed Schulz's distrust of frantic holiday preparations and garish decorations, such as the aluminum trees seen in the cartoon (a disease that never afflicted our household). The cartoon quoted liberally from the Gospel According to Linus (Luke, I later learned), and included two choruses of "Hark the Herald Angels Sing," sung by the kids after decorating Charlie Brown's scrawny tree. Schulz fought his producers to keep the religious messages in the script, and I'm glad he did – I've come to appreciate them for reasons beyond religious signification. They show that an artist can work within the system while remaining true to his vision.

A Charlie Brown Christmas introduced me to another religion, jazz. Namely, the smooth West Coast piano stylings of Vince Guaraldi. This was the same Guaraldi whom Mom had listened to in college, particularly his album *Impressions of Jazz Orpheus*, which featured his breakthrough pop instrumental, "Cast Your Fate to the Wind." Mom loved that song, and I always wondered if its title was a portent of the night a few years later when she would cast her fate with Dad.

Four feet from the TV, I drank the fizzy three-color radiation while scanning the cartoon's end credits for the name of the man responsible for the music. It flashed by, right after those responsible for "graphic blandishment," whatever that was. Guaraldi wrote the original music specifically for the cartoon, and they perfectly conveyed the holiday's hot and cold sides: the pent-up boil of my grandmother's living room ("Linus and Lucy") and the cool contemplation of her front lawn ("Skating"). They shaped not only my taste in jazz, but that of countless musicians to come; in fact, they were so popular that they bestowed a name to a new genre: "Charlie Brown music." (I have instructed my estate to play both "Linus and Lucy" and "Skating" at my funeral.)

The cover illustration of the *TV Guide* for December 25, 1976 is so noncommercial and naively drawn that even Schulz could not have complained. Belonging seemingly to another century (which it does, of course), it depicts a hallucinatory yet benign pop-art Santa hovering like a hummingbird under clouds of ribbon candy, above an evergreen forest decked with candles, sparklers, and firework starbursts of every color.

But for the good stuff, the peak-season Advent broadcasting, I turn instead to the *TV Guide* from two weeks earlier, the one with the cover portrait of Valerie Harper. Thumbing past cigarette and alcohol ads targeted at adults already besieged by the holidays, I read the sidebars:

The Bell System presents *The Tiny Tree*, "a story of love and sharing the whole family will enjoy."

Greer Garson narrates a new special, *Little Drummer Boy, Book II*.

Danny Kaye and Mia Farrow star in a brand-new stage production of *Peter Pan*.

And on CBS, Johnny Whitaker (of *Family Affair*) plays the lead in a made-for-TV production of *Tom Sawyer*. I remember that one well -- how I had a crush on its Becky Thatcher, Jodie Foster!

But what to make of an advertisement, placed by an organization named Vantage Youth, for a silk-screened satin "Leadership Banner" signed by "all fifty state governors and the president as of July 4, 1976"? (Had recent political events dictated that the President not be named?) It's hard to fathom a market today for such political reverence.

***

Now picture, as in a silent movie, a howling wind whipping calendar pages. With the years' passage, my preferred liturgy shifted from television to music. My new devotional became the Christmas carol.

Second through fifth grades, I attended The Peck School, a private day school in Morristown. Its campus lay behind a tall, black, cast iron fence bordering South Street and Route 287. Youngsters like me were educated in a modern, single-story building, but sixth graders and up – the formally attired "upper classes" in which boys wore ties and jackets, and girls wore knee-length white dresses – were instructed in a Victorian castle that had once been the Lindenwold Mansion, a mulberry-and-ocher fantasy in stone, studded with chimneys and turrets, one-hundred-percent Gilded Age. In 1900, it had belonged to William Skidmore, one of the first suburban New Jersey train commuters, most of whom resided on "Millionaires Row," which one day would be the stretch of Route 24 between Morristown and Madison. Their Wall Street flying carpet was a steam-powered train, replete with smoking, dining and club cars.

Peck's Art teacher was Mr. Green the Third, the headmaster's lanky, bearded grandson whose hair length greatly eclipsed his forebear's. One morning, *en plein air*, in Mr. Green's class, I sketched Lindenwold with a pencil, on a drawing pad, on an easel. I was proud of that picture, which represented the apex of my drawing career. I no longer have it, so I can't prove that it was good, but I still recall my astonishment that I could conjure crenelations out of nothingness.

The occasional visit to Peck's business office or library would take me to Lindenwold. The walk from the elementary school building was via a cloister with the flat roof of a carport, supported by regularly spaced wood columns planted squarely in a concrete breezeway, around which the hands of lucky boys and girls going steady would let go a moment as they said, "Bread and butter!"

Peck retained features of the English public school, most notably its seasonal traditions. For instance, on the last day of spring term, when we were giddy with the prospect of the gloriously long summer ahead, we would gather in the cafeteria to see a movie. Meanwhile, back in our classrooms, our teachers placed on our desks thick hardcover books, newly bound in the school colors, navy blue and white; our names were embossed on the covers in gold. They contained our scholastic year output -- spelling tests, math worksheets, short stories, book reports, drawings, and so on. After the movie, we'd grab them on the way out the door to our parents' waiting cars – and summer.

I don't know who chose the movie for the end-of-year assembly. Perhaps it was our headmaster, Mr. Green, who was tall and dapper with a rugged face like John Robinson's on *Lost in Space*. He was so tall, in fact, that at a school loath to mete out snow days, the saying was that the doors would not close unless the snow reached "Mr. Green's knees."

One year, the graduation day film was *Oliver!*, Carol Reed's celebrated musical adaptation of *Oliver Twist*. I was entranced by its spectacle, which painted England as a fairy tale land. As for the story, Oliver and Nancy were so pure, and Sikes so evil, that I was on pins and needles as I sat cross-legged on the cafeteria's rubber floor among hundreds of schoolmates: who would prevail? (The whole-school movie-watching scenario has been portrayed in films as disparate as *Au Revoir Les Enfants* and *The Cider House Rules*. I would not be surprised if communal movie going has precipitated many a filmmaker's birth: to see one's peers enthralled by art inspires one to make it.) As for me, I identified with Oliver, the poor waif, and inwardly hoped to be as pure at heart as he, and as worthy of the love of a good woman like Nancy.

But Peck's foremost annual tradition was the Christmas Sing, which took place on the evening of the last day before holiday break. It was another all-school cafeteria event. Bleachers were stacked on the raised stage to accommodate the entire student body, with sopranos piping stage front and basso profundo upperclassmen booming stage rear.

I still have a cassette tape of the 1975 Sing; when I play it, I am reminded of the large number of lesser-known carols in the program. That was due to Miss McCormick, our music instructor, who stoked my interest in the seasonal canon. We sang the nineteenth-century English carol "The Holly and the Ivy," the traditional French carol "Un Flambeau, Jeanette Isabella," and even the Catalan carol "Fum! Fum! Fum!" (not to be confused with the Beach Boys' ode to cruising, "Fun Fun Fun"). I spent weeks memorizing the words; Miss McCormick admonished us all to learn each carol by heart, so as not to be seen reading on stage. Her advice to soften our r's still resounds in my ears: "*Nevah evah* sing *neverrr everrr!*"

One year, as the Sing approached, I got sick. Not from overexcitement or a diet of holiday sweets, as might be expected, but from a stomach bug making the rounds. I despaired at missing the big event. The night before, I told Nana, who was over to babysit, in a voice borrowed from the waif Oliver, "Nana, I don't think I'm going to make it!" Nana told that tale for years.

The next night, merely queasy, I took my place on the bleachers, where my neighbors had been calibrated to be just tall enough to make me stand on my tiptoes and project my voice to the rear of the auditorium, where Mom, Dad, and Nana listened on folding chairs. I sang, and sang, and continued to sing as a student two rows back vomited on the boy behind me. But after the Sing was over, I beamed at a job well done. Christmas break was here, and at home a hill of bakery cookies wrapped in cellophane on the kitchen table, a gift from one of Dad's restaurant suppliers.

After I left Peck, I mostly gave up singing. I performed on occasion, anonymously, in the pews of St. Vincent Martyr, the family church, where rather than project my voice to the rafters, I kept it down, rounded my vowels, and tried to make our ragged congregation infinitesimally more mellifluous.

Of my family, I alone attended Church. I wasn't especially religious; I just liked the way the liturgical year marked the seasons. Like a sundial, one could gauge the month from the angle and quality of the sunlight streaming through the clerestory windows above the altar-in-the-round, but also from a dozen other details: the flower arrangements, the color of the priests' vestments, the hymns, the size of the handbell choir, the color of the collection envelopes. And during Advent, everything was heightened: chasubles went purple, votive candles multiplied, and incense streamed from thuribles, clouding the aisles. (The exotic vocabulary of Church hardware, learned in Confirmation classes, appealed to the word collector in me.)

Finbarr Corr, the senior priest with the snow white hair, a native of County Cavan, Ireland, lived next door in the rectory. During mass, he intoned in plain chant Isaiah's tidings of great joy, and I followed in the missalette that I removed from the seatback in front of me. One day, I slipped the missalette into my pocket so that I could transcribe the carols at home. I never returned it -- I hope that sin is venial.

Father Corr left St. Vincent's soon after I did. For many years, it turns out, he had been questioning Church tenets. Specifically, he could find no basis in Scripture for the requirement that the priesthood be celibate. Knowing in his heart that he wanted to marry, he resigned the ministry, becoming the first of a long line of Father Corrs to do so. He did marry, and as a layman continued to pursue his twin vocations of counseling and instruction, finally retiring to Cape Cod to write of his Irish childhood.

In the guest room at the top of the stairs that later became my brother Danny's room, I typed the carol lyrics from the missalette into my family's spare computer. Then I printed them on the pin-feed, daisy wheel printer that shrieked like the four horses of the Apocalypse, especially when I imperfectly threaded its sprockets with the fan-fold, green-and-white-lined paper. Those lyrics would join the ones that I'd previously transcribed from *Sing We Now of Christmas!*, a slim paperback for practicing carolers that I'd purchased at a Princeton bookstore. And for carols appearing in both sources, I cobbled together a definitive version, as though I were some kind of amateur folk song anthologist.

I was readying myself for the annual festival of carols that my childhood friend Clay and I observed each December 23. On that night, we'd attach our dot-matrix carol printouts to clipboards that Clay had outfitted with hand-built flashlights, built from Radio Shack components and housed in blue plastic soap bar holders. Then we would hit the road. Our destination was always Bethlehem, Pennsylvania – in particular, the star watching over "The Christmas City" from the top of South Mountain.

Along the way, we ate homemade cookies. Clay's were the good ones, baked from recipes from his test kitchen, which he sold by mail order. My own contribution varied annually; one year I made macaroons which, like evil souls, never rose. We washed them down with non-alcoholic eggnog while singing out the car windows for hours, whatever the weather. (One year, it was so cold that our flashlights failed.) If the roads were clear of snow, we'd take my Nova; otherwise, Clay would borrow his grandfather's pickup, to the grille of which he would string a set of white Christmas lights.

I believe our warbling went unheard, except at the odd stoplight. Small-town New Jersey then was pastoral, with the darkened December nights as desolate as the fields of the very first Christmas. One year, after a late start, we stopped at a red light to cross Route 24 at Robinson's Drug Store in the center of Mendham. It was utterly still. A few lights glowed wanly in storefronts, but the shops had long since closed. Street lamps, bright as theater spots, compensated to light our car, as we loudly sang "O Come All Ye Faithful" to no one at all. I assure you it really happened.

One year, we charted a course to Bethlehem via Mendham, Chester, and Long Valley (with a detour to Hackettstown one year, to see our high school classmate Rahn, who with his new bride and child were battened down that winter like the Holy Family), then forded the Delaware at the quaint burg of Belvidere. Its downtown was dark. After crossing the free bridge, we stopped at a restaurant on the river's far bank, in a former mill that had seen better days. Clay in his gray sweats and I in my blindingly bright yellow-and-red rugby shirt (Clay's holiday gift) were shown to a corner table, not that the restaurant had a crowd to hide us from. We amused ourselves with a menu riddled with typographical errors ("Michelop"), and I ordered a feta salad, for which I would later pay the price.

By Nazareth we'd be sung out, so, we'd put on cassettes of favorite Christmas tunes:

> *Mary and Joseph drove into town*
> *Searching for a place to stay*
>   - Squeeze, "Christmas Day"

or

> *Evergreens, sparkling snow*
> *Get this winter over with!*
>   - The Waitresses, "Christmas Wrapping"

or troll the dial to search for a radio station with a live deejay. One year, we came across an old codger playing 1940s music and reading weather reports to lost souls navigating the snowbound late-night lanes of western New Jersey. Like collectors who'd discovered a rare find in a dusty bookstore, we tried to appraise him. I pictured him in his chair, in a weathered shack in the middle of a field of frozen cornstalks, with icicles hanging from an "On Air" sign above a door. Clay and I listened to him with a mixture of disbelief and grudging respect.

Our pilgrimage never took the same route twice, because we never found a direct route to the star. Less like two wise men and more like Columbus' crew navigating uncharted waters, we kept our eyes glued to the horizon until the guy in the crow's nest (Clay) or the guy with the crow's feet eyes (me) spotted a five-pointed, eight-rayed beacon low in the sky, schematic as a drawing in a cartoon, considerably less complex than the thirty-point Moravian stars for sale in the downtown bookshop. The star!

Our final approach never varied: we ascended a hill on a local road bordered by blue collar businesses – delicatessens, pawn shops, TV repair stores – that proved yet again that the last step to a miracle is always mundane. The star was attached to the transmitter tower of local station WLVT, Channel 39. But even when seen from below through the metal infrastructure of a stanchion, the beacon had a kind of dignity.

Our tribute paid, we'd hit Perkins or Stuckey's on the way home. Over patty melts we'd play, on paper menus meant for kids, a game of "dots." Clay would give me a refresher on the rules of the game, one that he had played in elementary school and I had not. Then we would return by highway and, back in the Nostalgia Room, in my parents' basement, we'd spend the rest of the night playing chess, usually one interminable game that lasted for hours because we were too tired to think straight.

***

After television and music, my chosen medium for Christmas liturgy became literature. In my life, writers -- not political or spiritual leaders -- have been my moralists. They have defined Christmas for me as well.

And among writers, how could Dickens not be first? *A Christmas Carol* has shaped the Western world's Yuletide observation for one hundred seventy-five years. When I was young, I read it each advent, a seasonal rite like my August preseason football rereadings of George Plimpton's *Paper Lion*. Plimpton was an outsider with respect to professional sports; Dickens was a Christmas insider. Contemporaries testify that, like his reclamation project Scrooge, Dickens "knew how to keep Christmas well, if any man alive possessed the knowledge."

The inseparability of Christmas and Dickens became clear when I read *A Christmas Carol* aloud to my seven-year-old brother Danny. Our family had gathered at my grandmother's house in Roseland for a holiday dinner, and Danny and I sat on Nana's plush living room couch. From the kitchen next door, conversation crackled at the counter, where brothers, sisters, aunts, uncles, parents, and cousins shouted over music, but Danny stayed with me as I read. I was surprised at how well he followed the story. From a plum pudding of nineteen-century British archaisms, he was able to extract the modern notion of Christmas.

He could do so because *A Christmas Carol* is a fairy tale. And it lacks the verbal padding and head-scratching coincidences of Dickens' serialized novels, for which the writer was paid by the word. *A Christmas Carol*, in contrast, is a simple tale of a miser who, having chosen Mammon as his master, has come to a cold and lonely end.

A cry from the next room, where noise and light vied for supremacy: Andy Williams crooning "It's the Most Wonderful Time of the Year" on Ella's boom box; Robbie picking out carols on the upright piano; Dad's spaghetti pot whistling; and the hubbub at the counter surrounding a spread of desserts that included an authentic Manhattan cheesecake that cousin Donna had brought with her, along with a new boyfriend. Danny and I were reading Dickens, but our family next door was enacting him.

Meanwhile, Scrooge chooses reformation over an eternity in chains. Dickens' portrayal of Scrooge's joy at his own redemption is, for me, unrivaled in literature, the very definition of Christmas joy, alongside which the story of a manger, an ox, an ass, and a baby pale like a folk tale whose meaning has been muddied over time like other traditions of Merrie Olde England I never quite fathomed – maypoles, mummers, Morris dances. On the contrary, the plot of *A Christmas Carol* seems torn from today's newspapers. There are heartless, powerful villains; a wide gulf between the moneyed and the poor; and two children, Want and Ignorance, hidden in the folds of the robe of the Ghost of Christmas Present, foretelling revolution should the status quo remain. *A Christmas Carol*, if it were published today, would surely be decried as a liberal's scribblings.

This past December, for the first time in years, I removed the book from the shelf and reread it. It's a quick read. But I like lingering over words that sparkle, ushering in contrasting evocations of cheer and dread. Anyone who knows the story only from television and film adaptations should go straight to the source, as many dramatizations are not particularly faithful.

I was struck by its apolitical aspect. I realized that whole scenes in the 1951 film starring Alistair Sim, the version I know best, had been invented from whole cloth. Some examples: the purchase of Fezziwig's establishment by a financier with a thoroughly modern taste for the value of information, a scene intended as a metaphor for the ills of modern capitalism; the even shadier buyout of the firm by Scrooge and Marley; Scrooge's refusal to extend the maturity date of a loan to an indigent debtor. These scenes are simply not in the book -- but since the original story is not a broadside, its moral elements are heightened.

For Dickens, the most heinous crime one can commit is to turn one's back on humanity. Surprisingly running a close second is abstaining from the simple joys of society, which of course are heightened at the holidays. Dickens repeatedly brings the story to a lurching halt to indulge in lavish accounts of food, music, and merrymaking, which together are enough to make the weight watchers and stoics of the world – even the mildly antisocial – head for the hills. But Dickens was no hypocrite; his biographers confirm that he himself ran riot over the holidays.

Had Dickens lived to meet our 45th President, after overcoming his astonishment at meeting in the flesh the equal of his most malevolent creations, one with a surname wet with the indigo of his own inkwell, one so full of trumpery, I suspect he would have directed his criticism less at his policies (exploitation of the poor and dispossessed, thieving from the common treasury) than his character defects. It's easy to guess what Dickens might have said about a man who never laughs, fears food, dislikes music, despises pets, and never offers an apology – he said it all about Scrooge.

To read *A Christmas Carol* as an adult is to put one's conscience to the test. Does money matter too much to you? Does it somehow make you sacrifice your better nature? When I was young, I figured that whatever shortcomings I might have, I would have years to rectify them. In my fifties, I think rather: am I doing what I can? Do I treat people, as "fellow travelers to the grave," or are they rather "another race of creatures bound on other journeys"? After all, my character is pretty well formed, barring a miracle on the order of Scrooge's. But the most joyous moral in *A Christmas Carol* is that it's never too late for change.

***

When I was young, Christmas ran hot and cold. For every frenzied gathering with friends and family, there were quieter moments spent alone beneath the boughs of a Christmas tree, contemplating its lights.

Returning to the evening of the day spent at my grandparents: back at home, we three kids tore around the living room in a fever of excitement until our foreheads (and the tip of my brother Frankie's nose) beaded with sweat. To distract us, Mom and Dad assigned us an errand: take a gift up the street to the Rosenhauses. They didn't celebrate Christmas, but they were friends, and Sammy, the pug-nosed kid in Frankie's class, had a baseball card collection I envied. Sammy's older brother James, two years older than I, had made good use of the snow and ice that had fallen earlier that December to build the coolest ice fort ever. It was an architectural wonder, a real igloo, constructed so solidly that crawling inside on my stomach gave me a shiver – not just from the cold, but because its interior was a fortress of solitude, completely soundproof. That night, though, we bypassed the igloo to deliver our gift at the front door, then tore back home. This alternate sweating and freezing have fixed that night in my mind as the winter B-side of the torrid summer A-side of the day when I walked into the Morristown Pool clubhouse with my friend Robert and was greeted by an arctic blast of air conditioning, a shock wave that bestowed upon me an instant headache.

Today we bake Alaska differently. We warm the planet, then freeze it in discord as cold as the end result of the thermodynamic entropy that will one day turn out the universe's lights. Meanwhile, an entropy closer to home hurtles friends and family, move by move, across the continent like Christmas cards struggling to keep pace with unfamiliar zip codes.

It would be nice to reverse that entropy, but that isn't nature's way. I'd be happy just to revisit that first Christmas in Madison, when Mom was heavy with Danny and we three kids chose to sleep upstairs in the spare room until the stroke of six, when we were allowed to wake our parents. We stayed up late watching the Yule Log; I enlisted Robbie's help to count the number of different carols before a repeat. (As payment, I promised her a thousand "points," but since I never specified a method of redemption, she hasn't claimed them yet.) The next morning, waking at five, still too early, we watched episodes of *The Magic Garden* and *The New Zoo Revue* that were perversely set in the middle of summer, until the stroke of six and our mad dash downstairs.

Magic Realism

Wish I could find a good book
To live in
   - Melanie, "Look What They've Done to My Song, Ma"

I am *so* not a Platonist. I'd never claim that the life of the mind is the one true existence, and all else illusion. I'm too much a scientist to deny the material reality that guides our lives via cause and effect; besides, I love the senses and the pleasures they offer too much to consider living only in the mind.

And yet, I sense a deeper reality running underneath what we see. From my window, I can see the russet roof shingles of a neighbor's roof, a red beach umbrella, and the magenta flowers of a crape myrtle just beyond. Each, I feel, has a meaning beyond itself that affords the receptive mind unexpected discoveries. I'm a *magic realist*. As one dictionary puts it, magic realism is "a genre of art (literature, painting, film, theater) expressing a primarily realistic view of the world while adding or revealing magical elements."

Many people flirt with magic, even those who claim to deny its existence. Children most crave it (Dad knew this -- when we were young, he would don cape and top hat and perform tricks as "El Magico"), but in their way, adults also desire the inexplicable. This hunger might express itself in ways as various as a belief in precognition (intuiting the death of a loved one before receiving the news) or *déjà vu*. Even my mother, such a practical woman, believes she met Dad in a previous life, because she cannot explain their falling in love at first sight in any other way.

In Church, as a youth, I recited the Nicene Creed, or Profession of Faith. I should have declared right then for magic realism -- even then, I intuited that nothing is more real than Art, which is nothing more nor less than the mind's reaction to the flesh and blood within which we find ourselves. This recoil is the crux of life, and what makes it worth living. All else – hometown, workplace, occupation, and anything else the Census Bureau asks – is secondary.

My favorite childhood stories fed a love of magic. Sure, like many preteen boys, I burned through Hardy Boys mysteries, lining them up numerically on a bookshelf to count my conquests; but soon I moved to more idiosyncratic books. Each new favorite radiated an individual and troubled essence; it also invariably related a story in which magic enters unaccountably. I bookmarked their pages with my hours, and gradually became the person I am today. On a lawn outside a Cape May church, I recently saw a sign quoting the proverb about "training up a child in the way he should go." How true -- we *are* susceptible as children, and I'm glad I submitted myself to the tutelage of literature.

***

My earliest memories of books date to Peck School. First is sitting among a circle of children on the soft carpet in the school library in the upperclass building for "story time." As a middle-aged woman read aloud, we listened quietly, more attentively than in class. Perhaps our transformation was due in part to our sitting in a circle rather than the usual hierarchy of rows and columns; perhaps it was the story.

After story time, which I wished would have lasted longer, we were granted a few minutes to peruse the juvenile shelves. I looked at spines with enticing titles, craning my neck to see the ones above eye level, kneeling to read the bottom shelf. I would often borrow another *Encyclopedia Brown* mystery, but soon I found new favorites.

First among these was *The Phantom Tollbooth*. Its hero, Milo, a little older than me, is bored out of his skull one dreary, rainy day, when he unexpectedly receives a package in the mail. He unwraps it to find assembly instructions for a tollbooth and a small convertible, which he drives past the booth to enter a fantasy realm.

My favorite part involved Milo's visit to the marketplace in the twin towns of Dictionopolis and Digitopolis where, from pushcarts like ones used by street vendors to sell sugared almonds or roasted chestnuts, one could buy individual letters and digits that were not only edible, but iced in different colors and flavors. In real life there are prodigies with synesthesia, a condition in which numbers have colors and tastes, enabling the gifted ones to memorize a million digits of pi. Dictionopolis and Digitopolis made me feel special like that: I suspected that words' mouthfeels were linked to deeper meanings.

In contrast, *A Billion for Boris* was set in the New York City of 1974, a place I knew from my family's occasional visits to Radio City Music Hall. In this lesser-known sequel to *Freaky Friday*, Manhattan appeared as a realm of tall apartment buildings populated by doormen, latchkey kids, and absentee parents. The book was by Mary Rodgers, the middle link of the Broadway dynasty that spanned father Richard Rodgers and son Adam Guettel. Ms. Rodgers had written *Once Upon a Mattress*, the musical adaptation of Hans Christian Andersen's *The Princess and the Pea* that became a high-school drama staple in the 1960s.

A Billion for Boris was narrated by a teenager, Annabel. Having lived my life so far in suburbia, I considered her apartment life extraordinary. Directly upstairs was her crush, Morris, whom she mistakenly calls "Boris" because that's how he says it. Only late in the book does she realize that she has misheard his name, due to a nasal mispronunciation stemming from his allergy to his mother. Annabel's little brother Ape Face (her invented nickname) loves tinkering with machines in his bedroom; one day, he accidentally rewires his portable TV to receive *tomorrow's* news, embroiling the kids in madcap Manhattan adventures, including naïve attempts to fight crime and bet on horse races and baseball games.

I generally loved stories about time travel. Although this device can be a crutch, it was new to me, and so I appropriated it for my one and only award-winning short story, which I wrote to impress my fifth-grade teacher, Ms. Hunt.

Ms. Hunt had joined Peck that year. I learned that she would be my teacher when our class assignments arrived by mail on the day of summer that to me always felt like the beginning of its end. In the issue of the *Peck School Newsletter* that came in the same mailing, I read that Ms. Hunt was arriving with impressive credentials. That made me believe that she'd be a tough teacher, and my classmates felt likewise. It was Mac, the one who drew the crazy comics (who in a later day would have been prescribed Ritalin), who pulled me aside on the first day of class to say:

"The ultimate student meets the ultimate teacher! Boom!"

Mac smacked his right fist into his left palm, and I could see a thought bubble emerge from the pursed corner of his mouth. But when I shared Mac's comment with Mom that night, she said it wasn't "teacher versus student" at all. Good students benefited from good teachers.

Ms. Hunt was considerably younger than my other teachers at Peck. Mrs. Hurley surely had thirty years on her; Mrs. Zimmerman and Mrs. Moody, half that many. Ms. Hunt was tall and svelte, with the long, cool face and straight blond hair emblematic of the 1970s, like the young women in Kool cigarette ads on the back covers of *TV Guide*. And since she wasn't married, she could dedicate her energy to students like me.

Borrowing liberally from *A Billion for Boris* and a story I'd seen in a Saturday morning cartoon, I wrote my own time travel tale. It went like this: while at home just "minding my own business" (as the crime-fighting kids said in *Scooby Doo*), I was eating a cereal box of Winkies (a brand name worthy of Wacky Packs!) when I found a free toy at the bottom. It was like a TV remote, but with just two buttons. I pressed one and was transported to the night of Paul Revere's ride; one of the two lanterns at Old North Church had burned out, precipitating a near calamity, but I helped the patriot light it again. The other button took me to another famous historical event that I can't recall, and I returned home by pressing both buttons at once.

Ms. Hunt loved the story, and asked me to read it at Morning Assembly, a weekly whole-school convocation. I was nervous, and not necessarily from stage fright -- I feared that one of my classmates might have seen the same cartoon I had, the one from which I'd stolen my story idea. If so, no one said. I had got away with it, and was even congratulated afterward by a couple of upper school girls.

When Ms. Hunt returned my story, with an "A+" written in red pen, it included a puzzling marginal note: "You have a great gift for journalism." Even then I wondered at the word choice. *Journalism*? Wasn't that newspaper writing? Had I written so realistically as to make Ms. Hunt feel she was in revolutionary era Boston, or did she mean something different? Why hadn't she written "literature"?

In retrospect, I suspect that Ms. Hunt, like Peck's other teachers, was training us for practical careers. Our parents had ponied up too much tuition to support writers of fiction. One of my classmates was a Frelinghuysen (practically New Jersey royalty) – surely her parents didn't want her to write mere stories? (Perhaps she did: I left Peck after that year; when I next encountered her, it was in an English class at Princeton.) I suppose journalism was a more respectable career than "literature."

In a way, this short story indirectly made me a better reader. Having recognized my gift for *journalism*, Ms. Hunt took me aside, along with my classmate Gordon (with whom I shared high scholarship honors that year, based on grade point average), and assigned us Hugh Lofting's

The Story of Doctor Doolittle. This was by far the hardest book I'd encountered, a long story with difficult words, certainly no *Encyclopedia Brown*.

But I plunged in, determined to finish as many pages as I could each night. Gordon and I were not given due dates -- we were simply expected to read *Doolittle* in addition to our usual classwork. With the help of my parents' unabridged dictionary, the mammoth, leather-bound *Webster's Second International* that rested on a large metal stand in Dad's study, I plowed ahead. Gordon, less enthusiastic about the additional work, lagged behind.

I don't remember Lofting's book well, but it instilled in me a taste for challenges. I soon chose books based on one criterion: the longer, the better. At Peck's annual library sale, I bought abridged versions of Jules Verne's *Journey to the Center of the Earth* and *The Mysterious Island*; then, after I learned what "abridged" meant, I made sure not to do that again. Ever since, I've shunned page-turners, beach books, and quick reads. I want to savor what I read, word by word, sentence by sentence; I want to feel them on my palate.

Other books worked their various magic. In *The Lion, the Witch, and the Wardrobe,* I met four English schoolchildren who, having been relocated to a distant relative's country house during the air raids of World War II, found a portal to a fantasy world in – of all things – an armoire. (That humble detail, so English, is a great example of the sort of magic realism they practice across the pond.) Scenes that come to mind forty years later include the one in which Edmund can't stop eating cursed Turkish Delight: the more he eats, the hungrier he gets. (To this day, when I see that delicacy in a gourmet shop, I consider buying it, then think better of it.) Then there is the crucifixion of the noble lion Aslan, when he lays down his life on the Stone Table. His willingness to die despite his ability to escape death by merely raising a paw remains, to my mind, the best explanation – if one there can be – of the fundamental mystery of Christianity.

Then, in *A Wrinkle in Time*, geeky teen Meg and bookish younger brother Charles journey by tesseract (a four-dimensional path through spacetime) to find their father, a scientist, who has gone missing. They find him in a totalitarian world run by a giant computer (the nature of the disembodied brain is not specified, but what else is a disembodied brain than a computer?), named, presciently enough for 1962, IT. Once again: time travel, siblings, and magic realism.

And in *The Little Prince*, a disillusioned aviator, flying solo, crashes in the Sahara Desert. He meets a golden-haired boy from Asteroid B-612 who, before succumbing to a snakebite that he willingly seeks (shades of Aslan) teaches him to see beneath the surface of things. This book helped instill in me a taste for stories without simple resolutions.

I actually I saw *The Little Prince* before reading it. I was nine when Mom and Dad took us to Radio City Music Hall, where we saw, as part of the program, the movie musical that happened to be the final Lerner-Loewe collaboration.

We entered the grand hall, still beautiful during New York City's nadir. The red plush seats had seen better days; the seatback in front of me was torn, and someone had carved their initials in the wood armrest. Dad, who'd seen Radio City in its glory days, pointed out the graffiti to Mom, calling the vandals "animals." Little did he suspect that Manhattan would one day revive, and that his son would live there.

The lights dimmed, the movie began, and reality took a powder. I haven't seen *The Little Prince* since, but I was certainly engrossed then by its desert setting, filmed on location in Tunisia. And I was mesmerized by Gene Wilder's performance as the fox, the only friend the Little Prince makes on Earth aside from the aviator. Accustomed to seeing talking animals portrayed with animation, I was confused and delighted by the depiction of the fox by an actor wearing a brown suit, a tie, and absolutely no makeup. Artifice calling attention to itself adds an additional layer of meaning, and is so much more effective than art merely aspiring to be real. In this case, the suggestion was that people really were foxes or snakes – or vice versa. But the fox's mannerisms made me a believer, and when he said:

One sees clearly only with the heart
What is essential is invisible to the eye

the groundwork had been laid. Mom and Dad weren't impressed by the film, and I think it went over the heads of my younger siblings, but I took its moral – to see beyond appearances – to heart.

A quick aside for parents and teachers. Consider the films that you show children: they have unexpected, long-lasting effects. Ms. Hunt, as part of our fifth-grade mythology unit, screened a silent film called *Pandora's Box*. Its final scene, which I must imperfectly remember, terrified me. Pandora lies in profile, naked, back to the camera, lit so that her curves are obscure. Her body casts a long shadow over the desert landscape: by dwarfing nature, she personifies selfishness. That scene would make occasional appearances in my dreams for years, and may have inspired a slight distrust of women.

Looking back, I see that many of my favorite childhood tales had a unifying element – the resistance to evil, frequently totalitarian. The children in *The Lion, the Witch, and the Wardrobe* were war refugees; Meg, in *A Wrinkle in Time*, battled groupthink; in wartime France, *The Little Prince*, like all of Saint-Exupéry's works, was banned by the Nazis. It is important to expose children to stories about evil, so that they can recognize and resist it when they are older.

***

High school introduced me to adult classics. Some went in one ear and out the other (or, as the memoir by Sam Levenson, which sat on Nana's coffee table for many years, would have it, *In One Era and Out the Other*), but others had lasting effects. My favorite high school teacher – Mr. Russo, who taught American Literature – assigned many of these. A partial roll call:

- *Walden*, which I parodied in my college application essays by attributing Thoreau's desire to "drive life into a corner" to his love of billiards;
- *The Grapes of Wrath*, which more than any other book, made me lean left;
- *Huckleberry Finn*, often considered the foremost American novel, which paints an increasingly dark vision of our native land with each rereading;
- *The Catcher in the Rye*, that all-time classic of adolescent alienation, which steered me to other modern malcontents like Kurt Vonnegut;
- and the short story "The Diamond as Big as the Ritz" by that Princetonian *manqué*, F. Scott Fitzgerald. Mr. Russo said it

would become our class's favorite short story, and most of us (except the contrarians) agreed once we'd read it.

Thanks to Mr. Russo and the books he taught us, when the time came to choose a college major -- long before I knew what I wanted from life -- I chose English.

***

And so it came to pass one sunny September Sunday that Mom and Dad followed me in my orange VW Beetle to Princeton. We located parking spaces and then walked across campus to find freshman orientation, already underway in a residential college courtyard. Social and athletic clubs had set up booths to recruit new members, and I was immediately courted by, of all things, the crew team. Didn't they see my matchstick arms? Dad offered encouragement, but I declined that offer. My legs – Dad's, genetically – were the source of physical strength, and would have been underutilized in crew. Besides, scullers worked in synchronicity like machine cogs, in a sport entirely too hive-like for me.

We took lunch at J.B. Winberie's, a passable chain restaurant next to the historic Nassau Inn, which would have been a much better choice. (It would be decades before I ate there.) There we met the families of the roommates with whom I would be sharing a "quad" (two bedrooms off a common room, each furnished with bunks).

James and Cliff hailed from Birmingham. They already knew one other, having played for rival high schools where pigskin is king. They were ticketed for Princeton's freshman squad, but since the Ivies don't offer athletic scholarships, they were under no obligation to play. James took advantage of that freedom to abandon football after freshman year and pursue other interests: a rock band, a girlfriend, and a gig as a deejay at the campus radio station.

James and I shared a love of music; I had no such affinity with Cliff. To me, he was a Southern stereotype and the owner of a rebel yell that he'd deliver often, with gusto. I believe it was he who bestowed the nickname "Lavender" on the quiet fellow with the pencil mustache and pastel-colored Izod shirts who lived across the entryway from us. "Lavender" was also teased, or so I heard, by the sophomores who lived directly above us, whom I never met: the only thing I knew about them was their habit, each Friday afternoon after classes, to boom Aerosmith's "Sweet Emotion" out the window and clear across the courtyard. To this day, I have harbored an intense dislike for that song, which I still hear as an anthem of intolerance.

Cliff's first Princeton writing assignment was a social history of the acceptability of burping and farting. It was simply titled, "Burping and Farting." (I fancied I could hear F. Scott Fitzgerald turn in his grave.) And early that semester, Cliff received a phone call from a Birmingham buddy who was also known to James and attending a Southern school. As in an old Bob Newhart routine, I heard just one side of the conversation, so I had to guess at the context. It wasn't easy, because Cliff's utterances consisted mainly of a drawled "*Shee*-it," or "No way!" that he'd follow with a cupped hand to the phone and mouthed pantomime to James, then more listening. More indulgent than I, James shrugged his shoulders in incomprehension, his Burns to Cliff's Allen, then return to his bowl of cereal, over which he ruminated with minimal haste in the unconscious imitation of a Southern gentleman who was readying himself for a day at the office. He paged the *New York Times* and smiled blandly at his daffy friend.

Cliff hung up.

James looked up from the newspaper. "So?"

"He said it's party town down there! He's getting hole every night!" And then Cliff shook his head sadly, ruing his choice of college.

Notwithstanding, Cliff and I got along. It was Drew, the engineering major from Colorado who slept on the bottom bunk of my room, who made me bristle. He was precisely the type – we each have one – who, because he shares one or more of our least desirable qualities, instantly becomes the person we can least abide. At the lunch with our parents, he was silent; afterwards, as we all trooped up the sunlit sidewalks back to campus, his mother caught up to me. She told me how delicious my ice cream had looked, and how fortunate we young folks were, to be able to indulge. (I wondered at this. She was thin, and could have indulged.) I sensed that her maternal instinct was looking for an opening to clear a path for her maladroit son; she must have intuited a potential clash of personalities. She explained that Drew was a bit daunted by his first trip East. I listened, but had already decided – quite uncharitably – that it was up to me whether or not I would like her son.

I disliked Drew's world view. It was utilitarian, one fit for a budding engineer who measures every angle of life by the protractor of use. If something helped you to get along, it was good; everything else was a waste of time. Tone deaf in matters of art, Drew goodnaturedly teased me about my choice of major. He asked nothing more of his undergraduate years than a few weekend beers and the prospect of a Princeton degree and a good job. I scorned his complacency; I also envied it. Not knowing what I wanted, I strolled around campus at night, among moonlit flower gardens. Soon I began to go home on weekends.

Drew studied late. He worked in our bedroom at his desk, pushing me to the common room. He organized his texts on the two shelves of his wood hutch; Dad had built one for me and each of my roommates, painting them black and bright Princeton orange. All summer, until the fall semester, they resided in the basement of my house, next to a mammoth Princeton swimming block, also bright orange, which Cliff and some of his football teammates had stolen from the university pool on a dare.

The top shelf of Drew's hutch was also home to an alarm clock radio/cassette player on which he played what seemed to be his only cassette tape, *The Police's Greatest Hits*. Its first track, "Message in a Bottle," still has the power to make me wince:

Just a castaway, an island lost at sea
Another lonely day with no one here but me

Was it a cry for help? Or just mediocre taste in music? Either way, I ignored it, as well as Drew's frequent complaints about homework. Over in the common room I read, or listened to the Mets on my Walkman. In sum, I really had no problem with Drew... other than wanting to be utterly unlike him.

Returning to day one. After lunch, Mom, Dad, and I met up with a pretty sophomore with long, straight, blond hair who had attended my high school. I've forgotten her name: I assume she was a daughter of a card-playing crony of Dad's, and that Dad had arranged this meeting to help ease me into campus life. The sophomore gave us a quick tour that didn't register because I couldn't take my eyes off her face, upon which I could read a sense of obligation. Now it was my turn, following Drew's example, to clam up. She may have taken me for a cold fish, and so I interpreted one of her remarks personally: she said she disliked students who buried themselves in their work to the exclusion of all else. She lamented there were many such at Princeton. I voiced my agreement (I'd have agreed with almost anything she would have said), but had a sinking feeling that she'd already classified me with the "grinds" (the campus word for excessive studiers). Perhaps she vaguely remembered that, in high school, I wasn't a joiner. Too bad -- since we shared a hometown, I had more in common with her than most Princetonians. But perhaps she saw in me the person I saw in Drew, the person like herself that she didn't want to be.

Freshman year began with two placement tests. The first, oddly, was in swimming.

Years before, so I'd heard, an alumnus whose child had drowned made a bequest to Princeton with the condition that incoming freshmen demonstrate an ability to swim. This rumor was wrong. The swimming test was actually instituted in 1911 by the Department of Hygiene to imbue "manly virtue" in the student population. At first, students were required to dive, do the breaststroke and backstroke, and swim two hundred twenty yards. By the time I had arrived, however, the test had been watered down (so to speak) to a ten-minute dog paddle. I jumped in the pool and treaded water with a few dozen freshmen. The swimming test was dropped a few years later.

The second placement test was of writing proficiency. In one of McCosh Hall's immense lecture halls, I selected an antique desk, sat down, and steeled myself to write an extemporaneous essay. Should it turn out to be sufficiently well-conceived, I would "place out" of the writing requirement. For me this was irrelevant, since I would be taking English classes, but I still felt stressed, because I had never demonstrated an ability to write coherently under pressure. I was a creative writer – not a journalist! (Sorry, Ms. Hunt.)

The problem was, I couldn't neither resist the urge to dazzle with flashy words and unexpected ideas, nor could I build the scaffolding of a coherent argument. My mind flashed back to a similar situation in high school, in which I had been selected, with several others, to compete in a national essay writing contest. We met after school in Mr. Russo's class for an hour, which was enough time for me to write myself into a hopeless impasse.

That unpleasantness over, I wandered to my locker. A few minutes later, I saw Laura, another participant (who would go on to a successful career of writing under pressure), as she descended the short flight of stairs at the top of B Hall. Offering a faint smile, I asked how she'd done. She was non-committal, and asked instead about me. I opened my eyes wide and exclaimed:

"*Terrible*! I wrote the whole thing in the *second* person!"

Mr. Russo later took me aside. As much as he would have liked for me to have won, my essay was a mess. Only in the last paragraph, in which I described the bittersweet feeling I had regarding a particular Christmas tree, was well-written enough to be moving. If only, he lamented, I had written the whole essay like that!

I didn't place out of my college writing requirement. Still, English was an obvious major, if only because I enjoyed reading. At the earliest opportunity, the Monday of "orientation week," I visited the campus bookshop to buy my reading list. Selecting Andre Gide's *The Immoralist* more or less at random, I began reading, carrying the book around campus as I walked. I never "got" *The Immoralist*, nor Gide's sensibility, nor French existentialism in general. But it was Gide who ensured that I would be labeled a grind -- I had committed the *faux pas* of studying too much before the semester had properly begun.

My roommates wondered about me and, looking back, I can see they were right to do so. Though I got good grades for two years, my learning approach was half-baked -- I moved from assignment to assignment, class to class, with no big picture. That had worked in high school, but wouldn't fly here. And, socially, I made no friends. I didn't understand my schoolmates, and was too introverted to meet many of them. The ones I knew certainly did not inspire me enough to develop a new side of myself. Most of them didn't even seem to like school.

Fall of freshman year, I took physics, a course divided into lectures, classes, and labs. The lectures were fun. They were presented on a full-size auditorium stage by a cast of two, the principal course lecturer and his tireless assistant. The assistant, a short man with a wrinkly, prune-like face, did the hard work of setting up the machinery – winches, go-karts, roulette wheels – that would demonstrate the physical principle of the week. And each week, by lecture's end, you knew that somehow the assistant would get his comeuppance! Some sort of calamity would befall him; one week he was clocked by a giant pendulum on its downward swing. He was Super Dave Osborne -- before that character had even been invented.

After all you've done for me
All I really want to do
Is take the love you brought my way
And give it all right back to you
         -   Marshall Crenshaw, "Someday, Someway"

In contrast, labs were hell. And my lab partner had no more aptitude for the work than I did: one evening, while we struggled to simultaneously keep our composure and correctly position an inclined plane, our bearded teaching assistant stopped by. I assumed he would remark on a mistake we were making, but instead he asked:

"Are you having fun? Because if you aren't, why are you taking this class?"

The question stuck in my craw. No, I wasn't having fun. Certainly not like our course lecturer!

My roommates seemed immune to doubts like these. I took breakfast with them in Rockefeller Hall, where we were joined by several of James and Cliff's football teammates. I still remember many of their names and faces after all these years, having seen so much of those big, beefy linemen and tall and lithe receivers at meals and at football practices.

Recently, one of them unexpectedly reappeared in my life. On Super Bowl Sunday, Carol and I were idly watching television before the big game. Animal Planet was showing something called the "Puppy Bowl," a program designed to encourage pet adoption. It was hosted by a perky guy and gal who did the best they could to make the Brownian motion of small dogs racing round a miniature football field seem interesting. I found myself staring not at the dogs, though, but at the male co-host: I knew him from somewhere. Looking past his frozen smile and deer-in-the-headlights gaze to his long, thin, dark eyes and chubby face, it came back. I used to eat breakfast with him; he was one of my roommates' teammates.

His name, Dean Cain, flashed on the screen; I could still see him in the Gothic setting of the baronial, vaulted dining hall, seated at one end of a long wood table as thick as a beam of an eighteenth-century manor house. (I believe a not insignificant fraction of Princeton tuition went to the upkeep of these Hollywood settings.)

I caught up with Dean's career in Wikipedia. After failing to make it with the Buffalo Bills, he played Superman in *The New Adventures of Lois and Clark*. (The Puppy Bowl suddenly seemed an anticlimax.) He had taken up acting at the suggestion of his girlfriend, Brooke Shields, another schoolmate. I'd run into Brooke, literally, in a hallway once, but otherwise knew nothing of her except her memorable film appearances and blue jeans ads. And it turns out that I didn't know something about Dean -- according to Wikipedia, he was the beneficiary of Brooke's virginity. I paused to consider how authoritative Wikipedia might be on such matters.

I had less luck. I knew two gals, volunteers like me for the freshman football team, who (like Brooke) enjoyed being near football players.

Why do stars fall down from the sky
Every time you walk by?
Just like me, they long to be close to you
   - The Carpenters, "(They Long to Be) Close to You"

One was tall, thin, and plain-faced, with wispy, light blond hair; the other was short, dark-haired, and somewhat more attractive, though her upper lip was marred by a faint mustache. I bumped into the dark-haired gal one Friday night early in freshman year, before I began going home on weekends, at an ice cream social just down University Place. A band was playing and the noise was deafening, so we walked back to my dorm, which was dark, my roommates having decamped for a party. As street lamps refracted through lead glass windows, I spoke of my unhappiness at being away from home; she listened patiently, but offered little advice. Perhaps she had followed me to my dorm to kiss me (I never see these things at the time, my mind being elsewhere), but that wasn't likely given my low spirits and lack of experience in such matters. Oh, there was that mustache, too, visible even in the dark. She left to find someone more fun.

Another young woman, who lived across the grass commons of my residential college, was tall, blonde and conventionally attractive. She was also in my Physics class. Since I volunteered in class, she must have assumed I was an "A" student, and so she asked whether I'd be willing to stop by her dorm to help her with homework. Her roommate opened the door and kept an eye on us as we worked written exercises. But I had an off night; the assignment confused me, and my tutee, seeing me backtrack and rework the problems several times, concluded that however resourceful I might be, I was not the star student she expected. I was not invited back.

But it was not Princeton's student body but its dreamlike campus, flecked in light and shadow, that attracted me. As I explored its glades and gardens, I saw my footsteps in Scott Fitzgerald's, coloring the world via the dashed hopes of a romantic. I could never tire of walking the grounds at night, when lamplit flagstones alternately evoked cotillions and cookouts.

The campus architecture was a Noah's Ark of styles, two of every kind. Ivy creepers climbed old stone that had mellowed to purplish-brown, and dorms spanned from the neoclassical to the brutalist. Of course, Princeton's glory was the "Collegiate Gothic" it had purloined from English universities; at least that was the style of the dorms my side of campus, as featured in the film adaptation of *A Beautiful Mind*, about that other Princetonian, game theorist John Nash.

With such beauty to show off, I played tour guide to family and friends. I pointed out Witherspoon Hall, the administration building scarred by a Revolutionary War cannonade. I told tales of Alexander Hall, a rambling wedding cake crazy with rosette windows, which I'd heard was the senior thesis of an architecture major. He got an "F," but after becoming famous, he donated a large sum to his alma mater on the condition that his senior thesis be built. (Like the swimming test story, this was apocryphal.)

To your right, see those blocky cubes spiraling in a helix, like a lab-grown crystal, like bismuth? Those are dorms, believe it or not. To your left, the squat Greek Revival salt-and-pepper shakers are the locus of the Whig-Clio debating society – just don't ask me which is Whig, and which Clio. And this modern, airy dining hall was the commission of world-famous architect, I.M. Pei. These ideas made concrete were arranged across campus like chess pieces in an impossible position, making the campus more diverse and democratic than the student body. Gravel paths wound between dorms and classrooms, and led you, if you knew the way, to secret gardens and sculptures like Henry Moore's iconic

"Oval with Points," a tall, emerald block of marble with two protrusions halfway up, upon which parents posed future alumni for photographs.

Walks after class on quiet Fridays, or on somnolent Sundays, invited contemplation. The indolent air was supersaturated with potential. But it wasn't until I left school for good that I *really* savored Princeton's campus. Then I could linger as long as I liked, without a place to be and with no papers to write. It was, ironically, on these return trips to Princeton, when I was no longer obliged to visit the stacks and carrels of Firestone Library, that my desire to learn was rekindled. It was like meeting an ex-girlfriend: you forget her faults and can almost picture getting back together. Like John Nash after he'd gone crazy, I'd spend the rest of my days on campus. I would return to Firestone with big coat pockets and spirit away enough books – just as Princeton's uniquely black squirrels hoarded winter acorns – to read in the light of a partially open lead glass window in a garret atop a Gothic arch.

***

One Friday in the fall of freshman year, on my way to Firestone, I observed activity in the plaza out front. A student declaimed aloud from a thick paperback. Ah, that's right. My English preceptor had mentioned that the Department had arranged a daylong, campus-wide reading of Thomas Pynchon's *Gravity's Rainbow*, an infamously discursive and prickly novel, a sort of modern, conspiracy-laden *Ulysses* published in 1973. The proceedings were half relay race, half marathon; students read in half-hour intervals at various campus locations.

Pynchon was in the air. Laurie Anderson, a musician I admired, had recently recorded a song that alluded to him:

> *And at his funeral*
> *All his friends stood around looking sad*
> *But they were really thinking of*
> *All the ham and cheese sandwiches in the next room*
>   - Laurie Anderson, "Gravity's Angel"

The preceptor who had informed us of the public reading was a young and amiable man whose specialized in the poetry of John Ashbery. (A note on terminology: Princeton's undergraduate English classes consisted of weekly lectures, delivered by full professors, and breakout classes led by "preceptors.") The Department numbered several fans of Pynchon, who was a recluse on the order of J.D. Salinger. No one knew where he lived, though Northern California was suspected. On cluttered bulleting boards in the gloomy corridors of Pyne Hall, I had seen flyers touting a coming lecture on Pynchon's early science fiction novel, *The Crying of Lot 47*.

I did not take part in the campus reading; I did not see it snake across campus; I did not attend the lecture. So many missed opportunities for the sake of homework! But I bought a copy of *Gravity's Rainbow* at the campus bookstore, and made what little headway I could. My recollection is that it was a desperately pessimistic fable about the human condition, dense with metaphors of rockets and parabolic trajectories. But among those shadows was a luminous clearing, a humorous set piece I still think about to this day.

The protagonist, a kind of *noir* detective, visits the apartment of an old crone in London to collect information. She offers him candy from a coffee table bowl. He takes one to be polite, pops it in his mouth, and tries to resume his line of questioning, but the candy is so hideous he cannot speak. Reluctant to spit it out, he takes another candy to cancel its effect, but it is equally bad in a completely different way. And so, for three pages, we are treated to a lovingly detailed pharmacopoeia of the world's worst pastilles, lozenges, and drops, wretched sweets that ought to have been long ago classified as toxic substances. The humor of this exquisitely rendered scene, derived from the irony of a hardboiled gumshoe being foiled by a little old lady, had me in tears of joy. May I one day write something as funny.

The next weekend, home to see Clay, I read him this passage, and we both laughed. Each of us, thanks to grandmothers, could relate to the perils of accepting sweets from old women. When Clay was nine, his grandmother had taken him to see *Mary Poppins* at the Madison Theater. The show began; she unzipped a plastic baggie of something that she called "chocolate," and offered a piece. He bit into a square of the bitterest licorice he'd tasted in his young life, a bit of bridge mix. For the rest of the movie, he was dying for a spoonful of sugar.

My memory, more recent, pertained to the sweets that Nana kept in her cupboard, most of which had far outlived their expirations. I suffered many mishaps before learning to consult those dates -- tasting

Archway oatmeal cookies that had hardened to a rock-like consistency, Hershey Bars that had bloomed to chalk, and Lorna Doones that had crumbled into sawdust.

Liz Cutler was another preceptors. Short, with long and straight dark hair, she had ample energy for teaching, though she found freshmen frustrating because they seemed impervious to irony. She wasn't crazy about my essays, either, which she found dry. On occasion, though, I'd get a compliment -- she did cite one sentence that I had written about the city of St. Petersburg, Russia in Dostoevsky's *Crime and Punishment* as the "single best thing" I'd written. (I don't remember the sentence.)

One day, after another essay that she had doused in red ink, I spoke to her after class. I asked why I had been docked for using the word "opine." ("Not a real word," she had written in the margin.)

Oh, but it was! Here, I had her. I felt like Leo Durocher, the one-time major league baseball manager who, as related in *Nice Guys Finish Last*, had never won an argument with an umpire, but rejoiced on the day that he finally had what he considered incontrovertible evidence to present to an umpire who had blown a call.

(This mention summons a vivid memory. I was eleven years old when I read *Nice Guys Finish Last,* my first sports memoir. I noticed it on the shelves of a well-lit west New Jersey supermarket, next to a book about biorhythms that I perused for a long moment, fascinated as I was by the repeated appearance of my two favorite numbers, twenty-three and twenty-eight. Mom and I were taking Nana Edie shopping. My grandmother stopped by the shelf of books to point one out to Mom, and that's when I saw the bright yellow paperback with the cover photo of Durocher arguing with an ump. I read the first two pages, was hooked, and asked Mom if she would buy it for me. She didn't know if I was old enough, but after conferring with my grandmother, she let me put it in the cart. I began reading it on the drive home, by the light of the driver's side rear interior light, as Mom and Nana Edie discussed a book that Nana Edie had recently read about the coming "end times," in which she seemed to believe. Frightened by her words, I returned to my book of vintage baseball anecdotes, some of them sprinkled with eye-opening words I'd never seen before in print.)

To Liz Cutler, I respectfully submitted that "opine" was a word. She raised her eyebrows and said:

"Follow me."

We traversed a cluttered old passage in Pyne Hall, the square brownstone in the heart of campus whose walls wept of humidity. In her office, Liz extracted a dictionary from a wall shelf. I waited as she thumbed to the correct page.

"Oh, so it is a word."

I smiled.

"Well, it's a terrible word."

Durocher had lost his argument, too. Oh, well. But Liz was right: "opine" is a dumb and somewhat forced word. Sticking to sports metaphors, it's like a recent coinage so beloved of football broadcasters, "incompletion." (What, may I ask, is being incompleted?)

Returning to the preceptor who admired Pynchon. Having finished his lesson one day, he shared a secret that could be of use to those of us who travel to New England. (He was a Down Easter, himself.) North of Hartford, just off the highway on the Connecticut side of the Massachusetts border, was a restaurant with a sign out front advertising food and books. It was a favorite haunt of his, well worth a visit. I filed his advice away.

Years later, on my way to see a friend in Maine, I saw the sign. It was atop a very tall pole, and read: FOOD BOOKS. My preceptor's words flashed to mind. For the first of many times, I pulled over. Traveler Food and Books still serves food and books, and has changed little in thirty years. The food isn't bad, with Thanksgiving Dinner on the menu every day, but the main draw is books: each patron is entitled to three per meal, chosen from freestanding shelves scattered around the restaurant. These are the donations of individuals, libraries, and publishers; most are forgettable or long-forgotten, but there is the odd gem. And on the walls are decades-old, black-and-white signed photos of authors. No Pynchon, but many others who, like him, have lost their cachet, such as Charles Kuralt. There are also big names like Michael Crichton, Steven King, and others who stopped by the restaurant back in the day; and while you sip that cup of coffee you can idly look out a rear picture window to a charming little pond surrounded by bird feeders while you ponder the folly of lasting fame.

Another freshman memory. One day before our preceptorial, a curly-haired redhead – the vivacious type who appeals to me and then wears me out with her energy – told our class that we had to play a prank on our instructor. It was an annual tradition, she said. We believed her because she seemed to be a person who would know about such things, and because, I suppose, she was pretty. We hid in a dark classroom just down the hall as we awaited our instructor's approach. Right on time she arrived, stopped at the threshold of our empty classroom, and looked at her watch. A shrug of the shoulders betrayed her impatience. Catching sight of another preceptor in the hall, she initiated a conversation; two minutes later, when they were done speaking, she left. To me, it felt like the prank had fallen flat (our preceptor did not mention it at our next meeting), but we did get the day off.

It was another English preceptor, Catherine Esch, who posed a question that stuck with me:

"You're students of literature. You must be aware your major is not particularly marketable. You should be asking, 'Why English? Why is it relevant?'"

It felt like all the air had gone out of class, and we all fell silent.

To answer her question now with an unfair amount of hindsight, I'd respond that literature is a labor of love. It's what you do when nothing else matters as much.

It was also Ms. Esch who said:

"Literature cannot provide answers. It can only ask questions."

It was in Ms. Esch's classroom that my roommate James, who was also an English major, made a memorable mistake. We were reading one of the saucier of Chaucer's *Canterbury Tales*, "The Miller's Tale," about a suitor denied a visit to his true love, a maiden whose parents had imprisoned her in a castle turret. Undaunted, the lovers finally meet after the suitor climbs a very long ladder, and the maiden throws open her window. He steals a kiss, but is confused by the full beard that greets him, which he believes his beloved has grown since their last meeting.

This passage confused James, so he raised his hand for clarification. He wondered whether the awkward Middle English vocabulary and syntax had led him astray.

"Does she have a beard?"

There was a moment of silence, then some smiles and chuckles. I planted my head in my palm. A slow enlightenment stole over James's face, the first light following an eclipse.

"Ah, I see."

He should have asked Cliff's friend.

***

To arrange a one-year leave of absence was a simple administrative process. My hiatus might have been an inspiration: I could have hitchhiked Europe, tackled Pynchon's oeuvre, or considered Ms. Esch's question. Instead, I watched baseball; the Mets finally won the World Series. I also spent time with my family, which from the future's vantage point seems an excellent choice. But the seasons turned, as they must. The Mets fell from grace, and I was due back to school.

My friendship with James had been jeopardized a year earlier when I announced my impending leave, forcing him to scramble for a new roommate. By the time I returned to campus, I had no idea where or with whom he was living. I was lodged in a single room, a tiny chamber in one of the campus's oldest buildings, named after the late 1800s graduating class that had given it to the school. It had seen little renovation since. My room's principal design element was a huge, thickly insulated, putty-gray duct that bisected the airspace just above my head. Through a tall and narrow window, I had a view of the dumpsters behind the gym.

My new campus tour was shorter than the ones I'd given two years earlier. After I finished one for Mom and Grandpa Hines, my grandfather said upon seeing my dorm room:

"I've stayed in better jail cells."

It was worse than square one. My only acquaintances were seniors absorbed in theses, who had vanished to the library. (I ran across James precisely once, a chance meeting on a walkway behind the student center. We awkwardly talked about the latest record album by R.E.M.) And I'd built no bridges with teachers. I was randomly assigned to an advisor who would supervise my junior-year project. As in a bad dream, I had trouble finding his office; I climbed flights of stairs in an old building, the existence of whose upper floors I'd never surmised. After catching my breath, I stuck my head through an open doorway into a cluttered office. A man wearing a tea gown looked up from a book and greeted me with a wan smile. After asking me to sit, he asked whether I had a topic in mind. I suggested Dreiser. During my year away, I'd read *An American Tragedy* and *Sister Carrie,* which I'd borrowed from the public library. Mom had enjoyed those books when she was young, before she raised a family and no longer had time for novels.

He frowned.

"How is Dreiser relevant today?"

Again with the relevance! His question now calls to mind a favorite *New Yorker* cartoon: a man in a corporate boardroom stands before a flip chart, brandishing a pointer that indicates a trend line. Three people sit at a conference table; one asks, "Why must it always *represent* something?"

Why must books be *relevant*?

My second departure from Princeton was final. It was the result, to a small degree, of my major. As with math, I'd become disenchanted with literature after a view of its rarefied heights. I longed for simpler pleasures, and returned to reading whatever struck my fancy, no matter how insignificant or irrelevant it was in the eyes of others.

The Chatham Bookseller, that wonderful bookstore in downtown Madison that had once served as children's reading room for the public library, was still there. There, I chanced upon the books of Henry Charlton Beck, the former *Newark Star-Ledger* columnist whose weekend hobby was rediscovering New Jersey's vanished towns. These ghost villages had served as labor pools for canals, mills, and glass manufactories that were eventually killed by changing production methods, and were now buried beneath the shifting sands of time. Mr. Beck had crisscrossed the state looking for these places with occasional success; three decades later, when I tried to use his books, so light on specifics, as road maps, I was whistling in the wind. They did, however, serve as pretexts for long back road drives, which I spent in a haze of folklore and romance.

On another front, I read Kurt Vonnegut. His terse, astringent prose dealt in dystopias, not nostalgia. I binged on novels straddling science fiction, fable, and social critique. Vonnegut validated my feeling that the modern world was essentially insane. I particularly admired his debut, *Player Piano*, published in 1952 while Henry Charlton Beck filed weekly newspaper columns on vanished crossroads like Ong's Hat.

Player Piano was set in that scariest of times, the near future. It took place in a company town much like Schenectady, New York, the headquarters of General Electric. (This was not a coincidence. To make ends meet until his writing could support a growing family, Vonnegut worked in GE's Public Relations department.) It's a dark vision of a world run by technocrats who have automated nearly all meaningful labor out of existence. Sound familiar?

I particularly immersed myself in Vonnegut's middle period, mid-1960s to mid-1970s, an era when bestsellerdom promoted him to a series of TV appearances, and to the status of a midlevel celebrity. You may have seen his bushy eyebrows and mustache on Dick Cavett. Vonnegut even appeared on the CBS broadcast of the first moon landing: when he criticized the cost of the mission -- money that could have funded social programs -- he mystified Walter Cronkite. He earned enemies in high places like William F. Buckley, and admirers in low places like the countercultural youth, who began making pilgrimages to his Cape Cod home to camp on his lawn and seek an interview with a man they considered their Delphic master.

But what most impressed me about Vonnegut were two late-period novels that were published around the time I discovered him. In them, I felt he had regained his gift for narrative. First there was *Galapagos*, a fable in which natural selection eventually cures humanity of its oversized brain; then *Bluebeard*, which arrived at my front door, leather-bound, as a Franklin Mint Book of the Month Selection, a birthday gift from Mom to her bibliophile son. *Bluebeard* told of an aging abstract expressionist painter who lived in eastern, rural Long Island, as Vonnegut eventually did, who has been laboring for years in secret, behind the doors of a potato barn, on his grand statement, his life's summation, a monumentally large painting that is, horror of horrors, *representational*. To me, *Bluebeard* felt like a heroic vindication for Vonnegut the writer, who had pulled together the strands of his artistic DNA to make one final sweeping statement.

***

And then, of course, there was Proust, the writer who changed my life, who merits his own chapter.

Dream Two

The second of seven dreams I had while writing this book.

A rare dream in which, rather than being fate's plaything, I hold a position of responsibility. And yet I am powerless.

Carol and I are at a professional gathering, either a mathematics or chess conference taking place in an exotic city, possibly one in Central Europe. We have left our two teenage children (my first ever dreamed-up kids!) in the hotel room. They don't figure further.

I am tasked with shepherding a group of professors, or chess masters, to the next lecture, which requires taking New Jersey Transit. Before we leave the hotel, a courier hands me a package wrapped in brown Kraft paper, which I tear open. Inside is a new math text, hot off the presses, that I have ordered. The title on the book jacket is rendered in tall, German Expressionist block letters. A nearby colleague murmurs his approval; he has heard good things about the author, though he has never read him. Out of modesty, I joke that there'd better be some good stories inside. Otherwise, the book would just be too intimidating.

Our departure proves difficult. Carol and I must first navigate the grand ballroom, which is awash with people. In one wing, a podium has been erected for a press conference: Julia Louis Dreyfus is about to speak, or has already spoken, and the podium is empty. The ballroom is decorated for a gala, its tables set with fine linen and ornate cutlery. People circulate in fancy dress. I suddenly realize that I am barefoot; out of shame, to divert attention from my feet, I windmill my arms like propellers, as though to swat horseflies.

We cross a second ballroom. Arranged in a grid at twenty-foot intervals are six-foot-high microwave carousels, multitiered and transparent like dessert cases in a diner. Their spatial arrangement recalls the servers in the cavernous, blindingly white computer room of a financial firm where I once worked. (Servers grew smaller with time, so empty space increasingly predominated.) Earlier, Carol and I had placed our Thanksgiving dinners – sliced turkey, mashed potatoes, gravy – inside two of these carousels, and we can now see them slowly rotating, hot and ready to eat. They look delicious, but we are pressed to make our train.

The next detail is one I often dream: the train map, as seen on a wall in the station, is a long semicircle with many stops. To go from one end to the other ordinarily requires hours of travel, but there are ways to shortcut the semicircle via express trains. Any connection, however, requires split-second timing.

In the waiting room, the crowd is worse than in the ballrooms. I feel suffocated, and desperately want to be alone. The tide of humanity pushes and pulls as I make my way toward a ticket window, distant but clearly visible. I pass through subway-style turnstiles and hear trains arriving and departing, but do not know whether I have missed mine. I can't see because my view is obscured on every side by floor-to-ceiling cages. Carol helps me decipher a timetable posted on a large bulletin board, which says that I need to buy a ticket for Cedar Grove. On the platform, I ask a woman in uniform, the one fixed point in an eddying mass, who tells me to see another woman at the ticket window. Despite the chaos all around, she and everyone else in this dream are chivalrous and excessively courtly, as might be expected in a venerable, civilized European country out of the mind of Stefan Zweig. My ticket costs one dollar and eighty-three cents.

I board the train without Carol, once again in the company of a mathematical (or chess-playing) colleague. We walk to the rear car, which is frigid but brilliantly sunlit. This is the first time that I no longer feel hemmed in, and I exhale in relief. The bench seats are covered with inches of snow. As I used to do on old New Jersey Transit train cars when I was the first one aboard, I flip the seats to face the other direction. And though it is quite cold, I open the windows to the sun to let in the frosty air; then, using a shovel that I happen to have with me, I begin to dig out the seats, tossing snow into the aisle.

In the distance, I hear the whistle of an arriving train. I may not be on the right train. I wake, slowly, to the realization that the train whistle is really the tinkling of wind chimes outside my bedroom window.

Monsieur Proust

If only I could remember that sweet moment when we met
If I knew then that I would spend the rest of my life with you
I imagine I would have held your gaze a little longer
   - Billy Bragg, "The Fourteenth of February"

And I wish I could recall how and when I made the acquaintance of Marcel Proust, the man who wrote the user manual to my life. It would have been most Proustian had I done so in an unprepossessing way, perhaps at the home of a childhood friend whose family used *Remembrance of Things Past* as a doorstop. The determinants of our lives slip in when we aren't watching. In a way it's like – and, in another, very unlike – the *coup de foudre* that attended my parents' first meeting, that long-ago February the ninth.

All I know is that a little before high school graduation, I first encountered Proust's novel. I bought my first copy – number one of many – at The Chatham Bookseller. It was the classic two-volume, 2,265-page hardcover edition published in 1934 by Random House's Modern Library imprint. Inside the first volume's jacketless, two-toned cardboard cover, on a flyleaf of a slightly heavier grade of paper than the other pages', a penciled note still reads: "6.00, 2 vols." Not bad for a lifetime of reading: for the next thirty years, as I labored to finish this novel, I dug ever deeper into Proustiana. What began as two volumes eventually became two bookshelves.

My all-time favorite edition of Proust was a large-type edition that covered just the first of the novel's seven volumes, *Swann's Way*. Bound in a heavy cardboard cover of an old-fashioned lavender design suitable for vintage wallpaper, it contained a few watercolor illustrations, each protected by a sheet of tissue paper. I bought that book three times – all, alas, are now gone. I found each on a tall, slim bookshelf that juts into The Chatham Bookseller's main aisle; and each time that I needed a replacement, I found it in the same place. When the floodwaters of Hurricane Floyd destroyed my first copy, I bought the second; when I lent the second to a friend who lost it, I bought the third. Along the way, I lost copy number three, and my luck finally ran out. On the rare occasion when I return to Madison, I visit The Chatham Bookseller, which still plies its trade by that name under different owners, and check the shelf in vain.

I have Proust in French. Five paperbacks span the seven volumes. I acquired these in a variety of places, including La Librairie Française, a delightful three-story cultural exchange center in Rockefeller Center, when Midtown still cared about booklovers. Six years of school French enabled me to read Proust in his original tongue, as long I kept a dictionary to hand.

I can read French, but I was never good with the spoken tongue. I recall the time in eighth grade that my family stopped at a Quebec campground whose manager didn't know (or, pretended not to know, as Dad maintained) English. Unable to get through, Dad turned to me for help:

"How do you say 'sewer hookup'?"

I raised my eyebrows and snorted. How should I know?

My high school spoken French suffered because our teachers focused their instruction on reading and writing. In a last-ditch effort to make up for lost time, my senior year teacher, Monsieur Castaldo, gave us a last-minute tip before our AP French exam. He said that when we were at a loss for words, we should insert in our conversation (which was recorded for later grading) an occasional "bref." That's the sound that French speakers use to buy time when speaking, the way Americans say "um." Unfortunately I misheard him and instead peppered the verbal portion of my exam with the word "boeuf," which, bien sûr, is French for "beef":

"And so, beef, I took the train to Paris, beef...." My grader must have though I was crazy, or hungry.

I chose French before seventh grade from a list including Spanish and German. Mom suggested Spanish, the logical choice. True, Spanish would have been handy if I were to get by in a city. (The nearest I got to that was buying plastic bags of mango chunks from Greenwich Village food trucks.) Likewise, classmates destined for scientific and engineering careers signed up for German, the traditional language of scientific literature.

But I would never select a language based on the criterion of use: it needed to be beautiful. And so I chose French -- no other tongue so seductively combines mellifluence, range of expression, and logical precision. The latter might surprise folks whose only gropings with it have been on menus and party invitations, but for centuries French served as the international language of diplomacy.

Proust himself had a scientific bent. His father and brother were well-known physicians; the former helped France to formulate its epidemiological policy. Proust excelled in neither mathematics nor science, but he assiduously followed developments in those fields. (His novel contains enough scientific metaphors to furnish several theses.) The precision in Proust's style is evident in his famously long sentences, architectural marvels of grace that reward persistent readers who have the patience to follow their twists and turns; his syntax is so precise that translators can clearly render his ideas in any language. Thus, the language in which one chooses to read Proust is mainly a matter of education and temperament, or which part of the brain one chooses to exercise.

Back to my bookshelves. My two oldest Proust books, Léon Pierre-Quint's *Marcel Proust, Sa Vie, Son Oeuvre* and Pierre Abraham's *Proust: Recherches Sur La Création Intellectuelle*, are analyses of Proust's work that date, respectively, to 1925 and 1930. They look like antiques. They're paper bound, but not like modern paperbacks – their paper, as coarse as rag, summons via smell (the Proustian sense) the attic spaces where they resided for decades. Their spines are ragged, and their pages are clumped in groups: they must have been opened with a book knife. I picture them for sale on the shelves of the original Shakespeare & Co., on the Seine's Left Bank, where Hemingway and Fitzgerald loitered. I have them because long ago I knew a septuagenarian, Amelia North (more on her later) whose sister read French literature. I asked Ms. North if I might borrow the books, and then I never returned them. Now that she has presumably moved on to the next world, they have passed to me.

Another two-volume set, lithe, elegant, easily held, covers the third of the novel's seven volumes, *The Guermantes Way*. Published by Chatto and Windus in 1971, it is attractive because it has few words per page. The pages turn quickly, so one's progress seems brisk. On the other hand, I have an admirable three-volume hardcover edition published by a company named Oxford that offers ample white space between the lines, making each page easier on the eye. But there's always a trade-off: the easier the pages are to read, the more pages there are.

Then there are the graphic novel adaptations -- three tall, thin hardcovers that visually present the first two of Proust's seven volumes.

Stephan Heuet drew them in a sleek and vibrant style, capturing the novel's details in clean *Tintin* lines.

On another shelf are books *about* Proust. I've enjoyed them too, but here I must offer a word of caution.

The narrative arcs of memoirs and biographies can blind us to the significance and accomplishments of the life being described. Proust most likely would not have authorized a biography of his own life, because he was a professed enemy of the "biographical fallacy," the idea that a person's art is a reflection of his or her life.

Remembrance of Things Past germinated from an essay called *Contre Saint-Beuve*, in which Proust rebuts Charles Augustin de Sainte-Beuve, the literary critic. Sainte-Beuve believed that great art could be produced only by great men, or equivalently, that the morally deficient could not make great art. Proust believed the opposite. He asserted that masterpieces could come from boors (his fictional author Bergotte was modeled on Anatole France), philistines (his fictional composer Vinteuil was modeled partially on Camille Saint-Saëns) and salon-jumpers (his fictional painter Elstir was modeled partly on Whistler). To these I would add modern-day examples like Woody Allen or even John Lennon, who was beastly to his first wife, Cynthia, and son, Julian. (As Cynthia relates in her memoir, *John*, ten-year-old Julian once asked, "Dad's always telling people to love each other; how come he doesn't love me?")

Sublimation is the reason. Art's highest pinnacles were the work of deeply flawed individuals. Artists redeem themselves through art by speaking with the voices of the people they wish they could be. Because their public personae are flawed doesn't mean their fiction is any less meaningful.

Social climbing was an accusation Proust knew well; it was often leveled against him when he was young. It came back to haunt him later when André Gide, the author turned publisher, rejected Proust's first volume in the belief that Proust was still the man who had wasted his youth at balls in an attempt to cultivate acquaintances with society's *grandes dames*. (Gide later cited his rejection of *Swann's Way* as the greatest mistake of his life.)

So much for the disclaimer. I enjoy reading about Proust's life. One book on my shelf is *Proust's Way*, a collection of essays by Roger Shattuck occupying the obscure niche between literary analysis and self-help. (The best selling book of this type, which I have yet to read, is Alain de Botton's *How Proust Can Change Your Life*.) There is also *Paintings in Proust*, a *catalogue raisonné* of works of art mentioned in his novel, and *Monsieur Proust's Library*, a similar account of books read by Proust and mentioned in his novel. Then there's an odd little volume entitled *Proust's Overcoat*, a mystery story about what happened to the author's personal library and shabby overcoat after his death. I can't get enough of the stuff.

But it all began thirty-five years ago with that voluminous six-dollar edition at The Chatham Bookseller, the one whose length did not frighten me because I hoped to spend a good deal of time in the author's mind.

***

And so we begin: the title, stamped in a navy blue rectangle on a buff-colored spine, *Remembrance of Things Past*. I like it, but it wasn't Proust's. It was a flight of fancy by his first and greatest translator, the Scot with the double-barreled surname, C.K. Scott Moncrieff.

Proust had as much trouble naming his books as I do. It took an excellent reader, my wife Carol, to steer me to the title that fit my first book, *The Going Places Club*. And as I explained earlier, this volume had a number of working titles, until Carol found a better one.

Proust considered many titles for his masterwork, one of which was *Intermittences of the Heart*. That title does justice to one of the book's grand themes, that memory is recurrent (fading and revivifying at surprising moments of time) and that our feelings for one another, though grounded in the distant past, are never constant. It's a good title, but Proust felt it lacked the requisite poetry.

The one on which he ultimately landed, translated literally, was *In Search of Lost Time*. But this title was eschewed by Scott Moncrieff. His justification appears on the first page of the first volume, after the single flyleaf on which the owner of The Chatham Bookseller had written the book's resale price. There, Scott Moncrieff quoted:

REMEMBRANCE OF THINGS PAST

*"When to the sessions of sweet silent thought
I summon up remembrance of things past..."*

The beginning of Shakespeare's sonnet number thirty is an adequate gloss of Proust at his gentlest, but it doesn't really capture the novel's tone. Scott Moncrieff was criticized not only for this liberty, but for ones he took with the names of the novel's individual volumes. (For example, he bowdlerized Proust's *Sodom and Gomorrah* as *Cities of the Plain*.) Contrariwise, he added Victorian padding to Proust's lengthy, exquisitely proportioned sentences. But I forgive him all, and I'm not the only English speaker who has fallen in love with Proust through Scott Moncrieff's translation. Even if he wasn't a strictly literal translator, he mastered Proust's style.

Proust's sentences and paragraphs *are* long. (If I should ever teach sentence diagramming -- something I never hope to do -- I'll assign Proust for extra credit. Answers will require tiny handwriting.) Proust may have been the anti-Hemingway, but he began his novel with a short sentence, akin to the quartet of notes heralding Beethoven's fifth symphony:

For a long time I used to go to bed early.

So much is implied in that sentence, and not said:

That an "I" will tell the story of a life (making this a fictionalized memoir).

That the story will concern time, and unfold over years. The word "time," in fact, bookends the novel, appearing in its first and last sentences, linking the novel's end to its beginning like a melody returning to the tonic. (And this musical metaphor reminds me that the book's first word is actually the first chapter's sub-heading, "Overture," in which Proust asks us to consider his novel a sort of symphony. In pretentious homage to Proust, I began my first book the same way.)

That there has been an evolutionary (or revolutionary) change during the arc of the story, mirrored not only in changes besetting the novel's principal characters but also the whole of Parisian high society in an era encompassing 1870s Gilded Age France (Proust was born in 1871) and World War I's aftermath (he died in 1922).

And finally that bed, that home of dreams, will be a privileged setting in a novel that starts unfolding with a description of the narrator's dreams and a meditation upon the myriad ways in which we sleep and wake. An early character in the novel, Aunt Leonie, is confined to bed for much of later life, mirroring Proust, who suffered from severe asthma and other ailments (some psychosomatic, per his more uncharitable friends). He was bedridden most of the years he composed his novel.

***

From page one, I was hooked by the prose of a man who not only remembered the nineteenth century in detail, but was cognizant of modern art and the miracles of science that arrived with each passing year. Proust was certainly a modernist with a penchant for classicism. Consequently, the novel feels simultaneously old-fashioned and modern, like a sepia photograph of a bustling Times Square. It was certainly a mysterious point of embarkation for this reader's career. The world it described – on the one hand, heraldry, etymology, and nobility; on the other, radio, airplanes, and ice cream – made the familiar seem exotic.

And it didn't hurt that *Remembrance of Things Past* opens with some of its most vividly drawn characters, scenes, and stories. This part was fueled by Proust's memories of two childhood homes: his great-uncle's villa in Auteuil, a Parisian suburb that was then semi-rural, and his grandfather's home in the rural village of Illiers, in the vast wheatfields of the Beauce, near Chartres. I flew through these pages. My head of steam lasted through two more volumes, *Within a Budding Grove* (Scott Moncrieff's coy translation of *In the Shadow of Young Women in Flower*), which describes the narrator's adolescence, and *The Guermantes Way*, which describes his precarious entrée, as a young upper-middle-class artist, into the shifting kaleidoscope of elegant society.

Then the slog began. The novel's first half is Proust at his most accessible, but beginning with *Cities of the Plain*, the terrain gets rocky. The plot slows and dialogue dries up: long philosophical musings, never far under the surface of the novel's first half, increasingly predominate. Ideas are rung through changes like carillon bells. From Proust's letters to contemporaries, we know that he composed the middle of his novel last, after writing the beginning and the end more or less simultaneously. When he worked inwards, the novel's length far outstripped his original projection.

I suppose this method of composition accounts for some of the middle's aridity, and I suspect Proust felt similarly. We can see this by considering his fictional author Bergotte who, like Proust, died shortly after viewing a traveling art exhibition that included several Vermeers. After beholding the artist's *View of Delft*, Bergotte succumbs to dizziness, just as Proust did in real life. Proust later wrote that in *View of Delft*, there is a "little patch of yellow wall" with "a beauty sufficient in itself." When the old author Bergotte sees it, Proust has him say:

> *That's how I ought to have written. My last books are too dry, I ought to have gone over them with a few layers of colour, made my language precious in itself, like this little patch of yellow wall.*

I believe that when Proust wrote these words, he was thinking of his own novel's long middle, which he was still polishing on his deathbed.

Having failed to surmount this hurdle, I put Proust aside. Real life pinballed between college and work, work and college. Then, in 1999, I moved to Maine to spend time with my childhood friend Clay. I lived above his garage in an unheated loft, where I brought a few belongings, including my stereo and a copy of Proust.

Curiously, Clay had a distrust of Proust that dated to childhood, when he had been force-fed the author by his demanding mother-teacher. Still, he listened indulgently as I read aloud for hours from *Remembrance of Things Past* while he worked on my clunker of a car in his garage.

I must have restarted the novel a dozen times over the years. Sometimes I read in English, sometimes in French; each time it became easier, my eye following the path laid down by memory, anticipating the ends of long sentences by their initial words. But it looked like it would be a photo finish between the novel's end and my own demise.

As an adult, I empathized with the young narrator, who often reads by the burbling rivulet that ran through his family's garden park (in the real world, Proust's great-uncle's park), his mind lost in a book as the village church bells chimed:

> *And, as each hour struck, it would seem to me that a few seconds only had passed since the hour before; the latest would inscribe itself, close to its predecessor, on the sky's surface, and I would be unable to believe that sixty minutes could be squeezed into the tiny arc of blue which was comprised between their two golden figures.*

with the difference being that, in my case, a larger portion of life had elapsed. I sometimes wondered which was the real life: the one where I went to school, got a job, and changed residences, or the one where I read a book that I might never finish.

In 1999, fifteen years into Proust, I married a high school English teacher who didn't know what to make of my fixation. At Christmas, we went to her in-laws for dinner; at the dinner table, I casually mentioned I was reading Proust, then followed that up by throwing in his first name and a bit of biography. On our way home, my new missus pointedly told me that people knew of *Marcel* Proust, and that I needn't be so pedantic.

Because we married in December, we waited until the following June for our honeymoon, a leisurely two-week guided tour of Brittany, Normandy, and the Loire Valley. A gap in the schedule gave me the idea to squeeze in a side trip that I'd long contemplated. On the day we arrived in Chartres, my wife and I split off from the group to board a gleaming high-speed train, quiet as a hovercraft, that whisked us over the ancient wheatfields of France's bread basket. We were off to see Illiers.

More precisely, Illiers-Combray. The birthplace of Proust's grandfather had rebranded in 1970 to honor the grandson's reimagining of the town. This hyphenated, cartographic linkage of fancy and reality was unprecedented, and it mimicked, or so I believe, a major event near the end of Proust's novel: the cosmic wedding between the Swanns and Saint-Loups, the two families who in the mind of the young Marcel had lived in completely separate worlds, but whom he discovers much later to have been linked all along by a secret path (or "way").

I knew the way from the moment that my wife and I disembarked. The landscape was familiar from two sources: Proust's novel, and George Painter's 1959 biography that begins with maps of Illiers-Combray (then just Illiers) that overlay the actual town's topography with the fictional town's incidents. We circled the village, then dove in. Everything was miraculously familiar: the hedgerows, the church, the stream bisecting the town, and the marketplace where the weekly farmers' market was just closing as we arrived.

I knew we'd be recognized as "Proustiens" (the local term for "Proust pilgrims"), but to avoid playing too much to type, I did *not* buy a madeleine at the town bakery. Instead, I looked at the map and directed our steps to La Maison de Tante Léonie, the house of the fictional Aunt Léonie, on La Rue du Docteur Proust, named after Proust's real-life father. Again, fiction and fact inextricably intertwined!

We arrived at the rear entrance, where the tours begin, and I rang the bell. (Doing so, I could hardly avoid thinking of the little bell in the novel whose "double peal – timid, oval, gilded" announced Swann's arrival.) One minute later, a woman appeared. The day's tour had begun (there was one other visitor, a quiet, forty-something Frenchman), but we were welcome to join it in progress. Unfortunately for my wife, she spoke no English; still, when asked whether we wished to join, I said *bien sûr*.

We toured the charming and cozy house and lingered in the bedroom of the young Marcel, which looked out onto a former kitchen courtyard. It was furnished as at the time of the Prousts' family visits of the 1870s and 1880s. I strained to catch our guide's sentences before they shattered on the floor's ceramic tile, and caught enough of them to follow the narrative. (Only on the return trip to Chartres did I realize how much the strain of my undivided attention had exhausted me.) While I watched the lips of our guide, my wife watched me, and I caught her up between rooms, during lulls in conversation. This was, I believe, one of the few times in my short marriage when I thoroughly impressed my wife; I had managed to get us to a most inaccessible place, through a countryside populated by non-speakers of English, and achieve a lifelong goal.

Finally, as in every museum through the history of time, a gift shop awaited. There I purchased Celeste Albaret's *Monsieur Proust*, a first-person account by the one person who, more than anyone, knew the adult Proust. Ms. Albaret was Proust's live-in helper for his final ten years, when she arranged his topsy-turvy life per his instructions. She adopted his nocturnal schedule, prepared or ordered his simple meals (baked sole was one of the few foods he ate), and jealously guarded access to his person so that he could devote his remaining energy to his life's work. The tour guide complimented me on my selection, which she said corrected some of the more fanciful tales told about the reclusive author.

***

Four years later, I married Carol. She, more than my first wife, countenanced my love of Proust. In fact, she surprised me on our big day with hand-made wedding programs that quoted him. On translucent sheets of paper over a soft pink-and-white floral design, she had typeset:

> *Let us be grateful to those who make us happy;*
> *they are the charming gardeners*
> *who make our souls blossom.*

I was grateful for these words, but to my ear they sounded more like Proverbs than Proust. I didn't recall this aphorism from my reading; was it from a part I had not yet read? When I asked Carol, she admitted that she had found the words on a website of inspirational quotations, and couldn't swear as to their provenance.

I have not yet taken Carol on an Illiers-Combray pilgrimage. She did suggest another journey, though. While we were living in Manhattan, she encouraged me to take part in a several-month Proust class at the 92nd Street Y, an organization known for cultural programming. A notable Proust scholar would guide students through *Remembrance of Things Past* in its entirety.

"What has it been now, twenty-five years? You might not get this chance again. Why not settle down and find out how the story ends?"

From my reading about the novel I had an idea of how it ended, but there is no substitute for primary sources. So I signed up, and once a month that fall, winter, and spring, I schlepped to the Upper East Side and sat in a classroom with fifteen other Proust devotees. Most were older than I, with many crossing Proust off their "bucket lists." We read from a recently published seven-volume Modern Library edition. More books for the old Proust shelf, but they made a nice addition: when placed side-by-side, they did something that Hardy Boys books never did – their spines formed a single image, that of a starched white shirt collar, presumably denoting the entrance of a young man into society.

I made it to most of the classes, but spectacularly failed to arrive at the third one, the first Sunday of November. Dyed-in-the-wool Manhattanites know this as Marathon Sunday; being a new resident, I had forgotten. To take advantage of a beautiful fall morning, I took the subway up the West Side to 86th Street, then walked crosstown through Central Park. When I reached Fifth Avenue, I encountered a sea of runners kicking hard, buoyed by the looming prospect of the marathon's home stretch. Attempting a crossing was out of the question: even had I stormed the barricades and eluded the on-duty officers, it would have been a *French Connection* scenario. So I had to turn back.

Other months, I had better luck. The instructor knew his Proust, and my classmates, to judge from some of their particularly far-fetched contributions, were enthusiastic. All the same, it felt odd to be back in a classroom doing literary criticism. I thought that part of my life was over. My mind flashed back to my previous attempt at textual analysis, during my first marriage. My wife took us to a weekly Bible study group, which met in a poorly heated classroom under hard fluorescent lighting. After everyone introduced themselves, we tackled a Bible passage. I must admit that while everyone else tried to relate the words to their personal lives and shortcomings, I stayed on the high road of literary analysis. What can I say? They were there for the Jesus; I was there for the exegesis.

At the 92nd Street Y, I was on safer ground. Most of my classmates were Jews, so I stood little chance of offending someone who claimed a personal relationship with Proust.

And I finally finished the novel! With the final sentence, I felt the giddiness that accompanies the realization of a long-cherished dream. I also felt the disappointment of having attained it. Even so, the last part of the book was worth the journey: loose threads introduced in the earliest pages are tied up in surprising ways, thanks to the discovery of a children's book and an uneven paving stone.

***

Now that I think of it, I may remember how I first heard of Proust.

In high school, I was a fan of *Monty Python's Flying Circus*, the half-hour sketch show of absurdist humor that aired regularly on public television. (I wasn't the only fan of theirs at my high school; I distinctly recall a chorus of classmates performing "The Lumberjack Song" at a talent show.) PBS ran pledge drives around the show, when they would broadcast all forty-five episodes. (The first time I ever stayed up all night was, in fact, to videotape them on my aunt's primordial video recorder.) Of the skits, a personal favorite was the "All-England Summarize Proust Competition," in which contestants stand on a "summarizing spot" and attempt to encapsulate *Remembrance of Things Past* in fifteen seconds, once in swimsuit and once in evening dress. A series of risible failures ensues, including a notably misguided attempt by a choir to summarize the book as a madrigal.

Tickled by the skit's premise, I shared it with my artsy friend, Elyssa. We watched at the VCR at my house. She enjoyed it, though I recall being embarrassed in her presence at the risqué way in which the contest winner was decided.

May I offer my attempt?

Remembrance of Things Past is the story of one young man's apprenticeship to art. On the way, he learns that experiences never live up to expectations; that friendship and love are dubious propositions; that the only true life is one lived in art; and that all great art is a reflection of its creator's unique worldview.

How'd I do?

And if it's true that I found Proust via Monty Python, so be it. We make many sublime discoveries in inauspicious places.

Labyrinth

He who live on meditation
Never ever feel elation
Round and round he run and get nowhere
Ever chasing echoes in the air
  - Brian Protheroe, "Enjoy It"

Northwest of Philadelphia in quaint Doylestown is a museum that represents the legacy of an author I have never read -- James Michener. When I was young, Michener's books collected dust on my parents' bookshelves -- their friends', too. They stayed there, angled in repose, useful years gone, generational epics beloved of middlebrow America when its mind was sharper and eyesight more acute. Today, the Michener Museum, a bequest made possible by those books, features a school of art I never knew existed, Bucks County Impressionism.

Down a narrow road from the museum is a garden labyrinth, a sort of maze without walls. Its outer contour is the circumference of a circle roughly fifty feet in diameter; its path-defining inner partitions are slate-colored edging stones squarely planted in a bed of finely crushed plum-brown gravel. Though the labyrinth seems to serve no purpose but ornamentation, it was designed as therapy for distracted minds.

Labyrinths are sprouting in America's parks, gardens, and public spaces like civic crop circles. They propose to recall people from the distractions of modern life, to direct their attention to the dirt at their feet. The Doylestown labyrinth was created by Connie Fenty, a local artist and self-styled "labyrinth designer" who, on pagan days like full moons and solstices, leads community walks through labyrinths during which she explains how best to experience them.

I didn't know all this when I first encountered the Doylestown labyrinth. But its tranquil aspect persuaded me to put away my phone and do the one thing that anyone in my position could conceivably do -- enter the labyrinth and follow the path to its center.

Constraints have salutary effects. Rhyme, by limiting choice, distills a writer's most vivid creations; this labyrinth, by limiting mine, spurred me inward. I love puzzles, but this was not one, since there were no forks. In a nub, that is the difference between a maze and a labyrinth: labyrinths are unicursal, with but one path to follow. They are utterly unlike the paperback books of mazes with which I spent the summers of youth, which were nothing *but* choices. With only one path to follow, one proceeds meditatively, like a bride down a church aisle without a misstep to rue.

I gave Carol a one-turn head start so that we wouldn't get in each other's way. The path began by following the circumference, but turned in suddenly, like the involution of a honeysuckle flower or inner wall of a cochlea. I had trouble turning off my self-awareness. Had the partitions been walls, say in a harvest festival's corn maze, I could have proceeded invisibly to onlookers, but here I felt exposed to passers-by – library patrons, dog walkers, meter readers – so I reflexively turned my profile to them, as though shielding my modesty, pivoting on the outer edge of my left or right foot according to the winding of the path.

Perhaps I was being watched from a window of the grand, Tara-like manor next door, a large clapboard Colonial painted white with black shutters to keep up appearances in a pricey neighborhood. I imagined what I could not see, a wraparound porch with immense ceiling fans lazily pushing the humid air, palms transplanted from the tropics, drinks tables laden with iced teas and Pimm's Cups. Did this homestead from the Antebellum south belong to Michener, a dedicated globetrotter, or did it belong to Miss Havisham? I could almost see her bony fingers pull aside a heavy red damask curtain and lace liner to regard the curious young man twisting and turning on her lawn.

I followed the one and only way. Carol was in her world, clear across the labyrinth, facing outward. My thoughts had taken a peculiar turn: I was thinking of Michener's desk in the museum just out of sight down the street, which looked as though its owner had stepped away for a moment, laden with knickknacks and surrounded by photographs of the author with his celebrity and political friends. The desk was of metal, but preserved like the most heavily veneered and varnished hardwood. On it rested an antique typewriter and two baseballs, one smudged, one signed; correspondence from his publisher; and typewritten replies to admirers. Was the desk frozen at the moment of death, like the one in the famous photograph of Einstein's office, just down the road at Princeton's Institute of Advanced Studies? Or was it simply a period recreation, like Proust's childhood bedroom at his aunt's house in Illiers-Combray?

Such were my thoughts as I followed the labyrinth. Other, unconscious ones bubbled under, like an underground stream, but to bring those to light would require a dowsing rod, or a pen. Another thought: where was I? In a mathematical sense, I was everywhere, my path filling every part of the labyrinth in some order; but looked at from the labyrinth's point of view, it was filling every part of me.

I compared the labyrinth to others I'd seen. The one at the Coastal Maine Botanical Garden was smaller, with a flagstone path, but it occupied me much like this one did; it pulled me in until I was oblivious of other visitors following the same winding path, pausing like pollinating insects to examine the tagged and labeled plants.

Then there was the labyrinth on the road to Calistoga, California, near the outlying foothills. A minor roadside attraction, it sat in a dusty lot, squeezed between a laundromat and a hot dog stand. It was laid out with small stones directly on dry dirt, and had accumulated mementos: pebble cairns, miniature potted cacti, and beads from teens and aging hippies who worked at local wineries and gift shops. Carol and I walked that labyrinth, too, tuning out the sound of the cars whizzing by.

Three labyrinths – one in California, one in Maine, and now one in Pennsylvania – built by a grass roots movement, a well-endowed nonprofit, and a local artist. Three invitations to escape the quotidian and explore the folds of the cranium, the only place anything interesting ever happens, which we would remember if we could just tear ourselves away from cellphones and schedules.

Carol is near the labyrinth's center, but I'm still on the outskirts. Unlike the Calistoga labyrinth, but like the one in Maine, there's a beguiling garden along the rim. I beat myself up again for not having learned the nomenclature of flora; I can't name a single plant except the one with the waxy green-and-white leaves that I'm pretty sure is Hosta. I sit for a moment on a stone bench that has conveniently materialized near some flowers, and breathe in perfume. As usual, my nose isn't up to the task, sensing only a slight scent on the breeze. I wonder again why single flower buds emit strong odors but masses of flowers do not. I must have a small-picture nose.

Sight is another story. I admire a profusion of pinks and purples without seeing the details; that must have been Miss Haversham's intent when she planted the flowers at night, after the museum visitors were gone. The flowers were meant to divert, and I am indeed diverted, just as the labyrinth was made to rid my mind of care, which indeed it has. As Paul Klee wrote, "The eye follows the paths that have been laid down for it in the work." We fancy we're free, choosing our experiences, but our paths were laid out ages ago. Not just today, but since the day we were born. Enjoy it all – the *trompe l'oeil* of sight, the *divertimenti* of sound, the *amuses-bouche* of taste. Don't worry about destinations.

Here comes Carol, waking me from my reverie. She's on my side of the circle, tracing the outermost path but one, and as she passes she bristles without turning, like a preoccupied cat. Her lifeline absorbs her, and mine me. I consider rising and resuming my journey, but a memory arrests me.

A sunny day in late spring, thirty-three years ago. I'm in college, cramming for the final of an absurd Chinese history class, one semester covering four millennia. Having read that the Chinese issued the first paper money in 1024 AD – it's a power of two, so that should be easy to remember – I file the fact away for the exam. But what I really want to study is the beautiful, late spring day all around; I'd like to walk the campus and trace the deserted paths between formal gardens and medieval Gothic buildings that students have forsaken for the library, where they are cramming in study carrels.

I open my text to a photograph of a woodblock etching from one dynasty or another – I can't keep them straight – depicting a student in a flowing robe, lost in thought, sitting on a stone bench beside a wide path leading to a temple. He is supposed to be inside, taking his candidature exam to become a civil servant, but is lost instead in a moment he will never forget. Across ten centuries I identify with him and linger in a moment that will not stay. Here comes Carol again. I rise so as not to appear lazy.

We're next to each other, on adjacent tracks. Just before we cross, I raise my left hand to slap her five. She laughs. The joke is that she and I aren't close, in labyrinthine terms. She's way ahead, near the center, and I lag far behind. But for a moment, it looks like we're together. Isn't that life? We walk side by side, but once we put aside our daily tasks, we're alone. I'm sure someone in China said that conversation scatters like petals across sneakers. That's all we have a right to expect, the good fortune to walk with someone whose impressions differ from ours. If we're lucky, we'll meet at a wayside bench under a flowering magnolia.

What are decades but orientations? A child takes his father's hand upon entering a labyrinth, and exits leading him by the hand. A lover pursues a beloved, distantly absorbed in the garden's delights; in a later revolution their roles are reversed.

Suddenly Carol is in front of me! She must have reached the center and started backtracking. I don't need bread crumbs, but she offers me one:

"Just wait until you see the middle!"

She knows the labyrinth's secret, but keeps me in ignorance. I pirouette awkwardly on my right foot to let her pass.

Then it's my turn for *satori*. The center is no big deal, a single stone ringed by ticky-tacky four-leaf clovers, lime green, shiny as mylar.

I was hoping for something more, but so is everyone. It's the journey, not the destination -- a phrase we parrot without believing, but what of it? There may not be a pot at the rainbow's end, but the journey is neat. I'm reminded of an avant-garde short film I saw in college, Michael Snow's *Wavelength*, which consists of an exceedingly slow, forty-five-minute zoom to a small object at the other end of a long room. The film's meaning lies not in the inconsequential object finally revealed, but in the pattern of incidental sights and sounds (two people at the edge of shot discussing what might be a business deal; two others, at another time, listening to "Strawberry Fields Forever" on a phonograph) along the way. Our journeys make us.

The Lost Art of Wasting Time

The plan of the house
The body in bed
And the car that got stuck
It's the mud, it's the mud
      - Carlos Antonio Jobim, "Waters of March"

The bedroom where I lived for twenty years was situated at the crest of my family's home. Its two windows faced north-northeast and framed a parklike view, from the crown of the maple that edged the patio below (itself perched on the stone foundation of an old carriage house), to the trees and roofs of our neighbors' homes, to the green veins of foliage radiating to Samson Avenue, Rosedale Avenue, Brooklake Country Club, and points beyond.

For a better view, I'd climb the eave outside the windows. To reach the steeply-pitched roof required a jolt of adrenalin and not a little care, particularly after rain had made the asphalt shingles slippery. But once I was up, the view rivaled that of a Ferris wheel. To one side was our wooded, circular rear drive and enclosed yard; beyond that, the terraced ledge and disused stone fire pit; further still, the woods of the deep "dell" – the work of a glacier, so I learned in Earth Science – where I once lost a sneaker in the leaf pile that we kids added to each autumn. That sneaker must still be there. A careful turn to the other side of the roof offered a privileged view of my street, Crestview Avenue, winding off into the distance like a braid of ribbon candy.

Most of the time, though, the view from my bed was sufficient. I was never better at doing nothing than when I was a young teen, lying abed on Saturday or Sunday mornings. Unlike my peers, I seemed to lack the physiological imperative to sleep in; I'd wake before seven. On rare occasions, though, I would sleep so late that when I finally managed to gather myself and wrest my mind from the wall-to-wall carpet, sky blue paint, double-glazed glass and the rest of the collective unconscious of which I had formed a part, my neck would crack to orient itself the long way across my room, toward the built-in bookshelves Dad had made, on one of which sat an alarm clock with red numbers that slowly came into focus. It was shockingly late, maybe ten o'clock. I wondered at a world that had continued turning in my absence, and thought of George Harrison's mantra, "The world goes on within you and without you." That's a hard lesson for a young man to accept.

If I overslept, I missed the format changeover on the mysterious station that I'd recently discovered on the left end of the FM dial. I never knew its call letters, nor its point of transmission, but one spring and summer I fell asleep to the sounds of the Great American Songbook and woke to a crazy Jamaican dude playing rocksteady and ska. I had also missed my chance to flip the switch of the mini TV next to my bed to see the equally mysterious children's show that aired on Saturday mornings on a UHF station, in which four Claymation characters, two boys, two girls, piloted a spaceship to strange planets. Something about that show was askew: the children's accents didn't sync with their clay lips, making me wonder if the show was Japanese. Its name was something like "Interscope." What station was this, anyway? Was it Montclair State's public TV station? Was I watching a communication major's senior project? I'll never know, and the internet gives no satisfaction.

Late-rising mornings revealed that my presence on Earth, which I had deemed essential, was meaningless. Neither parents nor siblings noticed my absence. Dad hadn't, as he did sometimes, pounded the floor with a broomstick handle from the kitchen below to wake me. I considered what might happen if I expired. The clothes in my closet would pass to Frank, though he might not want them, with the exception of my bright red Widow Brown's windbreaker. (With a start, I reminded myself to dispose of certain magazines.) A guidance counselor would send my academic record to deep storage. How long would it take for all traces of me to disappear – a few weeks, a year at most? But the maple outside my window would continue to grow and slowly squeeze the patio's retaining wall in the vise of its roots, and the other trees outside my window would likewise thrive.

My insignificance was pleasurable, so I worried it like a wound, stewing on it like an affront. No one would remember me. Not Tommy, the cool cashier at Alwilk Records in the Livingston Mall who knew all the best Dave Edmunds records, nor my Bolivian pen pal, who wrote our family every few months, nor the girls at school. Not even my friends, not really. So, propping a pillow behind my back, I scooched up to face the windows and a day that was, as they said on television, "already in progress."

I was diverted by a cloud of dust motes in a ray of sunshine. They hovered, weightless in the rarefied air of my aerie, their existence betrayed by a sunbeam penetrating the windows. How astounding to realize that I walked through them, inadvertently inhaled them, like the microorganisms in tap water whose existence I would never have believed had Mr. Lyons not told me to place a droplet between two glass microscope plates. One corkscrewed down to my right index finger: just before landing, as it silhouetted against the concentric circles of my fingerprint, I saw its outline like that of an old chromosome, broken. It landed and disappeared.

Was this dust the result of human error? Soon after we moved to Madison, Dad had converted the far end of the unfinished attic with the huge louvered fan to two rooms, my own and my brother Frank's. Had he mistakenly kicked up the dust? Or was it my fault, the result of my faulty insertion, earlier that summer, of a window air conditioner? It didn't matter. The word "hypoallergenic" was not yet part of my lexicon -- besides, as a teenager, I was immortal. Every illness was as insignificant as a mote of dust.

I was always catching something, then sloughing it off like old skin. Poison ivy, oak, sumac – I never knew which, or how to tell – was an annual occurrence. I was sensitive to the oil of the vines that ran along our front yard's fieldstone wall, where on a hot and humid day I could catch a rash at twenty paces. Once aboard my body, it would establish base camp at my ankles, from which it would volley to every conceivable annoying spot, from crevices between toes to tips of eyelids, until Mom would drive me to the doctor (or once, the hospital) for some high-octane cortisone. Nana, on the other hand, took a more holistic approach, bringing a baggie of jewel weed from a patch of her shaded side yard. Jewel weed grew next to poison ivy, and was its antidote; rubbing it on the rash dried it more quickly than calamine lotion.

If on the other hand I had a cold, or flu, or "stomach bug," I gladly stayed in bed. It gave me a reason to dawdle, maybe miss a day of school. That in turn would fan my self-pity, and again I would wonder if my classmates would notice. At least in bed I could entertain that old doctor, nostalgia. He made house calls, bringing to mind childhood humidifiers: the milky white bedpan-shaped model that hummed like the wings of a guardian angel, and the larger dark brown cabinet unit that stood guard in the hall outside my room, watching over me with its piercing, constant, orange-red eye.

> *It's kind of like my body has a brain for itself*
> *It only uses just for health*
> *No matter what I try to do to stand in its way*
> *My body has the final say*
> *And it keeps me safe from harm*
> *It never fails, it never gives a false alarm*
>   -   Peter Murray, "Ears Make Wax"

As a teen, I added vomiting to my repertoire. That happened only when I was careless with food: too many clams at a cookout, too many rolls of Spree candy, a grape soda and pistachio dinner. Having never been drunk, that was the only path I had to the transcendence of evisceration that follows a night of praying to the porcelain god. After an extended sleep, I cherished the beatific feeling of complete peace.

Returning to the aimless motes falling silently as snowflakes into my deep, coarse pile carpet: I could summon a similar drift inside my eyelids by closing them tight. The reincarnation of Walt Whitman, I marvelled at the intricacy of my body: eyelids, phosphenes, gold hair picketing my arms as different from the hair on my scalp as golden raisins are from dark. All thriving without help from me. A mysterious thing, the body: if you listen closely, you can hear blood beneath the skin. The galvanic heart keeps time better than the mainspring of a precision watch. Better to listen to one's heart and less to the world.

***

Two years and done: I fetched my orange Volkswagen Beetle with the rust-flaked floor from the furthest Princeton parking lot, way out by the Ideal Course, the inlet of Carnegie Lake where the scullers, whom I had never joined, rowed daily. I took the time-honored route home – Route 206, Route 287, Madison Avenue. I would spend the next few years in the slow lane, in my old room.

Its furnishings were unchanged. The walls were still plastered with glossy reproductions of pop music charts, snapshots of weeks that I had fixed in amber, promotional centerfolds from *Billboard* magazine, posters of the "Hot 100" intended for in-store display. I had mounted them with Fun-Tak, a putty the color of wasabi with a thousand-year half-life that I now discovered could badly discolor the paint beneath.

> *I have your picture on the wall*
> *It hides a nasty stain that's lying there*
>   -   10cc, "I'm Not in Love"

On a wall of the bedroom next door, my brother Frank had, like many teenage boys, pinned up Heather Locklear. She straddled a motorcycle in a low-cut black swimsuit; she signed the poster in curvy handwriting with a lipstick-red note, a heart over each "i," ending in XOXO. I had my *Billboard* charts.

Fun-Takked to another wall of my room was a large poster I had bought years earlier at the Metropolitan Museum of Art Store, Edouard Manet's *A Bar at the Folies-Bergère*. My ideal woman *en décolleté* was a barmaid with a velvet frock cinching her waist, standing behind a marble bar laden with fruit and bottles of champagne. In her bosom, she wore a sprig of flowers; on her face, a look of impassivity. She was the picture of unavailability, the anti-Locklear.

"Tough day?" she seemed to say. "Mine's been worse."

On the other side of the windows was a robin's egg blue, floor-to-ceiling, commercial-grade-metal rack of Pepsi display shelves that Dad had given me years earlier, obtained from an East Hanover restaurant supply store. On them sat stacks of books and Mom's old record player, which I no longer used now that I had a quality stereo.

Under an eave, a large walk-in closet with a low ceiling sheltered a trove of possessions that, taken together, represented a perpetual negotiation with the past. I'd slide open Dad's homemade plywood doors, which always came untracked, and search for the switch for an antique frosted glass light that barely illuminated a large space that can only be inventoried now by the light of memory.

In a long and tall cardboard box that rested on its shortest side was a four-foot-high stack of tests, essays, and report cards that dated to the dawn of my school years. Along one wall, on a two-shelf gray bookcase that fit snugly beneath the pitched roof, was a haphazardly stored coin collection, slowly oxidizing next to a defunct backlit magnifying glass that I had once used to examine it. Near the coins, stacked on the floor, were two other past enthusiasms: *Dungeons and Dragons* reference books and "modules" with handwritten game notes, dusty as the universes they described, and a Fidelity chess computer in a creased brown attaché case that I hadn't booted up in years.

It was nice to be back.

***

I intended to take a year off college. For pocket money, I applied for a word processing job at a branch of the Metropolitan Life Insurance Company, in a small office on Main Street in Chatham.

The manager of the Policyholder Service Department was Geoff, a short man with a perpetually dissatisfied expression, a brown walrus mustache, and oversized matching brown suits that he may have thought made him look imposing, but instead made him look like David Byrne in *Stop Making Sense*.

I sat down in his office. Having never worked for a corporation, I was nervous. So nervous in fact, that earlier that morning I had attended mass at St. Vincent's. Clearly, my view of this job was different than my prospective manager's. After glancing at my brief resume, he asked why I was interested in the job -- surely an Ivy Leaguer wanted something with more responsibility. That was all I needed to loosen up. I mentioned my word processing experience, and said that I enjoyed typing. With no reason to turn me down, Geoff offered me the job. I had joined the professional world.

That evening, my eight-year-old brother Danny, a fan of MetLife's Peanuts-themed TV commercials, tweaked the company tagline:

"Get Met, it pays *John!*"

Soon, our office relocated to Eagle Rock Avenue in East Hanover, down the street from where Dad had bought my Pepsi shelves. Two weeks before our move, I got shingles from Danny, who'd caught chicken pox. I stayed home two days, but I was so eager to return to work that I showed up on day three with my face pocked with red, raw scabs. I was told to go home until I looked better.

So began an interlude when life asked little of me. I didn't dawdle at work, though. I processed words – tens of thousands of them – on an IBM Displaywriter, a dedicated word processor. My colleagues, the "correspondents" of our department, wrote responses to policyholder questions that arrived in the mail, and I typed them. This was before clerical positions were eliminated and white-collar workers had to learn their way around a keyboard.

Many questions concerned TEFRA, the Tax Equity and Fiscal Responsibility Act, effective August 14, 1982. The fourteenth of August happened to be the birthday of my coworker Mary, a soft-spoken, curly-haired brunette whose face still appears in my mental dictionary when I encounter the word "demure." Mary, a few years older than I, sat next to Ed, a tall fellow with a proclivity for his own sex that was so pronounced that even a naïf like myself, who didn't know Boy George was gay, could tell. Ed called Mary a "TEFRA baby." Each August fourteenth, I still think of Mary and TEFRA, even though decades have passed since I've heard about either. And despite typing hundreds of responses explaining the change in annuity tax treatment under TEFRA, I still can't explain it.

A funny thing. The more I recall my colleagues in the Policyholder Service Department, the more their names, faces, and idiosyncrasies arise from a thirty-year deep. Like a fishing line fitted with multiple lures trawling the river of Lethe, each hook baits the next: Mary recalls Ed, who recalls Jim, and so forth. Full names, first and last, return to me, because I typed them on the Displaywriter. Since that machine was not a general-purpose computer, it had limited autofill capabilities, meaning my brain was *not* softened, and every letter of my colleagues' names was keystroked directly on the carbon copy of my long-term memory.

I didn't socialize much with my coworkers, but for a while I went to their weekly "drinks night" at a Route 10 bar, where I'd order a gin and tonic, which I actually thought kind of gross. But it was what the guys ordered, and not knowing the names of other acceptable guy drinks, I ordered one too.

Next to Ed sat Jim, who in a word was a "gent." Just a little older than I was, he had a rugged, handsome face and short, dark, slicked-back hair. He was suave, a sharp dresser. He didn't exactly take me under his wing, but we did pal around a bit in the office. On my twenty-first birthday, at the little department party in my honor, he gave me a *Sports Illustrated* swimsuit calendar, which elicited general mirth because I was considered, in Gina's word, "harmless."

Across from Jim, in the corner, sat Jacqueline, a cherubic, slightly plump blonde. She had a serious demeanor; whenever anyone told a joke, she was a bit behind the beat with her laughter, like Sinatra's vocals. Not that she didn't get jokes -- she just didn't like laughing at the expense of others. One cold morning I drove to work in my Chevy Nova, which was then in its final days. Even its heater didn't work. On a whim, I drove to work with the windows wide open, sticking my left hand out the driver's side window, making both hands as cold as possible. Then, in the office, I headed straight for Jackie's desk (Barbara and Jackie, good friends and work neighbors, arrived early) and asked her to hold my hands. She hesitated.

"Why?" She looked warily at Barbara, who merely smiled and looked away. I told her I wanted her to feel how cold they were.

She gripped my two blocks of ice, let go, and stared at me with her wide-eyed, pretty eyes.

Barbara, a recent bride, had recently exchanged one Italian surname for another. (I kept reminding myself not to type her maiden name.) She wore her dark hair in a spiky do that made her look like a punk, but despite appearances she was professional; during my stint at MetLife, she was promoted to a direct reporting position to Lisa, the young, chain-smoking department head who spoke with an accent out of deepest Brooklyn.

Barbara enjoyed my mix tapes more than most people; she actually enthused over some of my finds. Alas, she was married. But one perk of joining a new cohort was identifying new mix recipients. I tried Warren, the bespectacled saxophonist and office bohemian who gigged in insurance for a steady paycheck; he was the only person I ever met who knew of Martha and the Muffins. (For more on them, turn the book over to Side B and read "The Class of '81.") Then there was the clever blonde with porcelain skin who worked one department over (sadly, I've forgotten her name), who reciprocated with a mix tape of her own, on which she had the excellent taste to include the Style Council. On that basis alone I should have asked her out, but I was too green.

The list of department veterans begins with Betsy. Old enough to draw from her own MetLife annuity, she had a long, wizened, aristocratic face that clashed with a commoner's conversation. She gossiped with anyone who would listen. The summer I was there, that was most often the department intern, a pretty young woman with no desk of her own who sat in the chair by Betsy's typewriter. Unlike me, this collegian lamented the time she had to spend indoors that gorgeous summer, recalling a past summer when she lived in a bikini and sipped her favorite cocktail, Sex on the Beach. (I worked hard to dismiss any images thus conjured.)

Betsy was tiresome, but good-natured, so I cut her slack. She got along with everyone. And I had plenty of time to talk with her because I typed my letters quickly, leaving me with lots of downtime. Betsy, in contrast, was an old-school typist who knew nothing of computers, so her usefulness to the firm was drawing to a close. Still, when tasked to type a letter on the old Selectric, she'd raise her glasses from the end of her lanyard to the bridge of her nose and slowly set to work. Betsy was MetLife's institutional memory when institutions still cared to have one; otherwise, not much was expected of her. She stayed on the payroll until the day she had a seizure in the office, effectively ending her career.

The other senior ladies included Catherine, who was lanky, ditzy, and alarmingly absent-minded; short, squat, chain-smoking JoAnn, who also did word processing and harped on me to work slower so that we would always have something in the inbox; and Katherine, a chain-smoking, honest-to-God Italian grandma with a raspy voice and salty tongue.

By me sat Donald, a middle-aged father who fit poorly in our group. He tried to carry himself like a manager, but was hamstrung time and again by his spelling mistakes and grammatical gaffes. He left MetLife during my tenure, but I ran across him years later during lunch hour at a temporary assignments at AT&T, in an office on Route 202 in Morris Township. We crossed the atrium from different directions, and he recognized me first. He hesitated, but when I waved (actually, I recognized his *briefcase* first, the one he had used at MetLife), he approached to shake my hand, explaining that he was on a sales call. After thirty seconds of small talk, we parted forever. I hope he eventually got that manager's job.

But wait, how could I forget Bill?

> *Maybe he went to get a sideways haircut*
> *Maybe he went to get a striped shirt*
> *Maybe he went to get some plastic shoes*
> *Maybe he went to get some funny sunglasses*
>   - Camper Van Beethoven, "Where the Hell is Bill?"

Bill, a few years my senior, had a boyish, freckled face, a dark quiff of hair that towered over a pale forehead, and the habitually lazy smile of the easily amused. In one word, he was diffident.

When Bill heard I was on leave from Princeton, his gaze went dreamy. His eyes may even have misted over. Because, as I soon learned, Bill had gone to Princeton. Exactly in what capacity remained a mystery. The way he described it, he had spent most of his time in one of the campus "eating clubs." In fact, he practically lived in one for a while – something I didn't even think was possible. To my mind, he assumed the aura of a member of Fitzgerald's lost generation -- possibly Klipspringer, the hanger-on in Gatsby's mansion.

Princeton had no frats. Instead, the venerable campus institution was the *eating club*, where upperclassmen who had dined for two years in cafeterias – however Gothic their appointments – took evening meals in greater luxury. A dozen such clubs were housed in ornate mansions on Prospect Street, at the east end of campus. I fancy at one time there were even bootblacks and smoking jackets, but in my time these institutions still projected class. Each eating club had a moniker (there were Ivy, Tower, Cottage, Tiger, and others) and a place in the pecking order from which its members derived a personal coefficient of exclusivity. To my mind, it was as byzantine as the heraldic titles assumed by the pre-WWI European aristocracy.

It my have been the looming specter of the eating clubs that prompted me to leave Princeton. My need to apply to one felt like having to choose a college all over again, the last thing I wanted to think about. It was necessary to apply to eating clubs. They had admission committees, and many required nominations, or at least recommendations. Some clubs were particularly *recherché*, and at least one had been sued for not admitting women. What bullshit. You had to know people, and I didn't; nor could I be bothered to figure out which clubs were compatible with mavericks like myself. To amuse myself, I wrote a computer program that ran for twenty-four hours on my dorm room PC: it would select, completely at random, the eating clubs to which I would apply. I moseyed over once in a while to check its progress, to see who was in the lead. When James, my roommate, asked what I was up to, I told him. He already knew which club he was going to, so he chalked up this exercise as another case of "John being John."

I never bought into the idea of eating clubs, but Bill had. I forget which one he had lived in, in some upstairs bedroom. He'd sleep the morning away, wake in his usual rumpled shirt, then head downstairs for a late lunch. He lived in that house long enough to become a fixture, or a mascot, and to attend some "legendary" parties. He mentioned, in particular, a local rock band called Flipper that had either performed in his house or one nearby.

I had never heard of Flipper, so on my next trip to the Princeton Record Exchange, I looked for their one and only vinyl album, *Generic Flipper*, released in 1982. It was there in the racks. The cover, following the "generic" conceit, did not describe the contents. It just said, on a blinding field of yellow:

ALBUM
Generic FLIPPER

I bought it, took it home to Madison, and put it on my turntable. An awful din resounded. A few seconds later, I lifted the needle to see if everything was alright. Had a mote of dust made the cartridge skate across the vinyl? No. I tried the other side. More of the same – tons of bass, no midrange: a rumbling, caterwauling, off-putting mess. This was before the advent of noise bands like Sonic Youth, so I didn't know what to think. I "dubbed" the album to cassette (leaving my room during the recording), and surprised Bill with it at work. He seemed pleased, but when I followed up later, he still hadn't listened to it. With hindsight, I believe he simply wanted not to sully the memory of his youth. To listen to that cassette would put it to the test.

***

Here I arrive at the one person who, alone among these ghosts, would significantly deflect my life. She was the newest "correspondent," a recent graduate of Douglass College, the women's college in the Rutgers system. She had an English degree, the major to which I still aspired, at least nominally.

Lisa walked her down my aisle to her new desk, catty-corner to mine. She smiled as she passed. Her dark hair was cut short, on a bias, slightly scalloped, complementing her olive-tinged skin. From her ears hung two small, discreet earrings, the only kind she wore. Once seated, she began to review the documents that Lisa had left behind. I wanted to make her feel at home, so I introduced myself. She listened with interest.

I had yet to learn her history. Her parents had escaped Hungary just before the 1956 Communist crackdown, crossing the Alps on foot in a scene not unlike the end of *The Sound of Music*. I would learn that though she was born in the United States, she had a Hungarian birth name. I asked her what it was, but she wasn't ready to tell me.

A week later, without any prompting on my part, she whispered her name conspiratorially while visiting my desk.

"How is that spelled?"

"Here," she said. She found a blank sheet of paper, folded it, and neatly tore off a narrow strip on which she wrote out her full birth name, which she said I should keep to myself. I beheld an improbable aggregation of consonants jammed up against one another in a way I'd never seen.

I was seduced by exotic orthography. We began to date, and on Easter Sunday, 1987, I kissed her, making her the first woman I kissed. Twelve years later, after we had lost touch for quite a while, she became my first wife.

***

Last but not least was Russell, Warren's manager. He worked in another group for whom I did word processing. One morning I typed one of his letters. Immediately after lunch, he waddled my way, his face as red as a marathoner's, or a tippler who'd had a few. He clamped my shoulders with one arm and placed the palm of his other uncomfortably in the square of my back. After a glance to see if anyone was looking, he pulled me aside.

In my transcription of Russell's handwritten letter, I'd included a marginal note that he'd written. Unsure whether it constituted part of his response, I typed it, figuring that I could remove it later. It said the policyholder could "go suck monkey balls."

"You weren't supposed to type that!"

I was unrepentant. I typed 'em like I saw 'em -- when in the zone, I sometimes typed so quickly that I didn't know *what* I was typing.

And though Russell's marginal note may have been odd, I had no other explanation at hand, so I reasoned that he must know the writer, must in fact be her personal friend, and that his comment was a private joke.

When he had stormed over, Russell was ready to tear into me. But after he saw my face aglow with innocence, he did a double take and laughed.

"It's a good thing for us both that I read your letter before I sent it to the mailroom. I usually don't – you're too good."

He let go. Then, on the way back to his desk, he said loudly over his shoulder:

"Slow down!"

I couldn't help it; I was an eager beaver. And at that point of life, I assumed that anyone in a position of authority – from President Reagan down to Russell – was so for a good reason, and must know their stuff. Looking back at my younger self, so happy-go-lucky and quick-to-please, I can only marvel at someone who had encountered so many depictions of injustice in *novels* but could not recognize their real-life counterparts. I blame a happy childhood; it must have made me assume that real-life injustice occurred with exceeding rarity.

My moral myopia may have also been the result of joining the workforce before the death of corporate feudalism. Large companies still had hierarchies of employees who scaled ladders rung by rung. Everyone knew their place: entry-level hires were not yet invited to brainstorming sessions to develop new products or improve operating procedures. It was simply assumed that they were too inexperienced to contribute in that way. And workplaces, like neighborhoods, were less segregated -- I worked with folks from a wide range of socioeconomic backgrounds. Consequently, workplaces were less stressful back in an era before the downsizing of middle management, before automation made clerks and secretaries obsolete.

And everyone got a birthday party. My assignment was usually the tortilla chips. One time, just before the party, I was nearly spotted by the birthday boy. I dropped the bag behind the microfiche reader and whispered to Barbara:

"Hey look, fiche and chips!"

Is it just middle-age crackpot thinking that makes me think fondly of jobs like that, ones that need little in the way of experience, just enthusiasm? Secretarial jobs, clerical jobs, word processing jobs?

> *Who will buy my sweet red roses?*
> *Who will tie it up with a ribbon*
> *And put it in a box for me?*
> - "Who Will Buy," Lionel Bart (from *Oliver!*)

From the perspective of one who has lived through the ever-accelerating centrifuge of modern corporate America, I can't help but think the old guild was pretty nice.

***

Evenings and weekends I spent with Clay, my former high school classmate. When not exploring the back roads and waters of New Jersey in a Chevy Nova, and after that the Ford Tempo that Grandpa Hines bought on my behalf at a dealer's auction, we hung out in the finished part of my parents' basement, which we dubbed the "Nostalgia Room."

Actually, the name was coined years earlier by Terry, another classmate, during a Dungeons and Dragons gaming session. The players had grown tired of the dungeon I'd taken such pains to construct – it may have been the larger-than-life *Mr. Rogers' Neighborhood* trolley that put them off – when Terry pushed back his chair and, exercising his sardonic wit on the musty knick-knacks, furnishings, and advertisements that surrounded us on every side, hit upon the phrase. (It's also Terry whom I must thank for a lyrical mishearing that plagues me to this day. Once, in gym class, he sang the first line of Steve Perry's "Oh Sherrie" – *should've been gone!* – in the way I shall forever hear it: *cinnamon gum!*)

After I graduated high school, the Nostalgia Room belonged to Clay and me. My parents no longer entertained there, and my siblings had abandoned it. But, as is usually the case, there was an exception. One summer Saturday, Mom and Dad were away and Nana was "watching the house," which is to say she was sound asleep at the other end of the upstairs hall. I, too, had drifted off to sleep after perusing a few issues of *Elle*, *Vogue*, and *Glamour*, which I kept in my closet for times when I fancied seeing young women of about my age wearing underwear. My wrists wore the spicy, floral notes of perfumed magazine inserts.

About midnight, I woke to loud music. Huh? The throbbing bass could belong only to the jukebox, two floors beneath me in the Nostalgia Room. I immediately surmised that Frank had taken advantage of my parents' absence to throw a party. Of course he hadn't thought to tell me: had he done so, I would have stayed at Nana's.

Up welled a fury that competed with my brain, which struggled mightily to place the bass line of the song rocking the house. Finally, I got it.

> *You're looking good, just like a snake in the grass*
> *One of these days, you're gonna break your glass*
>   - Electric Light Orchestra, "Don't Bring Me Down"

With Nana asleep behind a closed door, it fell to me to stop this. Hastily buttoning my chinos and plaid flannel shirt that I had cast aside, not even attempting to spruce up or run a brush through my hair in the hall bath, I headed straight for the noise. I surprised a couple of gawkers in the kitchen, then opened the door to the patio. (This was before Dad had enclosed the stairs to the basement.) The cool night air against my warm skin might, on another night, have inspired the contemplation of nature, but now I stomped down the stairs, turned right, and lifted the latch of the barn door that was the Nostalgia Room's side entrance.

> *It's like a party that happens sideways*
> *And you leave when you come in*
>   - Game Theory, "Dead Center"

I was momentarily blinded by the light. Three dozen kids were milling in groups, calling to one another across the room. I saw none of them; my radar was honed on Frank. Without looking at faces, I asked the nearest kid where he was. He pointed across the room, toward the pool table.

On the way, someone recognized me:

"Hey, John!"

It was Scott, a former high school classmate with whom I had never gotten along. Why was he here? (He was another kid whose house I'd seen exactly once – the One Visit Curse strikes again – in his case, to view a rare Bump Wills baseball "error card.") I stared daggers at him, a look that could only mean:

"You, sir, are guilty by association!"

And I shoved past.

Finding Frank, I strained to project my voice over the jukebox, saying in no uncertain terms that if everyone wasn't gone in fifteen minutes, Mom and Dad would know all. Frank frowned, but did not argue. I pivoted and stomped back upstairs. Angry as I was, I saw no face other than Frank's and Scott's.

Back in my room, my heart raced. I'd kicked ass! (And that, my friends, is the rhyme Jeff Lynne *should* have used.) It was Jesus and the money changers all over again. The house was soon quiet.

***

The Nostalgia Room owed its look and feel to Dad's love of Americana, the prevailing style of his restaurants. Its dim lighting was courtesy of Tiffany-style stained glass lamps demoted to domestic use, owing to chipped edges and bent mullions. They hung from improvised links of Jaeger Lumber chain above the pool table, ping pong table, and bar. Together, they bathed the room in a wistful glow.

A thick oxblood carpet hid every stain known to Man. One sofa, of glossy black leather, had large buttons that unerringly found the body's most sensitive regions. Walls were covered in traffic signs and advertisements that, whichever way one turned, caught the eye:

- SHAVES AND HAIRCUTS, 25¢ – leeching, cupping, bleeding
- Featuring Tonight: STEAKS AND LOBSTER
- POVERTY IS NO CRIME - But it's Nothing to Boast About
- DRINK BLUEBIRD – More Delicious than Grape Juice
- TO DOWNTOWN AND BROOKLYN
- NO MORE MALARIA – Coles Peruvian Bark and Wild Cherry Bitters Will Cure You
- PORTERS LAKE   14
- $1.00 Starts an Account at CITIZENS NATIONAL BANK, Netcong, N.J. (3½% on Savings)

The whole wall parallel to the front driveway was a huge mural that we kids had pieced together with Dad soon after we moved to town in 1977, a collage of *Sports Illustrated* covers dating to the 60s and 70s that offered a spectacularly diffracted vision of two decades of sport. It was much better, and more realistic, than the impressionistic LeRoy

Neiman murals that decorated the walls of the downtown Burger King. It required just a few paintbrushes, a bucketful of paste, and a stack of magazines from a friend of Dad's; we tore off the covers and discarded the rest.

Ten years later, under the same photographs of Vince Lombardi, Jimmy Connors, and Pete Rose (none of whom would have countenanced our idleness), Clay and I played games of dice and engaged in rambling discussions. Our response to the sports legends' disapproval might have been akin to Larry Csonka's: near the center of the mural was a photo of Csonka in Dolphins gear, kneeling next to teammate Mercury Morris, right hand on left, middle finger directed discreetly at the camera. Clay, a past master of doing precisely that in family photos, recognized it immediately, and admired Csonka's chutzpah for attempting it on the cover of a national magazine.

At the L-bow of the Nostalgia Room was a full bar. Dad kept booze there, but I didn't touch the stuff. I was more likely to fiddle with the immense antique gilt cash register, or admire the portrait of the long, leggy "barroom nude" behind the bar that depicted a reclining woman, back to the viewer, with not a stitch of clothing on.

The far end of the Nostalgia Room sported a restaurant booth and ping pong table. Years earlier, a Coca-Cola spill had damaged the table, leaving a discolored spot that deadened any ball striking it. Of course, that became the place to aim. The net was frequently askew due to a loose bracket, which required frequent in-game readjustments, and through long use the paddles had lost their rubberized surface, exposing unfinished wood beneath.

None of that needed repair, because Clay and I used the table not for ping pong but for "grovelball," an extension of table tennis that we invented. Had we done so a decade later, we could have called it Extreme Ping-Pong. Players were permitted to strike the ball as many times as desired, with no point ending until the ball had come to a complete stop. In furious battles against one other, or against our classmate Toto, we tore around the room, pursuing the ball wherever it had been struck, scooping it onto our rackets and dribbling it back to the table, only to smash it across the net to keep the point going. Though great for the metabolism, the game was terrible on the knees, and since I wore shorts, I suffered painful rug burns. No matter. The pain was well worth the trophy, which we called "The Medallion." It was a bronze charm that

Clay had received in the mail for some award or other, which he strung to a long silver necklace that belonged to his sister. Only the current champ could wear The Medallion, though when it was mine, I did not wear it outside the house. Unlike Dad, who had a nicely tufted chest, I couldn't pull off the Mediterranean look.

Clay and I spent most of our time in the Nostalgia Room's other wing, the one with a billiards table, a jukebox, a phone booth, a doctor's scale, and a barber's chair. They were all the real deal: full-size, monstrous pieces of furniture that mostly worked. The barber's chair groaned a bit when the hydraulic pump that raised and lowered it needed oil. The phone booth had a functioning phone.

The pool table served as combination game table, conference table, and war room. From bar stools on either side, Clay and I charted the passage of time, interpreting and quizzing each other about the past, describing and evaluating the present, and plotting the future. Our projects were myriad.

We played a season of Strat-o-Matic baseball, the dice-and-card baseball simulation game, after renaming the players after high school classmates. I called my team the Freeways after our junior school yearbook; Clay named his team the Porsches, because they drove all over the Freeways. I had the better team, but Clay was luckier at dice.

We developed a complex water fountain rating system that took into account variables such as flow pressure and consistency, switch type, refrigerant strength, and taste. We incorporated the NJWFTA (New Jersey Water Fountain Testing Authority), under whose aegis we spot checked public buildings and state parks to calibrate our rankings. (Our highest-rated fountain, dubbed "The Benchmark," turned out to be the one in the lobby of the Madison Public Library, a classic case of "no place like home.")

With a video camera no longer used by my parents, Clay and I storyboarded and recorded commercial parodies and comedy skits in the style of Monty Python: I did a ludicrous impersonation of Alistair Cooke hosting *Masterpiece Theatre*. It was all G-rated, but these videos could easily serve today as blackmail.

We mapped excursions to rural sites described by Henry Charlton Beck in his books about New Jersey's vanished towns. We tried finding them, sticking to the back roads indicated on gas station maps, the fainter the line, the better. From decades-old descriptions, we searched for Stockingtown, Double Trouble, Calico, Caviar, and Cranberry Hall. In Smithville, we managed to find a section of elevated bicycle track that workers once used to commute to factory jobs; we also happened upon the Pine Barrens obelisk marking the place where Emilio Carranza, the "Lindbergh of Mexico," had crashed and burned in the 1920s.

And of course we obsessed over music, always music. On the shelf of the bay window by my side of the pool table, I kept an old Radio Shack phonograph, on whose turntable I spun albums from thrift stores and record shops. These were the Madison and Summit branches of Scotti's, and two Morristown stores: the Rainbow Trading Post (just down from the Green), and Pellett Records, a wonderful second-story shop right on the Green, accessible by a narrow doorway and steep flight of stairs. Pellett's owner knew all the area collectors and aficionados. (He once kidded me for buying NRBQ's *Christmas Wish* out of season, telling me that when he was a boy, it was bad luck to play Christmas music before Thanksgiving.) To this day, certain albums that I played in the Nostalgia Room trigger memories of that time of life, for example Joe Jackson's *Big World* and Split Enz's *Conflicting Emotions*.

> *I don't want to say 'I love you'*
> *That would give away too much*
> *It's hip to be detached and precious*
>   - Split Enz, "Message to My Girl"

Today, when I play the digital equivalents of those vinyl albums, I hear them as played on that stereo – the wow and flutter induced by a faulty belt drive; the tinny buzz of cheap speakers: music illuminated by Tiffany lamps, and with it the scent of summer's cut grass, autumn's crickets, and the cold kiss of winter through open garage doors.

Food was never far from mind, but its procural paralyzed us. We dithered and deliberated for hours, arguing across the pool table. Eating out was not an option, since Clay didn't like it. Sometimes we got takeout – Stromboli King, located in an Airstream across the street from the Junior School, served up great greasy calzones with red food dye that oozed from pockets full of pepperoni – but more often we pieced together meals at supermarkets.

But that just kicked the can down the road – which supermarket? We continued the debate in the car. One possibility was Laneco, a proto-Walmart on Route 22 in Whitehouse Station, a good half-hour away. There, we'd walk the aisles until we realized we weren't hungry for dinner – what we really wanted was dessert. So, it was back in the car to Flanders, another half-hour trip, where Clay would buy a box of Klondike Bars. With no other way to keep them from thawing on the way home, he'd hold the box outside the passenger window, no matter the temperature outside, until his hand was numb.

Or we would go to Chester, to Taylor's Ice Cream Parlor. Laneco is long gone, but Taylor's is there as I write, a late-night beacon for travelers needing a sugar fix. Unfortunately, I can no longer go to Taylor's without confronting the memory of my first wedding proposal. The woman who would become my first wife was sitting with me at a table for two, beneath a wall of college pennants, when I realized that I'd forgotten the engagement ring in the trunk of my car, in her family's driveway. (I proposed anyway, picking up the ring later.)

But that was in the future. At Taylor's, Clay and I ordered extra-large hot fudge sundaes to go. We consumed them outside, in my car in the dark parking lot. They came in large plastic domes, continents of vanilla ice cream adrift in seas of chocolaty syrup, a maraschino cherry at the North Pole, in the straw hole. Once, having just begun his sundae, Clay realized he wasn't hungry, so he gave it to me, then watched in astonishment as I ate both his and mine, two pounds of carbohydrates.

In those days, I could not eat enough sweets. My metabolism required them. Clay, who had a weakness for meat, boggled at the sheer quantity of sugar I put down. To mess with him, I concocted meals like jelly beans over Frosted Mini Wheats swimming in milk. If such a craving came at night, we'd drive to an all-night supermarket close to home, like the Gillette Pathmark, which we called the "Pathological Mark" due to its late-night clientele and workforce. There, clad in sweats, we cased the aisles and weighed dilemmas like Little Debbie's Peanut Butter Bars versus Entenmann's chocolate-frosted donuts. But we were finally driven away by the music: the late-night lunatics running the asylum played over the store's speakers a paint-peeling spatter of heavy metal (likely Seton Hall's WSOU) and static.

Another choice destination was the Pepperidge Farm thrift store on Route 202, in Harding. I vividly recall a December afternoon when we pulled into the small parking lot; it was already dark, and we were listening to the football Giants on the radio. Inside the store, I was disappointed that my favorites, the Cappuccino crème cookies (sadly, discontinued), were not on the shelves. I turned to the freezer case and saw a bag of apple turnovers. Clay, who drove faster than I, was at the wheel, so we were just minutes from home, but I could practically taste those turnovers and didn't want to wait to warm them in the toaster oven in the Nostalgia Room. So I ripped open the bag with my teeth and gummed the pastries until they were close enough to room temperature to swallow. Clay told me I'd pay a price for doing that. He was right.

Seasons passed, but we were always working on something. We recorded audio montages in the style of Firesign Theatre that could have been amusing only to us, riddled as they were with nonsequiturs and layered over beds of ambient sound. We filmed a science fiction short in which I played a lunar explorer (my spacesuit a leaf blower, unrecognizable in long shot), and Clay the mother ship commander, frantically pressing jukebox buttons (his control panel) as he tried to contact me on his walkie-talkie, "Zinfandel! Zinfandel, do you read?"

Or we would spend an evening dreaming up the worst movies ever. I would be immobilized, shaking on the floor with laughter:

In *Three Moons Over Perth*, a sci-fi thriller, Gerald Ford plays a beekeeper and Diane Keaton a Russian scientist;

In *This Jukebox Ain't Playin' Saturday Nights*, a black-and-white drama, Henry Fonda plays the small-town mayor, Audrey Meadows a bank teller, William Shatner a teen idol, and Orson Welles a soda jerk;

In *The House the Big Man Made Over*, a sports biopic, George Steinbrenner plays himself, Angie Dickinson his wife, Dave Winfield his PR director, and Bob Vila a structural engineer.

All of this without alcohol.

In most seasons, the Nostalgia Room was comfortable. On humid summer nights, we left the garage doors ajar and ran a desk fan. On cold winter nights, I carried a box of matches to the ancient furnace down two creaky wooden steps in the unfinished part of the basement. To light the pilot, I'd rub a match against the strike strip – something that today I still do awkwardly – and reach into the blower to depress a button while holding the lit match along a long metal rod. After a moment, I'd flip the switch outside the furnace to activate the blower, which would ignite the flame, ffffroooom.

My problem was one of attention. Twice, either from fatigue or distraction, I performed these operations out of order, igniting the pilot when the blower was already on. When I did that, and peered into the furnace to verify the pilot had lit, my reflexes recoiled before I knew what was happening, and a blast of heat socked me like a shock wave. A moment later, dazed, blown two feet from the furnace, I caught the unmistakable whiff of burned hair, my own. I verified in the mirror above the bathroom sink that the lashes above my right eye had been singled and charred; a few stray ones garnished my right cheek. This happened twice, and each time my lashes were truncated by exactly the same amount.

***

In this way, for three years, I lived a second childhood. I didn't spend all my time with Clay, nor did he lack a life of his own, but our friendship defined those years. In retrospect, I'm amused that a pair of twenty-somethings never thought to go out for drinks or meet women. Instead, we built an annex to childhood. We acted like the real world was a place where it always rained, and put on dramas on a private stage set that remained dry. We needed no one else: not siblings, not classmates who'd scattered to every point of the compass to begin their lives, nor the folks upstairs paying the mortgage. Not even the Cat in the Hat.

We invented our world by redefining it. It's so obvious now. The clue was our penchant for naming everything: the Nostalgia Room, the Medallion, the Benchmark, the Pathological Mark; the renamed Strat-o-Matic cards, the fake movies.

If anything belongs to childhood, it is the act of naming. Children know that names not only signify, but contain reality. My first girlfriend won my heart by telling me her secret name. Clay and I renamed things to postpone life.

***

Clay broke away first, in 1990. He moved north and initiated a transformational plan that he called "Multifaceted." (Again with the names!) I, now alone in the Nostalgia Room, heard the winds of change pierce our cracking stone foundation, and whistled aloud. But then the wind found a gap and blew away the Strat-o-Matic cards, sending them, with me, hurtling into the future.

Stars and Stripes

They put the chairs out on the lawn
Grandma's got her new dress on
There's fresh flowers on Grandpa's grave
And Junior smells of aftershave
   - Timbuk 3, "National Holiday"

Red, white, and blue – the colors of the American flag. And Great Britain's. And France's. Australia's, too.

Among N's, the tricolor adorns the flags of the Netherlands, New Zealand, and Norway. C's include Cambodia, Chile, Costa Rica, Croatia, Cuba, and the Czech Republic. Let's face it: red, white, and blue aren't that unique. If you wear them to a party, someone else will, too.

And yet, judging from my street, my neighbors hold these colors sacred, especially when arranged in a rectangle of seven red stripes, six white stripes, and an inset nine-by-eleven grid of white stars on a blue field. This pattern is special because they saluted it as children. So did I.

It's the Fourth of July in Cape May and up and down my street patriotism runs amok. The spare tire cover on a parked car depicts an American flag beneath the words "There is Only One." Bunting filigrees porches. Sidewalk borders are studded with mini-flags sourced from China by discount stores, but that's okay: who can afford a flagpole and full-sized flag these days? Besides, the minis are all-weather, and may be exempt from those pesky Flag Code regulations that stipulate lowering, or illuminating, the flag at night. That's easier for our neighborhood seniors with bad backs.

Carol and I joined the party in a modest way, tying a tricolor bow to each of our six front porch columns. Unfortunately, the wind spun them round to face our own door. But maybe that's just as well -- more than my neighbors, I need to be reminded what patriotism is. Ever since Election Day, 2016, to look down my street is, for me, to look askance.

The morning after the election, I encountered a woman we see often see at the beach, where she walks her dog. For some reason, they were walking on our block. Before I could hustle inside, she called out:

"Some Election Night, huh?"

"Yeah. A complete disaster."

These were the first words that came to mind. She paused to weigh a response, then said:

"Well, my husband's pretty happy about it."

I already knew. He's a veteran, and has no problem making his feelings known. What I wanted to ask, but didn't, was:

"Yes, but how do *you* feel about it?"

In our neighborhood, I've noticed two variations on Old Glory. Both have blue stripes in place of red, except for the stripe directly below the field of stars, which is either deep blue or bright red. I wondered what they might signify so I went online, where I learned that they are flags of support for police and firefighters, particularly those who have given their lives on duty. I also read that they have been criticized as degradations, or even desecrations, of the traditional flag, because they politicize it. The police flag, in particular, has been a lightning rod for criticism, as a veiled criticism that our country's leaders are not doing enough to protect us from lawlessness. What a shame it is, I thought, to have our most potent symbol of unity dragged into fights. These new flags make me wary, like the picket signs that dot our neighborhood which proclaim, "I SUPPORT THE POLICE." Are the barbarians at the ramparts, or is Sting on a comeback tour?

Our 45th President, an expert at sowing disunity, has politicized all our acts. I resent that. It has come to the point that I wonder what my neighbors think of my *not* flying a flag, or my *not* planting signs in support of the police. Does that mean I do not support the police, the White House, or America? Down our street, a local hobby shop flies the Gadsden Flag, the rattlesnake banner bearing the motto "Don't Tread on Me." Does that mean that they support the Confederacy? The Tea Party? The NRA or KKK? All I know is it keeps me from walking in the store.

And it's not just me. Our country has never been so divided. Cape May County solidly voted Trump, which is unsurprising since it combines so many of his base constituencies, ones left behind by the modern world: the military, the rural, the aged. (There's a Coast Guard base three miles from here, and many veterans live nearby.) Never have I felt so disconnected from my neighbors, and they likely wonder about me.

So, when Carol and I ventured into town last night for some beach fireworks, I was also looking for patriotism and connection. I wanted some of that "olde tyme" feeling I get when I walk through the open screen door of the general store at Cold Spring Village, the nearby living history museum. You may recall the homey smells and sights of long-ago class trips to historic parks and museums, when such experiences were common: Revolutionary War coloring books; hanging calendars resembling Colonial samplers; long-wicked tallow candles; sticks of hard candy striped like barber poles in flavors like horehound (a bit like root beer, but more astringent). You know, boring Sunday afternoon things, homely and comfortable things, things odd to modern sensibilities, like antique pencils thick as twigs with circumferences ringed in the nubby bark of pitch pines. On each visit to the general store, I would pick one up, such a pleasure to hold, and wonder if pencils were truly fashioned that way once upon a time, or if these were gimmicks. I should check Thoreau: his family operated the first industrial pencil factory in the United States, with Thoreau himself instrumental (ahem) in reimagining the graphite implements of earlier eras.

Anticipating heavy homebound traffic, Carol and I parked across town under our favorite tree, a linden, whose roots are slowly lifting the asphalt off its street. From there we walked a mile to the beach, pausing at the grand old Virginia Hotel, once a haunt of Southern aristocrats. Topped with gingerbread, it has offered hospitality since 1879. The walls of its parlor are decorated with plates commemorating Colonial days; it was here, fifteen summers ago, that Carol and I were married, on an afternoon when everyone inexplicably ordered White Russians. We had a drink in the parlor as we waited for the sky to darken enough for fireworks – if the rain held off, that is.

This year's Fourth was a Wednesday, so the beach was not too crowded. More room for a beach towel! We draped one across an empty stretch of sand and settled in. Close enough to annoy me, I overheard the conversation of a nearby family, in particular a know-it-all twelve-year-old girl who pontificated nonstop to a quiet friend, most likely the awestruck family guest. The chatterbox went on about the crowd, current fashions, Instagram, and Trump, whom she proclaimed "our best President ever." I prayed for quicksand, or a string band, to swallow her words, preferably to the tune of the "Congress Hall March," written by one of Cape May's most famous visitors, John Philip Sousa, and named after the town's famous hostelry. But soon she piped down and my equanimity returned.

But at twenty past nine, the fireworks! From darkly silhouetted barges a hundred yards offshore, rockets streamed into the night. The colors and patterns were dazzling. Surely, in terms of sophistication and precision, pyrotechnics have evolved in my lifetime. This must be the result of automation: it's hard to imagine roustabouts running through the gloaming like they once did, lighting fuses one by one.

Another difference was that the colors of the fireworks outlined against the velvet night sky included saturated greens, blues, and violets. They came from a more vivid palette than I remembered. Perhaps they symbolized the greater diversity of today's world, a Rainbow Flag to fly in the face of a benighted desire to return to "old glory." The crowd delighted at the stage-by-stage unfolding of colors in complex starbursts. Even the smiley faces that appeared upside down due to the vagaries of the wind drew applause.

I'll take fireworks over flags. Flags stake out territory; fireworks, by sublimating patriotism, make it ideal. And despite their growing sophistication, fireworks cannot do what I did once with peg lights on a Lite-Brite, draw a flag. Only freeform pictures allowed.

Show over, our final adventure was the treacherous walk back to the car through bumper-to-bumper traffic. We finally attained our linden, got in the car, and took a place in the long caravan leaving Cape Island. I found Sousa on the FM radio and we listened as we inched by dark West Cape May shopfronts shuttered for the night. We waved to the traffic guards in their yellow jackets, and I found the feeling of inclusion I wanted. It had taken not only fireworks but a traffic jam, that common leveler, to prove that there may yet be hope for us, that we are in this together.

Dream Three

The third of seven dreams I had while writing this book.

A vast array of baseball fields, like what one might see at a major-league spring training complex, like Historic Dodgertown in Vero Beach. Uncountably many diamonds, a few soccer fields, and a running track around them all. The landscape is defined by diamonds, as a diamond is defined by a lattice of carbon atoms -- they stretch to the horizon. I say to myself, "This place goes on forever."

I pitch for the Toronto Blue Jays. Today is my start, so I amble to the field where my game is scheduled. I'm in full uniform, including a royal blue jersey. The game begins, and I am hot, lights out! But after five perfect innings in which no one reaches base, a teammate mentions my feat. This is bad karma, against every tradition of the game, and I don't want to hear it, so I shush him and cast his words from my mind. Then, after eight perfect innings, I hear someone in the stands say that I'm on the cusp of history, and I'm rattled – I take a bit off the first pitch to the leadoff batter, and it flutters to the plate, glancing off his hip. The perfect game is gone. But I pull myself together and retire the side without allowing a hit, completing the no-hitter. Not a perfect game, but still fairly historic.

Afterwards, I walk to the large fieldhouse with the lockers, gym, showers, and so forth. On other fields other games are in progress, and I watch as I walk. At one end of the complex, on the slope of a small hill, is a kid's clubhouse like the one that my cousins used as a fort when they were young. It's a ramshackle hut with a chipped slate tile roof and blackboard on one side, on which a score is etched in chalk. I recall a similar outbuilding astride the playing fields of Peck School, my school when I was young, where every year on Field Day, two teams, Red and Blue, competed for glory in track and field. The clubhouse scoreboard kept the running point total.

Near the fieldhouse is my aunt's house. It sits in a copse of trees and shrubs, the only ones in sight, on a property bordering one of the baseball fields. The occasional foul ball strikes it, usually on a bounce, more rarely on the fly. (Most likely, this is an echo of my grandmother's

Roseland home, which sat across a lane from the Essex County Golf Club. Golf balls occasionally landed on her lawn.)

I enter my aunt's long Colonial kitchen with wood center island, where the family congregates. My mother and sister greet me, and congratulate me on my no-hitter. I am carrying a tray of lemon cookies, presented by the Blue Jays in honor of my feat, but as I'm about to set it down, my cleats catch in a gap between two floorboards and I stumble. Some cookies slip from under the cellophane and fall to the floor, where they slide across polished floorboards. I stoop to pick them up, afraid that I've upset Mom, but she tells me it's okay. When I look in her eyes, I see that she's ecstatic: my no-hitter, she says, was a sign from her dead grandmother, Grandma Peccia. The clue is that the final batter I retired was named Puglia, which is the name of her grandmother's birthplace, where lemon groves abound. So, the lemon cookies, too, are a sign from beyond.

In the kitchen where Aunt Ro's maid Barbara always keeps the radio tuned to NewsRadio 1010, it is tuned instead to NPR, which covers the games still being contested outside. The breaking news is that my friend Laura, who pitches for the New York Yankees, has just thrown a perfect game, that rarest of gems. (Evidently, she didn't falter in the ninth as I had.) Laura is being interviewed by a woman reporter who draws attention to the fact that not only has she pitched a perfect game; not only has she become the first woman to pitch a major-league no-hitter; but her feat marks a complete recovery from a serious ailment. Then, for no good reason, she begins describing Laura's uniform, calling it her "outfit." She admires the light blue jersey that Laura has chosen to wear beneath her uniform top, and the pink undershirt just visible beneath the shirt sleeves.

"Oh, well," I thought as I listened, "I've been bested."

But I'm happy for my friend, and want to congratulate her. I leave my aunt's and walk with Mom to the fieldhouse, where I know I'll find her. Laura is sitting on an old, three-slat hardwood bench by the fieldhouse entrance. She's between George Steinbrenner, the fiery Yankee owner, and Steinbrenner's friend and business crony, Donald Trump, who's just finished congratulating her. Seeing her thus occupied, I'm ready to move on, but Laura sees me and jumps up, offering to take a turn around the fields. We talk a bit. Though it has cooled outside,

Laura is still sweaty from exertion. We circle back to the fieldhouse to find Mom waiting on the bench, and we take a seat.

Mom asks Laura about Steinbrenner and Trump.

"Steinbrenner's okay. And Trump said he'd do anything for me."

After a beat, I said:

"Well, did you ask him?"

We all laugh.

Inventory

Because we all knew that memories alone
Would never be enough
   - Peter Holsapple, "Inventory"

    I keep prisoners in my bedroom. Some I lock in closets, and others I file in a chest of map drawers.

    They're prisoners because they belong to the past. You can see it at a glance -- they lack bar codes, have quaint, archaic names, and are tinted in passé shades – ocher, umber, burnt sienna – that Crayola retired years ago. You might see them in a museum, but never a gift shop.

    It's hard to justify being a warden, but I'll try. By keeping things captive, I hope to rescue them from the ravages of time.

    Let's see what's in the closet.

1. *A folder containing:*
   - *Three cards and envelopes that once accompanied flowers*
   - *Instructions for preparing baby formula*
   - *A black-and-white photograph on card stock*
   - *A light blue matchbook embossed, "It's a Boy!"*
   - *An envelope with a lock of hair*

    The cards and envelopes, the instruction manual, and the snapshot date to my first hospital stay, and together represent the first proofs of my existence. They predate my birth certificate and the announcement of my birth in *The Bridgewater Courier-News*, both of which appeared nine days after I did.

    Two of the three flower cards are from Dad, via Ideal Gardens in Springfield. One is addressed to "Mrs. Betty Baldanza," and the other to "Betti Baldanza." My parents' courtship was a whirlwind affair, but Dad knew how to spell Mom's name: my guess is that the florist misspelled it the first time, and when Dad saw the misspelling in the maternity ward, he insisted upon more flowers.

    The other flower card, via Harry J. Burke and Son Florists in Union, is addressed to "Mrs. Frank Baldanza, Overlook Hospital, Summit, Mty.".

I didn't recognize the senders, Winnie and Howard Anderson, so I asked Mom about them, but she didn't remember them, either. This doesn't surprise me: when Dad married, he shed many acquaintances whom Mom would never meet. He'd even known Sarah Vaughn, the great jazz singer who lived in his apartment building, one of the two tall towers clearly visible through the windows of New Jersey Transit trains as they approach Newark Broad Street. And Mom learned upon her arrival out East that Dad's bachelor pad had no furniture except for a kitchen table – a pair of long, carved wood panels on sawhorses.

The baby formula manual is from Similac, a company still going strong today. My vital stats appear on page one:

- Name: Baby Boy Baldanza
- Birth Date (and birth year!): 1-9-66
- Weight: 6-13
- Length: 20 ½
- Discharge: 1-14-66
- Weight: 6

Clearly, my five-day hospital stay was no picnic; I'd lost more than ten percent of my birth weight. I also spent my first day in solitary confinement.

When Dad paid his first visit to the viewing room, from which he ought to have been able to see me through plate glass, he asked the nurse on duty which one I was. She checked her register, looked confused, and left for a minute; then she returned with the news that I wasn't there. She didn't know where I was.

"Let me see a manager!" Dad boomed.

I was in an incubator. Mom's doctor had overprescribed a drug to ease her through childbirth, knocking out not only Mom but me too. I got such a large dose that I couldn't cry at birth, something most newborns do to clear their lungs. I was, in effect, born asleep.

But not long after, I was ready for my first photo op. I now hold the result: a small picture on matte white card stock with rounded edges framing a stippled image more like a drawing than a photograph. The only visible body parts are my head (thin, expressionless mouth, gimlet eyes, scalp fringed with hair several shades darker than it would be in boyhood) and my left hand against it, propped behind the ear. I look pensive and not terribly happy.

I may have been listening for my name... after all, I knew it couldn't stay "Baby Boy"! Perhaps my parents decided it while Dad stood beside Mom's hospital bed. As my first name, Mom chose the name of her first brother, the one who died when she was still a girl. My middle name would be her father's surname. As for my last name, it would change only eighteen months later, when Dad shortened it to prevent the ethnic stereotyping of his children.

How much of who I became was determined in those first days? Did my isolation from a ward of screaming babies make me an introvert? Did the name change smooth my path in life?

P.S. After a threatened lawsuit, Mom's doctor's bill was discounted fifty percent. I was a bargain!

2. *One empty green whiskey bottle*

Front label: Product of Scotland / John Leslie B / Blended Scotch Whisky / Imported and Bottled Exclusively for Springfield Steak House / Route 22, Springfield, N.J. / Distilled and Blended in Scotland from 100% Scotch Whiskies

Rear label: Imported by Galsworthy, Inc., Newark, N.J. / Bottled by Dodge-Fielding, Nutley, N.J.

Embossed on the glass: Federal law forbids sale or reuse of this bottle / 4/5 Quart.

This bottle, which once held a "fifth" of Scotch, belonged to a crate that Dad ordered to commemorate my birth. Perhaps this was the bottle he split with Mom at home, earmarking others for his restaurant regulars.

At that time, Galsworthy was New Jersey's largest distributor of wine and spirits, so this was likely not the headiest, peatiest, marliest, smokiest Scotch ever to see the light of day. It probably wasn't even top shelf hooch. But it's the thought that counts.

3. *33 1/3 RPM record, Frank Baldanza on "The Joe Franklin Show"*

The most unusual item in my record collection sits in a sleeve the weight and color of an interoffice mail envelope. Heavier than vinyl, it is probably made of shellac, with a ten-inch diameter intermediate between that of a single and an album. There are grooves on just one side, the side with the light peach label that reads:

> Kong Recordings
> Customized Transcriptions
> Phone: Essex 5-5055
> 33 1/3 R.P.M. Microgroove
> Nov. 6, 1964
> SPRINGFIELD STEAK HOUSE
> RESTAURANT SALUTE
> "MEMORY LANE"
> WOR-TV Broadcast

When I put it beneath a stylus, I hear the sound of Dad just prior to meeting Mom.

Dad appeared twice on *The Joe Franklin Show*, a.k.a. *Memory Lane*. Fifty-five years later, I can't begin to explain how cool that is. Joe Franklin was a New York entertainment legend whose television show aired locally for forty-one years, the last thirty-one on WOR, Channel 9.

Joe's style was unmistakable. He dressed dapper, often in plaid, always with a jacket, tie and smile. His guest panels were diverse. There was always the chance his next guest would be Cary Grant, Salvador Dali, or Woody Allen, though more likely it would be a B-list actor on the comeback trail, or a local businessman or politico. It might even be They Might Be Giants, the alternative rock band that Carol and I bonded over during the summer we met. Joe promoted them when they were still unknowns, hearing in their songs and act the inner vaudevillians they would have been fifty years earlier.

Dad's appearance was courtesy of "The Canada Dry Man," as Joe styled him. Canada Dry was a sponsor, and their sales reps offered TV appearances to entrepreneurs who bought their product in bulk. I offer a short excerpt of a scratchy record, transcribed after numerous listens.

Joe: Our sponsor is Canada Dry: ginger ale, club soda, quinine water. This is the Dining Out guide, the very popular restaurant salute. I'm going to chat with a gentleman who appeared with me when I first appeared on the air. Your face is really familiar, you know that? You were with me about how many years ago?

Dad: Um, just about four years ago, Joe. Four and a half years ago when I first started over in Jersey.

Joe: I never forget a face.

Dad: Well, if I remember correctly, you were over there.

Joe: At your restaurant? Springfield House Restaurant. Well, I forgot, but I'll tell you one thing, it was great.

Dad: *(Laughs.)* Well, thank you.

Joe: You employ how many, Frank?

Dad: About forty people.

Joe: How many do you seat altogether?

Dad: Well, I have three buildings. I built two new buildings on the property. One seats five hundred, one about three hundred, and the other one about a hundred, so altogether we seat about nine hundred people.

Joe: Nine hundred? You're quite an operator.

I was very young when Dad owned the Springfield House, so my memories of it are mainly glints of sun, whitecaps on the ocean deep, scattered and saturated in atmosphere. I remember visiting with Mom and Dad on summer vacation mornings. We kids had the run of the place while Mom sat in the business office going through the previous night's receipts and Dad readied things for the day's opening.

The banquet rooms, quiet and still, smelled like a "flophouse" (the strange word Mom used when she insisted that we pick up our rooms), with traces of alcohol and cigarette smoke lingering from the previous night's revels. Windows were shuttered against the morning sun. After we spent a minute with Mom in the back office, Dad chaperoned us to the Lido Diner on the median of Route 22, which meant crossing two lanes of heavy eastbound traffic from the restaurant's voluminous parking lot. We sat in a vinyl booth and awaited our buttered, toasted muffins, or boxes of Kellogg's cereal from the colorful twelve-packs displayed on aluminum shelves near the ceiling, behind the chrome counter.

Back at the restaurant, while Mom and Dad worked, we played and explored. The main entrance was linked by an overhang to a valet booth where in the evenings, men in livery accepted keys, issued receipts, and sheltered during rainstorms. I loved exploring that booth, which was crammed with enough flotsam to furnish an itinerant's hovel. I especially enjoyed playing with the receipt pads whose alternating white and yellow pages were entitled "PRIME RESTAURANTS, Route 22, Scotch Plains," each pad with a movable carbon that enabled the making of one-time copies. An adding machine printed numbers in black and red on a roll of tape, and a large desk blotter framed a one-page calendar, Sundays and holidays marked in red, that advertised a local car dealer. This booth appealed to me in the way that any cramped, single-purpose space – submarine, tollbooth, radio studio – is romantic to the practitioner of an arcane art. I could see myself working there one day.

Inside the main restaurant entrance, a narrow hall led to the right, past cigarette machines, to the bathrooms. One long wall had been transformed into a mural of *Sports Illustrated* magazine covers, an idea Dad would reprise years later for our Madison rec room.

Dining rooms communicated by doorways no wider than those in homes, giving the restaurant the feel of an inn. From lintels hung makeshift curtains of translucent beads the size of costume jewels. And like the cereal boxes, they came in a beguiling variety of colors and shapes, fueling our zeal for collecting: emerald spheres, cobalt cubes, amber hearts, and others. Mom had given each of us a leather bank bag with zipper and lock, in which we kept excess strings of beads that we'd found in a big box in the rear of the coat check room. These remained legal tender until the day that Mom took us to a bank on Ridgedale

Avenue in Morristown and opened our first savings accounts. We received royal blue passbooks, the first pages of which were stamped with an initial deposit of five dollars, the first step on our journey to financial independence.

On my own, I explored a hallway that led to several rooms, a few with beds. During his long career in the restaurant industry, Dad had acquired a loyal group of employees that followed him from one business to another. He granted some temporary lodging, particularly cooks of long standing. (In Madison, they lived next door to the Widow Brown's in a derelict building that the cops – so a friend reported to me after hearing it on a police scanner – called the "Madison Hilton.") In the bedroom of one such employee I saw, above a headboard, a wall calendar from which smiled the picture of a completely naked woman. It was the first time I'd seen such a picture, and I was mystified by her unfamiliar folds and curves that I couldn't bring myself to view for more than a second or two. What's more, I was astonished that an undressed woman so evidently caught unawares would smile for the camera.

That photograph reminded me of certain cover photos of *Popular Photography*, to which my parents subscribed. Dad had created a wall collage of *Popular Photography* covers in the basement darkroom, a room that had, along three walls, countertops with rows of variously colored plastic bins for the chemicals needed to develop film. (On one wall, Dad had Scotch taped a detailed list of instructions, the last being, "Add salt and pepper to taste.") The *Popular Photography* nudes, however, were photographed in soft focus, with filters and tricks, so it was difficult to make them out: it was like looking through gauze. In contrast, the nude above the headboard, who wore impertinently pink makeup, was in clear, hard focus. Too young to find pleasure in this grotesquerie and too innocent to understand how her body differed from mine, I tried to dispel her from my mind. Since I remember her so well today, I clearly did not succeed.

In the fall of 2003, the year that my wife Carol and I were engaged, we happened to be in Manhattan one Sunday, in the Theater District, looking for somewhere to eat. This was Carol's home turf; she had lived there for many years. In fact, she was there when I first proposed marriage several years earlier. My proposal must have been unconvincing, delivered as it was on the spur of the moment in a restaurant that catered exclusively to the Broadway trade, which was nearly deserted on a theater "dark day." (Carol tabled the motion.)

At Forty-fifth and Eighth, a sandwich board invited passers-by into *Memory Lane*, the restaurant and performance space that Joe Franklin founded in 1993 after leaving TV. I suggested that we pop in for a look.

The dining room reminded me of Dad's old places, dimly lit, with linen tablecloths and walls of old photos and other memorabilia. But it differed in one key way: it felt like a museum, with ghosts outnumbering patrons. Only two tables were occupied. At one of these, a large group of merrymakers made noise and, among them, I recognized the man himself, Joe Franklin. His face was more wrinkled than I remembered, but he was still playing the gadabout. Hearkening from an era when entertainers *were* their careers, his private life and public persona had become one. He needn't have torn himself away from his long-time friends to greet an unfamiliar young couple, but he did.

I told Joe that it was an honor to meet him. And in my next breath, I said my father had been on his TV show, and that I had the phonograph record to prove it. His eyes lit up. Curious, he asked for details, and I told him what I knew from the record. He did his best to piece together the puzzle, but he admitted that he didn't remember Dad. He did say that he would look him up in the "archives" when he was back at home. After some more pleasantries, he bid us *bon appétit*.

Afterwards, on the sidewalk, Carol was amused by the noticeable glow in my expression. She was vaguely aware of Joe Franklin's celebrity, but couldn't account for my reaction. How was I to explain to her the "madeleine effect" of an otherwise ordinary hamburger?

It turns out that we had seen *Memory Lane* in its final days, shortly before it lost its lease. Today, the corner of 45th and 8th is occupied by a cookie-cutter gastropub whose widescreen televisions show round-the-world sports action in a never-ending, memoryless loop, disconnected from both space and time. None of them will ever play that epitome of old-time Manhattan, *The Joe Franklin Show*.

4. *A gold pocket watch and fob in a plastic dome*

When I was ten, my grandmother gave me a gold watch. It lives in my closet now at the end of a short gold chain suspended from a tin hook, beneath a plastic dome, over a cheap wood base, on the underside of which is affixed a scrap of bar code. It's a humble setting for such an ornate timepiece.

The Gothic numerals on the watch face coexist with minute tick marks on the outer rim. Only the "6" is missing, to allow for an inset second hand. The back of the watch is lightly etched with a long, flowing curlicue, and opens to reveal a thin compartment, also engraved, with one identifying mark: "Dueber Special 4169763." The back of that compartment opens onto the inner face of another compartment, lightly etched with a pattern whose colors change with the angle of refraction. Finally, beyond the innermost flat surface are the escapement and three engraved notes: "Hamilton Watch Co.," "Lancaster, Pa." and "Adjusted 122994."

It has been two decades and more since Nana left us. Does she know I still have her watch? I like to think so -- it's a happy thought that the departed keep track of us. Perhaps, living as they do spiritually outside time, they simultaneously see past, present and future. And I'm encouraged to think that Nana knows I'm writing about her watch, an object that has no use for her now. She always encouraged my writing.

On a Saturday of fourth grade, I wrote a report on birds at Nana's house. I set up in her downstairs parlor, a room she rarely used, a place as darkly furnished as a room in a living history museum, where one gets a sense of life as it was in the eighteenth century – quiet, solemn, restful to the eyes. (Nana never slept; she "rested her eyes.") To my right was a player piano with a roll in the cavity over the keyboard, to my left a long row of books as dusty as the ones Dad purchased by the pound to furnish his restaurants. Among these, I selected a thin volume at random and chanced upon an old diary. I turned its pages and read several weeks of terse, handwritten notes. Many concerned the weather, but others were more difficult to decipher, with references to names and places I didn't recognize. At one point, the entries became telepathic: brief sentences like "waiting," "no word today," and "still waiting." I never penetrated the mystery of those sad words, nor the identity of their writer. Before I thought to ask Nana about it, the diary went missing. Then I forgot.

In the center of that parlor atop a large, round wooden table, I thumped the encyclopedia volume that I had borrowed from school. I made room for it by turning back two heavy tablecloths of differing fabric that would have been at home in the eighteenth or nineteenth centuries. They might have been muslin, poplin, cambric, or something else with a delightfully outmoded Dickensian name that I knew only from books.

> *Calico and gabardine*
> *Satin, silk, and velveteen*
> *Sweet georgette and crinoline*
> *And everything in between*
>   - Peter Holsapple, "Cinderella Style"

I could hear, through two small windows letting in a ray or two of light, bird calls. How appropriate. For I was embarking on my opus number one, my report on "Birds." My first sentence, as I recall, referred to *Archaeopteryx*, the oldest bird in the fossil record; and by the time I was through, I'd written fifty pages of loopy longhand that covered every aspect of the avian order. As I worked, I felt Nana's pride. She had reminded her housekeeper, Ella, not to disturb me as I busied myself, repurposing and reordering the words of the encyclopedia, changing them just enough to make the work my own. A sore right hand validated my own maiden writerly flight.

I broke Nana's watch on the day she gifted it, a sunny morning of summer. She had come to babysit. I was playing on the flagstone patio behind our house in Morris Township, the one on the hilly cul-de-sac in the woods abutting Route 287, from which the whoosh of cars could be heard. (Those woods, though not sizable, were primeval to me. For remoteness, a rutted road within them still rivals any logging trail I have seen since. Through them one day, a neighbor's dog pursued me for what seemed like an hour, eventually nipping the back of my right leg. Those woods and that dog became dream archetypes.)

I was standing near a sundial tinged with verdigris, verifying that the sun was where it should be. I was slowly reading the inscription, "Grow Old Along with Me; The Best Is Yet to Be." That is to say, I was daydreaming. Not far from me was the shed where Dad kept his lawn tools, up the side of which a ladder led to an ornamental widow's walk. That was the shed in which, the following fall, I would stockpile several thousands of acorns for an epic neighborhood fight against the older kids up the street, who occasionally picked on us down-streeters. (The fight never happened, but I had fun enlisting siblings and neighbors to collect acorns and bring them to the shed, where I counted them. When they began to sprout, I dumped them in the woods behind the house. Perhaps there's a copse of oaks there today.)

Surprised by the watch, I immediately began playing with it, opening its compartments. Soon, in my excitement, I lifted it too quickly from its hook beneath the dome and dropped it. I can still see it falling, landing on a flagstone with a sickening crack, dial side up. When I tried to wind it, it no longer ticked. I ran inside the house to tell Nana, who became angry at my carelessness, and I cried.

But not long after, Nana had the watch restored to working order. To my recollection, it has worked since then, though the "122994" etched near the escapement gives me pause... did something happen to it around then? Or was it just a routine servicing? That date falls after Nana's stroke, so she couldn't have said: by then, I was the timekeeper.

5. *One ten-ounce jar of Best Foods "Real" Mayonnaise, two-thirds full of a fine gray powder*

May 18, 1980, another eighth-grade Monday. I was sitting in my first-period class.

Three thousand miles west in Washington State, Harry R. Truman, the owner and caretaker of the Mount St. Helens Lodge at the base of the famous volcano bordering Spirit Lake, was following the same routine he'd followed nearly every day for forty years, including the feeding of his sixteen cats.

The day before, state officials had paid him a visit. They had again urged him to leave; again, he had refused. It wasn't for fear of lost business: two months of tremors, venting steam, and evacuation orders had deprived him of his clientele. The only bipeds in the area were a few reporters and geologists.

The more the old codger resisted relocation, the more he became a folk hero. His friends and family told the press that he considered Mount St. Helens *his* mountain, Spirit Lake *his* lake, and the Gifford Pinchot National Forest *his* "arms and legs." Why would he run from them? He had survived the WWI torpedoing of his troopship off the coast of Ireland, and he would survive this as well, by airlift if necessary. If anything happened at all.

Two hundred miles east, my Aunt Margo was cleaning house. She and Uncle Mike lived in Pasco, a small town a quarter of what it is today, the runt of the Tri-Cities, smaller than its sister cities Kennewick and Richland, in Eastern Washington's arid semi-desert. Mike and Mom were raised in Pasco when it was crisscrossed by tumbleweeds; Margo had grown up in Burbank, a hamlet just across the Snake River. My uncle's green oasis of a backyard was just a block down a hot sidewalk from the wide, majestic Columbia River. On its waters, the locally famous speedboat competitions took place each year during my family's visit around July 4th, when "unlimited hydroplanes" battled the reigning champ, the Miss Budweiser.

When Mount St. Helens blew its top, fifty-seven people, including Harry R. Truman, perished. And presumably at least sixteen cats. The lateral landslide triggered by the explosion traveled in excess of one hundred miles per hour, so it was unlikely that Truman even made it to the abandoned mineshaft he'd stocked with food and liquor. But he was granted a posthumous wish: *St. Helens*, a made-for-HBO film, which was released a year to the day after the explosion. In it, he was portrayed by Art Carney, his favorite actor; Carney managed to make even the old crank lovable.

On June 2, Aunt Margo sent a letter. Here is an excerpt:

Dear Robbie, John, Franky and Danny:

Hi! We're sending one container of the volcanic dust for you to divide in portions among you to sell, trade, keep, give away or whatever. It's pure fallout, I laid newspapers out on our patio and then emptied them into the container; so, there's no dirt or anything in it. I'm also sending a chemical analysis and general information report that I got from work – show it to your mom and dad. Most of the dust has settled now that we've had winds and rain; so, things are almost like normal – we can even see some blue in the sky again!

I confess to not sharing the ash, but then again... I don't remember being asked! And since I have preserved it (and, more generally, the past) by imprisoning it, I don't feel too bad about it.

Aunt Margo's letter is young. Her cursive script, in red ink, is neat and vivacious. She used semicolons like I do. A quick calculation tells me that she wrote this letter when she was just setting out on motherhood's journey, exactly half my age now. As much as the ash, for which I've yet to find a use, I'm happy to have her letter, which rekindles in me an appetite for "snail mail." Computers may keep us in touch, but they rob us of memories.

Returning to the chemical analysis. The letterhead of the interoffice memo of May 21, 1980 identifies the office where Aunt Margo worked, the Applied Chemistry and Analysis Division of the Hanford Engineering Development Laboratory. The memo reads:

> *The following is an estimate of the chemical composition of the Mt. St. Helen's (sic) volcanic dust obtained from FFTF DHX (East Side). These results are in terms of the oxides and are based on x-ray fluorescence and spark source mass spectrometry.*

The referenced table has two columns: element, and percent by weight. As it is sorted on neither, I naturally wondered what it *is* sorted by. High school chemistry to the rescue! It's sorted by atomic number, familiar from the Periodic Table. Resorting it enables me to identify the most common elements: silicon (42%), aluminum (19%), iron (15%), calcium (13%), potassium (4%) and sodium (3%). That leaves five percent for twenty-two trace elements. With the help of the internet, I ascertained that this distribution mirrors the composition of the Earth's crust, with the exception of the most common element, oxygen, which does not appear. Then I recall and understand the phrase, "These results are in terms of the oxides."

What was the purpose of this report? I can't imagine these results would have surprised anyone, particularly the managers and scientists of the part of Hanford owned by Westinghouse, which was then tasked with building an onsite nuclear test reactor. My guess is that it was busywork pure and simple, an assignment for a summer intern to get his or her feet wet.

That fall, I showed the ash and analysis to my ninth-grade Earth Science teacher, Mr. Caprio. He asked if he could borrow them, and then commissioned a second chemical analysis. When he returned the ash, I asked him no follow-up questions. Why not? Had his test results matched the earlier ones? Was something novel discovered? What hypothesis was he testing?

My singular lack of curiosity had led to a lost learning opportunity. But that's life -- we run through our days, discovering but a fraction of what's important.

Wheatland County

In the same closet, a fraying, pale green rubber band holds together a brick of yellow photographs. Yellow, that is, not yellowing. They've been that way since the day I took them, overexposed, thirty years ago on the high plateau of Wheatland County, Montana. But that's the way I saw it: great expanses of overexposed wheat, barley, and scrub grass beneath a high sky. I figured the best way to capture it all would be to ignore the aperture.

Here's a line of Cargill silos – tall, pinched cylinders, immense cans of corn – on a railroad siding outside town. They were the first sign of civilization as one approached the county seat, Harlowton, from the west. Here they are again. And again: just a blue sky, silos, a telephone pole, and tawny grass.

Here, I believe, is the stocked trout pond where we fished as kids in Chief Joseph Park, named after the leader of the Nez Perce. (When I was young and ignorant of Native American history, I confused "Nez Perce" and "pince-nez," a word I'd seen in Dickens. I pictured an Indian tribe in old-fashioned eyeglasses.) I'm not sure, though, that it is the park -- due to overexposure, what I assume is water is barely bluer than white, and what I take to be trees are barely greener than blue.

Here is the high school field where the hometown Engineers played, something I never saw because we never visited during fall. A small set of bleachers abuts the far side of the field, beneath the only shade trees in sight. Looking at this picture, I can once again hear the ticking of the sprinklers struggling to keep the grass green, though once again I'm hard pressed to say if the whitish cast of the grass is real or just a trick of the light.

I purposely took photos at odd angles. One, of a tall gas station sign advertising the Western trinity (beer, ice and "pop" -- what Montanans call soda) isn't about the sign, but my attempt to capture the immensity of Montana's "big sky." By taking the photo at ground level, with the sign on the diagonal, I could let the sky overflow the sign from every direction.

But I give myself too much credit. The boy with the Canon was an amateur. My parents, having abandoned photography (Mom had moved on to video, and was capturing our trips in a new medium), had given me her old camera. With minimal instruction, I snapped anything that caught my eye during our annual summer visit to sleepy Harlowton, ninety miles northwest of Billings.

For most of the twentieth century, Harlowton was that point of the "Milwaukee Road" (the Chicago, Milwaukee, St. Paul and Pacific Railroad) where westbound trains switched from steam or diesel to electric, to mount the Rockies. Consequently, there was always railroad work in town; for decades, several great-uncles of mine worked for the railroad. By the time I knew them, they had become portly fellows; the big breakfasts and lunches that had fortified them during their working years had caught up in retirement with their waistlines.

Felix and Louisa Peccia, my great-grandparents, came to America in the early 1900s from Cantalupo, a landlocked village in mountainous central Italy, forty miles north of Naples. All but one of their children had been born in the Old Country; their youngest son, my Uncle Albert, was born right in their house in Harlowton.

As was Mom, decades later, in September, 1940. With no nearby hospital and the weather too poor to hazard a trip, there was no alternative to a home delivery. It turned out to be quite an ordeal for Nana Edie. She was in labor for forty-eight hours with nothing but aspirin to ease her pain. She prayed for a girl of her own; she had been the only girl among five children. As she later told Mom, "If you had been a boy, I would have handed you to the first person walking by."

Other than being small and landlocked, Harlowton was quite a change from Cantalupo. The landscape was so different -- broad vistas and wheatfields extended southwest all the way to the purple Crazy Mountains on the horizon. The Peccias' ranch house sat at the foot of a steep road descending from the main town crossroads, and was painted the color of pistachio ice cream. Its front screen door had a "P" inscribed in a circle, as though it were the branding mark of one of my great-uncle Tony's cows, which he called his "doggies." The house was small, and the lot barely wide enough to accommodate it, with just enough room left over on each side for a narrow cement walk. There being no exterior outlets, Grandma Peccia cut the lawn with a push mower; she was still at it in her nineties because she felt that "the kids didn't do it right." And the one spigot outside the house was used by Dad to gut and clean the trout that we caught at Chief Joseph Park.

When I was young, our great-grandmother's backyard garden was almost as large as the house. She made use of its every square inch - from the cement walkways to the garden shed to the weathered picket fence whose gate gave onto a back alley where the garbage truck arrived once a week – to grow the fruits and vegetables she needed for cooking, a habit she had learned during the Depression, when frugality was law.

The house plan was simple. Behind the screen door was a sun porch, where we hid from mosquitoes on summer evenings. Two steps further took you into the living room with a sofa and easy chair, the one in which Grandpa Peccia, in the only mental image I still have of him (he died when I was very young) watched television. To the left were two small bedrooms and a bath; to the right, another bedroom. On the wall, a cuckoo clock loudly marked each hour of the day and night, to the chagrin of light sleepers. A few steps further was the dining room; to the right, a fourth bedroom; to the left, a small kitchen. That was it, except for the unfinished basement where I slept in a bed under a tiny window near the ceiling that let in a modicum of light. I slept among castoff items like a hand-cranked washing machine that Grandma Peccia still used and a full-size icebox that hummed all night, which was stuffed with resealable bags containing meat cuts and frozen donuts.

Above each bed but mine, a crucifix. On the back of each chair, an antimacassar. On each side table, a lace doily saving the veneer from a host of framed photographs: the descendants. I could put names to only a fraction of the portraits, but Grandma Peccia, even in her dotage, would gladly take you on a house tour and name them all, one by one. (When she lit upon someone who had died young, however, she would only smile sadly and move on.) Then, if you had time, Grandma would open the drawers beneath the pictures, revealing a supply of linen and lace that would have furnished a dozen homes.

The kitchen at the rear was the home's one true heart, despite its small size. There was a stove; a double sink whose faucet issued an evil-smelling, sulfurous liquid that offended the noses of young suburbanites accustomed to fluoridation; a tiny counter on which Grandma somehow prepared meals for a dozen; the basement door; and a small, round kitchen table that seated only three because it abutted the wall next to a window that would have looked onto the garden had it not been forever draped in a curtain. On the wall to the right as you entered was a calendar courtesy of Saint Joseph Roman Catholic Church (as a child, it reminded me of Saint Joseph's aspirin, which advertised on *Wild Kingdom*) that listed all the saints' days. I looked up some classmates' names so I could inform them of their days when I returned to New Jersey.

And in the middle of it all was Grandma Peccia, a dynamo who towered above us at four feet, six inches, and shrinking. She was our measuring stick: the first thing we did upon our arrival in Harlowton was to hug her, if just to see how much we'd grown since our last visit. Surpassing her in height was our first step to adulthood.

After our hellos, Grandma would carefully descend the creaky steps to the basement to raid the icebox of homemade donuts, which she proceeded to warm in the oven. She would place them in a paper bag loaded with granulated sugar and shake them until they were thoroughly coated. Then they melted in our mouths. (So did her deep-fried cauliflower florets, the only cauliflower I've ever truly loved.)

Back to the photographs. I notice that some aren't of Harlowton but of Judith Gap, a much smaller town fifteen miles to the north. I know the distance for two reasons, the first being that *all* adjacent towns in Wheatland County are fifteen miles apart: they're evenly spaced, like necklace beads; this was apparent to me when I studied the old Rand McNally atlas. (Someone explained it to me by saying that a horse could cover fifteen miles in a day, and I believed them.) Also, the numbers on the Route 191 highway sign between Harlowton and Judith Gap summed to fifteen. I know this because that sign later graced the wall of our Madison rec room.

> *The good news out here on the highway*
> *Is the speed limit's just a suggestion*
> — Eddie From Ohio, "Number Six Driver"

In all Wheatland County, the highways between towns were wide open, with little traffic. The occasional pickup truck would appear a mile away, dropping into and out of sight as it followed the ribbon of road that shimmered like a mirage in the sun, up and down the chutes and ladders of the terrain. Vehicles made good time, with speed limits advisory, but thunderstorms, which are beholden to nature's law, took longer. One could follow their hourly progress via faint sheets of black rain on the horizon. Rivers, too, were visible from afar: the bendy

Musselshell, which one crossed a half-dozen times near Harlowton, was flanked by the only trees in sight – the ones that it watered.

Wide-open vistas were the physical analogues of the emotional space I preferred. I liked my school chums, but I also liked getting away from them. For much of each summer, I was content to send or receive an occasional postcard from a truck stop or Indian trading post. I actually competed with two classmates, Dave and John, to find each summer's "stupidest" postcard. We graded the cards not only for their photos but also the captions we improvised for them. John won every year; he had a knack for finding the strangest images and sealing them with zingers. One year, his winning entry was a card of Pope John Paul II flashing the A-OK sign, right thumb and forefinger encircling his right eye. On the back, John had written: "Eye of the Tiger."

Even on vacation, I clung to my personal space, avoiding new acquaintances. That wasn't hard in Montana, where a detachment of relatives served as my private guard. Even then, Montana politics may have been shot through with ideology, but if that was so, I didn't know it. Ditto the economy: I never considered that Harlowton might not have jobs for young people. There, the only youth that I knew there were my cousins -- and they weren't all that local. Harlowton's shuttered downtown storefronts told of a long and slow decline, but to me it was an Old West stage set whose remaining businesses advertised beer, sundries, western wear, saddles, and in one case, "vittles and grog." The grownups may have chewed over politics and the economy late at night around Grandma Peccia's dining room table while playing cribbage and pinochle, but by then I would have retired to the basement to fiddle with my transistor radio, trying to pull in a major league game. In the days before the Rockies joined the majors, my best shot was St. Louis.

I played games with my siblings and cousins. We gathered under the apple tree in Grandma Peccia's front yard, the one that tempted me once, never twice, each summer to try its tart and tiny crabapples. There we played "Monster," a variation of tag I'd devised, in which the person who was "it" chose a partner by tapping him or her on the shoulder while everyone's eyes were closed. I liked choosing cousin Jan, who was a year younger and shared a taste for some of my favorite books and bands, but who was otherwise my opposite – outgoing, extroverted, and full of life. Jan died very young, thankfully after Grandma Peccia's own death at the age of ninety-nine; my great-grandmother never had to pass over Jan's picture when giving her tour of the family picture gallery.

Sometimes Frank and I challenged Uncle Mike to basketball at the cracked, rarely-used half court up the street, where weeds grew through asphalt and the rim lacked a net. It was good enough for us. I was twelve, Frank was ten, and our uncle twenty-five, so as a two-against-one proposition he'd have been a three point favorite. Frank and I came up with various silly team names, but Uncle Mike was always the Tri-City Idiots. One day, Frank and I finally figured out how to beat him – by passing the ball back-and-forth until we could set up easy layups.

After all this togetherness, I needed to bury my head in a book. It was such a common occurrence that Dad would kid me about it. At unmarked fishing holes on unposted land along rural highways known to our ancestral outdoorsmen, I gave ten minutes of myself to the fish, gnats and no-see-ums before returning to the car for a book. Skeet shooting? No thanks. A movie? Pass. I never set foot inside Harlowton's movie palace, the only place in town other than the ice cream parlor where the town would meet teens halfway. Frank and Robbie went with my cousins. On one occasion, they came back disappointed because the movie had been canceled; the reel hadn't made it onto the bus from Great Falls.

Thirty years earlier, the ice cream parlor was a candy store called Betty's Corner. That gave Mom a kick -- Betty was practically her name! The store where she had once clamored for Snicklefritz Bars was now her children's hangout. I went there to play pinball, moseying up Central Avenue -- a gunslinger packing a roll of quarters, my sneaker laces trailing dust.

The pinball machine was in the back, next to a jukebox stocked with the current hits. Both machines were usually available, not getting the play of the ones in the saloons that lined Harlowton's main streets. I was a fiend for the silverball – had no use for new-fangled video games – and played it at every campground, rest area, and general store I could. I played it so much, in fact, that I'd injure myself; the repetitive motion of depressing the flippers and trying to steer the ball across the console would aggravate the muscles intermediate to my elbows and shoulders, leaving me with what I called "pinball elbow." When that happened, I had to give the game a rest.

One evening, having lost track of time, I looked up and saw that I was the only customer, and that the parlor was about to close. The two girls behind the counter, who couldn't have had more than a year or two on me, were toweling off dishes. The jukebox was playing Billy Joel's "It's Still Rock and Roll to Me." I liked the melody, but could not forgive the lyrics that disparaged "straight-A students" like me. On the way out, I smiled, and one girl smiled prettily back. It would have been nice to know her better, but I was too shy. Still, when I hear that song today, I have the consolation of her smile.

I tried to escape my loving family's embrace. At home I could go to my room, but in the motorhome's close quarters, or at Grandma Peccia's, I had fewer options. The year that we gathered in Harlowton for the big family reunion, effectively doubling the town's size (okay, a small exaggeration), was rough. The kitschy log cabin motel on Route 12 was full of Peccias; others were at the historic Graves Hotel, whose stone ramparts loomed over the hill above my great-grandmother's house. Family arrived from east and west: Mom's cousins Jean and Joan came from California, Uncle Al from Laramie, and Uncle Jim's "other" family (the one he had started after he disappeared for a number of years) from Florida, and of course my Helena cousins.

Returning to the photographs, I see my overexposed relatives in blurs of activity, coming and going on tractors, swings, and pickup trucks. I must have set the shutter speed incorrectly; things didn't move that fast in Montana! I mean, even my parents' near arrest for grand theft auto happened in slow motion.

Mom and Dad were gabbing with the family in Grandma Peccia's dining room when they volunteered for a grocery run, including ice cream (probably tin roof sundae) for Grandpa Hines. Their only conveyance being our motorhome, they needed a car. Uncle Tony tossed them the keys to his green Ford pickup, which he said was "out front." Sure enough, they found it unlocked, like every other vehicle in Harlowton, directly outside Grandma's house. They got in, Dad turned the ignition, and soon they zipped up Central Avenue to a small grocery.

On the way out of the store, they saw a man and woman standing near the pickup. They waved a friendly hello, but when they tried getting in, the couple interposed themselves, forcing them to shift their bagged groceries awkwardly from one arm to the other. The man seemed eager to make conversation:

"Hey, that's a nice fifth wheel you've got. Is that your truck?"

"No, it belongs to my wife's uncle."

Somehow, that answer didn't satisfy him. Mom noticed the woman had her arms crossed.

Then a squad car swept into the lot, lights flashing. Two young officers, a man and woman, got out; the man wore mirrored sunglasses like Rod Steiger's in *In the Heat of the Night*. Like Steiger, he wasn't smiling. He asked Mom and Dad for their names, then oddly asked Dad for his social security number.

"Do you know we have roadblocks set up for you on either end of town?" He meant Route 12.

My parents were flabbergasted. They were still holding their groceries, and Grandpa's ice cream was melting. After a perfunctory attempt to sort things out, the male officer asked for Grandma Peccia's home phone number. Grandpa answered the phone.

"Hello, do you know a Frank Baldan?"

After a beat, Grandpa said:

"Frank *who*? Never heard of him." He enjoyed a hearty belly laugh. Dad and Grandpa had that sort of humor. Over pinochle, they would call each other "Rasputin," or "Raz" for short, after the Russian monk who had survived one scrape after another, though I don't know the precise origin of the nickname.

Next Wednesday, the front page of *The Harlowton Times-Clarion* announced: "Couple Makes Honest Mistake." The story went on to explain how one ignition key had fit two green Ford pickups, the one my parents had taken (which was parked in front of Grandma's), and Uncle Tony's truck, which he had failed to mention was parked across the street by the butcher's shop (where the couple whom my parents encountered had been shopping).

I'm not surprised that two green Ford pickup trucks were parked across the street from one another. Back then, in America's heartland, one didn't see many foreign-made vehicles, the kind of cars that Grandpa Hines, who was a Ford salesman and veteran of the Pacific theater in World War II, called "riceburners." Nor am I surprised that Harlowton's police officers were so officious; I've listened to Arlo Guthrie's "Alice's Restaurant" enough times to know that they were merely acting like Officer Obie, the overzealous cop who turned a littering offense into "the biggest crime of the last fifty years" where "everybody wanted to get in the newspaper story about it."

Grandpa certainly never let my parents forget the mix-up. It may have had to do with the melted ice cream.

***

My memories of Montana are crowded with incidents and faces, but I keep coming back to the fact that nearly all the photos I took that summer are of landscapes, without a soul in sight.

A few were taken inside Judith Gap's elementary school, which was vacant over summer break. One day, Uncle Mike, Aunt Margo, and I walked over from Uncle Tony and Aunt Mayme's to explore it. (None of my pictures include my aunt and uncle, but I remember they were there.) Of course, the doors were unlocked. I took a few pictures in the empty gym: a backboard suspended above a lacquered wood floor, school logo at midcourt, and in the background, a royal blue stage curtain that hadn't been used since graduation.

And one more shot, a buzzer-beater: in a second-floor classroom, I snapped a picture out a window. Smoky glass blocks frame a single transparent center pane in which a dirt road recedes from town, heading straight for the horizon.

Roman Numerals

With apologies to Ringo Starr, it is *numbers*, not love, that don't come easy. Actually, they came quite late in our evolutionary time.

Recent studies show that bees count to four. Not only that, bees understand zero as a concept: in particular, that zero is the number that is smaller than all other counting numbers. That boggles the mind. Humanity didn't even recognize zero as a number until two thousand years ago, making us – until recently – less mathematically sophisticated than bees! And as every child can attest, counting is one of the most difficult intellectual skills to master.

But it is not only counting numbers that pose problems. Differences (subtractions) between them do, too. Here are some examples.

During my one semester in the teacher's education program at Montclair State College, I returned for three days to Madison High School to observe my former Calculus teacher, Mrs. Boepple. On the third day, she had me teach her remedial math class. I walked into the B Hall classroom that had once been the home of Mr. Kreger's typing class, and saw that it now housed rows of desktop computers exponentially more powerful than the ones I'd worked with just a few years earlier.

The classroom was also full of students afraid of negative numbers. Every generation of computers is born smarter than its forebears; every human starts from scratch. I was hopeful, having been told that I have a knack for explaining mathematical concepts, that I could lead these children up the mount of understanding, but dealing with the math-shy was harder than I expected. How does one explain what it means to subtract a negative number from a positive number? I drew pictures of a thermometer and demonstrated how the numbers straddled zero. (Would that work today with students who have never seen an analog thermometer?)

Years earlier, when I was the one in the student's desk, Mr. Growley, my algebra teacher, did not show up one day. A few minutes after the bell, Lou Blanchet, the Math Department Head, arrived, and posed brain teasers for the rest of class. One was:

"You begin reading at the top of page A and finish reading at the bottom of page B. How many pages did you read?"

We jotted down our answers, and he circulated around the room to check them. How easy, I thought! But then I saw that most everyone had gotten it wrong, even Dave, my one true rival, who had lamely written "X." (The correct answer is B–A+1.) Why is counting so hard?

In elementary school, I first met Roman numerals. Personally, I liked them because they resembled substitution ciphers (I=1; V=5, etc.), a hobby of mine. But when you calculate them, why do you sometimes add and sometimes subtract? And they're useless for calculation, being unmanipulable – just try multiplying two of them!

So ends my Montaignesque preamble to this chapter's topic, the Super Bowl. We go back a long way, the Big Game and I, and for a while we had quite a fling, but I'm afraid we're permanently on the outs.

***

My fourth-grade teacher, Mrs. Moody, assigned us autobiographies. I began mine by mentioning a unique tie that I have to the Super Bowl: we're the same age, and we sometimes share a birthday.

Fact check!

We're not the same age. The game now known as Super Bowl I, originally the "AFL-NFL Championship Game," took place a week to the day after I dove headfirst into my first birthday cake. The big game and I aren't the same age because of zero – I had been zero, but the Super Bowl had not. It was born on the day it turned one, though its birth was not recognized until two years later.

See how difficult this counting business is?

When I was young, football adhered to a strict liturgical calendar. It fell on Sundays, on the living room television. Dad's fanhood was somewhere between casual and involved; he watched when he had time, especially if he had a bet on the game. He watched; I absorbed. Up to then, my main TV interest – the only thing that made me glance up from my rocking horse – was commercials, because they were loud, bright, and full of music. I was also riveted to a locally syndicated program for toddlers, *Birthday House*. (Think *Romper Room*, but hosted by a B-list actor, Paul Tripp, who – according to Mom – obviously disliked children.)

When I was two, I was more interested in *Heidi* than football, so Dad and I naturally had different takes on the infamous "Heidi Game," in the fall of 1968. Dad had a bet on the Raiders against the Jets. Since the game pitted bitter rivals in the bad old days, it was a cockfight of premeditated violence and mayhem. So when the picture cut suddenly from a bloody helmet rolling on the turf to a young girl in pigtails skipping down a mountain path, Dad was stunned. NBC had pulled away from a game that was running late to begin its heavily-hyped TV premiere of *Heidi* on time.

The phone rang; Dad picked up.

"The Raiders are moving the ball. Don't sell your bet."

As soon as he hung up, the phone rang again.

"Hey, want to sell your bet?"

Such was gambling before the internet.

Though ignorant of that angle, I started watching games with Dad and Grandpa Hines, also a fan. When they watched together, they'd trade barbs. If a player went down with an injury necessitating a stretcher, Grandpa would bellow:

"Cart him off the field!"

The first game I remember watching was Super Bowl X (that's ten, for the Roman numeral averse), in which Pittsburgh's Lynn Swann made a series of acrobatic catches, one of which was captured on the cover of the following week's *Sports Illustrated*, to lead the Steelers past the Cowboys. Swann's heroics, and the drama of that game, sealed the deal: I was officially a fan. And so began a string of years when the Super Bowl meant a great deal to me. Reviewing the final scores of those games – their least interesting aspect from my perspective today – brought back memories that say as much about my maturation as they do about football's evolution. Here's the post-game recap.

Super Bowl XI: Oakland 32, Minnesota 14

The year the Super Bowl actually fell on my birthday – how exciting to wake to a day of sledding, presents, cake and football!

That morning, Dad took us to Springbrook, the country club where we were members. There, Mom and Dad played platform tennis in the winter, and golf and tennis in the summer. (I took a few tennis lessons but never joined the team. And swim team practice was the bane of my summers: I hated the "high dive" that seemed to sit a hundred feet in the air, and I hated the feel of my curled toes against the gritty edge of the swimming blocks. I also dreaded meets against other clubs' swim teams, when I always finished last. The only thing that made swim team practice worthwhile was the summer morning walks to and from the house and the country club. We would cut across the golf course, and I can still feel the peacefulness of a place utterly at rest, dew on my feet, seen only by my brother, my sister, and those strange pump-handled golf ball cleaners near each hole.)

Behind the clubhouse, by the putting green, was the steep slope that the neighborhood kids called Killer Hill for the lethal speed one could attain on a sled or toboggan. This morning, I was flying down the hill on my red roll-up toboggan when Frankie somehow got stuck on his, right in front of me; he was just getting off when I realized that he was in my path and mowed him down. He cried all the way home. Later, it was my turn to be disappointed, when the Raiders crushed the team I had adopted for the day, the Vikings.

Super Bowl XII: Dallas 27, Denver 10

What a drag! First, I was disappointed to learn that the Super Bowl had been rescheduled from mid-afternoon to early evening. I was a traditionalist even as a child; I felt in my heart that sports should be played under the sun. Played at night, they feel like just another TV show. Besides, it would have been easier to finish my math homework to *The Wonderful World of Disney*.

Second, my Broncos never stood a chance. I was born rooting for underdogs, and it was harder to imagine a sadder runt than Denver, who had surprisingly made it to the big game under quarterback Craig Morton, the hapless ex-Giant who at the age of thirty-five was considered over the hill. (In today's game, when players have the know-how and resources to follow full-year training regimens, that age is unexceptional.) On the other side of the ball was Dallas' vaunted Doomsday Defense. Another of my congenital qualities, my contrarian streak, dictated that I hate the Cowboys. Any team called "America's Team" could surely not be mine.

To pass the afternoon before the game – which was much longer than it should have been, due to the change in start time – I engaged in a peculiar form of calisthenics. I grabbed my two-toned Nerf football and placed on Mom's old phonograph one of my three *Music From National Football*

League Films albums. I had purchased them by mail order after seeing a direct response TV ad during the weekly highlights show that I watched religiously. These albums compiled the music that accompanied the highlight reels that transformed majestic slow-motion marches down the gridiron into Wagnerian epics. The selections, composed by Sam Spence and performed by The Elliot Blair Orchestra, began with "Sunday With Soul," a jazzy barnburner with thrilling blasts of kettledrum; track two, "Headcracker Suite," a plaintive melody oddly reminiscent of Mason Williams' "Classical Gas," shimmered with pent-up excitement. I began throwing myself touchdown passes, slow-motion lobs coming within an inch or two of my blue ceiling, the color of an afternoon sky, the color the sky should be during the Super Bowl, not the pitch dark of night or dead white underbelly of a dome. And now I was Lynn Swann making acrobatic catches, my arms outstretched, pulling the ball to my chest moments before crashing into the mattress.

As for the game, it was so dispiritingly one-sided that I went to bed early rather than see its end.

Super Bowl XIII: Pittsburgh 35, Dallas 31 – at Miami!

For my coming of age, Dad surprised me with a wonderful gift. As long as I kept up my grades (ha!), I'd see the Super Bowl in person!

Arnie Dahl, of Dahl Ford in Sumner, Washington, had received four tickets to the game. Having no interest in football, he gave them to his star salesman, my Grandpa Hines, who immediately thought of his football-crazy grandson. Dad told me that Frankie and I would be going to the game in our motorhome, along with Dad and his friend, Mr. Alofs.

That Friday afternoon, I left Torey J. Sabatini school early. I suspect my classmates were jealous! I ran down the concrete front walk to Woodland Road, where my ride awaited, engine running. I unlatched the motorhome door, hopped in, and we were off to Miami! I will never again experience such red-carpet treatment.

Being the first Super Bowl that I attended, this one is still clear in my mind. We stayed at a resort hotel, its lobby full of sunlight and palm trees. Near a revolving door was a Donkey Kong arcade game; Frankie and I played many games courtesy of Dad's roll of quarters, but we didn't make much progress against the big ape.

Since we were at ground zero, the Super Bowl seemed more vivid. Everyone wore Steeler or Cowboy T-shirts, and the local papers offered blanket coverage. I couldn't get enough of it: I read every sports section I could find, front to back, every article. On Saturday morning, over a diner breakfast, I pored over a listing of thirty bets that one could place on the game, not just obvious ones like margin of victory and total points scored, but unknowable things like which player would score first, or even who would win the coin toss. They made me laugh. Dad just shook his head, calling them suckers' bets.

On game day, we drove to the Orange Bowl parking lot, where Dad set up a grill and made his signature tailgate dish: sausage, onions and peppers on hoagie rolls. In the motorhome, the miniature black-and-white television played hours of local and national pregame coverage, but eventually I had enough. The waiting had begun to feel like Christmas Eve, so I went outside to drink in the atmosphere of the parking lots, anticipating the opening of the gates.

Finally, we entered the stadium. We climbed to the upper deck (our seats were high, but at the twenty yard line), where we had a good view of the field. I would, of course, be pulling for the Steelers. I think Frankie was, too, and though I'm not sure of Dad's allegiance (or if he had placed a bet), I knew Mr. Alofs was a Cowboys fan. I silently pitied him.

The Super Bowl has become unrecognizable from what it was then, in many ways. But I can summarize the differences by saying that back then it felt like a game, not an event. There were marching bands on the field during the pregame show, with not one pop star entourage in sight. Every fan was handed a large, glossy, square poster, color-coded by section, which we were instructed to hold aloft according to the instructions printed on the poster, at a certain point of halftime. We were admonished not to raise them early, because together they would form a surprise picture visible not only to those in attendance, but to the TV audience as well. How quaint it seems today to outsource the entertainment to the fans! Now fans expect their money's worth, and for the entertainment to come to them.

And I clearly saw, as it transpired, the pivotal play that still gets replayed today. Near the end of the third quarter, with the Steelers leading 21-14, the Cowboys' Roger Staubach found wide receiver Jackie Smith open in the end zone. Staubach short-armed his pass, and Smith had to reach for it; he lost his balance and dropped the ball that would have tied the game. Because I was shorter than everyone around me, I saw it all transpire beneath their upraised arms! Mr. Alofs, on the other hand, assumed Smith had caught the ball because he had been open, and because the crowd was yelling. Or so he thought for a split second, until I yelled over the crowd noise:

"He dropped it!"

I'll never forget his look of incredulity, then disgust.

The game ended happily, with the Steelers prevailing. It was the first time my team had won the Super Bowl – and I had seen it in person. We trooped back to the motorhome and then stayed put; with all the comforts of home surrounding us, there was no need to join the traffic. We had snacks from the kitchen cabinet and watched postgame coverage. I do, however, remember commercials for a scary movie. In what might have been the crassest cross-promotion in television history, NBC promoted John Frankenheimer's movie *Black Sunday*, about a terrorist attack at the Super Bowl.

Super Bowl XIV: Pittsburgh 31, Los Angeles 19

The one that got away. We didn't go to the Super Bowl because Nana Edie was ill. My parents repurposed Super Bowl weekend for a visit to my grandparents' home in Puyallup, Washington.

My grandmother had breast cancer. Mom had nursed her during radiation and chemotherapy, and had even taken her to Mexico, to a clinic offering an alternative therapy based on a chemical found in peach pits. But the cancer had spread. This would be the last time I would see my grandmother.

Watching the Super Bowl that night on television after seeing it the year before in person was a little dispiriting. As we kids watched in the living room, Mom kept her mother company in her bedroom.

The year before, I'd pulled for the Steelers, but now that they were favorites, I switched my allegiance to the Rams. The spread was ten points. Before leaving for Washington, I'd enlisted fifty classmates in a statistical experiment, polling them for their predictions of the final score, which I averaged to arrive at a consensus twelve-point Pittsburgh victory. We were right on target, a vindication of crowdsourcing before its time.

After the game, I paid Nana Edie a visit in her darkened bedroom. She kissed me good night and handed me a five-dollar bill. The next morning, I left the bill on the dresser in my bedroom. It was my way of saying that I would rather have my grandmother.

Super Bowl XV: Oakland 27, Philadelphia 10 – in New Orleans!

This was my first trip to New Orleans, a city I was very eager to see. Once again, we went by motorhome. This time our guest was Mr. Chipoletti, a well-known Madison patriarch, the snowy-haired owner of Chippy's Deli on Main Street. In New Orleans, we'd meet up with Dad's other buddies, including our next-door neighbor "Joe the Hawk" and a tall, thin, and tanned Chathamite I'll just call Mr. X. (He shared an Italian surname with a girl in my high school class. Perhaps they were related; that was always a possibility in Madison.)

The route to New Orleans led west, then south. Frank and I restlessly sprawled on our stomachs on our mattress perch above the driver and passenger seats, as we watched Pennsylvania highway signs passed overhead. As we approached the small town of Lenhartsville, out of sheer boredom I began to tease my brother, just to get a rise:

"Hey Frank, look, it's Lenhartsville! Bogley-ogley Lenhartsville!" Proud of my nonsense, I repeated it until Frank got annoyed.

"Bogley-ogley Lenhartsville! I bet they've got a gas station and store, and everything!"

But that got boring too, so we raided the pantry, the floor-to-ceiling cabinet by the kitchenette. It was jam-packed with snacks: cookies, candies, and more. Maybe Dad had bought them, or maybe Mr. Chipoletti had requisitioned them from the shelves of his store: either way, they were gone by the time we got to New Orleans. Mr. Chipoletti, with whom Frank and I exchanged barely two sentences over a thousand miles, gave us the *malocchio*, but I didn't care. Dad was on our side, happy to let us have our way as we headed to "The Big Easy."

The RV campground was practically downtown, a central base camp from which to see the sights, which we did more of this year than any other. Despite his buddies' presence, Dad spent almost all his time with us. He took us to the French Quarter, where we walked the streets for hours, long enough for me to commit to memory a ten-by-ten grid of exotic-sounding street names – Iberville, Bienville, Conti – and to sample several eateries, including an Italian bakery whose cannolis Dad proclaimed "authentic." We took them outside and ate them while we "people watched," a new concept to me. Then, for dinner, Dad took us to a seafood restaurant overlooking the Mississippi, where Frank and I tried oysters for the first time. I thought they were disgusting. They had the texture of jellyfish, and upon biting them, I felt something like an electric shock. These are delicacies? I'd take the cannolis.

The day before the game, we joined Dad's buddies for a ride up the Mississippi River on the Natchez, a paddle boat with a banquet-sized dining room. I have a photograph of Frank and me waiting to board ship that cool and breezy morning; I'm in a blue jacket and Frank has on his bright red Widow Brown's windbreaker. I remember standing on deck, watching the waterwheel sift the river like flour. But I better remember the practical joke that Dad and his buddies played on Mr. X.

I don't know if Mr. X. was married, but he'd struck up a conversation with an attractive woman at a table not far from the one where I was sitting with Frank, Dad, and Dad's other cronies. Dad asked Frank if he would do him a favor, and Frank was happy to oblige: he crossed the room, and as we all watched, tapped Mr. X. on the shoulder and said, pitifully:

"Dad, Mommy says you should come back to our table right now."

For a second, Mr. X. was startled; then he swiveled toward our table, where Dad and his friends had erupted in laughter. Dismissively jerking his head our way, he simply said:

"Jeez!"

The next morning, Dad took us back to the French Quarter so Frank and I could engage in some performance art. A buddy of Dad's had brought along two Radio Shack remote-controlled robots; Frank pulled an Eagles jersey over one (Philly was his pick), I pulled a Raiders jersey over the other (Oakland was mine), and we positioned them facing one other across a lightly trafficked street littered with the debris of the previous night's revels. It took some practice with the joystick to guide our charges, but we soon had them bull rushing, and when they collided, one or the other would buck up, teeter, and crash.

Sometimes the Raider prevailed, sometimes the Eagle, and soon we were performing to a large crowd. Some onlookers seemed to have been up all night; a few were clearly headed to church; but everyone stopped a moment to watch. Every volley, depending on the victor, provoked cheers and groans from different quarters. For once, I enjoyed being the center of attention. When Dad returned from his errand, we excitedly described our star turn. Mr. X. joined us and said that he and Dad had seen "Jimmy the Greek," the well-known pundit who handicapped the games each week for CBS, stagger out of a bar. I suppose he still had several hours to get sober, make his appearance on the pregame show, and call in some bets. Mr. X. already had his down.

After all the pre-game action, the game itself was something of an anticlimax. The Raiders won going away. I was happy to see the wild card team win the Super Bowl (the first time it had happened), but Frank again cried.

Afterwards, Dad took us to the hotel where his cronies were staying. We followed him down a long hallway to a room in disarray, where I peered in to see Mr. X. sitting at the edge of his bed, still dressed in the jacket he'd worn to the game. His head hung limply in his hands. Dad was saying something to him, but he wasn't answering.

On our way out, I asked what had happened.
"He lost a lot of money."
"How much?"
"Five thousand dollars."
I'm sure Dad meant it as a teaching moment.

Super Bowl XVI – San Francisco 26, Cincinnati 21 – at Detroit

Maybe Mom was tired of hearing how much fun we boys were having, because this year she came along. And not just Mom – Grandpa Hines, Uncle Mike, Aunt Margo, and their young children, Patrick and Meagan.

This year's game was in *January*, in *Detroit*, so we flew rather than drive the motorhome. It was the first time the National Football League had selected a cold-weather game site, and the decision was universally panned. Mom and Dad certainly didn't like it. The weather was cold and wet, with days of frozen rain, and Detroit seemed indifferent to our presence. In a token gesture, signs reading "Bourbon Street North" were put up in a bar-heavy part of town, provoking some mirth.

Mom's side of the family played it right, staying downtown in the same hotel as the 49ers. They had it all! Frank and I heard their stories of elevator double-takes: "Hey, Dwight Clark!" "Hey, Joe Montana!" My cousins even got autographs. I envied their being so close to the action.

The game was exciting, decided in the final seconds, though I had no strong rooting preference. More memorable were the odysseys of entering and leaving the Pontiac Silverdome. The trek in, undertaken with thousands of fellow fans like infantry on a forced march, was a frigid mile-long journey from a distant parking lot, over icy highway concourses bordered by chain link fences topped by razor wire. I could hardly believe how many people slipped and fell around me. And after the game it took an hour to leave the stadium, with the only means of egress being four revolving doors. Four revolving doors for eighty-one thousand fans! For Mom and Dad, it was the final straw, definitive proof that the event had been botched. (The Super Bowl would not return to a cold-weather site for thirty years.) But it was a memorable and mostly fun experience for us youngsters.

Super Bowl XVII – Washington 27, Miami 17 – at Pasadena

This was the year I was lovesick, so I don't remember the game at all. Frank, on the other hand, was thrilled to see his favorite team finally win the world championship.

This time, our guests were Mr. Alofs and his son. The fathers did their best, taking us to a number of well-known tourist attractions that did not impress me. We went to a Wild West town, where saloon doors whacked me on the way out; we panned for gold and found sand; and we saw Knott's Berry Farm. By that point, I'd had enough: while the others bought jam, I found the nearest bench and began the book my English class was reading. I was being a pill, but at least I was keeping up with homework, and in a small way I was communing with my unrequited crush, Gilberte, back home. We may have been three thousand miles apart, but perhaps we were reading the same words.

My most vivid memories of the trip were the hours spent driving California's highways in the rental car, listening to pop music. I'd just received my license, so it was debatable whether I should have been at the wheel – but the music was driver's choice. So I played the songs then climbing the charts, which I can't hear today without thinking of California and Gilberte. Every hour I heard "Africa," by Toto, which was okay; but my ears were more attuned to the latest songs by the British "New Romantics":

> *I have danced inside your eyes*
> *How can I be real?*

and

> *Straddle the line in discord and rhyme*
> *I'm on the hunt, I'm after you*

and

> *When your world is full of strange arrangements*
> *And gravity won't pull you through*

and even

> *The mist across the window hides the lines*
> *But nothing hides the color of the lights that shine*

One night while Dad was at the wheel, Frank in back, and I was in the passenger seat, I rolled the window down for some cool night air. The night sky was blanketed with stars, and I thought again of Gilberte. On the station Frank had selected, I heard:

> *Dream of a girl I used to know*
> *I closed my eyes and she slipped away*
>   -   Boston, "More Than a Feeling"

A few power chords later, my heart was toast. I asked the stars, the same ones shining over Gilberte, if she was watching. Was there a way to make her feel what I did – I don't mean *how* (that was too much to ask), but *what*? If I could make her sit still a moment and listen to these songs, would she hear what I heard, the promise of a new world? What if I made her a mix?

I didn't think: "Jeez, *Boston*. What a cliché." I'd already forgiven my heart.

Super Bowl XVIII – Los Angeles Raiders 38, Washington 9 – at Tampa
Super Bowl XIX – San Francisco 38, Miami 16 – at Stanford

Super Bowls began running together. I don't remember much of the one following my eighteenth birthday. With the game's popularity continuing to soar, Grandpa Hines no longer received complementary tickets, so upon arrival in the host city, Dad would find a scalper, buy tickets for his sons, and find a bar to watch the game on television.

The Stanford game was played in a vintage 1921 horseshoe-shaped coliseum reminiscent of Princeton's Palmer Stadium. Heavy rain a day earlier had turned fields used for overflow parking into a motocross course; cars churned up mud, spraying it everywhere. As we headed in to the stadium, Frank and I were handed padded seat cushions blazoned with the Super Bowl logo -- once we reached our seats, we realized why. The seat numbers on the old wood planks didn't even face the field. I didn't know it then, but this was the last time the Super Bowl would be played in such spartan surroundings; it was getting too big for that sort of thing.

Super Bowl XX – Chicago 46, New England 10 – in New Orleans

Our second trip to The Big Easy was less memorable than the first. Grandpa Hines joined us this year, so I guess he scored tickets one final time.

The game, a slaughter, was most memorable for its laughable denouement, the falling into the end zone of William "The Refrigerator" Perry, a 380-pound rookie, who scored the Bears' final offensive points. My other memories of the trip happened afterward. The first was the theft of Grandpa's wallet from the rear pocket of his jeans as he stood at a urinal, after the game, in a makeshift facility outside the stadium. He didn't know his pocket had been picked until he rejoined us. We went with him to file a police report, and then we drove him to his hotel.

I better remember our return home. Dad, Frank and I left on Monday morning; late on the first night, approaching the North Carolina border, Dad asked me to find a campground for the night. That was Mom's job when I was a kid, but I was happy to step into an adult role. I extracted the yellowing, tattered *Woodall's* directory from the passenger door pocket and found a listing that we would have begged to stay at when we were kids. It was loaded: swimming pool, shuffleboard courts, arcade, and more. Now, feeling like a beleaguered adult trying to keep to schedule on a dreary late January evening, I directed Dad to Heritage USA by cross-referencing the *Woodall's* against trusty old Rand McNally. We turned down a long and stately entrance road, and for a seeming eternity passed Christmas trees lit in every color of the spectrum, though the holiday was long past. I had a nervous foreboding, rechecked the guide book, and cleared my throat:

"Um, Dad, I think this is some kind of Christian campground."

We looked at one another, weighing the inconvenience of finding another campground against the discomfort that each of us felt in these surroundings. We made a U-turn before reaching the welcome center. I later learned that Heritage USA was Jim and Tammy Faye Bakker's private Disneyland.

The next morning, we stopped briefly at the campus where my high school classmate Laura was attending college. Dad and Frank cooled their heels while Laura showed me around campus. We compared notes about music (she liked the new album by Mister Mister) and movies (I wanted to see *This is Spinal Tap*), and college. Near the end of our walk, flurries began to fall.

Back on the road, driving up Delaware Route 13, we noticed that the southbound cars had their lights on, despite the sun's having reappeared. Was it a funeral procession? I turned on the radio to learn that the Space Shuttle Challenger had exploded.

Super Bowl XXI – New York Giants 39, Denver 20 – in Pasadena

The last hurrah, and I had the satisfaction of going out on top. My favorite team, the Giants, were crowned champions for the first time.

Two weeks earlier, Clay and I had saw first-hand the Giants' systematic dismantling of the Redskins in the NFC Championship Game. At its finish, I was colder than I ever hope to be again, but it was worth every icicle to see the 17-0 freezeout, followed by the spectacle of the Giants' three-hundred-pound nose tackle, Jim Burt, climbing into the crowd to lead an impromptu celebration of the faithful. As Clay and I finally struggled to our feet and then walked toelessly to my Chevy Nova which was parked in the most distant lot, we reviewed what a glorious day it had been.

In contrast, the Super Bowl, despite the result, was an anticlimax. My abiding impression is one of fatigue. Neither Dad, Frank nor I were enthusiastic about Los Angeles, where we stayed with Mom's college roommate, Anne. Instead of seeing the sights as a family, Frank hung out with Anne's daughter and I borrowed the yellow pages to chart a trip to every record store in a ten miles radius. My solo excursion, a series of blown turns and wrong-way driving, confirmed to me that L.A. is an interminable, formless, ugly sprawl. Even its record stores were lackluster, though I did manage to find a hitherto unknown Martha and the Muffins album.

I think that was also the trip when Frank mowed down a row of garbage cans when he backed our rental car too quickly down an alley.

What was once thrilling had run its course. I had changed, but so had the Super Bowl, which was now a multimedia event directed at the casual television viewer, not the true fan.

***

The year I was fifty, the Super Bowl should have been L. Except that it wasn't. The league's marketing department, feeling that a single "L" wouldn't be recognized as a Roman numeral, went with "50."

The following year, "L" made a comeback. The NFL just can't let go of Roman numerals, which is crazy. It's as if they want to convince us that today's game, which is all about touch, timing and analytics – utterly unlike the game I'd fallen in love with as a child – was still gladiatorial combat, and thus in need of macho, militaristic Roman numerals. One editorial nicely punctured the pretension: it said the NFL should stop "living a LII."

And this year, for the first time since I was too young to care, I completely ignored the game. That's not easy in today's wired world, where Super Bowl Sunday has assumed the status of a secular holiday. Instead, Carol and I dialed up classic football movies – *Brian's Song, Heaven Can Wait, The Longest Yard* – to honor the game as it was, or as Hollywood thought it was, at least. The stories were entertaining, despite or perhaps due to the odd casting choices: Eddie Albert as a sadistic prison warden? Warren Beatty as a quarterback? James Caan, *The Godfather's* Sonny, blubbering? But it was much more fun than watching another Patriots' Super Bowl win. And at halftime, I revived Dad's old tailgate recipe: sausage, onions, and peppers on hoagie rolls. Since Dad never wrote down his recipes, I made Rachael Ray's. It's always harder than you think to recreate the past.

Alone Again (Untruthfully)

> *In a little while from now*
> *If I'm not feeling any less sour*
> *I promise myself to treat myself*
> *And visit a nearby tower*
> 　　　　- Gilbert O'Sullivan, "Alone Again (Naturally)"

I'm in love with a seventy-two-year old Irishman with flaming red hair. Fifty years ago it was an infatuation; now it's the real thing.

He goes by Gilbert. Actually, Gilbert O'Sullivan – a preposterous name that I should have assumed from the start was assumed from the start. Gilbert, who adores wordplay like I do, would have liked that sentence. And though it may be unwise to assume faith in someone with an assumed name, especially one that's a terrible pun on the Victorian operettists whose work still burns the floorboards of high school stages, I want to believe. So, to find out about my crush, I did what any suitor does today – I turned to the internet.

There I discovered that "Gilbert" is a stage name. Having learned this, and Gilbert's place of birth, I put his biography aside, loath to knock the bloom off the rose. And so all I know for sure is that he was born in Waterford, Ireland, with a surname of O'Sullivan. Everything else I need to know is in my right brain, where the music plays.

When I was young, one could not avoid his big hit, "Alone Again (Naturally)." It played on the big speakers of our living room hi-fi, on the tinny dashboard radio of our motorhome, and later on the spherical, bright blue Panasonic transistor radio (with tin keychain) that my Aunt Ro gave me one Christmas. I always kept this radio tuned to one of New York's hit AM stations, WNBC or WABC, where I would hear "Alone Again" between rockers and disco grooves, though it neither rocked nor promised a good time. All it had going for it was a plangent melody and poignant lyric that starts sadly, going downhill from there:

> *And climbing to the top*
> *Will throw myself off*
> *In an effort to make it clear to*
> *Whoever wants to know*
> *What it's like when you're shattered*

This young music fan didn't hear the meaning of the lyric, just the sounds of the words and the catch in the singer's voice. Nor did I distinguish between singer and songwriter: if the lyrics were sad, the singer must be. I *did* know that the song had reached number one on the pop charts and stayed there for six weeks. Surely, success must have cheered Gilbert O'Sullivan?

Later, I heard the words. A man dumped at the altar. A father's death. The wasting away of a heartbroken mother. Finally, the loss of faith in a God who would permit such suffering.

But the song went to number one!

And it was always ready for another spin when I was a teen. I never owned it on vinyl, but I listened whenever it came on the radio. Its melody had a stately, logical, distilled despair. Either Aaron Neville or Allen Toussaint – one of those New Orleans bluesmen – when asked what song he would have most liked to write, chose "Alone Again." That attests to this sad little pop song's versatility.

On a day of my fourteenth year, I heard the song again on the plastic radio/cassette player that lived for years on our kitchen counter. I was drying dishes when Mom walked in the room, seeking something. When the song ended, I mentioned the story behind the song: that the singer, Gilbert O'Sullivan, was so heartbroken despite this big success that he abandoned his music career and become a recluse. Mom agreed that was sad, found what she was looking for, and left.

Humbug!

That brief exchange, rescued from a sea of oblivion, still rankles. My words felt true, but how could I not hear the lie within them? Was I merely parroting misinformation I'd taken on faith from a radio jock? Did Dan Ingram, to fill ten seconds before a commercial break, tell a lie that he never suspected a young fan would repeat to his mother?

Maybe I just needed the story to be true.

I was a serious boy. To improve my mind, I read what I didn't know. When not reading, I listened to music, usually upstairs in my room. I vanished so often that Dad called me Lamont (Cranston), after the man of mystery from the old-time radio show, *The Shadow*.

For a short while, I read the Bible. At my request, Dad took me to the short-lived Christian bookstore at the far end of the Penny Press strip mall so I could buy my own copy of the good Book. (Our family didn't own one, nor did we attend church.) I chose a leather New

International Version. Dad may have wondered at my sudden interest in religion. He wasn't against it, but he detected in me a tendency to see the world in black and white.

Another evening, under the lintel that separated our kitchen and front hall – I stretched to touch it, luxuriating in my newfound height – I casually asked Mom and Dad about the meaning of the passage that says, "It is easier for a camel to go through the eye of a needle than for a rich man to enter the kingdom of God." They were on the spot, but they answered diplomatically, showing me an ambiguity where I hadn't seen one. They needn't have worried about me. My becoming an ascetic was never in the cards. But that was the same kitchen where I had told Mom the lie about Gilbert O'Sullivan. I had implied that I knew his life story, though I didn't know him from Adam. I didn't even know his real first name! Why this need to make a hermit of a singer?

My guess is biology. Teens are hardwired to challenge parental beliefs. My parents believed in the American Way, that hard work brings success. So I mustered counterexamples. Jesus rejected wealth to serve God, and Gilbert O'Sullivan – or so I wanted to believe – believed that success was nothing in a world where parents die, women leave, and God does nothing. To remind Mom of life's unfairness, I presented Exhibit A, "Alone Again (Naturally)."

I had a happy childhood, but I'd read enough novels and heard enough love songs to know that things don't often work out, that people don't generally follow the Golden Rule, and that hard work isn't always rewarded. There was a distinct possibility that I would fail. Maybe that's why I wanted a Bible, as a hedge.

But about Gilbert's future... well, as the Beatles put it once, I should have known better. The next year, he returned to the top ten with "Clair," a breezy little tune about his niece, the only hit song ever about babysitting. I should have asked myself, what sort of hermit babysits? I still don't know why the part of my brain that knew of "Clair" failed to inform the part that wanted to believe that its singer was a recluse.

***

Forty-five years on, I know better. On the strength of an online review, I bought Gilbert O'Sullivan's 2015 album, *Latin à la G*. It was his eighteenth album -- not bad for a hermit! I then worked backwards, listening to his albums in reverse order, including imports that had gone unreleased in the United States. As I became familiar with his oeuvre, I pieced together the puzzle of his life – slowly, as one reads a compelling book, to sustain the suspense.

Latin à la G's cover photo has Gilbert facing the camera in a black shirt, its collar buttoned His arms are interlocked with those of two young toreadors in suits of light, their backs to the camera. Not until I opened the liner notes did I see the same picture from the other direction – the toreadors are, in fact, women. The notes explain that the cover is a tribute to Peggy Lee's album *Latin ala Lee!* (a personal favorite of Gilbert's), which won the 1960 Grammy for best album cover. Peggy had enjoyed the company of two male consorts, so Gilbert – who later collaborated with Ms. Lee – believed turnabout was fair play.

I looked closely at his other album covers.

Gilbertville, which preceded *Latin à la G*, has Gilbert alongside a highway, leaning on an upright piano, thumb raised, looking for a lift. *Piano Foreplay*, the album before that, shows a beautiful redhead of a certain age standing naked behind the same weather-beaten piano, which screens her charms from the lens. And on *Sounds of the Loop*, an album in which Gilbert experiments with loops and samples, a piano keyboard doubles as a UPC code.

It was clear, looking at his back catalog, that the piano is a key motif. Liner notes again to the rescue: Mr. O'Sullivan explains that he specially commissioned his piano from the only manufacturer willing to build a custom model tuned exactly one semitone low, to better accommodate his vocal range.

I missed, as I tend to do, that technical detail the first time I read it, but think about it for a second: you sit at the piano, depress a key, and get the note to its left. Black notes become white notes, and most white notes go black – the entwining of life's light and shadow. Dad's critique of my personality had been misguided, as had been my initial appraisal of Gilbert O'Sullivan.

> *Critics of all expression*
> *Judges in black and white*
> *Saying it's wrong, saying it's right*
>   - Joni Mitchell, "Shadows and Light"

Another Gilbert album, *Every Song Has Its Play*, is a self-penned musical in which the singer-songwriter reviews his career. Finally – as Paul Harvey would say – the rest of the story! The songs describe an apprenticeship at the hands of an unscrupulous manager; an unexpected success; and the good fortune to find a producer sympathetic to his goals. Finally – I hope this is in jest – he describes a current manager's suggestion to stage his own death in order to boost record sales. How ironic would that demise be in light of the effect that "Alone Again" had on me all those years ago!

All Gilbert's albums are worth hearing. His warm baritone voice complements any melody, and his melodies are so pitch-perfect that I hardly care what they're about. All his talents are on display on his brand new album, released last year, simply entitled *Gilbert O'Sullivan*.

Nothing in this world quite fills me with hope like an artist who has found a way to make a career of art regardless of the vagaries of fame and fortune. Though he's seventy-two, Gilbert's muse never left him. He loves the biz. And he's an obliging interviewee, all smiles in photographs. Most unascetically, he has surrounded himself with musicians who consistently bring his creative vision to life.

His most recent album contains a book of photographs. In them, his face seemed strangely familiar. Then the resemblance hit me – it was my own grandmother in *her* seventies! That pocked, wrinkled smile, warm as an overcoat.

It looked at me and said, "It was just a *song*!"

What's more, one of the few sad songs he's ever written.

Game Six

We haven't had that spirit here since 1969.
  - The Eagles, "Hotel California"

    I'm writing this in late October, 2018, a date smacking of science fiction. Baseball still exists, and I like it despite the changes that have turned it into something that would have seemed alien to my young self. But (most) games are still nine innings, bases are still ninety feet apart, and the Red Sox and Dodgers are still around. As I write, Boston leads Los Angeles in the World Series, two games to zero.
    This World Series reminds me that in my high school graduation speech of 1984 (the first futuristic sounding year of my life), I promised that the Mets would become world champions. I gave no timeline, but by October, 1986, two years had passed, and my promise was feeling stale. I was on the hook.
    Not that the Mets weren't getting close. In 1984, they led their division until July when the Cubs, led by ace pitcher Rick Sutcliffe, overtook them. (I still recall Sutcliffe throttling the Mets one Sunday as I listened unhappily on the kitchen porch to my transistor radio.)
    1985 was more excruciating. I tried my best. With my high school classmates John and Mike, I arranged a trip to Chicago's Wrigley Field to see a three-game series just before the All-Star break. Somehow, I talked Dad into lending us the motorhome for the trip. We motored to the Windy City with a minimum of preparation, and when we got there, I realized there wasn't a campground nearby. So we did the unthinkable: we parked downtown in the heart of the Miracle Mile, in a completely vacant parking lot directly behind the *Chicago Tribune* building. It was empty because the newspaper was on strike, and in retrospect I can only assume that both management and labor thought the motorhome was a security checkpoint. We stayed three nights, improvising mammoth games of handball off the *Tribune* building's several hundred foot high brick wall.
    Thanks to heroics like these, we kept the Mets in first place until mid-September. They were in a footrace with St. Louis' twin speedsters, Vince Coleman and Willie McGee, who between them must have outrun a hundred ground balls that summer. I shared Dad's distaste for those

rabbits, and how they used Busch Stadium's artificial turf to their advantage, pounding choppers into a parched, sunbaked field where the thermometer reached one hundred twenty degrees; the high hops took so long to fall from orbit that infielders had no chance. The final straw was the afternoon after class when I drove home from college with my roommate James to see a pivotal Mets-Cardinals contest that went the wrong way. (James thought my baseball mania curious; like most Southerners, he preferred college football.)

But in 1986, the Mets bolted from the gate: they left their competitors in the dust, winning their division by a staggering twenty games. They had jelled into a powerhouse – strong at bat, strong on the mound, strong in the field.

The Mets were yet another reason (I have documented the others elsewhere) why I took a year off from college. That summer and fall, I lived a double life – by day, mild-mannered word processor for Metropolitan Life Insurance Company; by night, rabid Mets watcher.

Mets games were carried on television by WOR, Channel 9, the employer of my cousin Karen's husband, Dan. Like his eponym, Dan was dapper. Whenever I saw him at my aunt's, he looked like he'd just come off the golf course, having broken par but not a sweat, Izod alligator on a pastel-colored shirt: tangerine, lilac, chocolate chip mint. Aunt Ro, knowing I adored the Mets, informed Dan that he would have to get me tickets to the playoffs and – if they made it that far – to the World Series.

On the first count, Dan came through. I had two tickets to the first Shea Stadium playoff game in thirteen years. It was played on a Saturday afternoon, so there was no need to call in sick, and as a bonus, I could take my little brother Danny, then in third grade. I introduced Danny to more than one of the finer things in life: I'd made him a music fan by playing him nonsense tunes like They Might Be Giants' "Chess Piece Face," and now I would make him a life-long baseball fan.

> *Train up a child in the way he should go,*
> *And when he is old, he will not depart from it.*
>   - Proverbs 22:6

We found our seats in the upper deck on the first-base side, and were barely in them by the time the Astros grabbed a 4-0 lead. In the sixth, the Mets evened things on a Darryl Strawberry home run. When the Astros regained the lead in the top of the ninth, it looked bleak, but in the home half, Wally Backman electrified the crowd with a leadoff bunt single. (Ah, for the days when players tried to do something other than hit home runs!) With one out and Backman on second, up stepped Len Dykstra, the Mets' bratty centerfielder, who connected with a Dave Smith fastball. The ball soared toward the right-field fence as the crowd surged to its feet. Knowing Danny had no hope of seeing, I lifted him atop my shoulders; he saw the ball land in the bullpen, a home run.

Mets win! *Gloria in excelsis*! Dykstra circled the bases, and at home plate he was mobbed by teammates jumping in place, up and down, up and down. His arms were raised high, his batting gloves stained with dirt, ready to high five everyone in sight, even those – relievers, coaches, bench players – who had donned dark blue jackets to ward off the late afternoon chill. Dykstra's expression was that of an eight-year-old, like my brother: more than anything, he seemed to be in shock, as if to say "I can't believe I just did that!" (in a postgame interview, he could liken the feeling only to Strat-o-Matic heroics), mixed with concern that his feet might not find home plate in the tangle of his teammates'. I know all this because I'm looking now at an autographed picture of that moment, which Danny gave me last Christmas.

I went back to MetLife. Four days later, the Mets nursed a three-games-to-two playoff lead. That afternoon, I was so eager to watch what might be the deciding game of the series that I am impressed even now that I didn't blow off work. I seemed to be treating my entry-level job like a career, but more likely, I went out of pure superstition, assuming the Mets would lose if I didn't honor my commitments. Not until I rushed from the office to my Nova in the side parking lot did I learn what was happening. Turning the ignition, I clicked the AM preset, and heard the roar of the crowd: Dykstra – him *again* – had led off the ninth with a triple to set things in motion. The Mets trailed 3-0, and a loss would mean facing Houston's ace, Mike Scott, the next day – not a happy prospect – but Dykstra had given the crowd hope, and as I took back roads to prolong the trip, the Mets scored three times to send the game into extra innings. There was no need to have rushed, it turns out. It would be hours before the Mets prevailed in the sixteenth inning, to earn a World Series berth.

Their opponent would be the Red Sox, the team that hadn't won it all since 1918, as James Taylor's grandmother knew so well. They'd be hungry, but so was I. I couldn't wait for the Series to begin, and would have loved to see a game in person. But how?

I can imagine the scene at my aunt's house, in her hardwood kitchen with the long center island, the home's true hearth, where Aunt Ro and Barbara, her long-time live-in maid, discussed the day's events, and Dad would pop by for a visit and a bite to eat. In my mind, I see Karen coming in, and Aunt Ro putting the screws to her – telling her that Dan would have to come through again with tickets. It wouldn't be easy.

I called John, my friend and fellow Mets' fanatic, with whom I'd whiled away many a high school evening in the parking lot of the Summit 7-Eleven drinking Slurpees while we listened to our boys. John, who unlike me planned to finish college in the standard four years, was beginning his junior year at Carnegie Mellon. We agreed that although the World Series opened in New York that weekend, we would try for Game Three in Boston on Tuesday night. I would drive to Pittsburgh on Saturday, where we would watch Games One and Two on television; then we would drive nine hours across Pennsylvania and New England to fabled Fenway Park, the cozy bandbox home of the Red Sox.

Saturday morning, I started with autumn in my rear window. To enhance the scenery, I shunned the Pennsylvania Turnpike and took its older twin, Route 22. From that two-lane road I had my fill of hay ricks, red barns, hex signs, and horse-drawn wagons, but I hadn't considered the downside of backroad travel, which is how long it takes to get places. Interstates are designed to be straight shots, but backroads aren't designed at all. Like coastlines or Proustian sentences, they twist and turn so often it takes twice as long to follow them.

By the time I neared Pittsburgh, it was dark and had begun to rain. My maps were useless in a dark car, and since John and I hadn't agreed on a meeting place (my plan was to drive to Pittsburgh, find Carnegie Mellon, then ask for directions to his fraternity), I reevaluated. Just before first pitch, I checked into a motel in the small town of Mars, and flicked on the TV. For three hours, against a backdrop of chintz, linoleum, and polyester, I agonized over a tense and ultimately dispiriting 1-0 Mets' loss.

The next day I reached John, who'd been puzzled by my non-appearance. He directed me to his frat, a large house that had probably been nice once. Near a grimy side entrance reminiscent of the back entrance to the Widow Brown's, empty beer kegs were stacked high.

I stepped into a living room full of yard sale furniture and one large television. John introduced me to some of his "brothers," all of whom had a hundred pounds and several inches on him: John, it seems, was the only non-athlete in an athletic fraternity. I was amused at how they treated him like their weird kid brother, the one who knew algebra.

I watched Game Two in their living room. Dwight Gooden, the Mets' ace, got knocked out early, and the Red Sox won going away, 9-3. To add insult to injury, I had to sleep in a room smelling of stale beer. The radiator heat made it uncomfortably warm, and it was impossible to orient myself on the short sofa. After hours of tossing and turning, I got up at five o'clock to walk the campus until dawn.

On Monday, John attended class and the Mets (and I) got some much-needed rest. First thing Tuesday, we hit the road for Boston in the Nova. We traveled by the seat of our pants, with no plan other than to find Fenway Park. By mid-afternoon, we claimed a dubious parking space a few blocks from the field, then followed the crowd to the stadium.

Having more experience in these matters than I, John started things by hypnotically repeating in a low bass voice the words, "looking for tickets." It was as if Mission Control were trying to establish radio contact with astronauts on the dark side of the moon, without letting the aliens (cops) know. Soon, John found his quarry. Or should I say they found us?

> *I once had a girl,*
> *Or should I say, she once had me?*
> - The Beatles, "Norwegian Wood"

Three dudes – older, taller, and stronger than we were – asked us to follow them around the corner and down an alley, away from prying eyes. They asked John how many tickets he needed, then named their price. I had a fair amount of cash in my pocket, but not that much! John talked them down, and soon we had, for two-hundred fifty dollars each, two genuine (we hoped) ducats for seats just past first base, down the right field line. For me, that represented a lot of word processing, but I was happy, at least, to be assured of admission. With the gates still an hour from opening, we milled with the festive crowd.

At one point, someone called out to us, asking if we had a minute. A local television reporter had seen our Mets' caps, and wanted to know our story. How had we gotten to the game? Where did we get our tickets? Pleased at our own ingenuity, we told the unvarnished truth, with no qualms about revealing the tickets' cost.

"Really?" he asked, with a raise of the eyebrows.

It dawned on me that we'd overpaid.

But it was worth it. One's first view of a major league field from the concourse tunnel is always a sight to behold, but Fenway's emerald green was stunning. Dazed, I followed John, more practical-minded than I, down a long aisle to our seats. Yes, they were past first base: in fact, they were much further down the line than our sellers had advertised. And when we got there, we found that they did not face home plate but third base, far in the distance, necessitating an awkward shift to take in the action.

As was his wont, John headed went for refreshments. I was still in a daze, but not just because I was *inside Fenway Park*. On the way to the seats, I had seen a familiar face. It belonged to a young woman in a gray pullover sweater with black lettering that bore the name of a small New England college, Trinity, a name that was vaguely familiar.

It took me a minute to place her. Finally, I did: it was Elizabeth, my first crush, whom I hadn't seen since fifth grade, when we moved away from Morristown. Was that her? She had Elizabeth's face: apple dumpling cheeks, fair skin, sincere smile. Even her ringlets of hair were as I remembered. I knew it was her, though I'd hardly glimpsed her on the way to my seat. Now, waiting for John to return, I craned my head down the aisle we'd just walked, but could not see her.

The game began. Len Dykstra – *him again!* – led off with a bang. He took a cut, lofting a fly down the right field line, near enough to make us rise from our seats before it tailed away to our left, nearer the infield. Foul ball. I sat down and sighed: a home run would have been a nice start. Then I turned to the field and saw Dykstra rounding first, head down, jogging for second. The crowd was stunned. I turned to John for an explanation.

"Home run!" he yelled.

Open-mouthed, I took my bearings. I fixed my eyes on the point where the ball had landed, then looked for the foul pole, Fenway's famed Pesky Pole. It was much further along the grandstand curve than I expected. I suddenly realized that not only were we "past first base," we weren't even on the right field line – we were in the outfield bleachers, and that was a home run!

I had no wish for a refund, not after the Mets won going away, 7-1. After a two-minute celebration, John and I set our minds to the next pressing problem, lodging. We discussed our options as we threaded through the disappointed crowd, Mets caps still on our heads, to the Nova. We got in, drove west, and stopped at a couple of motels. Each was booked solid, and at the second, the desk clerk said:

"You won't find a vacancy this side of Worcester."

So John, who had an early flight from Logan Airport, mooted the only possible solution: we'd sleep in the car. We drove to the airport, picked a random parking garage, and found a space. John took the reclining passenger seat, and I slept in the back seat. For the third straight night, I slept all folded up.

The next day I drove home alone. Already exhausted by the time that I reached the Massachusetts Turnpike, I forgot to apply the brakes at the tollbooth: fortunately, the eighteen-wheeler in front of me had a percussive rear bumper. I struck it and my car rebounded like a pinball. I came to and belatedly applied the brakes. The driver of the truck at the tollbooth opened his door, leaned out of his cab, and cast a confused glance back in my direction. I waved. Annoyed, he shook his head and got back in.

It was a relief to watch the next two games, which were also played in Boston, from the comfort of my parents' living room couch. The Mets won game four to tie the Series, but lost game five, putting themselves in a bind as they returned to Shea.

Then I got a call from Karen – Dan had come through! I had two tickets to the seventh game – if the Mets won Game Six, that is.

On Saturday, October 25, the Red Sox were one game from ending their seventy-year drought. I settled in to watch the game in the living room, which was quieter now since Frank had left for his freshman year at the University of Washington and Dad was on a hunting expedition (a rarity for him!) with his friend, Lou. I watched with Robbie and Danny, and Mom occasionally looked in on the action. Robbie was the one with the vested interest: if Game Seven happened, she would go with me.

There's no need to recount this well-documented game, but I can attest that when the Red Sox took a 5-3 lead in the top of the tenth, Robbie bolted. She stomped down the hall and slammed the door to her room. Since Mom had retired, just Danny and I were left to keep the faith, joined by our toy fox terrier, Mookie, named after the Mets centerfielder. (He patrolled center field, I mean the area by the sofa, for stray pretzels.)

I wanted to disappear too, but Danny was so engrossed in the game that I could not. Also, I was "scoring" the game on two large poster board panels, documenting each pitch with a method of my own design, one that requires a half-dozen differently colored magic markers. I couldn't very well leave the bottom of the tenth inning blank, so I stayed on task. Those posters would grace my bedroom walls for years.

The Mets rallied after staving off a defeat that was, time and time again, just one strike away. When they finally prevailed on a deviously twisted cue shot struck by the human Mookie under the glove of first baseman Bill Buckner, it was bedlam: Danny and I pogoed, yelling our heads off; Mom and Robbie appeared ("What happened?"); and the canine Mookie, confused by the noise, stood on his hind legs and barked without cease, his yelps reverberating through the house. This went on for a full two minutes while the Mets celebrated on the field and Vin Scully, the veteran announcer, turned his microphone off to let the crowd tell the story.

A half hour earlier, Dad and Lou were following the game on the motorhome radio, pulling in a staticky North Dakota AM station. When the Red Sox took their tenth inning lead, Dad told Lou to turn it off: in sympathy with me, he didn't want to hear the Red Sox win. But later, still driving, Dad turned on the radio and heard a sports talk show. The hosts were previewing Game Seven. After a moment of confusion, he realized the Mets had won.

"I don't believe it!"

The next night, Robbie and I prepared for our rendezvous with destiny. I was worried about the Nova, which was having one problem after another. Only my friend Clay, an automotive wizard, stood between it and the junkyard. Still, it was our only ride.

When we arrived at Shea Stadium's parking lot, a guy approached.

"Sir, I'm going to have to give you a citation."

That old ruse! I told Robbie to ignore him; it was an appeal for a charity that had been pulling the stunt for years, ever since I first started driving to Shea. To be fair, it was one of those annoying traditions that over the course of years had become endearing, so in retrospect I'm surprised that I didn't make an exception and donate that night, if only out of superstition. We must have been too eager to get to our upper deck, right field seats. (This time they were located as advertised.)

And then the Mets fell behind, *again*. Boston scored three times in the second, a lead they held until the middle innings. The crowd was restless, but they'd seen their team come back too many times to be despondent. I thought of the Nova in the big, floodlit parking lot. I had pushed it hard for a week, driving to Pittsburgh and Boston, and it was having trouble turning over. Perhaps, if we left now, we could avoid the worst of the traffic and baby it home. I said to Robbie:

"Come on, let's go."

She wouldn't hear of it; there was no way she was going to miss a moment so long in the making. I shrugged my shoulders -- what else could I do?

Of course, after the Mets rallied to win, 8-5, I was glad to have stayed. Robbie and I high-fived and celebrated with the crowd, who stayed on a long while, not wanting the season to end. We waited until most of them had filed out before we made our way to the car.

It didn't start.

But down our row, I spotted a tow truck operator jumpstarting another car, and he promised to be right over. He was in a good mood, as were the tens of thousands of folks around us, the biggest aggregation of happiness I have ever seen. He jumped my car, I gave him a hefty tip, and Robbie and I drove off into the night, world champions.

You have reached the end of Side A.
To listen to Side B, please turn the book over.

Side B
(Strawberry Fields Forever)

You are at the beginning of Side B. To listen to Side A, please turn the book over.

How to Play Guitar

I had a dream that we were rock stars
And that flash bulbs popped the air
And girls fainted every time we shook our hair
- Prefab Sprout, "Electric Guitars"

Guitar requires dexterity, persistence, and a musical ear. If you have two of three, you still have hope.

In my youth, the only instruments I played – briefly – were the piano and the recorder. The recorder was fifth grade: everyone in Miss McCormick's music class played one. My pipe, of shiny brown plastic, came in a velour drawstring bag. We played "Frère Jacques" and a few other songs, but I had trouble coaxing melodies from its holes. Woodwinds would not be my path to glory.

Piano was even earlier. I dreaded the lessons my parents had arranged because, first of all, I disliked practicing, and second, they hurt my small, seven-year-old hands. Despite Nana Edie's bold maternity ward prediction of future talent (for more on that, fast forward to "My Body," later on Side B), I found it painful to stretch for chords. My last lesson consisted of convincing Frankie and Robbie to hide with me behind the living room sofa as Nana repeatedly called my name, waiting with the instructor in the front hall. Eventually, the instructor left.

Then, for years, I renounced performing. I wasn't tempted. Mad for a hundred bands, I was a firm believer in the twin economic principles of division of labor and comparative advantage: leave music making to the pros and sit back to enjoy the fruits of their labor. The Beatles were better attuned to my own heart, anyway, than I could ever hope to be.

But for Christmas of my senior year of high school, when I was feeling kind of blue, Mom and Dad tried to encourage me with an acoustic guitar that they had bought in the small music shop in downtown Madison. It wasn't on my holiday wish list, nor was music making on my mind, but I was grateful. I promised to take lessons.

I had some catching up to do. My younger brother Frank had a head start, having taught himself monster riffs on an electric guitar that he channeled through a fearsome amp. (Maybe that's why Mom and

Dad bought me an acoustic.) Every so often, our bedrooms' shared wall would shake to the sound of Frank plodding through the introductions to Ozzy Osbourne's "Crazy Train" or AC/DC's "Dirty Deeds Done Dirt Cheap," or Rush's "Limelight":

Dah dah dah dah dah, DA DA DA DA!

Soon my digits awkwardly fingered the easy "cowboy chords." But it's not enough to swing the bat – you have to follow through. Within days, my fingertips sore, I put the guitar back in its hard case and stood it in the corner of my bedroom closet. From time to time, retrieving something or other, I saw it standing there. It offered no recriminations and harbored no grudges. It was just biding its time.

***

I went to college, leaving the guitar. I came back home and ignored it. Back to school, back to work, back to school, back to work. The guitar stayed put. I finally decided to finish school as a math major at Montclair State while living with my grandmother in nearby Roseland. Since I was now making good on old promises, I picked up the guitar one weekend in Madison. I pulled its matte black case from the closet, opened it, and removed the instrument.

Some gifts take years or decades to unlock. Mom and Dad must have sensed, long before I, that I would enjoy playing guitar. Or perhaps they'd simply drawn a conclusion based on the amount of time that I spent listening to music.

It had been so long since I had held my guitar that I didn't even remember what it looked like. I lifted it and observed its classic Les Paul concert-shaped acoustic design: three metal tuning pegs either side of the neck; four brass and two steel strings; fretboard, back and sides of chestnut wood; a light wood front; black plastic finger plate and bridge. Inside the sound hole, I read:

Yamaha FG-410
Made in Taiwan
Republic of China

At about this time, Nana returned from a day of thriftshopping with a gift for me, *The Complete Guitar Player Songbook*. Since she frequently misjudged the sort of thing I might like, at least when it came to pop culture, I initially viewed it with skepticism.

The book's crudely-drawn cover art depicted a gathering which, had it taken place, would have been historic. Musicians' heads appeared in ranks, as though they were sitting in the bleachers at a Rock and Roll Hall of Fame reunion. I knew them all: Dolly Parton and her teased blond up-do; John Denver and his granny glasses; Billy Joel and the skinny tie he wore in the video to "It's Still Rock and Roll to Me"; Elton John and his rhinestone goggles; Buddy Holly looking like Elvis Costello, but with boxier glasses (was rock bad on the eyes?); and a gentle woman with long, straight, dark hair whom I took to be Joan Baez. Finally, front and center, disproportionately larger than everyone else, was Paul Simon, sporting a slight resemblance to Charles Grodin. They all looked me in the eye as if to say, "You can do it too!"

Unimpressed, I opened the book. The flyleaf was splattered with first names and phone numbers, including one for "Arlo." (Guthrie?) The book's one-time owner was an "o-filler" (to borrow a word coined by Jimmy Stewart's character in *Mr. Smith Goes to Washington)*, having cross-hatched each one. Turning to the table of contents, I saw that the songbook was in fact a compendium of four earlier publications. The compiler, and the arranger of many of the traditional folk songs, was a Russ Shipton, of whom I knew nothing. (Even today, an online search yields little.) But thanks to Mr. Shipton's song selections and simple arrangements, this would be the book to inspire me to take lessons.

I chose a music store in an anonymous East Hanover strip mall on Ridgedale Avenue for no reason other than its proximity to Sorrento Bakery, the purveyor of a pastry that to this day remains my all-time favorite: two large toasted hazelnut cookies cemented with a thick layer of smooth hazelnut cream and dusted with enough confectioner's sugar to explode upon first bite in a massive powder cloud. Nana and her maid Ella used to buy them for me, but they'd recently stopped patronizing the establishment for a reason I never completely understood, because the one time they discussed it in my presence, I was too distracted to listen --

One morning before class, I was eating breakfast. It was winter, so Nana made me Cream of Wheat, which she claimed would "stick to your bones." She cooked it on the stovetop as thin as whey, then poured it until the meniscus met the serving bowl lip. It was now up to Ella to ferry the bowl across the kitchen without spilling it. She would walk extremely slowly, carrying the bowl in both hands, but some would invariably spill and prompt her to mutter beneath her breath, "Jesus Christ!" At the kitchen table, I would pretend not to notice and await her arrival. I had told her many times to carry the saucepan to the table and pour the cereal there, but she never took my advice.

While I ate, Nana talked of the old days. (She had already eaten her breakfast – coffee and a buttered Thomas' English muffin.) Had I only written down those stories! She told of the brief time that she had a desk job, her only one ever, as a sort of clerk. But she could not sit still, nor could she handle being "cooped up" inside, because it "bored her stiff." She admired my ability to do that, but she never could.

She talked of bygone family businesses. There was a pasta shop where a variety of shapes were hand cut, and she cranked the spaghetti through a pasta machine. If memory serves, that business failed in the Depression. There was also, I believe, a family liquor store. That was later, when brother Eddie ("Hotshot" per the *The Baseball Encyclopedia,* or "Uncle Ed" as I knew him in retirement, when he talked incessantly of his glory days) played second base for the Detroit Tigers. Eddie arranged for in-store visits by players such as Johnny Vander Meer (still the only major league pitcher to throw consecutive no-hitters), but they had to be kept on the QT; then, unlike today, baseball feared associations with liquor and gambling.

One year, after the major league season, Babe Ruth brought his "barnstorming" team to Paterson to earn some extra cash. (This was a time-honored practice, and Major League Baseball looked the other way.) Nana saw Ruth take on the local semi-pros, the Paterson Silk Stockings, named in tribute to Paterson's leading role in the manufacture of silk. Can you imagine a team today called the Silk Stockings?

Nana got another look at the Babe when Eddie made the majors with the Chicago Cubs, who faced the Yankees in the 1936 World Series. Nana saw Ruth "call" his famous home run before he hit it (still a subject of debate to this day, though she swore she saw it with her own eyes), and befriended many of the players' wives on the train to Chicago. At Wrigley Field, they were given the worst seats, but far from letting that dispirit them, they cheered lustily for the Tigers. That elicited boos, but the fans cut it out after an enlightened partisan explained they were Tigers' family members. Again, imagine that happening today!

But I cut Nana's stories short in my hurry to get to the Student Center cafeteria to study for morning classes. Since I also had evening classes, I frequently missed her on my return. She would have retired to the bedroom above the kitchen, from which the sound of her rabbit-ear bedside TV boomed. If it was Thursday, I'd recognize the voices of *Cheers*, a show Nana loved because she had lived it: at Dad's restaurants, she'd welcomed diners, bantered with barflies, and kept in the thick of the fun – the polar opposite of the secretarial career she had never pursued. Nana also watched *Cheers* because my sister Robbie went to Boston's Emerson College, and occasionally to the Bull and Finch, the model for the *Cheers* bar. So, when Nana told me that she looked for Robbie in the restaurant booths on *Cheers*, I laughed – then stopped short, unsure whether she was kidding.

The morning in question, the conversation was more mundane. Nana and Ella were rehashing their dispute about the amount of change due them on a twenty-dollar bill at Sorrento. Ella had complained so vociferously that she, or she and Nana, had been banned from the store. Or perhaps they'd just been sufficiently insulted to no longer wish to go. I left for class before sorting it out.

***

I took lessons at the back of the store, in a small space screened off by a heavy curtain. My teacher was a heavyset classic rock fan on middle age's far shore. I went a few times. Through him I purchased *The Complete Beatles Songbook*, from which I played a few songs. I still have the book, but don't refer to it much, since the arrangements are more complex than those in *The Complete Guitar Player Songbook*. I can still see, though, my teacher's occasional handwritten notes – mainly strum patterns. I got as far as making the chords to "Eight Days a Week" recognizable, but that's it.

A year later, I got the bug again. But rather than find a nearby teacher, I turned to the *Star-Ledger* classifieds and found one in Peapack. Peapack! That village near the terminus of the Gladstone Line was then so romantic to me: a bucolic glen, not just a pocket park for the landed gentry. That's where I should learn to play guitar, I told myself. I threw my Yamaha in the car and drove to my first lesson.

The idealization of place has always blinded me. Girls from upper-class, semi-rural towns, or villages with horse farms, like Harding Township, Basking Ridge, or Lamington, were instantly infused with the bouquet of mystery. Similarly, Princeton's sylvan campus seemed the ideal place to cogitate. All I required was a scenic view: if I could raise my eyes every so often from the page to gaze through a window at a forest, or sidewalk strewn with autumn leaves, I would be able to penetrate any scholarly abstraction. (Unfortunately, Mount Katahdin would not have sufficed.)

I found the guitar teacher's home in the one part of Peapack that was not scenic in the slightest, a ramshackle house near the train station. I parked out front, and walked right into a domestic quarrel being conducted in Italian. A middle-age woman on the phone finally noticed me standing at the screen door, which she jerked open, yelling to a back room:

"Nonno! Your guy's here!"

A white-haired gentleman appeared in an interior doorway. He wore a jacket and tie, and motioned me inside with an index finger. I walked into a bedroom that could hardly accommodate me and my guitar, and whose only window faced the tracks. The bed being the only place to sit, I sat down there, and for the next hour worked through a couple of songs in *The Complete Guitar Player Songbook*. That proved difficult because I had trouble hearing my strumming over an excited backyard dog and shouts from the kitchen.

I felt sorry for the old man, who didn't seem to be held in particularly high regard. I assumed that the cash that I'd hand him at the end of the lesson would go straight to rent. And because of the noise and distraction, I couldn't hear much of what he said, not that the little I heard was particularly useful. He seemed only vaguely familiar with the concept of rock and roll.

But I do remember the moment when he lifted the guitar from my hands and seamlessly played a melody in the classical style, some old Spanish folk song, perhaps a composition by Segovia. While he played, he smiled and his eyes assumed a faraway look, perhaps focused on his youth; then he returned the guitar with a flourish as if to say, "That's how you do it!"

***

Another year, another try: my senior year of college, I cracked open the case again, carried my guitar downstairs to Nana's parlor, and opened *The Complete Guitar Player Songbook*. Once again, I marveled at how the guitar stayed in tune: it was as though Mom and Dad, knowing how long it would take me to master it, had bought me the one enchanted self-tuning guitar in the world. With a smattering of notation gleaned from self-study and a few lessons, I teased melodies from the book into the air, as I had long ago teased a drawing of the Lindenwold mansion from a blank sheet of paper. (This is explained in Side A's "Sing We Now of Christmas!".)

Whoever he was, Russ Shipton had a sense for enduring melodies. His selections were now the new standards, the extension of the Great American Songbook to the folk and electric guitar singer-songwriter era. Despite occasional missteps ("Maxwell's Silver Hammer"?), the foremost popular songwriters of the 1950s, 1960s, and 1970s are represented by their best work.

Here and there, I found an hour to practice. My chords got cleaner, and I began stringing necklaces of melody, each note a bead. I played without a metronome, so I arrived at some notes early (most late), which made them sound better upon their arrival. There are few pleasures more edifying than the precise impact of the infinity of harmonious overtones on an eardrum attuned to hear them, resulting from the vibration of a guitar string. It's purer than speech. Rendered haltingly, without vocals or harmony, the songs in *The Complete Guitar Player Songbook* sounded more melancholy than originally intended, as though they'd been transposed to an instrument that no one plays anymore – harpsichord, barrel organ, the antique player piano in Nana's parlor. When I played them, trippy "Mellow Yellow" became plaintive, and melancholy "Mr. Bojangles" sounded downright lachrymose.

> *A winding tune on an old banjo*
> *You heard when you were small*
> *Still goes on for us all*
>   - The Lilac Time, "And On We Go"

***

Time for a confession. This chapter's title is tongue-in-cheek. I never got proficient on the guitar. On the other hand, I've never stopped trying. Recently I bought a second guitar, a solid body electric with a cool sunburst finish, to keep my acoustic company.

(Why do I struggle so to recall the word "acoustic"? I was racking my brain again for it now, like that time in the high school lobby when I was trying to describe the bridge of the song "Der Kommissar" to Wesley, a fellow classmate and musician: "It's played on um... a *manual* guitar." That made him laugh.)

But I keep going back to the Yamaha. It never fails to amaze – a slight turn of the pegs, and it's ready to go. It never needs new strings, or any kind of adjustment. Then I extract *The Complete Guitar Player Songbook* from the back of my closet, and I find that I can play those songs as well as ever. (Admittedly, not that well.)

Nowadays one learns online, so I purchased a course from a cheerful instructor at the University of Colorado who spends half of each lesson talking about the history of the guitar. Based on the course reviews, this annoys many students, but I like it. I was never in a hurry to get good.

Finally, wanting more than a virtual teacher, I looked for a flesh and blood one nearby, preferably one with common influences. I've had mixed success. Cape May is home to many musicians – many who play in cover bands for tourists, some who even perform their own songs – but few teach. I called up one sixty-something hippie, a local legend who plays blues, fusion, and other far-out, heavy stuff, but he didn't call back. Perhaps he could hear in my voice the sound of *The Complete Guitar Player Songbook*.

Then Dave, a youngish guy, opened a music shop ten minutes from my house. In my most concerted effort yet, I studied with him for several months, unfortunately without much improvement. Dave is a good player, but I believe our age difference got in the way, and in a way opposite to that of my earlier teachers. For someone so young, he knows a lot about sixties and seventies rock, but next to nothing about the music popular during my youth -- power pop and new wave -- which greatly influenced me. Conversely, a band far past my time, the Red Hot Chili Peppers, influenced him. *Tempus fugit!* When I made the mistake of bringing *The Complete Guitar Player Songbook* to my first lesson, he turned the pages diplomatically, but later kidded me about "my beloved James Taylor."

Malcolm Gladwell wrote that expertise requires ten thousand hours of practice. If that's true, I have nine thousand, five hundred to go. But Gladwell also said that practice must be *deliberate*, specifically targeted at weaknesses. That may set me back to ten thousand, because my bead-stringing isn't deliberate, at least not in Gladwell's sense. But I like stringing beads, and will continue to do so, uncoiling melodies through the repeated rearrangement of my fingers into the G chord's curly bracket, the F's ladder, and the A major seventh's arrowhead.

I have always drawn things out. Besides, the anticipation of pleasure always outstrips its attainment. The perfect spring day falls accidentally in January, and the giddiest Christmas gift arrives in an early November daydream. Happiness is best felt in the future, and best understood in the past. In the here and now, it isn't pleasure at all.

For now, I'll continue to play and dream of the day when I can finally say, "I'm a guitar player."

-

Radio Days

For a while, I was a disc jockey. It was the realization of a life-long dream that I didn't even know I had.

I was on WCFA, a low-power FM (LPFM) radio station in Cape May. LPFM stations were first licensed in 2000 by the FCC for the use of educational, non-commercial organizations, and operate at an effective power of no more than one hundred watts. WCFA runs at eighty-three. That's dimmer than a bright light bulb – or a bright deejay – but on a good night, eighty-three watts can take you ten miles up the coast, all the way to Stone Harbor.

The studio was in Cape May, but the antenna was a few miles away, in Wildwood Crest. Such separation is not uncommon. Here's how it worked: deejay at the studio console speaks into a microphone dangling from a boom arm; wires transmit the deejay's digitized voice and music through a soundboard, then a laptop; software streams the signal to the internet.

Then, in Wildwood Crest, a laptop in a shed streams the signal from the internet; its output wire runs through other boxes (one generates Emergency Alert System announcements, another ensures the signal is within operating specifications); another wire runs out the shed, across a lawn, and finally up the side of a municipal water tower to a non-directional antenna that beams it to old-fashioned radios in homes and cars everywhere – or at least as far as weather conditions permit.

I had a thing for the transmitter shed, as I once had for the valets' booth at The Springfield House, my father's restaurant. (Turn to Side A, "Inventory," for more on that.) Though it's just a prefabricated closet on a fenced-off spit of town property, it's a conduit for magic. And like the proverbial Pauline, it's in constant peril: the equipment inside can fail in summer heat, winter cold, hurricanes, storm surges (the shed *is* on an unprotected barrier island) and electrical outages. The antenna atop the water tower has a limited life, and when it requires adjustment, a professional must scale one hundred feet of rungs. The shed is dusty and littered with equipment, wires, and manuals and logs that should be tossed, but never are. Yet, for me this space inspires as much romance as a cathedral, since its only reason for being is the expression of the human spirit.

When I was a disc jockey, it was a kick to hear myself on the radio. This was possible when my show was rebroadcast. It took a while to get used to hearing my radio voice, pitched a major third higher than the one I hear inside myself. It isn't the *basso profundo* of a classic deejay, but it works. During my show's early days, I would invite Carol for a spin on Saturday nights to hear it, and see how far it carried. We'd drive up the Parkway, then turn toward the ocean, to Wildwood. One winter night, we were the only ones driving in that desolate town, its Doo-Wop hotels shuttered for the season, their neon signs extinguished. The only signals in town, other than the one crackling from our car radio, were blinking amber traffic lights that had been turned into pendulums by gusts off the ocean. But my radio voice was warm and loud as it ushered forth into the world the music I had to share with my audience – which that night was only Carol and me!

As for the studio in downtown Cape May, it was in no danger of an *Architectural Digest* photo spread. To riff on the expression "a face made for radio" (a reference to DJs' typically poor looks) our studio was made for radio. It did not resemble the MTV living room set that I had closely studied as a teen, the sunken parlor of a particularly well-to-do family, its wall-to-wall carpets carefully shampooed and vacuumed each night. I loved my MTV, but now I know that looks and character are generally inversely related. A studio should be small, dim, and cluttered with as many CDs, microphones, wires, and consoles as needed to get out the signal -- everything else is a distraction from the goal of messing with listeners' minds.

The studio was small, maybe ten by twelve. Two windows faced an alley, though one could barely see through the dingy slats of broken blinds permanently lowered against the sun, the rain, and the fire station across the street, which sprang into action at the most inconvenient moments, usually when one was live on mic. (The studio, needless to say, was not soundproofed.)

The walls were papered with posters, flyers, and memorabilia advertising long-past concerts and events. On one wall, nine vintage 45 RPM records were thumbtacked in a square pattern to a thin felt board. Another felt board was covered in newspaper clippings, obituaries of deejays who had died before I arrived. Yellow and dusty, they recalled the pilots' lounge at Edwards Air Force base, as seen in *The Right Stuff*, where a wall was dedicated to photos of test pilots who had died in the line of duty, before the lounge itself was consumed by fire.

I particularly liked broadcasting at night, alone, when the building was deserted. (By day, the station's nonprofit parent ran a small business office in adjacent rooms.) I was the late-night jock leading faithful night owls on their nocturnal flight; I was the spiffy "nightfly" DJ on the cover of Donald Fagen's first solo album; I was the captain of the pirate radio brig moored off Cape May -- I was "Johnny Wavelength," my larger-than-life alter ego, testifying to fellow music heads.

What I wasn't, was broadcasting to many people. Maybe two, maybe a dozen, listeners still trawling the megahertz with old-fashioned "terrestrial" radios. There was no way to know, because WCFA, being a small operation, couldn't afford the services that measure those kinds of numbers. Every local I had ever asked, had never heard of us. God spared a Sodom of ten virtuous citizens; I was willing to broadcast to just two listeners, and didn't even care if they were virtuous.

As a child, I conflated deejays with the songs they played: I assumed that each played the music he or she liked, and that the only reason they were on the air was to play their favorite songs.

I am a deejay, I am what I play
I've got believers in me
        - David Bowie, "D.J."

I have always loved sharing music. It's an intimate congress: better than book clubs, better than adjacent seats in a dark theater. Sound sets fancy free in ways images cannot, because ears do not discriminate like eyes, leaving the eyes, unencumbered by image, to follow reactions – eyes in a concert hall, bodies on a dance floor – an impossibility in media requiring visual focus. To pierce the ears is to mainline the mind. Steer a friend, a musician, a woman you want to wow to an easy chair, and play something: does the unexpected key change arch an eyebrow? The witty rhyme turn up the mouth? The angelic harmony shut the eyelids?

Beginning in high school, I made mix tapes – curated collections of songs on audiocassette – for musicians, friends and girls I wanted to impress with my sensitivity. I spent days auditioning, sequencing, and recording sounds that spoke for my soul. It was part art (as much as the actual music making, so I told myself), and part science. Regarding the latter, I needed quality audio components: receiver, turntable, dual tape deck, and speakers that let me not only monitor the recording but lose myself in its creation. I acquired them, one by one, from audiophile shops in Morristown, Morris Plains, and beyond, stores that went belly-up when music jumped the digital divide. The final piece of the puzzle was a two-track mixer from Radio Shack, which enabled crossfading of songs.

Like lovemaking to an insatiable partner, mixmaking pushed aside all other considerations. It left my bedroom a wreck, floor strewn with vinyl I was too distracted to put back in album sleeves. Oblivious to the rising heat in my room (I'd forgotten to turn on the air conditioner), I would work myself into a lather; my head full of music, I would forget to eat and drink. The only thing that mattered was getting the mix right, and in those analog days of real-time recording, a single mistake at the tail end of a cassette could mean a forty-five-minute re-do, unless I could salvage the glitch with an overdub.

I never won the girl's heart, but I tried. Each time I began certain that this would be the one, the mix to open her ears and synchronize our hearts. As the sun blazed through my dusty windows, I had dilemmas to resolve: Would an instrumental set the right mood? Or should I come charging out of the gate with the big hit? Where do I put "Six Weeks in a Leaky Boat"? Should "Everyday I Write the Book" precede or follow "My Ever Changing Moods"?

On one mix, I placed "Shaking Through," a buzzy, gauzy folk song on R.E.M.'s *Murmur*, in the same location on Side B of my cassette as it occupied on side two of the original album. That filled me with pride. It confirmed I had a producer's ear, a knack for sequencing. It also brought to mind something my cousin Donna had said, that I could script incidental music for the nightly news. That sounded like a horrible idea. I would rather work for Mitch Easter, the genius R.E.M. producer; apparently, he agreed with my judgment as to where "Shaking Through" should fall. But its false ending and backwards-tracked instrumental coda raised another question: should I include the coda on the mix?

After the girl returned my cassette without comment, I determined that she'd stopped listening right after the false ending but before the coda. How I read volumes into that! She must have especially liked that song for it to be the last one that she had played; in fact, by deliberately leaving the cassette in that position, she was telling me so. The strange thing was, I thought "Shaking Through" was about losing one's virginity (though determining what Michael Stipe's lyrics *were*, much less what they were *about*, was hard), or at least the pains of adolescence. The girl had left the cassette in that exact spot because she empathized. At the same time, by foregoing the instrumental coda, which seemed to undercut the song's feeling, she was casting a vote for sincerity and honesty over the difficulty of art.

I made mixes for people I hardly knew. At my first professional job, in Manhattan, all it took was for someone to mention music and I was off to the races: I'd submit a cassette for their approval on Monday. My taste nonplussed nearly everyone. One plain-faced young woman liked my mix enough to invite me to an outdoor lunch at a café on the plaza of the World Trade Center, but unfortunately her attention wandered incessantly to more interesting coworkers. A junior actuary, a tall dude who considered The Who's *Live at Leeds* the apotheosis of rock and roll, was underwhelmed by my mix's quieter moments. Another fellow gave my mix a guardedly positive review, saying that the songs "cut, but didn't bleed." And a fourth recipient, a junior manager, returned my mix with the cryptic comment that it sounded like "heavy metal elevator music." Music for heavy metal elevators?

Two years later, having left that job, I spent a winter in an unheated loft above a friend's garage in central Maine. Of course, I brought my stereo, and one day, drawn to the face of a checkout girl in a Yarmouth health food store, I was inspired to another mix. She and I had never spoken (other than "thank you, here's your change"), and I did not know what kind of music she liked, if any; but for several weeks, each time I returned to the store I carried a mix tape in my coat pocket. She never heard it, because she had left for a new job. But I was undaunted. My soulmate, whoever she was, would hear what I heard in music.

I later had a career building mathematical models for insurance products. People who are old enough – those who remember the 1960s and 1970s – will recall the phrase "computer dating," the fad of using computerized algorithms to predict human compatibility. (The models still exist, but not the phrase.) Should I ever build a compatibility model, I would prioritize two things – pets and music.

Pets are a must. Lovers of cats cannot truly love those who lack a feline affection gene. When I first visited Carol in her fifth-floor Hell's Kitchen walk-up, I immediately introduced myself to her cats Harley and

Dylan; I rubbed the outgoing one (Harley) on his head and clucked shy Dylan out of hiding. In this way, I instantly surpassed Carol's previous beau, Jay, a college professor and by-the-book libertarian who, like our recent President, is predisposed against God's simpler creatures.

Carol told me about Jay. He visited her apartment after a vacation in Greece with a gift bottle of ouzo, which he placed atop a small table in her galley kitchen. As they talked in the next room, Dylan, egged on no doubt by his older brother, jumped on the table and nudged the bottle, inch by inch, to the edge, until it crashed to the floor. Carol and Jay ran to the kitchen to find two very curious cats and an overpowering smell of anise! Jay was livid, but Carol laughed at the irony of this bottle, coddled a quarter of the way around the globe, meeting its demise at the paw of her kitten. Somehow Carol knew that had it been *my* bottle of ouzo, I would have been laughed with her.

Music, that other indicator of compatibility, also linked us. The summer we met, I played her my music collection. One album was *Flood*, the recent release by They Might Be Giants, a Brooklyn band that took its name from a movie in which George C. Scott plays a millionaire who believes he is Sherlock Holmes. The band specialized in ditties which, though absurd on the surface, contained pearls of wisdom. (Not everyone agreed with this assessment. When I played the band's debut album in my car to my musician friend, Elyssa, as we navigated postgame Mets' traffic, she heard only the absurd and requested something music.) For three years, They Might Be Giants had built an enthusiastic local following, and with *Flood*, they had a major label deal. They appeared on *The Tonight Show*, and I had the sublime experience of seeing them accompanied by Doc Severinsen and his band as they performed their new single, "Birdhouse in Your Soul," a strangely poignant song told from the point of view of a nightlight.

Carol so loved *Flood* and its follow-up, *Apollo 18*, that upon her return to school, she made them her first selections from the Columbia House Cassette and Record Club. She played them all semester, prompting her roommate Susanna, who didn't "get" the band, to hazard a guess that Carol must like the guy from summer school more than, say, Craig, the guy upstairs who blasted the Spin Doctors, a campus favorite, loud enough to rattle their radiator. At least you could dance to the Spin Doctors! Susanna reasoned that if Carol had liked Craig, she would be playing the Spin Doctors. But she had it backwards. If Carol had opted for the Spin Doctors, she would have preferred Craig to me.

***

At Princeton, my roommate James and I loved music. James had a show on the campus radio station, WPRB, which had one hell of a signal: at 14,000 watts (more than 100 times WCFA's power!), it could be heard on a good night as far north as Blairstown and as far south as Vineland, throughout western New Jersey and a bit of Pennsylvania. (On Sunday nights, I could even pick it up at Nana's house in Roseland.)

James hailed from Alabama. Though a football recruit, he wasn't much bigger than I. He retired from the game after freshman year, so he no longer weighed in regularly on the clubhouse scale, but he did keep his habit of lifting his shirt and patting his belly fat to see if he had put on weight. His chief extracurricular interest besides his campus girlfriend was music. A singer and guitarist of adventurous taste, he brought from home a square milk crate full of albums that were new to me but which later became firm favorites: Winston-Salem's dB's; Marietta, Georgia's Guadalcanal Diary; and San Francisco's Game Theory, the last of which became an obsession. James also started a band called the Noise Petals: a name simultaneously soft, loud, and psychedelic. If you look a bit, you can still find their one and only album in the stacks at the Princeton Record Exchange.

Our first semester, James joined WPRB. Unlike many college radio stations, it was a presence on campus, listened to and esteemed. Staffed by students and alumni, there was a spirited competition for time slots. As the new kid, James was stuck with the "graveyard shift," midnight to four a.m., one night a week.

Being early to bed, I never saw him leave for his show, but I can picture it now: he searches myopically for the thick-rimmed eyeglasses that lent him a professorial look like his doctor/father back home. He carefully selects a few albums to play from his milk crate, which will supplement the ones that he will choose from the station library. After resoundingly slamming the door to our suite (I do not wake), he turns, descends three steps, and steps outside through the old wood entry door. He walks across the Mathey College commons in the dark, that gentle, nearsighted former footballer, shoulders perpetually hunched, as though still bucking up against linemen. Treading the crackly, frosted grass that had been flattened by students taking shortcuts, he walks past the still-lit mullioned windows of the "grinds" who might actually listen to his show, then passes beneath a Gothic arch into neighboring Rockefeller College, past a row of manicured hedges (vegetable architecture unseen by seemingly all but me, who valued the peace they brought to our campus corner), then down the four steps to WPRB's unmarked studio entrance.

Occasionally, between classes, I accompanied James to the station to examine the record library. It was divided between floor-to-ceiling shelves in the studio itself, and the more voluminous shelves down the hall in a glassed-in room. WPRB was influential enough (and college radio had become a significant enough economic force, thanks to the burgeoning indie rock scene) to receive scads of promotional albums. I pulled one after another from the shelves, and wondered at band names that ranged from the bizarre to the profane. To each album was affixed a mimeographed form listing song titles, with check boxes beside each; the program manager or deejays would indicate which songs to feature and which not to play due to FCC regulations, and jot down comments. I admired a station with a staff who cared enough about music to do that. Some comments were miniature essays, true labors of love. One writer, eulogizing Laurie Anderson's *Big Science* (fast forward to the next chapter for more about her), had attached a supplementary sheet and even taken the time to thank Warner Brothers, the major label that had taken a flyer on a complete unknown whose music sounded like no one else's.

One day, after looking over the current station faves (led, that week, by the Dead Milkmen's "Bitchin' Camaro"), I suggested that James play "Sink with California," by the Canadian band, Youth Brigade. I liked how it began wobbly and slow, a demented, ridiculous, plodding march, then erupted into frantic punk. Its lyrics – at least, the ones I could decipher – were a comic book ode to international youth living in a world without borders. James said he would.

The next morning, over a slow, signature bowl of breakfast cereal, James told me that while he played the song, he thought he had heard an obscenity. Was there one, he wanted to know? I had no idea. Back then, there was no easy way to find out. I was amused that my roommate was actually concerned that I had landed him in hot water. How innocent it all seems in retrospect -- it's as quaint as a turntable technology itself. Today, a quick online search confirms that "Sink With California" does indeed contain the F-bomb, not that anyone listening to WPRB at three a.m. on a winter's day in 1985 would have noticed or cared.

Another time, from the outside of the plate glass window separating the studio from the entrance hall, I watched an ancient rite. A deejay slowly lowered a record on turntable two, which was not yet turning. Dropping the stylus to the beginning of a track, he lowered his ear to the platen, turning it counterclockwise until he could no longer detect any unamplified vibrations. (Oh vinyl, we miss you! Your heft, your scent of warm oil and plastic, the fun of spinning you before digitization offered instant gratification!)

Through the monitors in the hall, I heard the record the deejay was playing. He was the resident expert on British folk rock, so I suppose it should have come as no surprise that he was playing a modern take on an ancient border ballad:

> *And they will turn me in your arms into a naked knight*
> *But cloak me in your mantle and keep me out of sight*
> - Fairport Convention, "Tam Lin"

Many summers later, the year after we met, Carol and I saw Fairport Convention perform this very song at the Bottom Line, a venerable rock club near New York University. But this was the first time I heard it, and I was wowed. When it was over, and the "On Air" sign extinguished, I popped my head into the studio to ask the deejay what it was called. He was flattered to be asked.

On WPRB, you never knew what would play next. It depended not only on the day and hour, but the mood of the deejay at the moment you raised your antenna. It might be Celtic folk, raucous punk, or scratchy old rhythm and blues. That's still true today. WPRB (like WCFA) is freeform, dedicated not to one style of music but to as many as the knowledgeable air staff feel compelled to present.

It cannot be disputed that this bottom-up approach to programming reduces listenership. Most people who still listen to radio want to know approximately what they'll hear before they hear it. Freeform stations do not deliver eardrums to advertisers, and are not programmed by focus groups or algorithms. They are curated by deejays who only want to express their individuality.

Suppose radio played the same timeworn songs *ad infinitum*:

> *Imagine a world where this was the only song*
> *And against your will*
> *You had to sit and listen to it all day long*
> *Until it made you ill*
>   - Peter Blegvad, "The Only Song"

John Cage once said that in a more enlightened future, people would look back in amazement that they'd once listened to *recordings* – musical performances that never changed. His view is extreme (I never tire of some recordings), but I understand his point. I would renounce music altogether rather than face an eternity of hits.

***

I think it was in the early 1990s (Dad was still alive) when I awoke one night in my childhood bedroom. It was late. I'd drifted off to WFMU, the freeform East Orange station that I'd taken as my own in my early twenties. My eyes slowly focused on the amber blur of the warm stereo receiver display, illuminating not only the end table it rested on but the underside of the tape deck resting upon it. My stereo components were tightly stacked, separated only by several small, square, wood building blocks that I had played with in childhood.

I had awoken to a new song, an amazing song I wanted to know better. But when it ended, instead of "back announcing" the title and its performer, the deejay began talking about a new Manhattan donut shop he liked to patronize. *What was the song*, I wanted to know? It took me a few days to figure it out:

> *Looks like I'm going to end up in this life alone*
> *Don't know why nothing grows, I'm not a rolling stone*
>   - Michael Shelley, "Think With Your Heart"

Now I understood. Michael Shelley was not only a songwriter but also a WFMU deejay. The deejay who'd played my wake-up song was simply playing it cool, not hyping his comrade. Freeform stations don't do the hard sell, but they do make you sit up and take note.

Rhiannon

In *Remembrance of Things Past*, Proust describes one young man's fascination with place names. From a few syllables glimpsed in a book or, better yet, railway timetable, the boy conjures the essence of a town from the vibrations of his palate:

> ... gentle Lamballe, whose whiteness ranged from egg-shell yellow to a pearly grey; Coutances, a Norman Cathedral, which its final consonants, rich and yellowing, crowned with a tower of butter; Lannion with the rumble and buzz, in the silence of its village street, of the fly on the wheel of the coach....

Such distillations falsify reality, but what else has a boy to go on? Years later, when the boy finally visits these places, they lack the poetry with which he once endowed them, creating disillusionment.

Proust's term for words serving as repositories of spatial poetry was "place-names." In the same spirit, I propose the term "place-song": a link between a place and a song heard there. Like a food-and-wine pairing, song and setting can resonate wonderfully.

A place-song of mine involves the Fleetwood Mac radio staple, "Rhiannon," the one that goes:

> *All your life you've never seen*
> *A woman taken like the wind*

At the edge of fourteen, I stand in the dining room of my Aunt Ro and Uncle George in their rambling Essex Fells house, which idles the years away on a large property bordered by pink and blue hydrangeas. A swimming pool and tennis court doze behind the white house on a leafy, quiet, secluded street, on a crag between Caldwell and Roseland. Connie Francis, at one time a famous pop star and now a recluse, lives down the street, as do relatives of a girl, Karen, for whom I had a crush in sixth grade. At least I think the latter is true: once I saw Karen, or someone uncannily like her, playing on the lawn across the street while I watched her from behind the heavy, light-blocking curtains in my aunt's playroom.

The dining room is white, like the rest of the house, a relic beached miles from shore, bone-dry, sunbleached, and fossilized atop a mountain. The unrelenting glare is tempered only by the off-white and pastel accents of a watercolor of a Parisian flower market hanging over the seldom-used living room fireplace. All the carpets are white, and so is the furniture. Two overstuffed living room sofas, which loom beyond the top of the two carpeted steps on which I stand, are also white. Every morning, Barbara, the housemaid, fluffs their huge, poufy cushions, white as cumulus clouds, beating them with her fleshy arms like egg whites. In the dining room, a voluminous set of shelves, also white, with light bronze chicken wire screens, borders a wall, protecting the good china. Finally, near a bay window overlooking the front lawn, an old hi-fi cabinet encloses a record player. On it, I place side A of *Fleetwood Mac*, the band's 1975 self-titled album. I move the needle to track four, and in a moment "Rhiannon" fills the room.

Stevie Nicks wrote and sang it. She was the group's gypsy, the cape-wearing one who sang incantations of love. She was ethereal, the yin to the yang of bandmate Christine McVie, though I identified more closely with McVie because she seemed more grounded, and nurturing. Nicks sang this song about an "old Welsh witch" with such abandon that it prompted bandmate and lover Mick Fleetwood to comment, "It was like an exorcism."

Exorcisms don't happen in white rooms. Sunbeams pass beneath the placid green-and-white striped awning that fronts the semi-circular drive, then through the lozenge-mullioned windows; then they play across the wall-to-wall carpet and the surface of a grand piano, the room's white elephant. I push back the keyboard cover to check – there are black keys, too. "Rhiannon," in the key of C, doesn't need them, but it's nice to know they're there.

A song about the dark arts could not have found a less welcome home. The music cabinet stood near the head of the formal dining table where Uncle George took breakfast alone each morning, silently chewing on what Barbara had prepared: bacon, eggs, an English muffin, butter, freshly squeezed orange juice. He read *The Wall Street Journal* and ruminated, in his mind already at work, oblivious to my passage through the dining room as I crossed from one end of his house to the other, down a carpeted white hall as long and straight as an airport terminal.

I'd liberated *Fleetwood Mac* (the album) from my cousin Donna's record collection, which now occupied two shelves of an obscure hall closet beneath the stairs to the second floor. Donna no longer lived at home; she had escaped to Greenwich Village to become a writer. I suspected she found Essex Fells stultifying. Her record collection said as much: for every mainstream album like the Allman Brothers' *Eat a Peach*, there was The Zombies' *Odyssey and Oracle* or Joni Mitchell's *The Hissing of Summer Lawns*, that masterpiece of suburban discontent:

> *He bought her a diamond for her throat*
> *He put her in a ranch house on the hill*
> *She could see the valley barbecues*
> *From her windowsill*
> - Joni Mitchell, "The Hissing of Summer Lawns"

That album described lonely women, trapped in high society like flowers in Lucite. But that metaphor is too showy. It would be truer to say that Donna was a hothouse flower in need of wind and rain. Meanwhile, in a dining room she rarely returned to, I heard the legend of her escape in the song of a woman taken by the wind.

But that was long past, even then. By the time I found Donna's records under the stairs, they had gathered dust enough to obscure her signatures. (She signed her albums, something I had never thought to do.)

The album *Fleetwood Mac* was now five years old. In the interim the band that had recorded it had become an international brand. And Donna was a Manhattanite: I went with my aunt one day to see Donna's apartment on Horatio Street, on a block where James Baldwin had lived, in a dicey neighborhood that would one day gentrify and become my own. My aunt had brought along two pieces of furniture in the family station wagon. On her face, I read her perplexity at how to get them up the stoop and into a charming, but tiny, living room crammed with thrift store bargains. After all, what is the point of young adulthood than to prove to one's parents that there are other, equally valid, ways to live?

Donna reached escape velocity by doing what mattered to her. She met artists who would later loom (to me, certainly) as legends. She interviewed the musician Laurie Anderson, who had recently decamped from the Midwest to join a Downtown art scene that included John Cage,

William S. Burroughs, Robert Mapplethorpe and Andy Kaufman. Ms. Anderson was a "performance artist," meaning that she incorporated interesting constraints into her performances. For example, she invented a tape-bow violin, its bow strung not with horsehair but with magnetic tape that played different phrases on upstrokes and downstrokes. (How's that for a mix tape?) Or, in "Duets on Ice," she would play violin while telling stories about the art of balance, in skates whose blades were encased in ice: when the blocks melted, the show came to a teetering halt. These ideas were interesting, but music for me has always been about the songs, and when Laurie Anderson fully devoted herself to writing them in the 1980s, the results were revelatory.

I saw in Donna the artist that I might be. The difference was that she had taken chances I never would, like moving into a roach-infested Manhattan apartment. But Donna wasn't avant-garde, not a bit. She dressed conservatively, in long dresses, and her taste in music was not crazy, something I knew from occasional asides she made whenever I brought up the subject of music.

For example, one day at Caldor's Department Store (a rare seller of music near my aunt's house) I bought an album by Martin Briley that featured a Top 40 song I'd heard on MTV:

> *But I won't cry for the wasted years*
> *'Cause you ain't worth the salt of my tears*
>   - Martin Briley, "Salt in My Tears"

I liked the cover. In the foreground, a leggy woman in fishnet stockings sits on the edge of a bed; in the background, Mr. Briley tries to surface from a lake that has completely flooded the hotel room. Donna took one look at that cover and arched her eyebrows:

"This isn't one of those weird musicians, is it?"

I was disappointed. Wasn't weird fun? Besides, when it came to that, Laurie Anderson was way weirder than Martin Briley.

I had another insight into Donna's sensibility when I brought up *The Hissing of Summer Lawns*. Joni Mitchell, initially a folkie, had moved to pop, then jazz, and then to this album, a rare earth alloy of the three. I asked Donna if I might borrow it, to tape it at home. She hesitated a moment, exactly as she hesitated whenever I asked to borrow her

French phrase books (I still have them), then agreed. When I gave it back, I called it a masterpiece. Such songwriting, some musicianship!

> *Under neon signs a girl was in bloom*
> *And a woman was fading in a suburban room*
> - Joni Mitchell, "In France They Kiss on Main Street"

My cousin nodded and said, "It's a good piece of work."

I couldn't argue. I wouldn't have used her words, but in retrospect, I see what she was getting at. I heard *The Hissing of Summer Lawns* as a song cycle about an artist trapped by conformity – which it is. And while that must have resonated with Donna (particularly Donna), she saw it through the lens of an artist trying out something new. What the album said, or meant, mattered less to her than Ms. Mitchell's staying true to her muse through a period of stylistic change. That's why Martin Briley's album, with its cartoony cover, made her second guess my taste: it undercut its own seriousness. Joni Mitchell and Laurie Anderson, in contrast, were serious artists because they knew what they were about. Although I respect my cousin's opinion, I've always been partial to artists who don't mind goofing on their own seriousness. Then again, I'd never made a gambit to move from suburban Essex Fells or rural Illinois to big, bad Manhattan to be an artist..

Despite a wry sense of humor and a penchant for offbeat subject matter, Laurie Anderson *is* a serious artist. (She married Lou Reed; one must be serious to do that.) To that point, Laurie Anderson's only studio album was the idiosyncratic *Big Science*, the one with "O Superman (Song for Massenet)," an eight-minute, twenty-one second tone poem for voice, keyboard, and tape loop that inexplicably hit number two on the British pop charts, propelling Ms. Anderson, if only for a moment, from semi-obscurity to stardom. (Staying true to herself, she soon returned to the fringes of fame.)

I first learned of Laurie Anderson via my high school classmate, Elyssa, who played upright bass in the high school band, and bass guitar in her own band, Crystal Clear. She was one of the few girls with whom I felt comfortable; she was easygoing, and took the initiative to draw me out. I think she felt it would be a good idea if I stretched my horizons, looked beyond the comforts of the classroom, and listened to something other than the bells signaling the start and end of class. She disagreed with my father's assessment about my tendency to see things in black and white -- she said she didn't see that at all.

Elyssa was complimentary about a short story I'd written in sophomore year English, which our teacher Mrs. Phillips had read aloud in class. It concerned my fear of ringing a bell that sat on the reference desk of our municipal public library, near the periodical shelves. (That fear corresponded to another fear of mine that Elyssa also knew about: my reluctance to speak on the phone to anyone I didn't know personally.) Elyssa loaned me a few records, including Ravel's *Bolero*, and a recently published experimental novel by the Italian magic realist Italo Calvino, *If on a winter's night a traveler*, which was fascinating for being a book about itself. (Half of it is written in the *second* person!)

Finally, it was Elyssa who introduced me to Laurie Anderson's "O Superman." I soon located my own copy, a twelve-inch single, at the Princeton Record Exchange, and played it on my phonograph. Its *much* more lighthearted flip side was a song called "Walk the Dog," in which Laurie alters her voice to sound higher pitched, like a young girl, as she accompanies herself on ukulele. It was the rare Laurie Anderson song Elyssa hadn't heard, or so I thought, so to thank her for this discovery, I surprised her with her own copy.

> *Well, I came home today and you were all on fire*
> *Your shirt was on fire, and your hair was on fire*
> *And flames were licking all around your feet*
> *And I did not know what to do*
>   - Laurie Anderson, "Walk the Dog"

Laurie Anderson owns another of my place-songs, "Sharkey's Day," the soundscape that opens her second studio album, *Mister Heartbreak*. To hear its lyrics now, as read by William S. Burroughs in the voice of a hardboiled 1950s noir antihero, is to be transported to the Los Angeles night when I first heard it.

I was in the home of my mother's college roommate, Anne; we were there on a family trip to Pasadena. Earlier that day, I had borrowed the rental car to scope out local record shops; I returned with *Mister Heartbreak*. I put it on the record player that sat in the room where my brother Frank and I slept. Before settling in to a groove, "Sharkey's Day" begins with a scratchy guitar played as a percussion instrument, not as a vehicle for melody. That instantly turned off my brother. Like many listeners, he was not averse to songs with odd sounds, but he disliked this strangeness calling attention to itself – self-awareness proclaiming its own otherness. He left the room while I stayed with the song through its twists and turns, drawn in by Ms. Anderson's inventive way with words and music. It is a timeworn compliment to say of a great singer that you would listen to her sing the phone book; I would have listened all night to Laurie Anderson giving directions:

> *Go straight past where they're going to put in the freeway*
> *Take a left at what's going to be the new sports center*
> *And keep going until you hit the place*
> *Where they're thinking of building that drive-in bank*
> *You can't miss it*
>   - Laurie Anderson, "Big Science"

Those words made sense in the Los Angeles where I was then lost – an interminable sprawl, an endless, self-replicating grid of arterial highways pumping the land dry. It was, in fact, the landscape I'd braved in the rental car to buy *Mister Heartbreak*.

***

Truth appears slowly. For me that was true not only of Laurie Anderson, but of a punk band called the Mekons. The Mekons weren't in record stores like Sam Goody; my knowledge of them was via a brief discography in my tattered *Rolling Stone Record Guide*, which I'd flip through as a bored teen. It listed only one Mekons' album, *The Quality of Mercy is Not Strnen*.

For years, the oddity of that title stayed with me. What would possess a band to name its first album with a sentence, one beginning formally and ending in gibberish? Without a chance to hear the music, I could only muse about the title and guess at what it meant.

Later, when I learned that "The quality of mercy is not strained" is a line from Shakespeare's *The Merchant of Venice*, it had an unexpected effect: it bathed the still-unheard Mekons' album in a different light. The last word of the title, which I'd assumed was nonsense, was in fact an intentional misspelling; the album that I had imagined to be shocking

Dadaist art had gained a new meaning. "Strnen" must be "strained" uttered through gritted teeth. It was a kind of gag: someone trying too hard to be merciful was failing miserably.

But as happened to Proust's young narrator, I was wrong again. I know it now, because yesterday I went online to research this chapter. For the first time, I saw the album cover: a chimpanzee sits at a portable typewriter, paws on keys, album name freshly keystruck on paper: *the quality of mercy is not strnen*. Meaning shifted again. The title was a play on the statistical law that, given an infinite amount of time, a monkey would eventually type Shakespeare's works. The poor fellow on the album cover with the intense expression, after a promising start, had barely missed the mark.

As had I. The Mekons were not the surrealists I had imagined, but self-deprecating bookworms, artists hoping to achieve something they'd yet to accomplish, like Laurie Anderson, or Joni Mitchell, or my friend Elyssa, or my cousin Donna. Or the chimp just aping another's work.

Art takes one strange places: from noisy beginnings, the Mekons charted a decades-long journey through country music, reggae, and folk. Three thousand miles from home, I assumed Laurie Anderson's headspace. Elyssa went to school in Ohio, and Donna followed her muse to Greenwich Village, a long way from home and *Fleetwood Mac*.

Dream Four

The fourth of seven dreams I had while writing this book.

Back to school – *again.*

I'm in seventh grade, walking the junior high hallways. My two-floor school, formerly shaped like an ice cream sandwich, now has four floors, having sprouted new stairwells, elevators, and a conference center. The halls are buzzing with teachers and students changing classes on the first day of school. As in most of my school dreams, my body is young but my mind knows things it could only know now.

In the cafeteria, I recognize a few classmates. At the far end of a long table, I sit by John; then I turn toward a neighboring bench, at one end of which sits a girl I've always liked. Every so often I look her way and sense her gaze, but our eyes never meet.

After lunch, I refer to the schedule written on the inside cover of my three-ring binder. Intermediate French.

"Intermediate?" I wonder aloud. "I've read Proust in French. There goes the curve."

But I can't find the class, and my handwritten schedule is missing room numbers. In the hall I see a girl who I believe is in my class, so I follow her. She enters a stairwell that is truly a *well* – narrow, dark, steep, windowless – and I fleetingly glimpse her face. She's aware of my presence, but faster than I am, she vanishes.

I suddenly realize that I'm barefoot (another dream archetype). I would like to fetch sneakers from my locker, but there's no time. In the middle of the ground floor hallway, there's a folding table with the room numbers that I need. I strain to read them, but as is usual in dreams – and if we only remembered this, we'd know we were dreaming – the type is too small and blurry. (I'm seeing shadows inside my eyelids.) The names of the teachers, which are in boldface, are legible, but not the small, faint room numbers.

> *I suppose that's the disadvantage*
> *Of not speaking a second language*
>   - Wire, "French Film (Blurred)"

I head for the Guidance Office, because clearly I need guidance. On the way, I pass my high school calculus teacher, Mrs. Boepple, who is speaking with another student. She waves a distracted hello. Then I pass Mayer, the only person in this dream who isn't from my schooldays, but rather my professional life.

I worked with Mayer for two years, while I was training to be an actuary. He was short, and had a congenital disorder: his thick lips and lopsided face, one half more concave than the other, gave him the hint of a smile even when he was in a bad mood. On two occasions I recall, he had a reaction to his medications while at work, precipitating seizures that sidelined him for weeks.

I changed departments, and for years I no longer saw Mayer. Ten years later, after my promotion to a managerial position, he called from out of the blue. After some brief congratulations, he asked a few technical questions that I could not answer, which amused him. Perhaps he was testing my mettle. After that call, I gave him less of my time; when I saw his name on caller ID, I'd deliberately not pick up, or answer to say I was heading to a meeting. Eventually, he stopped calling.

In my dream, Mayer is smaller than I remember, a homunculus. He's also quite ill. In my dream, I'm comforted by the thought that I previously videotaped an entire school day, so at least I will have footage of him when he was healthy.

In the Guidance Department, I see the same classroom numbers that I saw in the hall, and again cannot decipher them. At a loss, I walk through a side door into the school store, which is better stocked than the real one ever was. It resembles a university bookstore, with an array of souvenirs, paraphernalia and clothing emblazoned in Dodger maroon and gold. Then I wake.

My first thought is of Mayer, and the professional relationship we never resolved. I'm left with questions: did he consider me a protégé, though he taught me little? Did he want a job in my new unit? Was he lonely, wanting to speak with someone from the past?

Like most of my dreams of school, this one has an unfinished quality. Sometimes I return because I need one more class to graduate; other times, my whole class must graduate a second time. Perhaps these dreams stem from unresolved relationships, like the one with Mayer: my id wants a do-over. Will they continue until the day I can inform my subconscious that I have no more unfinished business?

The West Village

As a young teen, one day I glimpsed the real Greenwich Village. I was with my cousin Donna as she ran errands on Hudson Street. She picked up her professional mail at the seedy West Village Post Office; we walked by the strangely-named restaurant, Rubyfruit Jungle; then we ducked into a tiny bakery just beyond, perfumed with the luxurious aroma of hot yeasty bread and dominated by a glittering *étagère* of jewellike pastries.

Later, when I lived in it, I saw the real Village only in snatches – unexpected, privileged moments, usually before daily life began in earnest, when the sun scratched at the edges of wet cobblestones, making me think I had washed up on a European shore. From unmarked medians devoid of traffic, I saw brownstones, gargoyles, chiseled stoops and cast-iron railings, but not a trace of real estate. In the real Greenwich Village, art prevails over commerce, or at least goes down swinging.

Before our Manhattan residency, Carol and I lived in suburban Madison, New Jersey, the town in which I grew up. Our married home was a boxy, unlovely, 1920s thing, a cheap house in an expensive town. We lived there two years, long enough for me to realize how much Madison had changed since I was young. It seemed old and lonely, no longer in step. Mostly, it felt cramped. What had been vistas when I was a child were now jumbles of structures on fragmented lots, and everything was narrower than in my memories, like old school halls. New outbuildings, even whole houses, had been shoehorned between and behind spalling driveways. On my morning walk to the train station, I would pass what had once been the Prospect Street home of my childhood best friend, Clay. It no longer resembled the imposing structure that I described in *The Going Places Club*.

> *And your youth is like a dog rose*
> *Only blossoms for a day*
>   - Martin Newell, "A Street Called Prospect"

Potholes riddled streets, and sprawl had made my once parklike town into the Caldwell and Verona of earlier decades, with one difference: it was full of frustrated Type As who couldn't quite swing the mortgage for a shorter commute from posh Summit and Short Hills.

Carol couldn't help but notice in brief encounters with neighbors that, like me, they'd grown up in Madison. Joanne, our neighbor to the east, was a single woman who spent more time at her shore rentals than in town. Our neighbors across the street were a single woman and her teenage daughter; the only time we talked with them was soon after we moved in, when we were all getting in our cars at once. Carol and I introduced ourselves at the foot of their driveway. When I heard that the daughter's name was Logan, I most awkwardly remarked:

"We have a cat named Logan!"

My words dissipated without further comment.

To our west lived a retired Italian couple whose surname agreed with that of a former high school classmate's. (At the next class reunion, I confirmed the blood tie with Carmen, their nephew.) They owned the empty lot between their house and ours; we relied on that patch of sunlight for tomatoes and well-being. One day, they casually mentioned development plans; the next, I went to Town Hall to examine blueprints and calculate the distance of their proposed structure to our property line. It was the exact legal minimum.

> *Our house in the middle of our street*
> *Something tells you that you've got to move away from it*
>   - Madness, "Our House"

Our house with white stucco walls was centered on a small lot, just down the street from where I'd attended sixth grade. Its pitched roof created charming but useless angles upstairs; outdated knob-and-tube wiring ran beneath the walls; and most of the casement windows didn't open, so we spent a small fortune replacing them with double-glazed ones that did. Each morning, I drained through a small spigot the rusty scale from our basement hot water heater and carried it daintily, like night soil, to the grass at the far side of the backyard, which I was either fertilizing or killing.

***

I recently revisited Madison. After walking awhile in a drizzle, I headed for the library and its comfortingly familiar grounds. On the way in, however, I became disoriented. I was looking for a brass nameplate on one of the wood courtyard benches that had become damp with mist, and came up empty. The plate I sought commemorated the father of a childhood friend who had been a library benefactor. Only on my second pass did I find it; time had nearly erased a nameplate that I had initially assumed was blank. I was saddened by this failure of infrastructure – or was it negligence? Was it a lack of will, or funds, which had kept the library from updating the nameplates? Wasn't that part of the bargain?

Downtown, chain stores had made inroads. Independent shops were threadbare. E-tail was strangling what malls hadn't killed, and residents were either too busy, poor, tired, parsimonious, or lazy to visit stores displaying posters urging people to "shop local." I tried doing my bit, but was buffeted at the first door I entered, a new bakery, by a headwind blowing from a television perched atop a refrigerator case: it was showing Fox News. Though I had nothing against the shop owners (or the person tending the store that day), the sound of the television affected me viscerally, like the cacophony of heavy metal music. The bakery mood had vanished, and I turned heel.

Madison had once let in the sun, but now its only undeveloped spaces were crowded by scraggly trees beneath transformers and high-tension lines linked to more interesting places. If it is true that all human effort is vanity, and that nature alone is capable of renewal, Madison had bet on the wrong horse.

***

One day, Carol read about an upcoming chocolate walking tour of lower Manhattan. She worked in Midtown, and I in Jersey City, but though we lived along a commuter line, we rarely availed ourselves of the City's bounty. Carol signed us up.

Fuel, in the volatile form known as chocolate, fired my desire. Instead of waiting to be buried alive in a dying suburb, one without a bookstore or café to call its own, we could ditch our pre-dawn commutes and move to the heart of the hive. With no children and only a modest need for space, we'd be good. Nothing in our basement, mostly pickups from others' yard sales, needed to follow us.

I could see us in a Manhattan apartment, maybe a small studio overlooking a cozy, sun-dappled scene of cobblestones and lampposts. I would lie comfortably on an L-shaped sofa with blue denim slipcovers, book in hand, small end table at my side bearing a half-finished box of artisanal chocolates awaiting my next selection. For furniture, we would require only bookshelves: one for the recently dispatched, one for the soon-to-begin. That, a small bed, and window overlooking a Montmartre street scene was all we needed!

I'd never thought of Manhattan as a place to live: in my twenties, it was a hunting ground. Even now, with record stores being historical footnotes, I can mentally retrace my shopping route: PATH train to Christopher Street, left three blocks, then right on Bleecker, the main vein zigzagging through Greenwich Village. In the 1960s, Paul Simon sang of paying thirty dollars a month to live there; our rent would likely exceed that, even allowing for inflation. Though Bleecker's west end was no longer the sketchy street it had been in Simon's day, it was not yet Manhattan's Rodeo Drive, when Michael Kors and a wave of upscale fashion designers converted every available storefront to eye-catching boutiques – then sold them after realizing that even as loss leaders, the receipts didn't justify the rent.

I would approach my first stop, Rebel Rebel, its windows obscured with posters of David Bowie and his followers. Peering between them to verify that the store was open, I'd ring the buzzer for admittance. Rebel Rebel's locked door policy wasn't designed to protect the owner, the customers, or the records, but to regulate traffic flow. The store, with its every cranny occupied by boxes and milk crates full of vinyl, could hold only six customers.

Year after year, the same guy behind the counter buzzed me in. Thin, of average height, with a Mediterranean complexion and dark hair that time had begun to frost at the ends, he was always listening to music at the counter, usually with a client. While I browsed, I would eavesdrop on conversations about European electronic dance music, of which I knew little. The shopkeeper would play a song on the sound system, and he and his buddy (nearly all the customers were men) would listen for ten or fifteen seconds before moving to the next. That seemed nuts to me then, but from the perspective of today's streaming world, I now recognize that it is an efficient way to sample a virtually unlimited selection of music.

But if I was looking for a particular record, maximally entropic Rebel Rebel was not the place, having too much inventory and too little alphabetization. I could have asked for help – the shopkeeper would have known at least where to search – but I did not want to interrupt him, and was wary of asking for something not cool enough to justify his time.

But my tour had just begun. On East Eighth Street, a block north of the townhouses beloved of Henry James which line the sunny north side of Washington Square, was Venus Records. On the second floor of a most un-Edwardian building, it was accessible only by an arduous set of stairs, the steepest I recall in Manhattan. I bought the first Ben Folds Five album there from a Goth gal behind the counter who paused while ringing me up to compliment me on my smile. She rarely saw them, she said; most of the customers were too cool or intense.

Venus is gone.

Subterranean Records, on tiny Barrow Street, got its name from a considerably shorter but equally treacherous set of stairs, a slippery half-flight down from street level. There, I bought They Might Be Giants' compilation album, *They Got Lost.*

Subterranean is six feet under.

Bleecker Bob's was a cultural landmark, already misnamed by the time I knew it, after its relocation to West Third Street. It featured releases by local artists, mysteries to me, in a glass display case by the register. One day, my eye was drawn to the retro design, dorky band name, and humorous song titles of a disc named *Brian Woodbury and His Popular Music Group.* I learned that the musician's wife, Elma Mayer, had drawn the schematically rendered cover art: a yellow sunflower superimposed on an eye. Songs included "The Oranges" (not about the New Jersey towns, but rather the manic, giddy feeling that's the opposite of "the blues") and "Everything's New in the Sun" (I got the joke: *in* the sun, fusion ensures that everything *must* be new). Without hearing a note of music, I bought the album, which became an all-time favorite. Fortuitous discoveries like these are rare today, when everything can be sampled and purchased online except the experience of buying. That is, not until the day when someone creates a virtual reality store in which one can shop shelf by shelf, and bin by bin, lifting and manipulating virtual records. Even then, I'm not sure.

Bleecker Bob's, R.I.P.

Several discount music shops surrounded St. Mark's Place. Top of mind, I recall Norman's Sound and Vision, Kim's Video, and Sounds, but there were others, like the tiny store near the Lithuanian Church whose name eludes me. Inside that shop, it was quiet, cool, and dark. To venture in was to travel ten years or more into the past, into a collector's lair of punk and indie records that dated to the heyday of CBGB, the famed lower East Side punk club down the street that is now a high-end clothing boutique.

From there, my sneakers guided me to other stores specializing in imports and independent releases. Two, Academy Records and Generation Records, amazingly still exist, but a dozen others do not.

House of Oldies, the record store with the tall, narrow, forbidding entrance that is famous for refusing to sell CDs, is still there on Carmine Street. In 1982, it was featured in a music video by a band called the Flirts that can still be viewed online in all its awkward naivete.

> *So I saw you in the pizza place*
> *You were with another girl*
> *Little things remind me of you*
> *Cheap cologne and that damn song too*
>   - The Flirts, "Jukebox (Don't Put Another Dime)"

To revisit 1982, just watch that video in all its Day-Glo splendor. It serves as a reminder of how amateurish – in a good way – MTV was in its early days, and how important hairspray was to my generation.

1982 was the year that I convinced Dad to drive me to Manhattan to visit House of Oldies. I needed the single of "The Breakup Song" by the Greg Kihn Band, which I'd missed during its chart run of the year before, for my next Name That Tune. (I periodically hosted competitions in which my music-mad buddies competed to identify songs and artists. Back then, just acquiring the music was a major investment of time and money!) If any store would have a year-old minor hit, it would be House of Oldies.

It felt awkward to penetrating the store -- a narrow passage, door to rear, between two long, ribbed album troughs. There was no safe harbor, no place to survey the landscape without roiling the eternal stream of collectors filing in and out of an aisle as turbulent as a waterfall pool, as loud as an aircraft carrier's landing strip.

On the left-hand wall, all the way to the ceiling, was a gallery of vintage album covers, family portraits of a nineteenth-century friend of Connie Francis and Bobby Darin. Where a drawing room ceiling would have sported crown molding, here were moldy tin tiles. Unlike oil paintings, the albums had price tags. I craned my neck to read them, but I was not a collector, and the prices gave me vertigo. The right-hand wall was crammed with shelves of 45; I wondered if House of Oldies, like that famous record collector, Joel Whitburn, owned a copy of every hit ever waxed. I hunched my shoulders and gazed at the wall, idly pawing the bins. Had I been alone, I might have lingered for hours: fortunately, Dad was there to suggest that I ask a sales guy for help.

I did, and got a stare. The Greg Kihn Band? No, they didn't have "The Breakup Song" in the store. If they had it at all (but they must!), it would be in the basement. I pictured an immense catacomb, a former Underground Railroad stop, a Prohibition wine cellar, running the length of Carmine Street. My heart sank. I guessed the salesman would have sent a runner after a rare record by Howlin' Wolf... but the *Greg Kihn Band*? Not worth it.

Dad stepped forward. He calmly but forcefully explained that he'd spent half an hour looking for a parking space so that I could get this record. The guy behind the counter dispatched a flunky, a kid no older than I was, and five minutes and five dollars later I owned the most expensive single I have ever purchased. Thanks, Dad!

Further east, at Fourth and Broadway, in a district resembling the TV images I'd seen of Beirut, beside rubble-strewn lots where dudes in makeshift stalls sold some of the world's first hip-hop cassettes, soared the new flagship location of Tower Records. Improbably enough, I'd first read about it in my grandparents' quiet living room in Puyallup, Washington. Grandpa Hines subscribed to *USA Today*, and one day in the early 1980s, while idly perusing its purple-masted "Life" section, I saw a sidebar mentioning that the California-based chain was ready to open Manhattan's biggest music store. In my solar plexus, I instantly felt a visceral excitement. I could not wait to check it out.

My music-mad friend Dave and I disembarked from the PATH train to go to Mecca: four floors of recordings in every style I'd ever heard of. Entire rooms were devoted to niche genres like folk, Broadway, jazz, and world music, and throughout the store were domestic, import, major, and indie releases. In one room was a mammoth wall of 45s, even ones that failed to hit the *Hot 100*. It was a Metropolitan Museum of Modern Music, too much to see in a day. On Dave's recommendation, I bought Squeeze's *Argybargy*, which became an all-time favorite; on another visit, I bought They Might Be Giants' debut, a platter that puzzled Dave mightily when I put it on the turntable in his family's dining room. Each time I left Tower, just before shoving through one of the perpetually revolving doors, I stopped myself and pirouetted for a copy of *Pulse*, the free in-store magazine chock-a-block with music reviews – required reading for the train home.

But wait, there's more! I learned that Tower, despite its claims, wasn't comprehensive. Directly across Fourth Street, a store called Other Music opened. True to its name, it carried music that Tower did not. My taste in music was still too provincial to appreciate what they had, but I enjoyed browsing. Like Tower, it had stacks of free publications near the door, though in this case they were strange little art zines that profiled artists who didn't give a damn whether anyone understood the art they were compelled to make. It gave me a frisson of excitement to think that between writing, music, and every other sort of art, there were *whole worlds* out there whose existence I had not surmised. It was like discovering an infinity of notes between two adjacent piano keys. And it was liberating to know that no matter how big the box, or box store, art could not be contained within; the delights I'd sampled to date might be but a fraction of what I might one day savor. Through a gap in the fog of my soul, I glimpsed a place where I, too, might one day become a holy innocent casting aside security and common sense for the sake of art.

Other Music is history. Thanks to its dedicated staff, though, it lasted longer than almost all of its contemporaries, certainly longer than Tower. A worthy documentary, *All Things Must Pass*, chronicles Tower's rise and fall, and there's one in the works about Other Music, too. For one, I'm proud that on my final visit, a few weeks before the store's unexpected closure, I bought a CD box set, a compilation of early recordings by the Cleaners from Venus.

I'm racking my brain for other stores. I once made a map for my music buddy Dean when he made his first visit from Milwaukee to

Manhattan. Perhaps I still have a copy. In the meantime, some mental jogging brings to mind Rose's Secondhand Records, Revolver Records, Disc-o-Rama, and a store on Mercer Street, near NYU.

There was also a memorable trip that I made in March of 1989, shortly after the release of XTC's *Oranges and Lemons*, an album I'd been on pins and needles to hear. That day, I escorted ten Japanese college gals into the City. Two of them, Tomie and Youko, were staying as guests of my parents through a cultural exchange program sponsored by our church. I prepared for their arrival by tackling a blue paperback called *Teach Yourself Japanese,* purchased at Kinokuniya Bookstore in Rockefeller Center. Between my secretarial tasks at AT&T, I worked the exercises, chapter by chapter. The book didn't teach the written language, but at least I'd be able to speak some phrases.

Since I knew Manhattan well, at least by Mom's standards, she suggested that I play tour guide for a day. Accordingly, one Saturday, ten gals joined me aboard a Hoboken-bound train. They enthused over the prospect of a mostly unchaperoned shopping trip, and I tried out my phrases on them. They were impressed, though I could not understand their replies: they said too much, and way too quickly.

I did admire their choreography. They did almost everything – finding seats on the train, climbing and descending flights of stairs – in lockstep. They were like the troupe of seaside girls in the second volume of Proust's *À la Recherche*: it was impossible to single out any one as a romantic interest. (There was a night, though, listening to music with Tomie and Youko in my bedroom, when Youko rose, complained of a headache, and left for the guest room down the hall, not without a significant glance at Tomie. It was probably the only time all week that they weren't together. The only result was that Tomie got to hear more of my record collection than Youko did.)

From Christopher Street, rather than take the gals on my usual route, I led them to Soho, where they were most eager to shop. I would have to content myself with just one record stop, at Tower (which the gals knew due to its strong retail presence in Japan), to buy the new XTC. To visit any other store would have been like stuffing a phone booth.

Like the Lower East Side, SoHo was waking from a long, dissolute night, like a disheveled young woman with bedhead. It ached with beauty. Photographers could – and many did – capture the quality of sunlight that bore in suspension the crumbling plaster of the ages. For years, artists had been snapping up cavernous SoHo lofts at negligible rents, but change was in the air – luxury chains were purchasing vacant buildings; racks of dresses were wheeled outside for perpetual sidewalk sales; and in vacant ground floor spaces yet to be remodeled, "pop-up" shops sprouted, long before they were called that.

I led the gals to one store after another, ladies' choice. For lunch, I could think of nothing better than my usual, so we found a pizzeria large enough to accommodate us, and ordered slices. I sat back, tired but content, idly asking about the name-brand bags the gals were toting, ignoring quizzical looks from other patrons. Then back to shopping. At one pricey boutique, one gal splurged on a winter coat, spending over three hundred dollars. Imagine! The others flocked to examine it. This gal, the one who dyed her hair platinum, seemed different; she must, I figured, be the artist of the bunch. Finally, I had a way to select one figure from Proust's seaside frieze – I immediately chose her as the recipient of a mix tape. (The others were jealous when I presented it to her!) On the train ride home, as she nonchalantly carried the coat in its box, I could see in the other gals' faces a mixture of scandal, admiration, disapproval, and worship.

***

On solo trips, I'd stop in Hoboken before boarding a train for home, to visit two more record stores: Tunes, on Washington Street (still there as I write), and the sorely missed Pier Platters. The latter had two parts, one fronting Newark Street and the other a block away, accessible by a cobblestone alley. It was in the rear store that I scored another all-time favorite album, Kirsty MacColl's *Kite*, then available only as an import.

> *Happy with your 2.2*
> *What else is there for you to do*
> *But turn and wet the baby's head*
> *And pray he will be happier than you or me*
>   -   Kirsty MacColl, "Tread Lightly"

Kite's front cover was a dramatic monochromatic image of the back of Kirsty's silvered hair, reminding me of the artsy Japanese gal.

But sometimes, Hoboken was superfluous. If I was tired or already laden with bounty, I'd call it a day. I'd grab a slice at a Christopher Street pizzeria and watch the sun set on the gleaming, oily Hudson, garbage afloat by the piers, then direct my legs down the subway steps beneath a groaning backpack of music, sweets, and magazines. Peeling it from my shoulders, I'd feel bands of sweat, the residue of the straps, cool and dry on my T-shirt. Then I'd prop the pack against a metal column and sit ninety degrees from it, my sweaty back against cool metal. I'd pop open a Snapple, exhale, and feel the throbbing of feet that had walked many miles. Eager to hear my new CDs and LPs, I reviewed their liner notes as I waited for the train. I wondered what discoveries awaited me – and my music buddies, via the mixes I would make – but in those days before instant gratification, I had to wait until I got home.

***

Like I did, Carol had New York City history.

Before she and I met in 1992, Manhattan was still for Carol a *terra incognita*, a place not to tread lightly. An old envelope of Polaroids at her parents' house in Pennsylvania – one taken at Rockefeller Center, another aboard the Liberty Island ferry – proved that her mother and grandmother had visited in the mid-1960s, before the City had developed a dangerous reputation. They'd stayed at the Waldorf-Astoria (also vanished) where, through butterfly eyeglasses, they appraised the fashion sense of its worldly citizenry. (Carol's mother revised that assessment decades later when she would come to visit her daughter.)

Carol's parents met in Cleveland, on a church outing to see *La Bohème*. Her mother wore a hefty, pear-shaped diamond engagement ring, but her fiancé, not an opera fan, stayed home. In further proof that harmony is not only part of music but that music is part of harmony, the man to her right either didn't see or overlooked the ring. He engaged her in conversation, then in marriage. A few years later, after the pair had paid off their furniture loans, Carol was born.

The year after we met, Carol graduated from college and decided, rather than go back to the strip malls of Pennsylvania, she would rent a room in a house on a small, suburban South Orange street. Each day she walked to and from the train station to take the Morris and Essex to her internship at Comedy Central, which was then headquartered on

Broadway. One day near the end of summer, I stopped by the house where she was renting, but she had yet to return from work. I carried a ring with me – a neon glow ring from the fireworks show we'd seen in Chatham the previous Fourth of July – which I slid over the antenna of her parked car. When she got home that night, she saw that her car had been lassoed. Not yet her heart.

That fall, Carol began a full-time job in the Development Office at Seton Hall University, just down South Orange Avenue. To make ends meet, she also took an evening job at the Livingston Mall outpost of World of Science. With every move she made, I was watching her, admiring her willingness to try new things and her determination to make them work. I paid occasional visits to the mall and her new apartment, in a building that housed many college students. There we watched videos like *Cinema Paradiso* (my call) and *So, I Married an Axe Murderer* (hers).

Then Carol got a break: Comedy Central offered her a position as a research assistant in Advertising. She moved to the City as quickly as she could to ditch a commute that was costing her time, money, and energy. Through a coworker, she found a rental agency that specialized in roommate placements, and they steered her to an East Thirty-First Street lodging shared by two young women looking to economize.

Curious about her latest move, I took the train one Saturday morning to the narrow, multistory townhouse that was clearly someone's investment property. While Carol readied herself, I waited on a settee in a little common room on the second floor. The TV was tuned to Bravo, which was then still dedicated to art. Since it did not play commercials, it showed short films between full-length features; and while I waited, I saw a silent black-and-white film about a day in a dog's life.

The camera panned room to room through a suburban home. The film was shot from the dog's point of view, with little of its torso visible, and never its face. Instead, there were upward-facing shots of its owners as the dog snuffled behind them, occasionally crossing between their legs. The owners were busy, paying the dog only intermittent heed. Near the end of the film, the dog settles into its doggy bed as the picture fades to black – and then, quite unexpectedly, erupts in color to the view of a windswept field of grass where the owners cavort with the dog they'd previously ignored, frolicking with it, tumbling and turning cartwheels. Remembering that today, I still get goosebumps and chills.

With her job going well, Carol looked for a place of her own. (Roommate Suzanne, who worked for a Manhattan government agency and attended therapy five times a week, had begun to flake.) But how to afford Manhattan on an entry-level salary? Through an agent, Carol found a fifth-floor walk-up, positioned snugly in the rear corner of a West Forty-Fifth street building, for $975 a month. It was relatively inexpensive because, in 1994, Hell's Kitchen had not entirely outgrown its name: the far side of Times Square was still seedy and shunned.

To call Carol's new place an apartment would be charitable; to call it legal would be a lie. Nevertheless, she made the best of fewer than four hundred square feet by paring down her belongings, erecting a wood-frame loft above her desk, and leasing a tiny rental space at Manhattan Mini Storage, where she stored her air conditioner for nine months of the year and her Christmas ornaments for eleven.

In time-honored City style, Carol ignored her neighbors. The one exception was Paul, who lived directly upstairs in an identical shoebox apartment. Carol knew he was a pianist because he practiced each day. For the first half hour he played scales, then a simple melody, always the same (Chopin's Etude No. 25), and finally, other music. Though he had occasional engagements around town, mostly private parties, he didn't earn much. He invited Carol upstairs for a glass of wine on the day she gave notice to take a new job with a large media company's information technology department, which turned out to be her entrée into the field where she found her professional footing. Carol observed that almost all Paul's floor space was dedicated to an upright piano, a twin mattress, and books in neat little stacks – the garret of a Bohemian.

One day, Carol realized that it had been weeks since she'd heard the piano. She climbed the two half-flights to check in on her neighbor. His door was ajar. She looked in cautiously and was surprised to see an empty room. Soon she learned that Paul had died of a heart attack. That was another facet of Manhattan life, where social ties are gossamer to the point of nonexistence – as with spider webs, one brushes against them, discovering later that they have been destroyed. Anonymity defined city life, which for Carol was a positive. Only in a metropolis can someone without family or history fit in as well as anyone else; as opposed to, say, a small heartland town. Or, come to think of it, a seasonal shore town like our future home, Cape May, which has more Mayflower descendants per capita than any place outside Massachusetts. Manhattan, in contrast, was – as the gyms advertised – a judgment-free zone: young, old, black, white, gay, straight, artist, square.

In 1999, the Super Bowl was on January 31. It had been three years since Dad had died, and much longer since he and I had gone to see the Big Game. I felt like company, so I paid Carol a visit, and got to see her new digs. She had a TV, but it was hard to find a place to put it where we could watch the game without sitting on top of one another. We put it on the windowsill. At halftime, with the game running long and Carol sleepy, I headed home. The train was on its weekend schedule, and the return trip took forever, but I wasn't in a hurry. I walked the final leg from Chatham, enjoying the surprisingly warm evening, grateful for the placidity of suburbia after the bustle of the city. Back home, I flipped on the TV and saw, to my amazement, that the game was still on.

Two years later, on September 7, Carol moved around the corner to West 47th, to a legal apartment more than twice the size of her former studio. The move was precipitated by a minor disaster, a fire caused by renter negligence. Carol smelled smoke beneath her hall door, opened it a crack, then slammed it shut. She dragged Harley, the cat she'd adopted two months earlier, from the dresser beneath which he was hiding, shoved him in a duffel bag, opened a window, and climbed down the fire escape to safety. Harley repaid the favor the next week by offering Carol consolation, after a much larger disaster.

***

With the City calling us again, Carol and I began shopping for apartments. By this time, Manhattan had changed. Most of my favorite record stores were memories, the victims of changing listener habits, rising rents, and e-commerce.

On the other hand, it was the golden age of cupcakes! Pastel-colored boutiques had popped up everywhere, and bakeries retooled production lines to meet the insatiable demand for little cakes fueled by *Sex and the City*'s featuring of Magnolia Bakery, a West Village fixture. Outside the real-life Magnolia, lines snaked around the corner and down the block, with tourists clamoring for the big, puffy, iced cakes that the shop turned out by the trolleyful. The tourists may also have been hoping to glimpse neighborhood locals Sarah Jessica Parker and her hubby Matthew Broderick; personally, I would have preferred to see

Philip Seymour Hoffman, another neighborhood resident who attracted less attention. (Not long after we moved, I saw packages addressed to him behind the counter at our branch of Mailboxes, Etc., but I never saw the actor.)

The West Village wasn't all empty calories; museums, cinemas, and independent bookstores cast a spell. I admit, though, that it was that chocolate tour that stirred the pot, making me eager to move.

We met one Saturday morning, not too early – this *was* the East Village, after all – outside Chickalicious, an artisanal shop owned by two young women seeking empowerment through ownership of the means of production of chocolate. Our second stop, on Spring Street, was Vosges, the chocolatier that had made it fashionable to put bacon into chocolate bars. Third, on Broome, was Mariebelle, whose nacreous white and canary blue packaging was as luscious as its chocolate; behind its retail store, in a back room, was an elegant tea shop where well-heeled aunts and their *Madeleine*-loving nieces sipped hot chocolate at café tables of white veined marble beneath frosted glass chandeliers. Fourth on our itinerary was a hole-in-the-wall boutique known only to true aficionados - which I have not since been able to relocate – where petals of candied rose and violet adorned truffles less than an hour old that were as light as whipped butter. Finally, there was the playfully deconstructed factory of Jacques Torres, run by human oompa-loompas who ensured the consistent production of mammoth chocolate chip cookies weighing in at a thousand calories apiece.

Inspired by our five-course meal, we hied ourselves to a no-fee realtor on Eighth Avenue to see the first available agent. We soon learned that this is not how to rent a Manhattan apartment: ones worth seeing are seen at a cost. We did, however, get to see a variety of dispiriting hovels – ones on sordid streets, ones with little natural light, ones with windows giving onto air shafts, and ones with water damage, piles of drywall, and holes in the ceiling. Unless we wore hard hats with our slippers, we'd need a pricier realtor.

We chose one on Fifty-Seventh Street, near Tiffany's. Then, after raising our price point, we began to see places where we could picture ourselves. That's when we found the apartment on West Thirteenth, which we were told would be gone by the end of day if we didn't move fast. Realtors everywhere say that, but it's true in Manhattan.

Our one-bedroom apartment was proximate not only to good chocolate, but to interesting neighbors. Many in our building were long-term residents. In general, they were private, but we did get to know our next-door neighbor Mark, an exceedingly courteous older gentleman. Mark was nocturnal: we would hear his television, faintly, through our common wall whenever we got up early or stayed up late. And though we were never in his apartment, we occasionally glimpsed it through the open hall door when his maid did her level best to clean; it was overrun with tall stacks of newspapers and periodicals.

When we crossed paths, Mark would entertain us for five, ten or forty-five minutes, asking after us and our cats, whom he adored and would stroke whenever they followed us into the hall. He didn't talk much about himself, but would occasionally let drop that he was going to a theater premier, or opera. Though he was infirm, and talked and moved more slowly than just about anyone in Manhattan, he didn't let that prevent him from getting around.

On Thirteenth, just past the local pocket park, Jackson Square, was the Integral Yoga Institute. One of its two entrances led to a school, where Carol took classes in Hatha; the other opened into a health food store, where I shopped despite long lines. One day, Carol and I were leaving the store when I noticed that the woman in front of us had just exited the school with a yoga mat. Her thin, chiseled face was the profile of a woman a little older than we were, but very hale. What I could not ignore were her leg warmers: they were straight out of the 1980s – neon, prismatic, concentric bands bound to her legs like psychedelic bandages. I nodded significantly to Carol; then I was surprised to see the woman enter our apartment building. She walked past the lobby aspidistra and boarded the elevator just before we did. We staked out the other side of the ascending carriage, and I nodded a silent hi. I was terribly bothered. Somehow I knew this woman. Then it hit me – I recognized the legwarmers, and the woman in them, from the cover of one of my record albums! It was Suzzy Roche.

I'd been listening to sisters Suzzy (rhymes with "fuzzy"), Terre (sounds like "Terry"), and Maggie Roche for years. I'd first heard them on WFUV, Fordham University's radio station, during college, but they had been recording and performing much longer. (My cousin Donna had a couple of their albums from the late 1970s, and it wouldn't surprise me if she had interviewed them as well.) The summer Carol and I met, I had taped their song "Ing" off the radio, from their then-current release, *A Dove*. I played it in the car for Carol and Mary Dana, another summer math student (more on that later) as part of the elective seminar I was teaching, Songs to Impress Young Women:

> *Will we be marrying*
> *Instead of parting*
> *Or are you still singing*
> *The praises of waiting*
>   - The Roches, "Ing"

Mary Dana, a classic rocker, thought the song was gimmicky, since each of its lines (but one) ended in "ing." But Carol got it.

When the Roches split up (as a band, not as sisters), I followed Suzzy's solo career. She tried acting, appearing in the charming romantic comedy *Crossing Delancey*, which was set in the East Village. Then, on her solo album debut, *Holy Smokes*, she wrote a song that described the effect that New York City has on introverts:

> *People who live in eggshells*
> *Have only one alternative*
> *They can get hardboiled*
>   - Suzzy Roche, "Eggshell"

But it was Suzzy's second album that I looked for when Carol and I got back to our apartment: *Songs from an Unmarried Housewife and Mother, Greenwich Village, USA*. That was the one whose cover photo I'd remembered, with Suzzy in her rainbow legwarmers being dragged for a walk by her black dog, a shelter mutt whom she later told me was named Bunny. It all clicked; I had, without realizing, seen Suzzy and Bunny in the neighborhood, often by the Hudson River bike paths. It tickled me that I had moved into the building of a woman whom I had idealized for years. (The young narrator in *Remembrance of Things Past* had the same experience when his family took an apartment in a building owned by the Guermantes.)

Starting the next day, each time I left or returned to our building, I kept my eyes peeled for "Suzz" (as I had begun calling her in my own mind), hoping to introduce her to one of her biggest fans. What would I say? I could rattle off the names of favorite songs, like "My Winter Coat," the greatest eight-minute epic ever about a coat. Or maybe "The Death of Suzzy Roche," a ballad about the stabbing of Suzzy in a laundromat by a customer who'd become incensed by her habit of leaving her laundry unattended in a washing machine. On second thought, not that one.

Soon it happened. I was descending the stairwell when I saw Bunny walking Suzzy up. On a landing intermediate between two floors, practically face-to-face, I buttonholed her:

"You're Suzzy Roche, aren't you?"

She froze. She nodded and awaited my next move; I fancied that I saw her look up, then down the stairs, to gauge the nearest exit.

"I just want to say I've been a fan of your music for a long time. It's great to be living in the same apartment building!"

"Which floor do you live on?" she asked.

"The sixth. My wife and I saw you walking back from yoga the other day."

At the mention of a wife, she visibly relaxed, and smiled slightly.

From time to time, Suzz and I met by chance – on the elevator, or on a sidewalk near our building. Each time, I endeavored to strike up a conversation, not the easiest thing for two introverts, but I was encouraged by a shared love for music. I'd ask about recent gigs, favorite venues, or an upcoming album, but I don't think she ever completely warmed to my exuberance. My reaction to her fame (modest as it was) differed greatly from that of our fellow apartment dwellers, who either didn't know she was a musician or simply took it in stride.

I fear that musicians like Suzzy, and heterogeneous apartment buildings like the one we shared are becoming rarities in Manhattan. I think of Westbeth, the first federally subsidized "live-work artist colony" in the United States, just down the street from us: it occupied the former campus of Bell Labs, during the era when it invented radar and television, before it relocated to the Jersey suburbs. There, in tiny apartments, courtyards, and common spaces, gray-haired folks sculpted, drew, and made music, and painters stacked canvases seven deep under mattresses while the modern world passed them by. How long could artists remain in Manhattan without extraordinary subsidies such as Westbeth?

***

Carol and I recently saw Manhattan after eighteen months away. From Cape May we drove to a Park-and-Ride lot along the Parkway, then boarded a bus – a seven-hour round trip for a day in the City.

Arriving at Port Authority without umbrellas, we braved a chilly mist and dashed several blocks to the curved portico of Worldwide Plaza, where we took shelter. We would breakfast at the Blue Dog, a favorite nook, which in our absence seemed to have become something completely different.

> *They fixed up the corner store*
> *Like it was a nightclub, it's permanently disco*
> *Everyone is dressed so oddly, I can't recognize them*
> *I can't tell the staff from the customers*
> - They Might Be Giants, "Man, It's So Loud in Here"

A young woman greeted us at the entry, now draped with a floor-length velvet curtain. "Even as I speak," she said, a table was being cleared for us, or at least that's what I think she said. But I had trouble hearing her over the soundtrack of 1980s hits by the Cars, the Bangles, and Madonna.

Stepping inside, we were further disoriented by a continuous loop of Oliver and Hardy films playing on the bare wall above our table. I glanced at my watch: ten o'clock. The place was packed. Who were these folks? They couldn't be blue-collar or retail workers, or paralegals from Cravath, Swaine and Moore, the law firm upstairs. They must be – tourists! (I paused, being a tourist myself.) Or maybe they were well-to-do Manhattanites, slumming. The City's a wonderful place for the leisure class.

After breakfast, Carol and I parted. She headed uptown to a museum, and I set my course south to see old haunts. My expectation was that everything would have changed during the time we were away. But I was wrong. Inexorable change has a strange tendency to move very slowly.

> *It'll end in ten minutes*
> *And too much wine*
> *Or it might struggle on*
> *To the end of all time*
>   -- John Wesley Harding, "The End"

We had left Manhattan when it was on the decline, albeit in a different way than in the 1970s, and from what I'd read online, the pace of change had only accelerated. Neighborhoods were losing their characters (in both senses of the word) to rent increases. Landlords were evicting longtime independent stores – community linchpins – to court deep-pocketed clients like chain stores that could absorb the fixed cost of a prestige address. But the suitors had not come in the numbers that the landlords had hoped, and the losers of the lottery were boarding up shopfronts. Addresses that had served neighborhoods for ages were vacant, shuttered for one, two, three years. Landlords could play the waiting game in the hope of landing the big one, but that was little consolation to residents who had to walk past plywood every day.

    The developers were coming. Certainly to the West Village, after an old railroad spur was refurbished and rechristened The High Line. In Midtown, bank branches claimed every other corner, and I wondered if Manhattan was destined to be a giant safe deposit box, a place to park assets while abroad. Shops peddling everyday wares - hardware, art supplies, groceries - were going the way of the Automat.

    By pure chance, I was in Rebel Rebel at a pivotal moment. I was flipping through records in a bin when two men walked in to introduce themselves to the shopkeeper, the same guy who always played music behind the counter. They were activists, collecting signatures for a petition in favor of legislation that would protect small business owners from corporations and real estate moguls who, with the help of City government, had rigged the game. The shopkeeper then did something I'd never seen him do – he turned down the music. He and his guests talked earnestly for a while, and he asked questions that made me realize that though he was an expert on music, he was a novice in economics.

    That memory, still recent, returned as I retraced the Village. Rebel Rebel was gone: I knew that. I expected that other establishments had joined it in oblivion. What I found was quite the opposite, and I cannot overstate my surprise. For each store that had changed, twenty others were as I remembered. Also unchanged were sundry small details, like no-fee rental signs hanging off fire escapes and sidewalk conversations of young professionals lamenting busy schedules and too many visiting friends and relatives. I popped into Sockerbit, the store that sells Scandinavian gummy candy. I was the only customer, and I scooped gummy skulls and coke bottles into a paper bag to the usual Eurodisco beat.

Also familiar was the sidewalk scaffolding on alternate blocks. Here was the office building in which I scored a zero on an early actuarial exam. There, by the cash register of a familiar bodega, the same fig bars – Manhattan walking fuel – in Saran-wrapped bundles of three. On a bulletin board, the flyer promising "Dan Smith Will Teach You Guitar!" that I'd seen for twenty years, with the same black-and-white photograph of a jeans-clad Dorian Gray cradling a Stratocaster. On a Union Square sidewalk, a relay team of heavyset men hawking comic books, bootleg DVDs, and spiral-bound screenplays. And around a bend, my eyes recognized the long-time purveyor of miniature cheesecakes before my brain could even register it.

In SoHo's cast-iron landscape, I was reminded how our built environment comforts us, and how little we notice it. Then I was truly surprised – there was McNally Jackson, my favorite New York City bookstore! Online, I'd read it had lost its lease, but here it was in bricks and mortar. I stepped inside a store whose titles, unlike an e-tailer's, are expertly curated. I lingered in each section; in periodicals, I admired literary journals I had never seen. One confused me with its format: do I begin with the captions, or the text? Which side was up?

In the back stood three bookcases, twenty-one shelves in all, full of memoirs. I love memoirs. I picked one up at random, then another, spending a few sentences in each. Montaigne wrote that a few sentences are all one needs to appraise a writer's skill, and I concur. I came across another book that I knew a friend was currently reading; I gave it a try, but was put off by its fussy, old-fashioned diction, so I returned it to the shelves. The next book had too much dialogue. Others were more promising, but not enough to pull the trigger.

Nearby, another wall of twenty-one shelves was stocked with essays and "creative non-fiction." One benefit of a contrarian taste in literature is that you get part of a bookstore to yourself. McNally Jackson was crowded with folks fleeing the cold (all day, the sun played hide-

and-seek with the clouds), browsing bestsellers and picking up what the store cafe labeled a *"pan* au chocolat" (for shame, in a bookstore!), but I had plenty of elbow room. On occasion, the door of the staff-only backroom near where I was reading swung open, and once a black-and-white dog emerged. I assumed he was the store dog because he was comfortable with my presence; he lay in the aisle as I continued to try out essays. One discussed rap and reality television. One may write interestingly about anything, but I'd rather read about loftier subjects.

My belly awoke with a growl. I put the book in my hands back on its shelf, then left the store. Turning a corner, I walked into Balthazar for a cookie and scone. *Au hazard, Balthazar!* I then turned north, toward the neighborhood where Carol and I had lived. Along the way, I saw new street signs – old roads with new secondary names that commemorated historic figures linked to these locales. In a word, place-people. The signs reminded me of the cobalt blue Parisian plaques that offer, along with street name and *arrondissement*, a one-sentence biography of the person lending their name to the street. I passed one named for Gilda Radner: her I recognized. Another was named for Margaret Sanger, but without a helpful Parisian gloss, I stayed ignorant.

The street signs told me that the Manhattan I loved, the part that wasn't changing, was like the museum where Carol was walking. Yes, a metropolis is an organism, and needs to breathe and change; but as we are defined by our memories, a city needs a part that never changes, so that its residents and explorers can orient themselves. My Manhattan consists of cornices, signs, shelves, frames, and phyllo dough. Some of these things may yet be saved, if not for me, then for those who are left behind.

> *I could have been a signpost, could have been a clock*
> *As simple as a kettle, as steady as a rock*
>   - Nick Drake, "One of the These Things First"

***

Walking by our building, I saw her again, leash in hand – Suzzy!

Not having seen each other for a while, here we were again. I stopped and waved hello. After another awkward start, during which I marveled at the role of pure chance in bringing about another encounter (did she doubt it was chance?), I told her that I hosted a radio program in Cape May. That piqued her interest. She said she would send a couple of tracks from her new album.

"Great, I'll play them. Would you like my e-mail address?"

"No, just friend me on Facebook."

Then we parted.

Five minutes later, we ran into each other again. We had circled a park in opposite directions. Another awkward nod.

At home, I tried friending her, but was rejected because she had reached her five-thousand-friend limit.

Maybe one day she'll write a song about me.

My New England

As there exists a real Greenwich Village, so there is my ideal New England.

Every fall, Carol and I visit the land of Down Easters, Yankees, Holsteins, cheddar cheese, lobster rolls, brown bread, clam chowder, and hermits. (By hermits, I mean the spicy, raisiny sweetbreads, not the locals who shun visitors.) In my New England, memories are pressed like butter or cider. Or maybe like dead leaves in almanacs, their veins faded like those of the hands of my grandmother, also a Yankee by birth.

> *Where we're going in this verdant spiral*
> *Who's pushing the pedals on the season cycle*
> - XTC, "Season Cycle"

There's no better time to contemplate autumn than the dawn of a worldwide summer. A "heat dome" is parked over our house, one of the few on our block still unmarked by solar panels. The dome focuses the sun's rays on the eastern halves of the United States and Canada, and we're like ants under a magnifying glass. Like many of my neighbors, I've chosen to remain in air conditioning, but I see an occasional jogger or cyclist move past my window as they traverse mirage-like heat waves amid a background hum of condensers.

If I lived before, it was as a New Englander. How else to explain a predilection for Norman Rockwell, Henry David Thoreau, E.B. White, and Edith Wharton? Though I can't hold a candle to their writing (I can't even burn one at both ends trying), I pride myself on my descent from sturdy New England stock. Being the scion of an oak like my long-lived grandmother, who was born in Northborough, Massachusetts, may ensure that my veins carry enough sap to withstand long winters.

One Saturday, when I was in college and Nana was in her golden years, we drove to Massachusetts to see family I did not know. We took the Merritt Parkway, not the interstate, because that had been Nana's antique trail when she was younger, looking for furnishings for Dad's restaurants in the days when you could really get a deal.

Our first stop was Sturbridge, Massachusetts, at the New Yankee Workshop, which I knew from the PBS woodworking show of the same name. After a look around, Nana bought us some fudge. Then we went to lunch.

I really wish that I could recall the restaurant's name. I want to say it was Sturbridge's Publick House, but it may have been on the way to Worcester. Most of all, I wish I could remember whom we saw. But my memories are only hazy with well-being. We got out of the car, walked to the restaurant's white-and-green striped awning, and were greeted by a party of white-haired women smiling beatifically, a convocation of angels welcoming me into heaven, early admission. I didn't know them, but they knew me. I was the golden boy, the one who went to Princeton, the one who could not, apparently, get enough of learning. That day I could do no wrong.

We lunched for hours. I talked to the ladies and tried to piece together their names, like puzzle pieces, into a family tree. I explained what I was up to, and they told me that I reminded them of their children and grandchildren. But I can't recall a single word we said, or any of their names. That meal remains one of the biggest mysteries of my life, to the point that I can't be sure it really happened. And I'm beating myself up because all I remember is the chicken pot pie.

I didn't know it then (though Nana must have, in her heart), but that was the last time I would ever meet that side of my family, until the hereafter of course. Now that link is broken.

***

My dream New England home crouches like a cat on a generous two-acre lot straddling nature and culture. It's fashioned from old-growth wood and locally hewn stone that moderate, at either end of the calendar, the exterior temperature. Fieldstone walls, mortised with rock extruded from the soil by tectonic forces at work since the Ice Age, border a quiet country lane shaded by an alley of trees that pickets the property line. Post-and-beam fencing keeps me, like Robert Frost, in good stead with neighbors I never see. Part of my land is open, part wooded, but no timber has been harvested in decades.

On the ground floor is a small study, one corner of which is amply filled by a gloriously anachronistic writing desk. My laptop needs little room, so the desk holds mementos: a paperweight snow globe, a hand-thrown ceramic bowl cradling a confetti of guitar picks, a Currier and Ives tin replete with corks dated in magic marker. Above the desk, an open window frames a stand of mature trees that shades the room in summer, and through their gaps recede three distinct tiers of hills – the classic foreground, middle ground, background. Here's where I spend a good deal of time, only a fraction of it writing. Mostly I look through the window, or within the frames of wall-mounted paintings, drawings, and photographs, at birches, nude in winter and fully clothed in summer, or sugar maples lightly stippled in spring and regally arrayed in autumn red and gold.

When not in my study, I'm out walking. At a bend at the foot of the driveway is a country lane. I pass the one neighborhood concern, an apple orchard run by a several-generations farm family. It's a major attraction in fall when it offers apple picking, hayrides, and a maize maze; more importantly, it is the steward of two dozen species of apple trees, including many heirloom varietals. I've tried them all, but my favorites are those that will never make it to the supermarket. Speckled, mottled, oblong, unpolished, they are alive, not embalmed. Each apple announces itself like a citizen at Town Meeting: the juicy Ashmead's Kernel, the firm, fine-grained Black Oxford; the dense, syrupy Graniwinkle; the historic Esopus Spitzenburg; the tart, aromatic Northern Spy.

From the lane, an unimproved path climbs to the Appalachian Trail. I tramp it in all weathers – snow, rain, sleet, even sun – to reach a rickety table that I've placed near the Trail entrance, which bears gifts for through-hikers, our only regular visitors, whom I rarely see. Cookies in fall, soda in summer (though a working, albeit rusty, hand pump stands nearby), and books for the lending library. I shed books that have grown too familiar, and run marketing A-B tests to see what sells: Fitzgerald or Hemingway; *Rolling Stone* or *TV Guide*, my book or Stephen King's.

Into the woods. Sometimes I walk the big trail, the Appalachian, such a good friend by now that I no longer notice its markers – single white blazes or plaques depicting paths winding among stylized tree trunks. In good weather, I walk miles before reversing field. Timeless New England paintings are framed by overhanging boughs: Holsteins browsing a pond's marsh grass; a red barn in a field; last winter's ski lift chair suspended halfway up a slope like the stylus of a record player whose power has been cut. In the woods at my side, a thicket of plastic maple sugar tubing sleeps soundly through summer.

I'm roused by a whoosh. A bird? No, a hot air balloon. Shielding my eyes with my right hand, I can make out four haloed outlines gawking down as an ear-flapped, goggle-toting pilot tends to the flame. I wave tentatively, not quite the greeting recommended by the local Chamber of Commerce. The balloon disappears over a rise.

Carol and I traveled once by balloon. Having misread a road map at our bed-and-breakfast, we sped up Interstate 91 to make the flight; because we were late, we missed out on the group labor of inflating the balloon. Our pilot, who was clad in a bomber jacket, had logged more hours in a balloon than any other pilot in the United States, beginning with his college days on Long Island, up to his rural Vermont present.

Once aboard, we lazed over vistas of log cabins, some retrofit with solar panels – net exporters of energy – and some completely off the grid. An easterly wind carried us further than our pilot had anticipated, beyond all his usual landing sites, so he had to improvise. Our touchdown happened in ultra-slow motion, as lightly as a feather, in the waist-high thatch of someone's unmown backyard. Our bodies were folded like freshly washed laundry, stacked like bales in a rick. We dusted off the chaff, convened at the pursuit car that had tailed us cross county, and enjoyed a customary post-flight champagne. Our pilot knocked on the door of the nearby house in case the owner wished to partake, but no one was home.

Now I was the exotic local under scrutiny, the one that city folks wondered about. Carol and I get to town, she more than I, but I've packed my memories of commuting into deep storage, getting behind the wheel as seldom as possible. I can find everything I need in the nearest village.

Almost all of it is at the general store, that uniquely New England institution that has somehow survived the onslaught of a blockchain world. Young couples who want to be more than Walmart greeters have taken possession of old buildings at graceful village crossroads that wear old wood like a badge of honor, asking only for a new lease on life. These entrepreneurs learn their trades from the ground up: sales and marketing for the wife, butchering and carpentry for the husband. The key to success is getting to knowing their neighbors' preferences for newspapers, cough drops, macaroni salad, and fishing lures. And do they like craft beer? Here customers vote with their feet.

What I want is always there. Hard by the freezer aisle, above uneven floorboards, near a bulletin board plastered with ads for tutors, tricky trays, and snow removal, is a narrow set of shelves, two of which support an array of locally baked goods in Saran wrap, bearing primitive logos of local entrepreneurs. Whoopie pies run the gamut of flavored cakes and fillings; fig, date, and raspberry bars are sprinkled with oats and coffee cake crumbles. Then, of course, there are the hermits, a regional specialty made of molasses, brown sugar, ginger, cloves, cinnamon, and raisins, which power my rambles.

My dream village has other amenities. There's a post office, of brick, its large exterior wall bearing the numerals of the tiny zip code from which I send and receive "snail mail" to and from folks who value the written word. There's the cozy pub serving comfort food – meatloaf and mashed potatoes, shepherd's pie – but here, too, the winds of change have arrived, and there are farm-to-table and vegetarian choices. Its walls sport maps, photos, and old license plates. Locals drink at the bar, while couples and families occupy booths along the outer wall. There is only one television, and it is always tuned to the weather.

The center of the village is the bakery, the town's doughy heart. French has distinct words for bread shops (*boulangeries*) and pastry shops (*patisseries*); "bakery" just doesn't do justice to a place doing both so well. The morning shift, which arrives before dawn, readies the shop and opens the doors at seven a.m., releasing a scent of croissants upon a morning breeze. It reaches my front door a quarter-mile away on quiet, chilly autumn and winter mornings before the deep blue, starry sky has appreciably lightened.

I arrive soon after. In the summer, the front door of the bakery is open, so I need only push the creaky, counterweighted screen. I forget to close it gently, and it slaps back percussively, prompting an eye-roll from a regular. "Next time," I tell myself, then examine the offerings. What scones, with what preserved fruits and icings, have been contrived for me today? Apricots and currants, I hope? And what did Carol want? I can never choose quickly enough, before the young ladies behind the counter arrive in their beguiling frilled aprons. I have long wished to fall in love with a bakery maiden. One steps up briskly to take my order, but her sense of duty has made her voice officious and commanding, so I stammer out a request and step aside for the next in line.

Bearing a bag that sags under its own weight, I step outside and stop a moment at the curb for an oncoming car. It stops for me instead – a New England nicety that still catches me off guard. I cross the street to find that overnight the pub across the street has transformed into a breakfast nook. The bakery's coffee is just okay; the pub has the good stuff. I sit at the counter and request a high-octane from the counter matron, likely the mother of one of the bakery maidens – the simplicity and complexity of small-town life right there in a nutshell. My coffee arrives in an avocado-colored mug; I cradle it in my hands. Its warmth pervades me, a sensation I never properly appreciated until I moved north. I abstain from a sip until its warmth circulates inside me, warding off the morning chill, climbing my arms to my head and then back down my neck and shoulders to the arms holding the mug, one circuit of a perpetual heat machine.

One sip, and I admire again a framed poster above the counter, which I study each time I'm here. It's a poster print of a painting exhibited in 1982 at a nearby gallery, now defunct. In the foreground, a lone tree stands in an open field of winter stubble, a white metal bucket hanging from one branch, a red bucket suspended from a slightly higher one. In the distance, a farmhouse gleams. The artist is identified as David Armstrong, whom I have looked up online. He apparently still paints, not far from here. I don't suppose the owners of the pub have met him, but to them I too am just a nodding acquaintance.

Another sip, and I turn the pages of a free local paper. There *is* a world out there, and this publication ushers it into my consciousness, raising it like a hot air balloon. I appreciate the lack of national and international news, and pore over local color spanning two counties and then some, anywhere with designs on our discretionary income. Unlike the national scene, everything is cooperation: pot lucks, beef n' brews, car washes, health food co-ops, benefit concerts, open houses. This is what I admire about our little enclave within the larger confederacy: despite a rural aspect, it bucks the trend and votes progressive. It must be a legacy of old-time Yankee democracy (small "d") that dates to the republic's earliest days.

Not far from here is the strip mall lot in the medium-size town where Carol and I fetch our Christmas tree each December. It isn't the idyllic pasture where one chops down one's own tree with a hatchet, but I was never good with a blade. And that shopping center is the site of a wonderful independent bookstore where I do much of my Christmas shopping. Each time we arrive, my eyes dart nervously to the sign out front to see if Amazon has done it in yet. The store's staff, all of them actual readers of books, post recommendations on index cards beside the books. There is also a section for local authors, where I discovered the rewarding essays of Verlyn Klinkenborg.

Two other stores at the edge of town sell used books. One is a marvel; it houses tens of thousands of volumes, stacked to the rafters of the former millhouse. Each room is furnished with a chair from a different epoch – Louis XIV, Eames, beanbag – from which one may read and look over the backyard, where a stream flows and birds feed. Nowhere is old literature more redolent than in this literary tree house attendant with the chemical decomposition of parchment and its notes of jasmine and vanilla.

Progressive politics is joined at the hip to education and literacy. A diadem of liberal arts schools crowns New England, where there are more institutions of higher learning per capita than anywhere else in the United States. Carol avails herself of this bounty by taking continuing education classes at a local college offering certifications in the fine arts. Here's an advertisement for one, right in the local rag. She and I also volunteer at the regional radio station, connecting us in another small way to the world beyond the coffee cup.

But it's time to go. Before leaving, I pay for the area's one real newspaper, the one touching on topics I'd rather ignore, big world issues and local stories that don't mesh with my idealized vision of New England: battles over zoning and development, and the impacts of unemployment, poverty, and drug abuse. They, too, are a part of New England, and I may consider them when I'm back in my study, eating my scone.

Searching for Dolphins

I've been out searching
For the dolphin in the sea
Ah, but sometimes I wonder
Do you ever think of me
        -- Tim Buckley, "The Dolphins"

    We lived once at New Jersey's tail end. Picture the Garden State as a giant horseshoe crab wading north: that's us at the pointy tip of the telson, the long aerial that is the crab's hindmost part. A photograph taken on a sunny day from high above Delaware Bay hangs above our living room fireplace, showing quite clearly the shoreline receding from Cape May's resort beaches. It jumps the canal, skirts the streets of our neighborhood, then traces the bay to a point west of Sea Isle City, where it finally bows west into rural Cumberland County, a place forgotten by time.

    Time has forgotten horseshoe crabs, too. These living fossils, among Earth's most primitive animals, have scarcely evolved over several hundred million years. Long before months had names, they paddled ashore to lay eggs every May and June. On our morning walks, Carol and I find a few strewn on the sand, beached, flat on their backs. A nudge from our sneakers tips, and their myriad legs kick up a fuss; that is our cue to flip them gently with fingers or toes so they can slowly find their way back to the water, as testified by the curved tracks and occasional backtracks that festoon the sand.

    We want to see them thrive, because their eggs are a bounty to migrating red knots, birds desperate for sustenance to power their several-thousand-mile journey to an Argentinian winter. In a small way, we are undoing the pernicious influence of mankind, that ultimate invasive species. Horseshoe crabs (and, by association, red knots) are endangered because humanity has commandeered their habitats and discovered medicinal uses for their eggs. (Synthetic alternatives have been developed.)

    When Carol and I looked for a weekend refuge from Manhattan, we were attracted to this neighborhood because it, too, seemed to have been forgotten by time. I, in particular, found it refreshing that big chains and box stores were forty-five miles distant, and that the nearest large airport was two hours away. (I have since come to better understand the trade-offs.)

We found our house late one autumn. It was tucked away among modest lawns and wide streets blanketed by sere brown leaves that the wind had swept, like woodsmoke, into curlicues. Our private seclusion, our Land's End, our Finistere, paralleled a quiet, undeveloped beach where houses huddle like penguins in winter. Many of them, nicknamed "Mitnicks" after the developer of a 1950s planned community, had not been updated since; others (particularly those nearest the beach) have gone pituitary, ballooning to hotel size, with balconies and wraparound porches that sunbathe all year while their owners work off mortgages in distant cities.

On a fine morning, Carol and I strap our kayaks to the car and drive ten blocks to the bay. At water's edge, we shove off into an incoming tide, then paddle briskly to reach open water. We head north, against the telson. Our bonny bright boats, green above and white below, look like key lime biscotti. They sift the salt water, which in the morning light has a shade between taupe and brown, with grains of tan like crushed graham crackers – the sand churned by the waves' action.

I survey the bay, looking at the big picture, like the one above the fireplace. Astern, in the distance, a ferry to Lewes, Delaware pulls out slowly from a slip; from a distance, it resembles a huge paddle boat, displacing water with less effort than our own labored strokes. Another ferry, further off, arrives from Delaware: its profile, due to the mirage of distance, resembles that of a square-rigged galleon, sails billowing in the wind.

Past my bow, perhaps two miles away, on private property, the slender petals of a lone wind turbine trace a nearly imperceptible motion. Delaware is too far to port, but at the hazy vanishing point I see thumbnail sketches of vessels as big as islands in the bay's deepest, bluest water; they might be oil tankers cruising one of the busiest petroleum channels in the United States. The modern world nags at me – we aren't really at the end of the earth. Market forces are at work, traveling accelerated world lines. I wonder if more distractions will come. With the recent shift of the federal government to the right, and the consequent rollback of environmental protections, offshore derricks are a real possibility. Might we see more wind farms and solar panels?

Or is our destiny billboards, retail stores, and drones delivering beach umbrellas?

> *Feathers hit the ground*
> *Before the weight can leave the air*
> - R.E.M., "Fall on Me"

An unexpected flash of light rescues me from the rabbit hole – a dolphin! Unmistakably so. I signal Carol with upraised paddle, but she has already seen it and is signaling me. Dolphins rarely appear alone, so I scan the bay for more and, sure enough, a hundred feet away there is a pod of juveniles and adults at play, some on backs flapping fins atop bellies, others swimming sidesaddle. They vent their water gracefully, putting my junior swim team spitting to shame, and do the backstroke, breaststroke, and Australian crawl. They are quickest, however, at freestyle, sluicing the water one bottle-opener-shaped fin at a time:

> *This summer I swam in the ocean*
> *And I swam in a swimming pool*
> *Salt in my wounds, chlorine my eyes*
> *I'm a self-destructive fool*
> - Loudon Wainwright III, "Swimming Song"

I now know where I got my strokes – how much more I might learn from nature if I only had a mind! I don't speak dolphin, but as I watch these vivacious mammals cavort, I suspect they have a specialized jargon devoted to play. Douglas Adams ranked humanity third in terms of intelligence, after mice and dolphins; I suspect he was joking about the former, but I believe he was correct about the latter.

> *You may not share our intellect*
> *Which might explain your disrespect*
> *For all the natural wonders that grow around you*
> - Joey Talbot, "So Long, and Thanks for All the Fish"

For a second, I fear a dolphin might strike my kayak's dorsal side and capsize me, if only by mistake. The thought of this suspension of mammals shivering past gives me a chill, and when I see shadowy traces in the nearby surf, I give a start. But I reason that dolphins are too agile to collide with kayaks.

Meanwhile, Carol wants a closer look at the action. She paddles bayward toward the taller waves. Behind her, I see a large adult dolphin surface, vanish, then resurface beyond her with a splash. It must have gone right underneath.

The show goes on until the dolphins clear out for deeper water. They have diverted us, taken us further than expected, out of our comfort zone. As is always the case, the return trip proves more arduous than the outbound journey. Funny how the waves are always against you on the way back! We slacken our pace. I feel the muscular burn that follows a workout, and try to shorten my strokes, and strike along a path of least resistance. Taking a cue from the dolphins, I let the incoming waves carry me home. When I was young, I didn't know how to relax, to let life's tide carry me. Senior year of high school, trying out for the varsity baseball team after several years away from the game – my own George Plimpton act – I ran laps inside the school too quickly at first, and was chided by more experienced athletes, "Pace yourself!" And on tennis courts, I wearied myself with footwork only to be told by the gym coach, "You take ten steps when three will do." With age, I have improved my slackening.

Our leisurely return gives us an opportunity to scan the shore. With a summer day settling in, people are hitting the beach. The early birds – dogwalkers and crab-flipping good Samaritans – give way to sunbathers. I let my mind drift, listening to the plastic handle at the kayak's stern beat a rhythm, hollowly striking the hull like a drum. I am surrounded by nature's music: the soughing wind, the laughing of seagulls, the clanging of the ferry chime, even this plastic clacking. But beneath it all, I realize that a song has been straining at the back of my mind all along.

> *This old world may never change*
> *I've been searching for the dolphin in the sea*
>   - Fred Neil, "The Dolphins"

More tone poem than song, this languid ballad floats along not so much by its melody as by the incidental wash of phrases and chords, like the water on which I bob, in which the dolphins swim. Following a brief career that was praised by critics but ignored by much of the record-buying public, Fred Neil gave up performing publicly in the early 1970s. Then he did what he had always wanted to do – he went searching for the dolphins in the sea. He moved to coastal Florida to devote the rest of his life to founding and working with organizations devoted to dolphin research and preservation. He had found his dolphins.

Colleen

Montclair, New Jersey, where I graduated from college, was two towns. To the south was the urban moonscape of Bloomfield Avenue, an east-west thoroughfare of nail salons and Italian food suppliers; to the north was the village of Upper Montclair, where back streets sheltered stately residences under the somnolent boughs of centuries-old trees.

Amelia North, septuagenarian, lived in a dark brown Victorian house with a turret and wraparound porch. She was born in that house and had never married. A few weeks a year, she vacationed at her other ancestral home, a coastal Connecticut bungalow that she and an unmarried sister kept up on limited funds, closing rooms in winter to save on heating.

The rest of the year, Ms. North lived in Montclair. She maintained a backyard garden and compost heap of kitchen scraps, and followed the tug of world events from a high-ceilinged living room, where each wood chair had its own throw rug for warmth – the room got ample summer shade, but little winter sun. There she read *New Scientist*, a magazine of abstracts and reviews, and *The New York Times Book Review*, which she always said made books sound better than they were.

To afford home repairs and the services of her African-American maid Bertha who, though pushing ninety, walked several blocks daily in fair weather to the house she had cleaned twice a week for seventy-five years, Amelia took on two boarders from Montclair State. She gave them kitchen privileges and big, drafty bedrooms on her home's second and third floors. One was my good friend Colleen, the most kindhearted person I've ever known. She and I were atypical undergraduates, several years older than our classmates, and for six years we were good friends, before she left this world too soon.

Familiar photographs can be hard on the eyes. Long exposure, like sunlight, burns retinas: before one can see the subject, memories overtake it. There is a picture of Colleen in a flowery blue and green summer dress, taken at Sears where her family used to sit for portraits; she had it taken for the benefit of her far-off parents and for me. Another photograph, taken by her younger brother, has her in a red windbreaker among the saguaros of the Superstition Mountains. But what is the point of looking? I know these pictures before I see them, and know more about them than can be seen.

Montclair State students were like Bloomfield Avenue; Colleen was more like Upper Montclair. She was old-fashioned, timeless. I loved her name, and teased her about it because to the Irish it simply means "girl." (She had Irish blood.) I kidded her that she reminded me of Crystal Gayle, and nicknamed her Coal, as in "coal miner's daughter."

What do I mean? Hmm, let's see. Crystal Gayle, the kid sister of Loretta Lynn, had hip-length, razor-straight hair. Colleen had Crystal Gayle's long, straight hair – brown, though, not black – and blue eyes. Crystal and Loretta were daughters of a victim of black lung disease, which explains Loretta's famous country ballad, "Coal Miner's Daughter." But Crystal, like Colleen, had a sunnier disposition than Loretta, and drew attention to her eyes in "I've Cried the Blue Right Out of My Eyes" (penned by Loretta) and "Don't It Make My Brown Eyes Blue." Got that? It's how my mind works.

Colleen was rather proud of her long hair, despite its tendency to develop split ends. When I came to know her better, I would gather it in strands that I would hold to my eyes, and say:

"Just look at this bunch! Lots of split ends!"

We first met in the Student Center, on October the second. I'd left my grandmother's house early – before Nana had a chance to make my morning Cream of Wheat – to look over my Calculus III notes. Having recently changed my major to math, I was sitting in the large, still, quiet cafeteria, where only a few students chatted, to exercise my mind's rusty left side at an otherwise unoccupied table for four. My cafeteria oatmeal sat in front of me, untouched.

A long-haired girl in a baggy sweatshirt dropped her melamine tray on the table next to mine.

"Aren't you going to eat?"

I looked up to recognize a classmate. Like me, but unlike most of our classmates, she sat willingly at the front of class, unafraid to interact with Professor Koellner.

"Well, it needs salt."

Without a word, she left. A minute later, she returned with a plastic shaker that she slammed down in front of me. Grains of salt leapt into my oatmeal.

"There you go!"

Soon we met regularly at Ms. North's. Colleen introduced me to her landlady, whom I liked immediately despite her penchant for propriety. I wasn't permitted in Colleen's room, so we talked downstairs in a drawing room at the foot of the stairs, in the ground floor of the old turret, to the left of the front hall and the old table with a rotary phone. When Colleen wanted to show me something, she'd leap up and tramp upstairs to get it. Sometimes she returned with Ms. North's orange tabby, Benjamin, with whom she would sleep. She would toss him over her shoulder like a knapsack and juggle him in the air, but he never complained of the rough handling.

We would spend a half hour or more on the overstuffed settee, behind the long drapes that separated us from the hall. There we would hold hands and kiss; I had to remind myself not to kick the antique table near the settee. Sometimes I let my eyes wander to the pictures on the walls dimly hanging in gilt frames. Colleen later said she knew I would make a good boyfriend by the way I lightly caressed her hands.

Ms. North soon called me Colleen's "beau." I guess that made Colleen my "belle." I liked the words; they sounded refined. I agreed with Ms. North that "boyfriend" and "girlfriend" were juvenile terms.

***

Colleen smiled a lot. We were, in fact, Montclair State's sunniest, smilingest couple: kindred spirits, twenty-five years old, returning to school after protracted breaks. Mine stemmed from immaturity, but hers was due to illness. She had dropped out of Notre Dame, a setback she avoided discussing. My equanimity regarding the years I spent at Princeton, which I talked about when we visited its campus, astonished her. How could I not feel a twinge of regret? Why had I not fought tooth and nail to stay? I shrugged. It wasn't meant to be. I wasn't ready. I didn't belong. She listened indulgently.

Colleen called them her "meds," the medications she'd been on since her late teens. I couldn't keep them straight; I hoped she could. I was also unfamiliar with her diagnosis of bipolar disorder. Colleen was coy about how serious it was, and suggested that I ask my teacher, the white-haired fellow who taught Introduction to Psychology. I agreed. He invited me to his office, where we sat down and I told him what I knew. I could sense him equilibrating between a concern for my feelings, a duty to be forthright, and the probability that I would repeat his words to Colleen. I left the interview with a guarded optimism and a deeper appreciation of what Colleen had been through. When I told her what he'd said, she laughed, amused to be the center of attention.

Lithium was one med; the others varied with puzzling rapidity. Every week, Colleen drove to Wayne to see her therapist and her doctor at the "Center." When her symptoms flared, the doctor would prescribe a new pill or adjust a dosage; when she felt tired or unfocused, he modified her cocktail another way. It seemed unscientific, so I simply assumed the science had not moved beyond trial and error. Colleen kept me apprised of the details of her treatment, most often in long letters, but I admit the details made my eyes glaze over. She also invited me once to the Center to meet her doctor and therapist. The therapist was cordial, serious, and a bit guarded; the doctor strangely jokey.

In retrospect, I'm unsure whether I'm more impressed or aghast at my nonchalance. I think impressed. My downplaying Colleen's illness made things easier on her, and boosted her confidence. In any event, since I knew little of her condition, I left it to the experts. Colleen didn't want sympathy, anyway. She just wanted to get on with life, to live it fully. College would take time – unlike me, she attended school part-time, not only due to her illness, but because tuition and rent came from her waitressing paychecks. She found my easygoing attitude toward life, which I took day by day, a relief and an inspiration.

And yet there were times Colleen was surprised at how cavalier I was about mental illness. One example was Joshua, a classmate of ours in Calc III who was always free associating, offering correct answers to wrong questions. He rented a room from a landlady in Nutley. Joshua didn't have things together like Colleen: he came to class in rumpled, oversize, button-down white shirts with collars stained nicotine yellow, though he didn't smoke. His unruly red hair corkscrewed from his scalp; teasing it with his right hand was his only attempt to tame it. When Colleen chided him about his appearance, it elicited only a distracted smile and far-off look in his eyes.

One day, Joshua suggested we meet at the main campus library, Sprague.

"I'll see you at It's Only a Sprague Library," he said.

I laughed at the pun, but when I repeated it to Colleen, her expression was one of exasperation:

"That isn't funny! That's something only a psychotic would say."

One Saturday that semester, he and I took the train to Manhattan to see a world championship chess match, Karpov vs. Kasparov, in a small Midtown hotel. Joshua insisted on bringing along a pocket chessboard so he could play while we watched. This wasn't strictly allowed, but our seats were in the last row of a dark auditorium, so I figured he would get away with it. But a flashlight-toting usher appeared and pointedly told him to put away the set. It seemed authoritarian to me: there was no way in the world that Joshua's noodling could be seen, or be of interest, to the best players in the world sitting two hundred feet away.

That winter, I invited Joshua to Nana's to watch a Lions-Redskins playoff game. At halftime, hungry, we went to my aunt's, where a good sandwich could always be had. I fell into conversation with Aunt Ro in the kitchen, losing track of Joshua; I searched the large house and found him in my uncle's private study, watching the game with Uncle George and my cousin Karen's husband, Dan. They said nothing, but looked at the disheveled young man in their midst, and then at me, as if to say, "Who *is* this guy?" I shepherded him back to the kitchen.

Colleen and I often met at the Student Center cafeteria or at the campus library. She brought gifts, often sweets, perhaps a package of Jelly Bellies she'd picked up with her prescriptions. After my Tuesday night abstract algebra class, I'd go to Friendly's, where she waitressed. There I was a known commodity; either the thin, young greeter on duty or Janice, the chubby, bespectacled manager, would spot me at the "Please Wait to Be Seated" sign and croon:

"Colleen, Loverboy is here to see you."

I'd be shown to a seat in her section, and in a moment, she would stride from the back of the restaurant, purposefully walking toward me with a big grin on her face.

"What are you doing here?" she would ask, out of breath.

Then she would disappear as fast as she had come, because she knew what I wanted.

As my eyes adjusted to the bright lights that made the restaurant glow like a jewel in the otherwise dark suburban Cedar Grove night, I sat back to observe the crowd. On a weekday night, Friendly's might be a quarter full. It was way too late for two of the regular patrons, "Statler" and "Waldorf" (nicknamed for the eternally dissatisfied *Muppet Show* vaudevillians) and their world-weary criticism. High schoolers, some in varsity jackets, acted rowdy. At another table, Mr. Fish, a glum regular, sat in silence. Colleen was teased by the high schoolers and by Mr. Fish for the perky way in which she recited the daily specials. I understood the kids' teasing; not so much Mr. Fish's mean streak.

Colleen would set down my Reese's Peanut Butter Cup Sundae with a flourish. She'd contrived as always to have it served with an extra scoop of ice cream and a small avalanche of toffee crunchies. What had I done to deserve this? I felt a twinge of guilt for not showering her likewise with gifts.

I did made her lots of mix tapes. Musically, she was on my wavelength. One song I played for her, which she loved, was a rocker by an Irishman named Francis Dunnery:

> *I always believed that if I never missed a yoga class*
> *Read my horoscope in the dailies*
> *And recycled bottles, and knew a red Indian,*
> *I could make myself a great spirit man.*
> *But I was only doing yoga 'cos I fancied the teacher*
> *Stars 'cos it looked good on paper*
> *And I only went to church 'cos my Granny gave me*
> *Money when confession was over*
>   - Francis Dunnery, "Too Much Saturn"

We heard it as a sensible rebuke of perfection.

Colleen loved music like I did. After hearing it all shift long at Friendly's, she'd play it at home. Mainly she played the radio. Her taste was more catholic than mine, encompassing sappy ballads as well as rockers like Alice Cooper's schlocky "School's Out" and Jim Carroll's morbid "People Who Died." And she had access to a psychosomatic dimension of music that I could only imagine: she said that before we had met, when she was quite ill, there was a time when music was extraordinarily vivid to her. It was as though it were being mainlined to her hypothalamus, every song a message directed personally to her. One hit she heard this way:

> *Ooh, baby, I love your weight*
> *Wanna tell you I love your weight*
>   - Peter Frampton, "Baby I Love Your Way"

Music appealed to the inner voices that counseled her anorexia and bulimia. Of course, after her confession, I had to tease her whenever Peter Frampton's hit came on the radio, singing it her way. She took my kidding gracefully, but I noticed a wistful look hinting at a lingering fondness for a time when music could be such an affirmation of the psyche. She'd fought demons to reach her ideal weight, a goal she had since relinquished. With some embarrassment, she blamed her current weight on her meds. She would try to trick her body into satiety by drinking lots of fluids: water, diet soda, Slim-Fast.

Another of Colleen's psychosomatic pop hits was "Time," by the Alan Parsons Project. She told me about a time, in the waiting room of an outpatient clinic, that she was transfixed by a large mural of a river running through a glen. "Time" was playing on the radio, and as she listened, she saw the river stream through the mural. She stood up to examine the wall more closely, but the illusion ended with the song.

Beyond music, Colleen loved letter writing. Being her favorite addressee, I struggled to keep up. Letters bearing extra postage in thick envelopes arrived one or two at a time at my grandmother's house (weekdays) and my parents' (weekends). When we met, if Colleen happened to be in the middle of a letter to me, even in mid-sentence, she'd tear the pages from her spiral notebook and hand them over. She liked nothing better than to sit in fast food restaurants, especially the McDonald's at Montclair's Brookdale Park (which doubled as a Garden State Parkway rest stop), and buy the largest available container of Diet Coke, nursing it while she wrote to family and friends, some of whom she saw occasionally and others of whom, through life's vicissitudes, had become strict correspondents.

Colleen would write her friend Mary, disabled since childhood and living with her parents in Rockaway, and to an aunt in Cedar Grove, who lived down the street from the Friendly's where she worked. She also wrote to her three brothers, who in an equal-but-opposite reaction to their father's life as a corporate wage slave, lived lives as footloose as possible, trading one resort-town job for another so they could maximize their time snowboarding, cycling, and hiking in national parks.

Colleen also wrote to her parents, who had moved away from her childhood Blairstown home after her father retired. His long commute and desk job at a Manhattan finance firm had so sapped him of time and energy that he spent the weekends of Colleen's adolescence crashed on the living room couch. Now her parents lived east of Phoenix, in the desert, where they waited for urban sprawl to track them down. Colleen had no desire to follow suit. As much as she loved her parents, she wanted to live life on her own terms.

Colleen's letters were as prolific as Mozart's scores, and detailed her surroundings with great care. She described the mannerisms of all she met: classmates, coworkers, fast food patrons. Her pen stayed in motion, and she didn't fuss over handwriting, even when her e's and o's unraveled due to her medication-induced fatigue. She was particular about spelling, but didn't carry a dictionary, so she wrote "(sp?)" when she was uncertain about a word. That habit made me smile.

When I could, I'd slice open an envelope, revealing a sheaf of college-ruled paper heavily inked on both sides, with confetti left over from notebook tears. Sometimes the pages were stained with Diet Coke. I read them all. With the vagaries of postal delivery, sometimes three or four letters would arrive at once, so I would start the one with the earliest postmark. And I could always count on a long letter to ring in the new year, because Colleen insisted on spending New Year's Eve at home alone, writing. Her taking stock of the year was for her a bittersweet but essential, ritual.

> *Same old man living at the mill*
> *The mill turns around of its own free will*
>   -- The Dillards, "Old Man at the Mill"

The years passed. I spent two of them in Ohio getting a master's degree in mathematics. I didn't date during that time, managing to resist the charms of Audrey, the petite redhead graduate student whose office was next door to mine, who seemed interested. Colleen flew out once to see me, but the trip wore her down, and she napped much of the time. She said she had seen *Groundhog Day* with a guy from the Center, but was annoyed by the movie's repetitive structure.

When I returned from Ohio, I found that life had changed little for Colleen. She still lived at Ms. North's and took occasional classes at Montclair State. There were stretches when she'd had to withdraw from classes due to illness, but I was always there to offer consolation, and to help her shrug things off.

***

Almost thirty, I found that life wasn't quite so carefree. I tried to keep it that way. I went back to my old temp agency, which found me a job in the mailroom of Kern McNeil International, a Morristown firm that ran clinical trials of new medicines. And during lunch, I stopped at the Swiss Chalet Bakery, catty-corner to my workplace.

In a youthful stroke, I commuted to work via the Loantaka Brook Reservation bike paths. My sweet ride was a three-speed 1950s Hercules British racing bike I bought for five dollars at a garage sale I went to with Nana. The pedals charged the headlight, lighting my way as autumn days grew short. Engaging the charging mechanism induced drag, but I was proud of my classic, frugal transport. It did make the trip longer, though. One night, I returned home to find Colleen asleep on my bed, still bundled in her winter coat. She'd fallen asleep waiting for me.

One Saturday that fall, after running errands in Madison, I cycled home. To climb the driveway, I stood and pedaled – and the next thing I knew, I lay dazed on the asphalt with a bloody arm, still grasping the handlebars that dangled from the handbrake cords. Advanced metal fatigue, years in the making, had sheared the handlebar support.

Colleen and I began seeing each other less often. She never gave up hope for a more formal, long-term relationship, but it was something we didn't discuss. I wasn't ready, fearing the obligation implicit in a serious relationship. I was hardly a womanizer, but I just didn't know where life was going. At one level, Colleen was relieved by my unhurried approach; it meant that I wouldn't be impatient with her slow progress toward recovery and a degree. But every so often her patience slipped. One letter arrived with a full-page pencil sketch of a fieldstone country home, woodsmoke puffing from the chimney. That was what she wanted.

Instead, she lived at underheated Ms. North's. One February in 1996, I paid a visit, making the drive from my grandmother's. It was cold in the little sitting room, so we moved to the living room. Colleen wasn't feeling well. But a light snow had begun to fall, and I wasn't confident in my Ford Tempo's ability to climb the ridge back to Nana's, where I would spend the night. The next morning, a Saturday, I planned to return to Madison to begin a mix I'd long been planning, so I kept my visit short, disappointing Colleen.

At Nana's, I was the only one awake. Ella was upstairs, and Nana was at my aunt's, where she had lived ever since her stroke. I went to the living room, turned on the television for some noise, and collapsed on the overstuffed sofa. Nana's house was better heated than Ms. North's, and I was glad of it.

Colleen called. She was upset, and asked me to return. But the snow had gotten heavy, and I was settled in. It took some convincing, but I persuaded her that things would look better in the morning, and that we'd see each other soon. Colleen told me she was typing me a letter on an old typewriter that Ms. North had recently given her. I encouraged her project, and we said good night again.

As planned, I drove to Madison the next day. The snow had ended; the roads were fine. I went directly upstairs to my old bedroom, shouting a quick hello to whoever was around, then surrounded myself with the tools of my trade: vinyl, CDs, cassettes, stereo.

At the top of the hall, the telephone rang. Someone yelled from downstairs to pick up. I knew something was amiss, even before Ms. North's distraught voice came down the line. She said Colleen seemed to be asleep and would not respond to her efforts to rouse her: I should come immediately. I ran to my car, then sped to Montclair, sensing the worst. Strange thoughts flooded my brain, which in an effort to save itself had momentarily shut down all limbic functions. I was running on pure logic, and logic advised me to get through the approaching days as quickly as possible. Other than that, I was numb.

Except for flashes, that day remains a blur. The police were at Ms. North's. I waited in the living room where Colleen and I had talked the previous night. Benjamin was missing, likely hiding from the commotion. When they carried Colleen's body downstairs, I turned away. Ms. North's face was one of devastation. At the police station, before my interview, an officer said in passing that I should mention the typewritten letter. I nearly forgot, but remembered when the interviewing officer asked, "Anything else?" I told him, and he said, "I'm glad you mentioned that." Naively, I told him that one of his colleagues had suggested I do so.

Back in Madison on the living room couch, I was watching television, the great anesthetizer, when Dad popped his head into the room. His expression as he stood in the hall was full of sadness and concern, utterly unlike his habitually cheerful manner. He'd rushed home from his cajun restaurant in Springfield to see if I was okay. I told him I was, though I didn't really know, because I felt nothing. Little did I imagine that three weeks later I would grieve again, when I lost Dad.

The next day, I cleaned Colleen's room. Ms. North insisted it be done immediately. I arrived to an empty house, and climbed the stairs to Colleen's second-floor room, which I had never seen for more than a minute at a time. As usual, it was a mess. I looked for the typewriter, but couldn't find it. I triaged: things to keep, things to donate, things to trash. I don't remember which keepsake it was, which memento of our time together, that burst the dam; but for the first time since I had lost her, at the threshold of the closet door, I sat down and cried. I was surrounded by so many things I hadn't seen in ages – things connected to me, things meaning something to Colleen, markers of hope. The ones I didn't recognize were now orphans, because they no longer held meaning: still, they implored me to take them home.

By the time my game face was back, I'd been joined by an uncle of Colleen's whom I had never seen before. He was there to have a look for himself, and to cart away some larger items. While he went through her closet, he too had his watershed moment, and it was my turn to console. I told him I'd cried too, and smiled.

Damn that smile. It has been a bane since childhood, always near my lips. I can't help it. What likely began as a defense mechanism, as a way to conciliate, to not make waves, had become an unceasing campaign by my subconscious to put the sunniest possible face on reality. It's good for you: scientists have shown that an upturn at the corners of the mouth induces happiness. Colleen knew this. But circumstances now militated against it, and I needed to stow it.

I'm pretty sure I was smiling when I greeted Colleen's parents at the arrival gate at Phoenix Sky Harbor Airport, despite my determination not to. I had followed her body to Arizona to attend her second funeral. At the first funeral, which had been arranged by her aunt in Cedar Grove, I had seen most of her friends and family. But Colleen's parents wanted her near them.

In Arizona, I spent three days with her family, whom I had met only briefly. I hiked with her athletic-minded brothers in the Superstition Mountains, recognizing the landscape where she had stood in that red windbreaker. Back at her parents' condo, her father kept a stiff upper lip, but her mother broke down more than once in tears. At one point, I believe she was going to share some family history, but her husband cut her off, patiently placing his hand on her shoulder until she trailed off. She looked utterly broken.

Colleen's funeral happened on a warm and sunny day in February, the reason people move to Arizona. The low-slung funeral home was in the ubiquitous whitewashed adobe style. As we returned from the grave, we passed through a portico encircling a verdant courtyard, and I was arrested by the sight of a dove perched on a slab of ornamental stone, cooing. I stopped walking and listened for a full minute, hearing laughter; the laughter of the stars at the end of *The Little Prince*, the laughter I'd heard from Colleen at the most inappropriate times, part and parcel with her belief that things were never as bad as they looked. I stored that memory away.

Back in New Jersey, I was near the end of the tunnel. I had two Marys to see. The first was Colleen's childhood friend whom I'd never met. Her spinal injury kept her in a wheelchair, so we hugged awkwardly. We talked for a while in her mother's kitchen, and I said Colleen would be happy to know we had finally met. She replied, "I'm not so sure about that." The oddness of that remark stayed with me, but since this would be my only visit, I'll never know what she meant.

The second Mary was Colleen's aunt, whom I'd seen with Colleen several times, but never for long because she was always in a hurry to go somewhere. Married and with three daughters, she exercised the iron discipline of the Irish matriarch who did not condone fooling around, having seen too much of it in her life. (This only encouraged Colleen to tease her at every opportunity.) On Colleen's last birthday, her thirtieth, her aunt had given her an expensive necklace and remarked – with an eye toward me – that the day was a big deal. Perhaps she felt my gifts to her niece didn't measure up.

One night, Aunt Mary called. She wanted to return Ms. North's typewriter, which had come into her possession. I wondered if she had the letter that was found in it. I said I'd stop by after work the next day.

It was nearly dark when I arrived. One interior light hinted at life inside; through a window I thought I saw one of Colleen's cousins. I knocked, but there was no answer. I knocked twice more, louder each time. The cousin came to the door, but did not open it. I tried to explain my errand, but she shook her head negatively, said something I couldn't hear, and disappeared. I went home.

I waited for Colleen's aunt to call again, but she never did. So ended a disorienting, dreamlike era devoid of emotion.

Memories of death come too easily, overwhelming the more significant memories we should instead remember. It's too easy for me to recall Nana's final two years of life, after the stroke that deprived her of her speech (except for the catch-all "oh, boy!" she would utter to express either pain, surprise, disgust, happiness, or fatigue). I should instead bring to mind the time when, despite a broken arm, she batted baseballs to Frank and me in our Mendham front yard, or the times she led us in a chorus of "whee!" as we drove down the steep slope of McCosh Road to Applegate's Ice Cream.

As for Colleen, I should remember the many times we hung out at the Student Center, where we started each weekday, before it filled with students. Or the times at the library, at our favorite desks, where I rigorously adhered to my routine of never studying hard for more than fifteen minutes at a time, a philosophy she found endearing yet ridiculous. Or the times we sat on the hallway floors of our math building, backs to the wall, waiting for the previous class to empty.

The times at Friendly's and McDonald's. The times listening to the car radio. The times in Ms. North's sitting room. All of these more important than the last ones. Because if I focus on the end, I have to recognize the irony of my not having read her last letter after thousands of others, and of her not having heard the cassette mix I'd gone home to record. Those idiosyncratic final communications were left hanging like unresolved chords when Colleen left this life too early, a first fallen leaf in August. And so, despite a few photographs, I never see her except in memory, or one of Carol's chance tics or expressions, or the defiant, humorous act of a housecat that makes me wonder about reincarnation and doves.

Dream Five

The fifth of seven dreams I had while writing this book.

I'm at the firm where I worked for twenty years, in a conference room full of colleagues. I'm seated at a table, waiting for a meeting to begin. Karthik, the senior actuary whose professionalism, acumen, and sartorial elegance I always found daunting, presides. He distributes two sheets of paper on which we will be briefed; one is a tree diagram of a project I worked on for years without reaching a satisfactory conclusion. Karthik is ready to relaunch and "productize" it, so I wonder how closely it resembles the concept I made such a hash of. Honestly, it's been so long since I've thought about the idea that I doubt my ability to contribute to the upcoming discussion, or even understand it at a high level.

To my left sits Joe, my boss from before I was an actuary. While we wait for the meeting to begin, he and I discuss a coworker, Leonard Cohen, the famous musician. Joe tells me that Cohen had several big hits, but I can't remember any of them. And if he was such a star, I ask Joe, what was he doing in our department?

The meeting has still not begun when the public address system summons us to a company-wide event in the auditorium. I suddenly remember that I have a role to play, so I hurry outside, to a very green park, to meet a young woman whom I have been tasked to coach, to help her learn dialogue. We walk in the park and take turns trading lines, but my mind freezes; I've forgotten my part. She takes my absentmindedness in stride, but I sense her disappointment.

As we walk, the wooded path becomes the long, white, carpeted hallway of my Aunt Ro's home. At the end, where the bedrooms should be, are doors to the auditorium. Standing just outside them, our Chief Executive Officer and Chief Financial Officer welcome us like priests greeting their flock. They don't see me, so I duck in to avoid them. I have always assumed that our CEO was born with a silver spoon, but I recognize the CFO as a true-life example of someone who has worked his way up from the mailroom, or at least a junior position in Finance. As always, he radiates confidence; his hair is slicked back, his dark eyes are set in expensive eyeglass frames, and a frozen smile hovers on his close-shaven face.

I take a seat by the stage. The chairs are very plush. To my left, Leonard Cohen is slumped in his seat, asleep. To my right, through an open glass door, I see a balcony topped by a bright yellow padded railing such as an up-to-code Little League fence would have, nineteen floors above a raging ocean. I step outside and notice on closer inspection that the water below isn't moving. Though crested heavily with waves, the waves are frozen, and the indigo blue water is studded with massive chunks of ice, Antarctic floes with stiff meringue peaks. I return to my seat, wanting to describe this image to Cohen, but he is now performing on stage. I leave.

Padding back down my aunt's hall, I duck through the door into my uncle's private study. I find myself in a gymnasium where bleachers have been erected. I recognize Rich and Andy from high school; I also feel I know some of the girls, but can't name them. My friends tell me of an alternative event taking place in the annex next to the concert hall where Cohen is performing. I'm eager to see it, so I immediately run back down the hall, my underwear briefs beneath my left armpit (I'm not wearing them under my pants, but am otherwise clothed). I ball them in my fist to conceal them as I enter the smaller performance space. It is nearly full, and I take the only available seat near the door, an easy chair upholstered in coarse fabric.

On a small stage, a trio of women sing political folk songs. They're in the middle of a long ballad, a history lesson. Behind them is a screen displaying a PowerPoint presentation. The audience is not the uncritical, adoring mass under Cohen's sway; they seem restless. I sense that they consider this hootenanny old hat. But the band soldiers on, singing about injustice – past, present, future – while cartoon stills projected behind them jokingly punctuate their songs with jokes about shipwrecks and something called the American Cheesecake. When their song reaches the verse about the future, a slide depicts a cartoon showing three young women in yellow raincoats, standing at the end of a puddle-strewn driveway, their faces upturned to the rain. They are meant to represent the real-life trio before me, the Roches.

I wonder, how can the Roches be the future? They are long past. Maggie is dead of cancer, Terre has retired, and Suzzy performs infrequently with her daughter. How are they the future?

I awake from a dream where I do not belong: a failure in love, business, and event planning. And I'm glad to have kept my self-respect.

Flatland

While walking around the block yesterday in a light rain, Carol saw, beneath a mature tree, curled in a C, an adult black-and-white cat, asleep. Or so she thought until she got closer and realized it was dead. Its eyes were half open, but it was otherwise ready for taxidermy. Too unblemished to have been struck by a car – a common fate of cats in our town – it may have died of poison after nibbling on the wrong pest.

When I saw Carol arrive at our front door, I could see that some of the water on her cheek was saltwater, not rain. She was sorry for the unlucky cat that would go unburied, its body pelted by rain, next to the gas company trucks servicing the neighborhood. She foresaw workers unceremoniously disposing of its body as they replaced gas mains. If that didn't happen, a vulture, another common resident, certainly would.

We waited twenty-four hours for its owner to claim it. The next morning it was still there. Maybe, as a housecat of a summering family, it had made the fateful decision to hide during the confusion of Labor Day packing. But those were morbid thoughts: it was time to act.

In our shed I gathered gardening gloves, two heavy-duty garbage bags, and an empty cardboard pallet. I took these up the street, turned the corner, and found the tree. Up close, I marveled at the cat's long, sleek body, its otherwise unmarred hair clumped from exposure to rain and soil. It offered no resistance to my touch, which as any cat fancier knows, feels strange. And its body was heavier and flatter than I expected, like a cake that hadn't risen. Is this not true of every body from which the breath of life has departed? Our breath keeps us light.

I placed the body in the pallet, draping the bags around it, then walked home past the everyday sounds of automatic garage doors and combustion engines.

In 1884, the theologian Edwin Abbott composed *Flatland: A Romance of Many Dimensions*. In that slim volume, he describes how incomprehensible a three-dimensional world must appear to a 2D creature. Imagine a sphere passing through a page where a line lives: the sphere materializes as a point, expands to a circle, wanes to a point, and vanishes. All the line knows is its cross section. By implication, reasoned Abbott, we inhabit a world we cannot fully understand. Twenty years later, Einstein proved our universe has a fourth dimension, time; today, many physicists study string theory, a model of reality with many more dimensions than four.

Physics aside, consider (as Abbott did) the spiritual dimension. The cat we intended to bury had no idea of mortality, nor any view on life's ephemeral nature. It did not regard the past with nostalgia; it did not view the past at all – time was inaccessible to it. That cat lived in Flatland. Only humans fear the future and rue the past.

Our eldest cat, Moose, an old black female with long white whiskers, loves to sleep in cardboard boxes, particularly those that once held wine. We keep one on the floor near the sliding glass doors to our backyard. Her current modular home bears the imprint "Beach House," after the bargain wine brand. Carol and I get the joke, but Moose does not: to her, the box is simply her house. Its constraints put her at ease, like one of Temple Grandin's "hug boxes," or the two dimensions of Abbott. But if we recycle that box tomorrow, she'll find another niche. In Flatland, ignorance is bliss.

Jools, our younger black cat, is one year old. He likes to gnaw on Moose's beach house, slowly ripping it apart. First he scallops the front porch (the overhanging front flap), making it a gingerbread house. Soon, after further deconstruction, it's a wreck. Concerned for Moose's comfort, we promise her a new box, but she simply moves on to the sofa. Too many dimensions! Past, present, future – emotion's playground – are our baggage, not hers.

It occurred to us that the burial of Kitty Cat, as we had taken to calling the deceased, was affecting us more than a human funeral. I suppose that we were compensating. Carol and I were the only ones to grieve Kitty Cat, so we felt an excess of sorrow. In contrast, I was stoic at my father's funeral reception, my counterbalance to the presence of so many friends and family. When my coworkers unexpectedly arrived *en masse* from the nearby Morristown office where I was then temping, they found me in a strangely jovial mood.

Our potentialities are activated differently, in different settings. A husband behaves one way among his high school buddies, and quite differently around his wife. A second son, as smart as his elder brother who has gone to graduate school, directs his energies toward work.

At four o'clock, Carol and I walked to the hole that I had dug earlier that day in a shaded corner near our back property line, and held a funeral. I laid Kitty Cat out on a pillowcase that we no longer needed because it didn't match anything in our linen closet, and Carol placed a starlight peppermint toy, which she had crocheted, at its paw. We read from a children's book, *Cat Heaven,* which Carol's sister had given her years earlier, to console Carol for the death of Harley, her first cat. Then we committed Kitty Cat to our common home.

It was time for dinner. We walked to the kitchen, taking the shortest path through the four dimensions we knew.

My Body

The life of the body is something relatively unimportant which can be sacrificed to the inner part of the self, the real vital core... its personal existence is of value only as a protective outer skin."
   - Marcel Proust

    The recent chaos in the news having triggered something in my mind, I suddenly needed to know if my passport was due for renewal. I found it in a hanging file folder where it had collected dust since the last time I flew, over two years ago; flipping past its official-looking federal blue cover, I regarded the face of the man I was ten years earlier. The same hanging folder contained two earlier passports canceled with hole punches like cutout record albums marked for discount. I opened them, too, to look at their photographs, a portfolio of my past beauty.

    I've always felt my body is not part of me – or rather, not my characteristic part. I've lived mostly in my mind. Anyone might have my looks (in the 1980s, a second-tier tennis professional did; his name escapes me, but he played in several major tournaments, and even Mom saw the resemblance), but no one shares my thoughts. The rest of this book anatomizes those thoughts; here, for completeness, is one chapter about my body.

    I was twenty-three when I applied for my first passport. I was contemplating a trip to Kyoto, to see a friend. Looking at that photograph, I can confidently say that it looks like me. However old that we grow, our mental self-image remains fixed in our fruiting years, our teens and twenties, when looks actually mattered. Unless one is a "distinguished gray" or has the chiseled jaw of a movie star, that's the best we can hope for.

    In that first passport, I have clear skin and a Beatle bowl of thick, dark hair. My eyebrows are prominent. I'm wearing my first tie, the one from the old Madison haberdashery The Locker Room, its red and blue stripes diagonally slanting down to the right. My mouth is open in a half-smile, as though I've just recognized someone on the street and am about to say hello. That was allowed then: now when I visit a passport processing facility, I am told to refrain from smiling, in order to fight terrorism.

My current driver's license says I'm five foot ten. That was indeed my maximum height, but I've since shrunk an inch, after a brief fling at being taller than the average American male. I'm happy to have even made average: until my freshman year growth spurt, I didn't think I had a chance. (Disclaimer: I cannot check that memory, because the only evidence – the frame of the kitchen doorway where Dad recorded his children's heights in carpenter's pencil – has undoubtedly been repainted or replaced.)

Much of that spurt occurred during Christmas break, when I shed baby fat like a Butterball under an electric carving knife. As I stretched, I thinned. Seeking to capitalize on this exhilarating development, I gave up holiday sweets and did hundreds of sit-ups on the carpet of my aunt's television room, sweating off the pounds like Richard Simmons. When school resumed I waited for the girls to notice, and it happened on the very first day in first period English: Vendy, who sat behind me, was the first to take note. (A woman among girls, Vendy was highly esteemed by my peers, though she was not my type.) I sensed her eyes on the back of my neck as she said in an offhand manner:

"John, you look different."

I assumed she meant that I had blossomed.

***

I've always been drawn to the guy in the mirror. When I was a toddler, before I had much of a vocabulary, I'd quiz Mom by pointing at things in my bedroom window:

"Uts dat?"

Mom named the trees, the birds, the two cars in the drive.

"No! Uts dat?"

She realized that I meant my own reflection.

"It's John!" Only then was I satisfied.

I still have a framed baby portrait from Sears. I'm sitting up, teddy bear in arms, wearing red-and-white vertically striped pajamas, with a beaming rosy-cheeked face that is lighting the world, my parents' sun. That portrait hung in my room when I was young, confirming my position at the center of the universe.

As a teen, I still fancied myself. One junior high schoolday, after class, I skipped down Main Street's cracked, uneven sidewalk to Widow

Brown's. Dad was outside, touching up the paint on the restaurant sign. He saw me in my bright red sweater and flushed cheeks and announced:

"Here's Jack Armstrong, the All-American Boy!"

Jack was the hero of a Wheaties-sponsored radio serial that Dad listened to as a young man. I didn't know that, but I understood his compliment.

What Dad had overlooked was the oddity of a treble-voiced teenage boy skipping down the street. I was his son after all. Others weren't as quick to dismiss my habits and attributes: years later, the custodian of our math building at Miami University said I should really temper the bounciness of my gait. Then there was the day my first wife chided me as we walked down Main Street in New Hope. I was smiling broadly because I was enjoying our day of shopping; to her dismay, she noticed some young men smiling back at me, so she told me to tone it down. My habitually lazy smile has always been for me an impediment, but I try not to think about it much, lest it paralyze me.

Actually, I mentioned to my wife before our marriage that I had always considered myself handsome. I was saying this in the spirit of full disclosure. She said, "That's one of the most conceited things I have ever heard." She didn't smile while she said it, not even a half smile like the one in my first passport.

Soon after my first wedding, I got my second passport. The photo inside reveals the first shadow of my having passed my prime. Or was it because I no longer bothered spiffying up? I'd ditched the tie, and instead worn a solid brown shirt. At least my dark hair still matched the collar.

***

Why is my body, which isn't important, worthy of note? Let me count the ways.

My hair is straight, with a tendency to curl before haircuts. One day, when it was on the long side and I was looking for a compliment, I called to Laura as she passed my locker after school to ask whether she thought my hair was curly or straight.

"It's *wavy*," she said. The way she said it, it sounded cool.

My eyes are hazel, though my driver's license says brown. For a long time, I didn't know what "hazel" meant. My eyes aren't the color of hazelnuts. I now know it means an outer rim of blue, a middle ring of green, and a center of chestnut brown, concentric on a black dot.

More importantly, my eyes are powerful. They are the eyes of a professional athlete, which is what my father was. A favorite parlor trick of mine was to read highway signs aloud as soon as I could, before anyone else in a car could discern them. I amazed my friends and, later on, the father of my first wife:

"What sign?" he'd joke.

Thirty years of occupational close work haven't yet fit me with prescription lenses. At my most recent eye exam, at a New York City teaching hospital, the presiding doctor told an intern:

"You're looking at the pupils of a twenty-year-old."

My nose is straight, not too prominent, and well-proportioned – a draftsman couldn't draw it better. Even Russell, the day he graded noses in gym class, pronounced it satisfactory. (He caviled that it *was* a bit long.) But unlike my eyes, it doesn't work as well as it looks; my olfactory sense has never been subtle, not like most women's, which on occasion can be a problem.

A half inch beneath my left eye, a small crow's foot is the remnant of a mole removed in my mid-forties. Carol thinks that it is unnoticeable, but I feel it makes me look sallow, nearer my true age. Consequently, more than any other decision that I have made about my body, I've regretted having that mole removed. I was just following the advice of my general practitioner, who first noticed its jagged outline, and my dermatologist, who convinced me to let him operate. He was following the rubric of good sense, but I should have followed my vanity and kept the mole as a beauty mark.

In contrast I have had, since birth, a glorious mole. Round as a button, it resides on the back of my scalp, just beneath my hair, an inch from my left ear. My hair has yet to recede, so it remains hidden. Each time I sit for the barber and brace myself for a cascade of gray locks that can't possibly be mine, I indicate it with my index finger and advise her to avoid it. I'm not sure what would happen if she failed to do so. Would blood gush forth? Would it pop? Actually, I doubt anything much would happen – it's too old to be tumescent. But it's oddly satisfying to probe with my fingertip: it shifts under pressure like a convalescent's squeeze toy. That mole is a bequest of my father, who had one at exactly the same place on his scalp. I will never put it under the knife.

My lips are average.

My mouth, while not terribly interesting, was for years crowded with teeth. The lower incisors, in particular, were barely hanging in there, like straphangers on a runaway subway train. My dentist, Dr. Callahan, who rarely suggested surgery and never performed it himself, finally told me to see an oral surgeon. The resulting surgery was so successful that each of my subsequent dentists has assumed upon initial inspection that I have a full complement of teeth.

"Count again," I say.

But for forty years, Dr. Callahan was my only dentist. He and Mrs. Callahan (who also served as receptionist) ran a practice from the ground floor office of their Mendham home on a pretty cul-de-sac just off the main road to Chester. They were friends of my parents, with whom they had socialized when young.

> *The years run too short*
> *And the days too fast*
> *The things you lean on*
> *Are the things that don't last*
> 　　　- Al Stewart, "Time Passages"

It was at the Callahans', more than anywhere, that I felt time's passage. It was the sundial, the one fixed point, the Foucault pendulum, from which I measured Earth's motion. The single, mature, deciduous tree shading the waiting room's front window instantly told the month according to whether it was in flower, in leaf, both, or neither. And since my appointments were scheduled at intervals of slightly longer than six months, they precessed through the calendar like a lunar festival, enabling me to see that tree in every season.

Just inside the front door, one was confronted with a showroom of juvenile furniture. Every piece, from chairs to end tables to benches and bookshelves, was slightly too small. In winter, I'd lean over to hang my coat on a miniature brass hook in the closet, then crane my head around the partition wall to tell Mrs. Callahan I had arrived. I'd sit in a child's chair, peruse the magazines for grown-ups, then visit the low bench and its stacks of *Highlights* to read the Goofus and Gallant comic strips. I thought that Gallant, who was always sharing his possessions and helping old ladies to cross the street, was creepier than his selfish brother, and I hoped I didn't overly resemble him. Then I would pick up one of those unwinnable puzzles in which one tries to put ball bearings in holes, or guide magnetized balls through a labyrinth, and struggle with it until I grew bored. Finally, I was called into the examination room, where WQXR, "the classical music station of *The New York Times*," always played, impervious to decades of change in popular music.

My pretty brown-haired hygienist eventually got a touch of gray. She was my hygienist for as long as I can remember, so another way to measure time's passage was by my changing feelings for her. On each visit, the first thing she did was to remove from a drawer a stack of multicolored index cards summarizing each dental appointment I'd ever had, back to the first one, the April that I was five years old. She removed the cards from an elastic band and flipped through them. After some small talk, cleaning would begin. Though I hated the pain that her thoroughness provoked, I liked the sensation of her slight bend over me as she probed my mouth. I recalled Steven Wright's joke about the man in love with his hygienist: he would eat a whole bag of Oreos before his appointment. When I was in my twenties, my hygienist must have been in her mid-forties, with two children in high school, but her shoulder-length hair was still pretty, and I was flattered by her maternal solicitude for my teeth.

Finally, the dentist made a cameo appearance, like the last guest on a talk show for whom the others on the couch can't be bothered to make room. He would pat my shoulder and pronounce everything to be ship shape. From my reclined position, I could admire his distinguished bearing from below: tall, silver haired, with a face of a slight feminine cast, perhaps owing to his surgical mask, or maybe the biological fact that men's and women's faces converge as they age. With a never-ending practice in his own home, Dr. Callahan seemed to hold the key to immortality.

Back to my body.

My chin is ordinary, though touched by the vestige of an accident that happened when I was four. Mom was vacuuming the downstairs hallway when she saw me at the head of the stairs, my little legs working. Without knowing exactly how she knew, she could see that I did not intend to stop – and like a slow-motion runner in a nightmare, she arrived too late. I tumbled down the stairs, and landed on the floor with a badly bleeding split chin requiring dozens of stitches. That event is commemorated by a ghostly line that is permanently obscured by razor stubble. My body remembers it better than I do.

Dad saved me from an even earlier spill. Behind the house in Scotch Plains, which I barely recall because we moved away when I was four, I was determined in any way possible to cross the patio and get to the swimming pool. This time it was Dad who experienced the slow-motion nightmare of seeing me at the precipice – but at the same instant that I plunged, he dove into the pool and scooped me from the water like an osprey nabs a fish. I never had a chance to practice my underwater breathing.

Those two falls, into the pool and down the stairs, were my first of many brushes with fate. Some Mom and Dad knew of, but others I kept to myself. In reverse order, they are:

In graduate school, playing tackle football with classmates, I hyperextended my right arm reaching for an overthrown pass. The campus doctor prescribed rest.

In college, dashing across an icy West Orange sidewalk to my parked car, my feet flew out from under me and I landed so hard on my back that I knocked the wind out of myself and lay dazed a full minute.

In high school, I accidentally locked myself in the motorhome's clothes closet, and had to kick my way out to breathe. I should mention that my baby brother Danny was with me: we were playing hide-and-seek with our siblings. I later overheard Dad wondering aloud at how the closet lock could have broken; I kept silent.

Around the same time, on another adventure with Danny, we were riding Dad's moped about the property. I was cradling my brother in my left arm and gripping the handlebar with my right when I lost traction with the gravelly front drive, near the basketball backboard. We went into a long skid. I wound up with several cuts, a bruise, and a burn on my right thigh from the moped's muffler, which scalded me as it lay momentarily atop me. Danny was completely unharmed – he loved it and wanted to do it again!

In junior high school, roughhousing with Frank and Robbie in our parents' bedroom, my head was thrown onto one of the wood bed knobs, giving me a bloody head of hair, a dazed look and a big, dumb, prizefighter's grin. Robbie was horrified, and ran to get help, but I felt no pain. Ice soon worked its magic.

In fifth grade, at night, riding on Route 287 with Mom, Frank and Robbie, I was in the front passenger seat when the windshield in front of me suddenly exploded, spraying glass everywhere. The culprits: two teens dropping something from an overpass. Mom immediately headed for Morristown Memorial, but I told her I was fine; though surrounded by glass, I was unhurt. (I suspect that this incident, along with another from about that time in which a teen on a Morristown street saluted us all with a volley of adult language through Mom's open driver-side window as we waited for a red light – Mom remaining stone-faced, never acknowledging the speaker – precipitated our move to Madison.)

In second grade, I severed the tendon of my left big toe when I stepped on a piece of glass. More on that later.

And that's not even counting an earlier incident in which no one was hurt. We were living in Mendham, and I must have been about six; Frankie and I were in the family room. I climbed to the top of a bookshelf, where I found a gun. I picked it up, climbed down, and pointed it at my kid brother:

"Hey Frankie, look!" I said.

He started to cry. Mom ran into the room and grabbed the gun from my hand, telling me I shouldn't play with dangerous things.

I'll bet Dad heard about that afterwards.

***

Time to move to my chest, the source of much embarrassment. I didn't obsess about body hair to the degree that other adolescent boys did: to me, it was a matter of indifference whether my chest tufted out. But enough folks drew attention to my hairlessness to make me wonder. One was my father's friend, Mr. Alofs. On a sunny Saturday, he took us all sailing on Lake Hopatcong, and I removed my T-shirt to swim. Mr. Alofs, who was tall, hearty, of Dutch extraction, and fairly hairy, kidded me:

"Hey, John, where's the hair?"

Well, it was just hiding. I found it here and there, like patches of pachysandra in sandy soil. There was some on my lower arms, and a decent amount on my fairly muscular legs (another legacy of Dad's), but hardly a trace on my upper arms or chest. On good days, hair ringed my nipples; on bad ones, a stray hair sprouted in the midst of my cheek or on the bridge of my nose. Where did they come from? Where did they go?

Nor were my hands hairy. All my life they've been small, delicate, soft, supple, and fine-jointed – but not hairy. They weren't the hands of Jack Armstrong, Boy Wonder, and a lifetime of office work have ensured they won't be. But it was my hands that got all the attention on the day that I met my grandparents. Nana Edie took one look at me and said:

"Why, he has the hands of a pianist!"

To which Grandpa Hines answered:

"What do you mean? He's got the paws of a lumberjack."

Neither guess was right, and despite my father's genes, my hands weren't those of an athlete, either. Dad may have wondered whether his son would go on to play pro ball, but he never complained: he loved my mother too much to criticize her son's hands for being like hers.

Under the tutelage of Ms. Creange, my elderly high school typing teacher who wore her spectacles at the end of a long ribbon, I put those hands to work. After a semester of Typing I, they flew across an IBM Selectric at fifty-five words per minute; after Typing II, they neared eighty. Ms. Creange asked me whether I intended to become a secretary. That wasn't my plan, but it would come to pass. And hands too small to throw a tight spiral had found their métier.

Years later, they received a different sort of compliment. I was still living at home when Mom hosted a middle-aged Frenchwoman and her tween son as part of a cultural exchange program. They were from the sunbaked town of Perpignan, on the Côte d'Azur. One day, the mother, taking a break from the book that I had lent her to practice English (Anne Tyler's *Breathing Lessons*), told me that she could read palms. Would I like mine read? (Why can't I hear that phrase without seeing Bugs Bunny painting Elmer Fudd's hand with red paint?)

She took my left hand in her right and considered it carefully. After a pause, she looked at me. There was a *soupçon* of hesitation – was she finding the words, or simply weighing the wisdom of saying nothing? She said:

"This is the head line, indicating intelligence and wisdom. Yours is as long as I have seen. See, it begins here, at the edge of the palm, and goes across your hand to here, where it turns down and continues here, below your little finger."

I don't handle praise well, so I changed the subject. I tried some French on her son, who responded so quickly that I couldn't understand a word he said. His mother, annoyed, told him to stop the "l'envers."

"L'envers?" It sounded like the French word for backwards.

"Yes," she said. She explained that it was slang used by inner-city hoodlums and bratty French teens. The smarts I had were of the book, not street, variety.

***

The more distant I get from my brain, the weirder my body gets. As a teen, my fingers were my tools – my forceps, my lunar rover's robotic arms – that explored those alien lanes. I proceeded with deliberation, first flexing and calibrating my instruments.

When I couldn't sleep, I played a game of my own design with my hands: I paired my fingertips as if to play "church and steeple" then rotated one hand with respect to the other by one finger – right thumb to left index, right index to left middle, and so forth. The steeple having buckled and warped, the parishioners having fled, I'd offset my fingers again by another finger so that my hands were twisted like a Christmas cracker. In this way I continued, seeing how far I could go, contorting my hands ever further in a game of cat's cradle without strings.

Only then would I burrow beneath the comforter, which I knew was another name for the Holy Spirit. I made my laboratory in a snug cavern of body heat, just as physicists dig miles underground to create dark reservoirs in which they hope to detect faint splashes of neutrinos.

I began with the little toes, those disconcerting appendages, so extraneous, so maimed in daily life; they were easy to reach then when I was nimble. The bulbous, florid amorphousness of my pinky toes made me shudder. They were nearly devoid of toenails. To probe them with my deployed thumb and forefinger was to detect just a trace of keratin, a melee diamond set by a fastidious jeweler in pink flesh.

Working through my toes, I compared their lengths. My second piggies, the ones who had roast beef, were nearly as long as the big toes. As a teenage boy, I of course immediately wondered whether that was normal. Like most of my concerns about my body, I needn't have worried, but it turns out that I *was* onto something.

I have since read of an analogous measurement, the "2D:4D ratio," the ratio of the lengths of index fingers to ring fingers. That ratio, it turns out, correlates with the amount of testosterone to which one is exposed in the womb, which in turn (for men) correlates with aspects of masculinity. That's why men have longer ring fingers than index fingers, and women the opposite. (Go ahead and check; this book can wait.) The smaller the 2D:4D ratio, the less testosterone. My ratio is *low*. In a way, I'm glad I didn't know that then; on the other hand, I would have had a ready explanation to Mr. Alofs' jibe about my chest hair.

There was once, on the underside of my left foot, where the big toe met the second toe, a faint scar. It has now vanished, subsumed by pink new skin, but for years it was a bookend of sorts to the scar on my chin. It, too, resulted from a youthful accident.

The summer I was eight, I spent part of my vacation at my aunt and uncle's Westchester County summerhouse. One morning, playing barefoot in their driveway, I felt a small prick. There was no pain, just a sensation like the sting of a small bee; but when I raised my foot, I was stunned to see its entire underside painted bright red. I calmly walked to the front door to ring the doorbell. (I didn't want to track blood in the immaculate white hall.) I told Aunt Ro that I thought I'd stepped on something, and showed her my foot. She nearly swooned. But she hurried to the hall telephone to call Dad, who arrived in record time to whisk me to Morristown Memorial.

I was smarter then: I knew my injury was of little importance, because it touched nothing that mattered. Besides, Dad would tell the doctors what to do. So I was calm on the way to the hospital, dwelling on my usual preoccupations – television, books, baseball cards, coins, bottle caps – and a new one, the school where I'd begin that fall. Dad, who *was* nervous, later told me how he was struck by my calm. Even the ward nurses complimented me, calling me a "trooper" for not fretting about the operation. Why should I? They knew their stuff; my body was *their* department. I didn't care, as long as I had a book to read.

A piece of glass had snapped the tendon of my big toe. Surgery was scheduled for the next morning; I'd stay overnight in the hospital. That evening, Mom and Dad paid me a visit. A nurse wheeled me to the rec room so that we could play games. My parents had brought a new game called Perquackey, like Boggle, in which players formed words using the upper faces of thrown dice. We played while a ceiling-mounted television in the room's far corner played an old episode of *The Adventures of Ozzie and Harriet*. The Nelsons had nothing on us.

Next morning, I was wheeled to the operating room, where a kindly nurse told me to count backwards from ten. I got to seven.

I can't be sure how much later I awoke in the clouds. The wind whistled, and the air was moist. It felt like I was flying. Was this heaven? I tried to turn my neck, but was too woozy. Soon I realized that I was surrounded by netting, in some kind of tent. A hyperbaric chamber, to be precise.

The souvenirs of my stay were a heavy, full-length plaster leg cast and two crutches with white rubber pads that supported my armpits. I wore the cast for weeks, into the beginning of second grade. It turned out to be a great way to break the ice with my scary new schoolmates – they all signed it. Then, when it came off, I attended physical therapy sessions at the hospital. I still remember the terror of the first one, when I supported myself on parallel bars as I prepared to walk for the first time in weeks. That hurt like crazy. I told my parents that I never wanted to walk again, which must have thrilled them.

When I healed, Dad spraypainted my crutches gold. (I'm not sure why.) They stayed in my bedroom closet for twenty years, like Tiny Tim's; once in a while, I'd take them out for a spin, locomoting around my bedroom although they had become far too short for me. The rubber pads were cracked with age.

As for Perquackey, after its one night of purposeful use, it sat in its box for years in the closet beneath the center stairs of our Morristown home. Likely, it never made the move to Madison.

***

May I linger a bit on my middle?

For ninety-nine percent of my life, I've been dissatisfied with my weight, though I've never been more than chubby. I don't blame peer pressure for my self-image; I blame Special K. Specifically, the misleading claims made on Special K commercials during the Saturday morning cartoons of my youth. Could I pinch an inch? Sure. What I didn't know was that *everyone* could. Years later, I got the honest truth from

Daryl, a kid one class ahead of me in high school. Our physics teacher, Mr. Bucher, teased him for his putting on weight, and he responded that those were just "love handles" anyway. Bucher laughed – *touché*.

When I was young, Mom showed me how to take a shower on my own. Quite reasonably, she suggested toweling off my middle last.

"You wouldn't want to dry your face after drying off down there, would you?"

Of course not!

Years later, I discovered I liked toweling off down there first, last, whenever. That was, not coincidentally, about the time I discovered the *Sports Illustrated* swimsuit issue.

Like every *Sports Illustrated* issue, it sat in the stack of magazines in my parents' bathroom, among *Reader's Digest, Architectural Digest, Photography Today,* and the Sunday mass church bulletins. The only difference was that this particular issue had a cover photo of Christie Brinkley in a white bikini, smiling at me with the sunkissed girl-next-door face of a girl who could never, ever, live next door.

> *When I was a young boy*
> *My mama said to me*
> *There's only one girl in the world for you*
> *And she probably lives in Tahiti*
>   - Wreckless Eric, "(I'd Go the) Whole Wide World"

Christie leaned complacently against a palm tree in the British Virgin Islands. Listing slightly to starboard, she braced herself with her right hand against the palm's massive rings. She wore a V-shaped bikini bottom that went all the way down to *there*.

I careful noted the magazine's exact position in the stack before extracting it. It would come in handy in conjunction with another recent discovery, one that had momentous, far-reaching consequences. With no tutelage from books, movies, or peers, I had discovered a hitherto unknown realm from which no one, so far as I knew, had returned alive. My initial sorties were death-defying, but I had become familiar enough with the terrain to hope that they would not prove fatal.

> *My hand's a five leaf clover*

> *It's palm Sunday over and over*
> - Jellyfish, "He's My Best Friend"

Now here was Christie, my congenial tour guide, to help me find *terra incognita*. And not just Christie! There was Elle, and Paulina, and Kathy, and Rachel, and Stephanie, and many others who would be happy to help me find myself. The February *Sports Illustrated* swimsuit issue became my Pandora's box; but unlike the one of which I'd read about in mythology, or seen in the silent film that had provoked such nightmares as a child (for more, see Side A, "Magic Realism"), this one was in glorious living color, and full of *good* things, not bad. Unlike the backlit woman at the end of *Pandora's Box*, these women looked directly at you – and smiled!

Alas, the only thing I'd later regret was all that lost time....

The Class of '81

As a deejay at WCFA, the local community radio station, I not only presented a solo show, but teamed up with Carol for a weekly program that we called "Brunch Box." For three hours every Saturday morning, we profiled the pop music of a different year.

Planning the 1981 show was giving me fits.

How to keep it to three hours? Or rather, one and one-half minus talking (since Carol also chose songs). 1981 was the year when music opened my ears to new vistas, confirming to me that my love of sound would be lifelong. Until then, I'd been a strictly by-the-charts listener of AM pop radio, not yet a devotee of FM's "album-oriented rock," much less music's other delights.

It was the memory of that sense of unlimited possibility that made preparing a 1981 playlist so difficult. So many songs, so little time! I decided, to Carol's surprise, that we would need *three* shows to do the year justice, though we hadn't devoted more than one to any other. That would give me the time to play a representative cross-section of every strain of pop music that made an impact on me and the larger culture, but also time to consider: what were my schoolmates listening to?

That required research. From a bookshelf I pulled a compendia of *Billboard* charts, and in the back of my bedroom closet I located my 1981 high school yearbook. I was a freshman then, but more interested in the seniors whose "write-ups" I wished to examine.

The typical senior write-up went like this:

Nickname(s) (if any)
Things that rate
Things that don't rate
Friends and activities
Abbreviations and acronyms that no one, not even the student-writer, will be able to decipher ten years hence
Plans for the future
Inspirational or provocative quote

I didn't want to read three hundred write-ups. But I needed to know what the kids were digging. So I speed-read, tallying every mention of a musician or band. I took attributions at face value; that is, I didn't fact check the student who cited Ray Davies as the author of the words, "Success walks hand in hand with failure along the Hollywood Boulevard." (He was right.)

Two hours later, I had results. What surprised me most was how *reactionary* the seniors' taste was: what I saw as a watershed year for pop looked very different from their perspective. By and large, they had shunned their generation. Their allegiance was to 1960s-1970s classic rock: Led Zeppelin, the Grateful Dead, Jackson Browne; the Doors, the Who, Pink Floyd; The Beatles, the Eagles, the Stones; southern-fried boogie from the Marshall Tucker Band, the Allman Brothers, and the Pure Prairie League; and singer-songwriters like Dan Fogelberg, James Taylor, and Crosby, Stills, Nash, and sometimes Young.

Equally notable were the omissions. Punk never happened. Neither had disco, except for an occasional mention of how much it was *hated*. And new wave barely registered – aside from the Cars, the B-52's, and Elvis Costello, there wasn't much evidence. In 1981, new wave and disco were prominent on the *Billboard* charts, but largely absent from the radar of the senior class.

Why the disconnect? The charts had long been the province of teenagers, but ours had soundly rejected it for the tried, true, established and old. I formulated several hypotheses.

Conservatism. Morris County, then as now, was a Republican bulwark, and this was the Reagan era. (Heck, even *I* voted for the Gipper in my only GOP vote ever.) Young Republicans established *bona fides* by championing establishment musicians. And while I doubted that Jim Morrison, the lead singer of the Doors, the *fifth* most popular group among the seniors, would have voted for Reagan, his having been dead for fifteen years ensured he would not pose a threat to the orthodoxy.

> *Meanwhile at the White House*
> *Everyone who wasn't extremely rich was* persona non grata
> *Nancy Reagan said to just say no*
> *To everything except Frank Sinatra*
>   - Wally Pleasant, "I Was a Teenage Republican"

Groupthink. Those who liked disco were suspect, so they kept quiet. Personally I liked many disco hits; many ("Le Freak," "Knock on

Wood," "I Will Survive") were juggernauts of production. And though disco lacked the idiosyncratic songwriting I tended to favor, it was a long way from that point of view to the parochialism of reflexively chanting "Disco sucks!"

Resignation. One senior quoted the following lines of a brilliant song – but how do they work as a life motto?

> Say a prayer for the pretender
> Who started out so young and strong
> Only to surrender
>   - Jackson Browne, "The Pretender"

The Class of '81 had grown up fast. They'd lived hard and loved hard. They drank, smoked, caroused, brawled, and before they could vote they liked their rock and roll straight, no chaser. Was our Bedford Falls, Pottersville? Wasn't it Nick the Bartender who said, "Hey, look mister, we serve hard drinks in here for men who want to get drunk fast. And we don't need any characters around to give the joint atmosphere."

Or was it like that other coming-of-age classic set in a small-town, dead-end world, *The Last Picture Show*, with classic rock in place of lowdown Hank Williams blues? No smart-ass new wave for the Class of '81, thank you: keep the chords simple and the riffs familiar.

That last theory, while intriguing and quite possibly true, did not describe my own experience. I was not tempted by drink; my mood-altering substance of choice was music. And by junior year, I'd begun looking further afield for it than FM radio.

In the summer of 1983, I landed a job in the new field of word processing, an amalgam of two skills I had studied in high school, typing and computer programming. I worked for a kindly gentleman, Sam, who ran a home business that he'd started with his daughter as a means of bridging the generation gap. He called it Jenny Gapp.

It was Mom who saw the advertisement in the *Madison Eagle* classifieds. She started working for Sam on Saturdays, and suggested me for weekdays. Though Sam was reluctant to hire a high school kid, Mom convinced him that I was more responsible than most. (Mom later bought the business from Sam and ran it out of our house, making me her employee.)

Having gotten wind of this, my classmate Dave told his mother, who asked me if I would lend her a hand with her math tutoring business, which she also ran from home. She had quizzes and worksheets that needed data entry – would I like some extra cash? Well, sure.

Thus began the second least rewarding job I've ever had, just ahead of the three days I spent in a Morris Plains warehouse assembling gift baskets for The Body Shop. The worksheets were a pain, particularly the entry of mathematical symbols on an antiquated computer running primitive software. As for working conditions, I sat for hours in a hot, stuffy attic without air conditioning. In the end, I earned twelve dollars, but rather than pay in cash, Dave's mother asked her son to buy me a record album. So, we drove to the Short Hills Mall and its upstairs music store, Record World. (Ah, for the days when malls had "upstairs" and "downstairs" record stores!)

Taking my time like a kid in a candy shop, I finally opted for *No Parlez*, the debut album by a young Brit named Paul Young. *No Parlez* contained his cover of "Love of the Common People," a British hit that I'd heard on Scott Muni's Friday afternoon WNEW show, "Things from England," which was sponsored by an import record store of the same name in Cliffside Park. I'd been to the store; a classmate, Toto, drove me there from time to time so I could check out the hits from "across the pond" while he stocked up on singles, posters, and calendars by his two lady loves, Nena and Madonna.

On the US charts, "Love of the Common People" stiffed. Perhaps the culprit was its odd, stuttering choir sample, as conceived by Laurie Latham. Latham was a record producer whose star rose and fell in the 1980s, when his signature synthetic buzz-and-bass went in, then out, of fashion, like a distant radio station.

No Parlez cost $9.99, saving Dave's mom two dollars. I played it a few times for "Love of the Common People" and its *American Top Forty* follow-up, "Come Back and Stay." Not great value, but I doubt I was the target audience. The album cover showed the young Mr. Young looking right at me, right hand on right cheek, hair greased and teased a foot high, extending right off the album cover. He wore what looked like an undershirt, a ploy to seduce unwitting female fans.

After I got my own driver's license, I could often be found at the malls, in record stores, particularly Record World, for its import section: four bins of twelve-inch records along the west wall, far removed from the store's more highly-trafficked profit centers. I lingered there, studying covers, absorbing cover art, reading song titles, imagining music unlike any I'd ever heard. At that time, artwork on import albums was more interesting than that on domestic releases; imports were carefully crafted as cohesive artistic statements, not eye-catching messes meant to shift units. (Paul Young, I'm looking at you.)

It was in the import bins that I discovered the extended mix of "A New England," Kirsty MacColl's British hit with the over-the-top yet intricately textured production. MacColl teamed up with well-known rock producer Steve Lillywhite, who later worked with headline acts like U2, to transform a lachrymose song by folkie Billy Bragg into a galloping seven-minute dance-pop epic. And they did it without sacrificing the message about the difficult transition from adolescence to adulthood, albeit shifted to a female perspective. Behind it, a massively multitracked choir of Kirsty's own vocals was awash in harmonics. Never have I heard a pop singer harmonize better with herself.

I didn't know Kirsty from Eve. I did not know she was the daughter of Ewan MacColl, the noted British folksinger and composer of "The First Time Ever I Saw Your Face." I didn't know she would one day marry Lillywhite. Nor could I have extrapolated the arc of her career, which began with "They Don't Know" (a single I bought at Things From England, later a hit for Tracey Ullman) and "There's a Guy Down the Chip Shop Swears He's Elvis," her first British hit. (Again, the Americans didn't get it; some lame marketer had her sing "Truck Stop" instead of "Chip Shop"). After collaborating with the Pogues, those Irish barnburners, she would flex her songwriting muscle on increasingly sophisticated solo albums, culminating in *Tropical Brainstorm*, still an all-time favorite. Finally, I could not have known that Kirsty would die young in a hit-and-run speedboat accident, when a craft owned by a high-ranking Brazilian government official struck her while she was swimming. All that would come later.

I had just the sleeve to go on. As with many British records of its era, the cover photo is simplicity itself, making good use of negative space, with album and artist names sandwiching a grayscale letterbox photo of Kirsty. Had the record been a crass American one, she would have been dolled up like a peacock, like Paul Young; but here she looks fixedly, unsmilingly, and a bit off-camera, with her feathered blonde hair mussed and a homemade bead earring dangling from her only visible ear, the right. Her fair, freckled complexion is apparent even in grayscale. I see the beauty Steve Lillywhite saw, but her expression is one of annoyance, as if loath to pose or be captured at all.

The back cover is even more enigmatic. We move from letterbox to full screen, to a photograph of what looks like a job site strewn with sheetrock, gravel, cinder blocks, and fragments of wood. Amidst it all, front and center, a man with tousled hair, back to camera, rights a pole atop which waves the Union Jack, the only thing in the photograph rendered in color. It's torn in half. I could wonder all day about how these images related to the song. (And when MTV came out, I did just that: some of my favorite songs were videos.)

Like the front photograph, "A New England" is part come-on, part protest, part provocation, part mystery. The protest part refers to "prams" (baby carriages, to Brits), bringing to mind another British hit of that era:

> *Let's talk about prams! And washing machines!*
> *Let's talk about the end of childhood dreams!*
> - Vital Disorders, "(Let's Talk About) Prams"

In that age of Thatcherites and neoconservatives, British artists – men and women alike – strained against conformity, stereotypes, and traditional gender roles. Madison High School's Class of 1981 might have been more self-empowered had they heard some of this new agit-pop instead of resigning themselves to reliving their parents' lives, sins, and record collections. As for me, I would have been happy to let Kirsty go off to the studio as often as she wished while I stayed home to do the dishes, as long as I got to hear her albums first.

***

Same bin, different day: I found an even more unusual record which had a similarly long-lasting impact.

Once again, it was an import with a spare cover. The front photo was letterboxed, but vertically, with a blank right margin except for a few tiny words near the top:

"This is the Ice Age"[1,2]
MARTHA AND THE MUFFINS[3]

Three questions immediately sprang to mind. What sort of band calls itself "Martha and the Muffins"? Who puts footnotes on album covers? And to what do the footnotes refer? I flipped the album front to back, front to back, then back to front, to examine it more closely. The front photo was nothing like what one would expect from a band with such a silly name.

The lower half, partially out of focus, is the top of an old home or apartment building in an old city district. The masonry's russet-colored paint has been peeling for quite some time, exposing red brick near the roofline and, a bit lower, a whitish layer with flecks and patches of russet. The building is in a state of advanced decay, like a once fashionable dress that has ripped, exposing petticoats beneath, the middle one gingham.

Beyond its flat roof looms the salient feature of the photograph's upper half: a distant skyscraper set like a jewel in a faded, early evening light blue sky. Just a few wisps of cloud are discernible. Where the home is fuzzy, the skyscraper is crystal clear. The office lights of its top dozen floors (the height is hard to gauge due to the obstruction of the nearer building) are already lit against the evening sky, and from its rooftop, amid a clutter of skylights, a tall antenna injects a needle into the sky, a faint pink pinprick at its tip. It must be an aircraft beacon on the city's tallest building – but which city? I couldn't say, knowing nothing about the band. The only clue (other than the record's location in the import bin) was the skyscraper, whose two camera-facing sides blazoned a bright blue "B" lying on its side, resembling an infinity symbol.

Turning the record over again in my hands, still wondering what it could possibly sound like, I saw the same composition from the same perspective, but in the early morning. In the foreground, the nearby apartment building has been eclipsed: no light falls on it. Beyond, in the peach sky of first light, the skyscraper keeps its vigil. All its lights, except an abbreviated row on the second-highest floor and an entire row a few floors further down, are extinguished. And here's something I see only now, thirty-five later: if you take the B's to be eyes, and the illuminated rooms as a nose and close-lipped mouth, it looks like the building is impassively watching *you*.

When I first saw those photos as a high school senior, the album, *This is the Ice Age*, was going on two years old. I'd found it because it had languished in the import bin for two years. How different from the favorite albums of the Class of 1981! Here all was ambiguity, unlike the cover of, say, *Sticky Fingers* – to name just one album by a Class of '81 favorite, the Rolling Stones – a close-up of the crotch of a pair of jeans, zipper ready for pulling. *This is the Ice Age*, on the other hand, had the quality of an indefinable dream.

To deepen the mystery, the band had gone out of its way to be anonymous. Clearly, they didn't seem interested in broadcasting their hometown: the only clue was an address for "correspondence," printed in a tiny font near the bottom of the back cover, a postal box in Toronto. (Ah, they're Canadians!) There were no band photos, front or back. Somehow they had managed to persuade their label to go along with marketing suicide.

Then there were the song titles:

[1]*Swimming*
Women Around the World at Work
Casualties of Glass
Boy Without Filters
Jets Seem Slower in London Skies

[2]*This is the Ice Age*
One Day in Paris
You Sold the Cottage
Three Hundred Years/Chemistry

Now I understood: the footnotes referenced album sides. Without having heard a note, I was beginning to understand this record's strange logic. The rest would have to wait until I got it home and put it on my bedroom phonograph.

When I did, I was arrested by the oddest pop music I'd ever heard: insistent and melodic, a little dissonant, yet still beguiling. It begins with the looped sound of a car crash, then settles into "Swimming," a rhythmic, synthesized loop over which arpeggiated guitars wander. A man begins to talk-sing, leading to a male-female duet of:

We're afraid to call it love
Let's call it swimming

I told myself to make a copy for Elyssa, the member of my high school class most likely to share an enthusiasm for "alternative" music. This was clearly alternative! And she did like it. She also told me, with a chuckle, how she'd played it one morning while driving her mother to work, provoking the question, "Could we listen to something else?"

I will refrain from a song-by-song review in deference to the 99.9999% of the human race who have not heard *This Is the Ice Age*, but I'll mention some highlights.

"Women Around the World at Work," sung by one of the band's *two* Marthas (they could have gone by "Marthas and the Muffin") was a minor hit in Canada. It has angular riffs and, for this band, an above-average guitar quotient. It also has a venomous lyric that blames men for heartless predations in and on the battlefield, the boardroom, and the bedroom. In short, it is of a piece with "Prams," but more political and less absurd. Despite this, it has a strong melody. In the early 1980s, that was not yet a sin; musicians still paired politics with catchy melodies, and in the process created memorable music.

The album's standout, "You Sold the Cottage," with its propulsive beat and weird keyboard squiggles, sounds like the B-52s with the kitsch surgically removed. Martha sings of a lakefront cabin in rural Canada that her parents rented each summer, where she suffered every kind of indignity: bloodsuckers between toes, tumbles from tree forts, bites from chipmunks living under the boathouse. And yet, in the chorus, when she addresses herself to her husband, or perhaps a brother, she acidly reminds him that it was *his* idea to sell the cottage.

The key to her disappointment must lie in the repeated phrase, "but it's a lifestyle" – the song's only lyric sung by a male. The man who sold the cottage has robbed Martha not only of trees and chipmunks, but identity. The malefactor may have cashed in to finance a lifestyle boost: a sports car, or a new kitchen. (What isn't marketed as a lifestyle boost?) Whatever it was, the way he says "lifestyle" can only be heard as hollow.

In my room, as I listened to this penultimate track, I turned back to the front cover and reasoned as follows: the eclipsed building in the foreground is the "cottage"; the distant skyscraper is the future. We're destined for a modern, well-lit, antiseptic future run by the Infinity Corporation.

One disclaimer. As lawyers of media conglomerates are fond of saying on DVDs, these interpretations are my own, not those of Martha and the Muffins. I don't *know* that this album is about the victimization of an underclass left behind by the new global economy, mostly women and rural folk, though I think it may be. I don't *know* that this is a protest album, though I think it is. It may simply be protesting human nature.

There is foreboding in the eerie instrumental "Jets Seem Slower in London Skies," the perfect soundscape for watching a fading contrail in a blue sky. And there is, I believe, a glimmer of hope in the album finale, "Three Hundred Years/Chemistry," especially its strange cheerleader chant in the second half. It may take three hundred years, but we may eventually figure out what life is about.

Those were my thoughts on the album, at a time when I was contemplating my own future. I was about to go to college. Which future did I want – the one in the cottage, or the one in the skyscraper? My friend Dave, and most classmates I knew, wanted the skyscraper: they couldn't wait to escape our hometown. I wanted the cottage. I wanted to live at home as long as the roof kept out the rain, to postpone the day when I'd work in the finance department of a soulless multinational. Perhaps the Class of '81 and I weren't that different, after all. We both feared the future.

I looked again at the yearbook write-ups, particularly the future plans. Aside from optimistic predictions of coveted careers – business school, law enforcement, nursing – I saw the wisecracks of dissidents:

> *Teaching yoga*
> *Elevator operator*
> *Draft dodger*
> *Eternal numbness*
> *Space travel*
> *Golden smog*
> *Abolishing cretinism*
> *Buying new batteries for his radio*
> *Moving to Colorado*
> *Being an artist*

We had more in common than I knew, but we differed in the role assigned to music. I embraced new sounds that, at least tangentially, addressed my fears head-on, or at least acknowledged my worldview. They sought in music a comfort, a crutch, and a hope that there would still be a place for them in the world of their parents.

***

The beauty of writing about 1981 in 2019 is having the internet at my fingertips. I can instantly query the provenance of the front and back cover photographs of *This is the Ice Age*. I am not surprised to learn they were taken by Mark Gane, the band's principal guitarist, out the window of his Toronto apartment. The skyscraper in the distance was the headquarters of the Bank of Montreal. All well and good. But the internet cannot tell you what the photos *mean*.

Communications Breakdown

For my peers, college was a given: it followed high school like fall followed summer. But I wasn't ready, and it took three tries in three years for me to figure that out: two stints at Princeton and one whirlwind week at Drew University, Madison's small liberal arts college.

So I changed tack. I spent the rest of the 1980s at entry-level jobs, mostly at AT&T. The telecommunications giant's heyday had come and gone, but it still dominated the Morris County landscape. Its offices were everywhere, and I worked at several.

But AT&T never cut me a paycheck. Instead, I worked for Focus Management Group, a hole-in-the-wall employment agency behind the Morristown Green, near Bamberger's. Week after week, year after year, I recorded my hours on triplicate forms: white, blue, pink. Keeping the pink copy, I dropped the others in a mail slot in the office door after hours on Fridays. Pay began at nine dollars per hour, climbing to twelve. After a year, I got paid holidays. It was all I wanted or needed.

The seasons passed, and I enjoyed the routine. I had dismantled the pressure cooker of life. I read Thomas Mann's *The Magic Mountain*, and saw myself in Hans Castorp, the young man who one day visits a friend at a sanatorium and winds up staying longer than he expected.

For a year or more – I'm unsure because, like Hans, I lost track of time – I worked in an office building in Harding Township, across Route 202 from Wightman Farms, the market where at lunchtime I would buy cider donuts and flavored honey straws – cinnamon, clove, lemon. I worked in the office building's Telecommunications Center, a windowless room in the rear of the second floor where all day faxes came and went, a Grand Central Station of glossy paper. I was part of a small team servicing the building's seventy-five-odd middle managers and secretaries. Thirty years on, I can still bring to mind the names and department numbers of many managers listed on the bulletin board directly inside our office:

    Pelliteri, Frank – 1
    Van Cleef, Liz - 1
    Bouska, Amy - 2
    Ng, John - 4

Frankly, I'm amazed that I remember this trivia, because I never knew these folks, and rarely encountered them for more than a minute at a time. Most managers dispatched secretaries to collect and deliver their faxes; others wandered in distractedly, scribbled cover pages, and tossed outgoing faxes in a wire basket on the credenza, then collected incoming faxes from a department cubbyhole.

A few managers I remember slightly better, the ones who hung out with us between meetings. Mr. Pelliteri, for example, traded gossip with our manager and matriarch, Florence. He told one story about a coworker, a Japanese woman, with whom he traveled on business. He said she worked nonstop; once he glimpsed the inside of her hotel room, and her bed was covered with stacks of papers she intended to read. This vapid but psychologically significant anecdote has remained in my mind for thirty years. At the time, I'm sad to say I was disposed to side with Mr. Pelliteri, against the woman who worked so hard. I suppose I was projecting my own need to relax. Still, shame on me.

I was on a team of six. Looking down time's long corridor from a world defined by automation, the Internet, and the Cloud, our back office seems remarkably Dickensian. Imagine: half a dozen people sitting around, waiting for faxes to spool off ticking machines, page by page; making long distance calls to request resends after paper jams and power outages; physically discarding spam mail from office supply companies; and committing for0eign countries' area codes to memory.

And we sent telexes, that secure alternative and predecessor of faxes. I knew the address protocols. I knew the country codes. I could compose, send, and check the status of messages that failed due to network congestion. And I could use the telex machine to have fun: for example, I knew the address from which one could print out the current *Billboard* pop singles chart. In fact, I was probably the only Squeeze fan in the world who followed the weekly chart progress of their 1987 comeback hit, "Hourglass," by telex:

> *I feel like I'm calling on a telephone*
> *No one can hear the ringing*
> - Squeeze, "Hourglass"

That was the golden era of my Squeeze fixation. As a member of their fan club, every other month I received by air mail a newsletter and memorabilia from their quaintly-named London business address, Bugle House. (I still have my own club pin.) It was around that time that I wrote a short story about a young man and woman who fall in and out of love, their shared love for Squeeze serving as backdrop. And though I liked "Hourglass," which echoed the classic songs the band had recorded before it had broken up and reformed three years later, it was the record's B side, "Splitting into Three," that I really liked. In fact, that tale of family breakup told from a child's perspective inspired my one and only limerick:

There once was a band called Squeeze
Who played all their songs on their knees
Though the half of them liked it
The other half hiked it
And that's how they split into threes

I took the time to e-mail the limerick to the band's principal songwriter, Chris Difford, but I never heard back.

***

I lived slowly and sped through work. Only when I'd finished my daily tasks would I again slow down. The rest of the time, I mulled over hobbies and talked with coworkers whom I still remember despite seeing them only in the office and having little in common with them. I believed in human nature then, accepting people for who they were, not wishing to change them in any way.

Each day I worked with Florence, Rose, Becky, and Jim.

My manager Florence signed my timesheets. Cheerful, middle-aged, African-American, and obese, she remained at her desk, letting her staff handle the physical labor of loading and unloading the machines. She smiled a lot and enjoyed gossip, and was never mean-spirited. Her manager Vivian, white and older, maintained a patrician bearing and profile. She rarely bothered us; perhaps she sensed that we considered the Telecommunications Center our personal domain, and that we were handling things just fine. Only when Florence was out on a Friday – a frequent occurrence since she had so much accrued vacation – did I hunt down Vivian to get my timesheet signed.

Rose was an Italian nonna, a youngish sixty, with close-cropped, salt-and-pepper hair. Our windowless room's powerful air conditioning kept her in thin sweaters the year round. She would gingerly arrange a wrap over her shoulders with index fingers and thumbs as she stood to collect a fax and carefully dial a phone number with one fingertip. She walked erect, shoulders back, and her sweater's loose folds gave her the self-contained fullness of a Madonna in a niche. Her hands incessantly and unconsciously worried a large gold crucifix that hung from her neck at the end of a long gold chain, a stand-in for the rosary that she was required to leave at home.

Rose was tolerant, but Vivian occasionally had to remind her to check her religious opinions at the door. The only problem I had in this regard was the day Rose brought in a petition protesting the release of Martin Scorsese's new film, *The Last Temptation of Christ*. My coworkers signed it, but I did not. Rose was initially surprised at my refusal, but moved on. A slight curl at the corner of her mouth was all that hinted at her incomprehension.

Rose took a maternal interest in Jim, who was close to my age. He was biding his time until he could find a job nearer home. Jim was so Italian that he might have walked right off the screen of a different, earlier Scorsese film, *Mean Streets*. A bit short, thin as a rail, with dark cheek stubble, he dressed to the nines, eschewing a tie; his loose shirt collar hinted at a quantity of dark chest hair. He sported tailored suits, always dark, usually pinstriped, with the pants baggy around the middle and tightly flared at the legs. When he felt like work – sometimes he just sat and directed the rest of us, outstretched legs crossed atop his corner desk – he executed his maneuvers with a dancer's grace that complemented his outfit. For Jim was a dancer: on Mondays, he'd tell us where he'd gone dancing the previous weekend, and on Fridays we'd hear where he intended to "go out dancing" with friends.

His follies made Rose smile. Perhaps Jim reminded her of a son, or a beau. But she betrayed an occasional concern for the way he led his life, and chided him about his dancing obsession. One day, a secretary who flirted with Jim despite having ten years on him ensnared him in a conversation about chest hair. Jim naively admitted that he had a lot – even below the navel. She said:

"They call that the trail of pleasure."

After a long pause, Jim glanced nervously down, then away, and chuckled. I could hear Rose grind her teeth.

Jim had many admirers among the fresh-faced young secretaries who dropped faxes off for their bosses; they would hand faxes personally to him rather than drop them in the wire basket. I don't believe he saw them outside the office. They mainly ignored me, whom they viewed as a curiosity, though I recall one young woman with plump, rosy cheeks, whose name I've unaccountably forgotten, who smiled broadly at me each time she entered the room, which of course had the effect of making me freeze. One time after she left, Florence pivoted in her squeaky manager's chair and said:

"She likes you."

I blushed. "Do you think so?"

"*Oh, yes.*" Florence was tickled by my innocence.

Eventually that secretary stopped coming, sending another in her stead. I hope I didn't break her heart.

Finally, there was Becky. Petite, blonde, plump, and in her early thirties, she was the first person of my acquaintance to speak in a rounded and mellifluous Southern accent straight out of North Carolina. Becky was a reader, the only other in our group, and I enjoyed talking with her during downtime. She could see I was capable and quick; why wasn't I trying for something better? I told her I was content, and that my job let me do as I pleased. She had read that intelligence could find happiness in any situation.

That was our team. It had surprisingly little turnover.

There was one brief hire who couldn't hack it: a pale, thin young man who'd been recommended by a manager. One morning, as I typed a telex, I caught him looking over my shoulder. When I turned to face him, he said in an affect-free voice:

"RU 2000?"

I smiled nervously and asked him to repeat himself, but he just stared and remained silent. I glanced around the room in an appeal for help, but no one was looking my way. A couple of minutes later, Vivian collected him. She later explained that he'd had an "episode," and would be seeing his doctor.

With no obligations – no one to support, no hot dates, no dance buddies – my schedule was flexible. So, when asked if I would take the flex shift from eleven to eight, I agreed. There was far less work at night, though managers occasionally required after-hours assistance.

At night, my coworkers were two gals who alternated evenings. One's last name was Dinacola, a charming name to say. She was petite, with dark eyes and curly brown hair. Younger than I, she was finishing her undergraduate degree by taking part-time and summer classes. She brought her homework, and I would distract her with music talk. Not having heard my favorite bands (who had?), I made her a mix tape that must not have overly impressed her since she returned it with little comment. I struck another name from the marriage list.

The other gal was Pam. She was older, dark-haired, probably in her thirties. She bragged about her niece's precocity; she cited her facility with metaphor, such as a robin's "topknot." Our tastes in music were closer, and when I made her a mix of exclusively Squeeze songs, she said:

"It's good. I would have been into this when I was younger."

That didn't make sense to me then, but now I understand that taste can change with age.

***

Inside the Communications Center's thick walls, calendar pages turned. Outside, unseen seasons passed. I worked steadily with little thought of advancement, biding my time until life itself changed. In retrospect, I'm happy to have had that time: just writing of it and the people I knew then makes me happy. Fate scattered them to the wind, but not before adding texture and consistency to my life.

This stage of life felt different than any other, being as simple as it could be. My only consideration was the daily round. How lucky to have been born when jobs like that still existed: certainly, no one sends telexes anymore! Middle management, what's left of it, must send their own messages. It's a shame, because jobs like mine were good places to dip one's toes in life before taking the plunge.

And so it came to pass that my job ended, and I moved to another position within AT&T. Here's what happened:

In the late 1980s, unions pressured AT&T to stop filling jobs, particularly long-term jobs with benefits, with temporary employees.

The short-term/long-term cutoff was taken to be one year, and since I'd been at my job longer, my position was axed. So my temporary agency immediately placed me at another AT&T location.

Making ten dollars an hour, I did not heed labor politics. Was I depriving someone of a salary and benefits, someone who needed it more? Should I have been doing something meaningful with my life? Should I have been making the world a better place? I don't know.

> *I'm stupidly happy, with idiot grin*
> *I'm stupidly happy, it's surely a sin*
> - XTC, "Stupidly Happy"

My new office building was not just another AT&T site: it was Headquarters, an immense V-shaped complex, somewhat akin to the Pentagon Building and Newark Airport. Its nickname was the Taj Mahal, though I don't know why, since it had neither minarets nor a dome. Rather, it was a long, modular building on which ivy ran rampant, a huge stack of balconies in need of a good power wash.

Headquarters occupied two hundred acres near the small-town crossroads of Basking Ridge. On a fine afternoon, particularly when the Mets were playing, I'd take my lunch outside – perhaps a sandwich and Snapple from the deli next to Pepperidge Farm. (I was partial to their baguette sandwiches with brie and honey mustard horseradish.) I'd put on headphones and listen to the team's enthusiastic rookie announcer, Gary Cohen, as I traced a long circuit around my workplace. Sometimes I'd extend my walk to neighboring roads that resembled Connecticut hill country, then return by way of a small reservoir carpeted in lily pads, with algae blooms the color of split pea soup.

That year, the day before I flew off to my family's annual summer reunion, it occurred to me that my destination – Harlowton, Montana, the seat of Wheatland County – could fit in my building five times over.

First-time visitors inevitably got lost. They'd pull in one of the garage bays running the length of the complex, then call their contact from a call box to ask which elevator to take. Once in the huge central atrium, they'd wait several minutes for a corporate Sherpa to guide them down interminable concourses, off which entire departments hid like rabbits in warrens, down aisles which even long-time employees would miss if they weren't watching carefully for the particular piece of corporate art that marked the turn. Finally, along a narrow passage, one found a hive of desks and offices where the actual work got done.

One day I escorted a heavyset woman from the parking garage to an interview with Joe, my boss. When we reached his office, she was so out of breath that she could barely speak. She didn't get the job. On our return trip, while I babbled to pass the time, she kept mum, wearing the wide-eyed look of someone who'd survived a house call to the Addams Family, or the Munsters.

Headquarters was where AT&T's middle management went to die. The late 1980s had not been kind to the corporation: deregulation, new technologies, and belt tightening had everyone on edge. As one of a legion of secretaries, I typed letters, completed spreadsheets, and made airline reservations for my boss and his small sales force. Most of his team was local, but there was a gentleman from Marietta, Georgia named Roger, a big, jovial, round-faced super-extrovert, who taught me how to pronounce the name of his hometown.

From memory, I would have guessed Joe was fifty then. After a few keystrokes online, and a quick calculation backwards from his age of death as posted on a funeral home's website, I now know that he was then forty-five. He had chubby cheeks and a paunch, but otherwise the hale physique of the former Air Force officer that, in fact, he was. In his office, he kept a walking stick fashioned by a Native American woodworker, with a matching one at home that he used while he walked his dog on Schooley's Mountain. (When Joe learned that I intended to walk from Madison to Pennsylvania in a single day, via Schooley's Mountain, he told me to acquire a similar piece to fend off wild dogs.)

The world was changing, but ties and jackets were still *de rigeur* at Headquarters. I had several sport jackets, mostly from Nana's thrift shop excursions, but my most unique one, the color of rosé wine, came from Kurtz's Men's Shop in Madison. It stood out like a beacon at AT&T, catching the eye of Beth, another temp who worked in my unit. Beth wore her hair in dramatic spikes, like a punk. She must have sensed a potential confederate in a guy who chose to wear rose, but after a lunch or two she could see we didn't have a lot in common.

Besides, I preferred Patti. She was the young, married secretary who, in our corner of Headquarters, sat next to me. We were fortunate to have our own desks, since managers' offices outnumbered secretaries' desks, forcing assistants to double up in shared offices and niches. The coming revolution would bring not only dress code changes but open floor plans.

Thirty years later, I still see the adorable porcelain face that complemented Patti's wispy, light blond hair. Always a bit cold due to her thin, small-boned frame, Patti draped her shoulders in soft sweaters. Her sweet temper and smile revealed a Midwestern origin, but she was no hick: when we were alone, she smiled wickedly at coworkers' foibles. Her viewpoint was Jane Austen's, and her looks reminiscent of Audrey Meadows in *The Honeymooners*, another specimen of the type I've fallen for across decades. Patti and her husband lived nearby, without children. I surprised her one Christmas with a card bearing a local photograph, a Morristown winter scene of conifers bending under the weight of snow. She reciprocated belatedly with a card in which she wrote that she'd no idea that there were such lovely places nearby. High praise (not without snark) from a Midwesterner.

If Patti was Audrey Meadows, then Ken, her boss, was Jackie Gleason. Patti did her best to rein him in. Ken was older than Joe, with a feminine, almost grandmotherly face, full white eyebrows proving the convergence that men's and women's faces undergo at his age. But Ken still fancied himself a man's man, telling jokes for which Patti chided him, sometimes with bemusement, sometimes exasperation. Some she just shrugged off. I can see the cashmere billow on her shoulders.

Once, when Joe and Ken talked near my desk, Ken referred to the "chicken farm." He seemed to mean another AT&T office, but I was clueless, so I asked for clarification. Joe, as he habitually did whenever finding himself in an awkward spot, smiled sideways, grunted once, and looked at his feet, shifting from one to the other, awaiting Ken's words. Ken, who never quite knew what to make of me, smiled a completely horizontal smile, becoming for a moment the straight man: he carefully explained that he meant AT&T's Morris Plains office on Route 10. Many young secretaries roosted there.

I should have known. Ken never did stop joking about the time that I happened to mention I had Koni gas shocks installed on my Tempo. Every Monday thereafter, he'd raise his eyebrows and ask what I'd been doing over the weekend in the back seat. Then there was the lunch with Ken, Joe and Charlene (another manager) at Basking Ridge Country Club, where Ken laughed so heartily at a joke of Joe's that I thought we'd be shown the door. Joe had awkwardly told the story of a naive young housewife who had inexpertly followed a girlfriend's advice about how to perform a certain intimate act, misinterpreting her friend's analogy of removing ketchup from a bottle.

But I was nearer in age to the secretaries than the managers, so I mingled more with them. Carol, who wore glasses, had mousy brown hair and was married. Hearing that I was a reader and had no girlfriend, she lent me *Dona Flor and Her Two Husbands*, the risqué 1966 novel by Jorgé Amado in which a woman has an extramarital love affair with the ghost of her first husband. I'm still trying to figure that one out.

Another secretary, one with feathered blond hair and a cherubic face that was lightly dusted with freckles, took an interest in me. I can't believe that I have forgotten her name, since I remember so many others; besides, she was the only gal I saw outside the office, if just once. She invited me one Friday to her home in Essex Fells, actually the home of her parents, who were out for the evening. She greeted me at the door in flannel pajamas. We stayed up late talking about life and morality, though I remember just one specific: she'd taken under her wing the new Latina in our department, who was quite religious and strongly believed that premarital sex was wrong. The blonde agreed.

I was greatly confused, therefore, when I heard soon thereafter that the Latina had stopped talking to the blonde. The blonde had gotten pregnant, and the Latina was devastated.

Could one understand women? Was I a terrible listener, or a terrible psychologist? Or was there some deeper uncertainty principle at work?

Dream Six

The sixth of seven dreams I had while writing this book.

A dream of movies, movie stars, and just plain *moving* that may have been inspired by last night's *Columbo* rerun featuring the lovely Molly Hagan.

It's a sunny day. I'm in a theme park or possibly a studio backlot, in a crowd gathered on an elevated platform without guard rails, like the gantries that once launched spacecraft to the Moon. I am puzzled by an immense object hundreds of feet tall in the near distance, which is not the rocket I expected. Analyzing it more closely, I conclude that it is an immense sculpture of a sandwich. The white layers that I'd taken for rocket stages are, in fact, slices of bread; the dark layers, turkey; and the red and green accents, ketchup and relish, matching the colors of larger-than-life plastic bottles rising like smokestacks in the distance. Tall, upright yellow cylinders, bundled like church organ pipes, frame the sculpture – replicas of french fries.

As our tour leader addresses us, the platform slowly lifts us to the top of the sculpture. I'm reminded of a similar visit I once made to the Gateway Arch in St. Louis, where I'd gone to see a Mets' season opener; this feels similarly grand, though not without raising a similar question about the point of it all.

Outshining everyone in our group is a statuesque beauty with the brilliant highlighted tresses of a Medusa. Consumed with romantic love, I study her every gesture and comment. I long to meet her, but circumstances conspire against it; someone keeps interposing themselves at a crucial moment, or I zig when the tour zags. I think she senses my interest, but she's hard to follow.

Suddenly, it isn't a tour group. It's summer camp, and after six and one-half months, it's drawing to a close. The whole time, I've made no progress whatsoever toward meeting the statuesque actress. Today we are teammates in an arduous competition, something involving water – running whitewater rapids, or playing Slip n' Slide. In any case, I spin out of control, overshooting the rapids or the end of the slide, and I flail madly, reaching for anything that might arrest my rapid progress, but my efforts are futile. I spin to a stop. Someone lends a hand, and I get up. My beauty, more adept than I am, has moved on, and is no longer in view.

My family joins the dream. Having lent the studio a great deal of furniture for use as props, they want it back. (So, we *are* on a studio backlot.) But it has been destroyed in the rapids. Just one settee, whose square, black, plastic seat cushions resemble those used by bleacher sitters, remains. Frank and I discuss the best route to carry it home across Madison. Mom and Dad are also talking; Mom tries to recall a foreign word she once knew whose English meaning is "mother-in-law." Neither Dad nor I can help.

A second piece of furniture has survived the rapids, a treadmill. Frank and I opt to move it first. He pulls from the front, tugging a cord that stretches hundreds of feet, and is soon so far ahead of me that I lose sight of him. I try to push from behind, but am having difficulty getting traction. I then realize that I've left the treadmill plugged in – another cord, retractable like that of an Electrolux vacuum cleaner, extends tautly behind me. That is what has impeded my progress. My stupidity embarrasses me.

My route across Madison has become a long tunnel terminating at an underground subway stop like the one at Manhattan's Christopher Street. I am younger, a teen again. I lie down and arch my side against a low stone ledge running the length of the platform, back to the wall. A strange, dissolute man pesters me for money. He reaches forcibly into my right pants pocket looking for some, though he may have a more sinister intent. He finds only a key; I carry no money. I begin to worry for my safety, but two burly cops appear, marching in lockstep down the subway steps, filling the tunnel entrance. The brass buttons of their bright blue uniforms bulge, as if over flak jackets. My tormentor runs, and I take the opportunity to bolt up the subway steps.

At street level, in the sunshine, I am again an adult, in the middle of a busy Greenwich Village intersection. My crossing is blocked by a long bus making a right-hand turn. It is stuck, blocking traffic in every direction. But I still feel pursued, so I take a chance: I dash around it, then down half a city block into the entrance of a quiet Italian restaurant.

By dim candlelight, two steps down from the lobby, I see a dining room arrayed with tables topped by traditional red-and-white checked tablecloths. At one is the beauty I have been pursuing, lunching with her mother and sisters. She seems downcast; she picks at a plate of french fries, dipping one in bright red ketchup and the next in a brown sauce. She's lost in thought, oblivious to the conversation around her. One by one, members of her family depart until she and I are alone. I sit down and, without asking, try fries in each sauce. I prefer the ketchup. I look at her again, and she has aged. No longer as glamorous as in youth (at the beginning of the dream), she is still pretty. We talk, and her mood lightens.

Great Results of Mathematics

Proposition 1 (The Four-Color Theorem): Every map can be colored with four colors.

Statement of Problem
Given a two-dimensional map, it is possible to color each region in such a way that no two adjacent regions share a color, with four colors sufficient to color the map.

Interpretation
Before the computer, there was the brain.

Proof
Before mathematics had a sense, it had a smell. Or should I say that smell was my first sense of math? Math smelled like dice and playing cards; like construction paper, tracing paper and adding machine tape; like colored pencils, rubber erasers, and glue.

Mom curates my earliest memories of math. She tells of the time that I numbered the bricks of our childhood home with chalk. Or, earlier, of the time that I stopped bobbing on my rocking horse long enough to ask Grandpa Hines what time it was. He looked at his watch and said:

"Nine fifteen."

I pointed to a wall clock and said:

"Nine *seventeen*." I went back to riding, satisfied.

Mom also remembers the time I was one year old and she was feeding my baby brother in our living room at 2648 (a great number, by the way) Crest Lane. As usual, Frankie was depriving me of Mom's attention, so I grew peevish. To keep me from pestering her, she said:

"Go get me a five."

She didn't need to say "playing card." A deck of cards had been my constant companion ever since I'd begged for one, having seen Mom and Dad play bridge with friends.

I brought back a five of diamonds.

Beginner's luck?

Mom continued the experiment by asking for a three.

When I returned with a three, I had Mom's attention. Forgetting that this was just a diversion, she put Frank down in his crib. Victory! Then she fanned the deck of cards on the living room table and began quizzing me. I knew all my numbers; I could even tell sixes from nines. I'd been watching my parents' card games more closely than they knew.

That day at the local bookstore, Mom bought two books, one of numbers and one of letters. I dragged my new best friends everywhere. Mom was happy to know that her first-born had a love of learning, but also had a concern: she hadn't considered early preschool for me, but now she felt it might be necessary to keep me from getting bored.

It's hard now to appreciate how difficult parenting was in the 1960s, before WebMD and a publishing industry geared to parental advice. Mom and Dad learned on the job. Not recognizing their luck at having a baby who loved to sleep, they'd wake me in the middle of the night to feed me. (Dad later blamed this for his encyclopedic knowledge of every bad B-movie ever shown on *The Late Show*.) Regarding my schooling, Mom could consult either her pediatrician or Dr. Spock. She chose the former, and we drove to his office.

"Should I enroll my son early in school?" she asked.

"No, I'm a firm believer in home time with mother. The bond formed early in life is essential. There's always time later for school."

Mom was unconvinced.

"The only time I ever recommended early preschool was a very special case, a boy who could spell difficult words. I'm not talking about 'dog' or 'cat.' He could spell words like 'bakery.'"

Mom turned to me.

"John, how do you spell bakery?"

"B-A-K-E-R-Y!"

The doctor reconsidered.

But that was beginner's luck. Had the doctor asked me to spell "cat," I might have fallen short. But I'd seen "bakery" over the display case in my favorite grocery department too often to not have committed it to memory.

I loved preschool, especially Miss Glusa, my teacher with the bobbed dark brown hair. I knew she loved me too, because she let me do what I wanted. True, it was Montessori school, where students were encouraged to follow their bliss, but Miss Glusa may have been inclined to treat me particularly well because, for a while, she lived in my family's red brick guesthouse, near the stable. That was the guesthouse that Mom and Dad later rented to a family whose son, Nicky, offered me my first cigarette puff when I was seven – the only time so far that I have smoked.

I attended preschool and kindergarten at Westmont Montessori School, in Mendham. Today the school occupies a permanent structure, but in my day it was just a trailer on a gravel lot along Route 24, which was then a country road. Behind the school was a long stretch of woods that we explored with Miss Glusa and her assistant, Miss Pullman. In it, streams burbled in swamp meadows, and I still recall the smell of skunk cabbage. (One day, returning from our party of explorers in order to use the bathroom, I caught Miss Pullman hiding Easter eggs. She asked me not to say anything; this is the first time that I've mentioned it.)

Miss Glusa encouraged my interest in numbers by letting me use the large blackboard at one end of the classroom to write out, then add, the longest pair of numbers I could fit. What a show-off! Large numbers are no harder to add than small ones, but I enjoyed making a stir. Later, to generate similar hype in a high school study hall, I resorted to the quadratic equation.

During downtime, we worked on our number rolls. On strips of graph paper the width of adding machine tape, we wrote the counting numbers in order, beginning with 1. At the end of a strip, we pasted a new strip to the roll and kept going. By the end of kindergarten, in my zeal to impress Miss Glusa, I'd gotten further than any previous student. She rewarded me by taking my number roll to a talk she gave at a teacher's conference.

I still have it. Its inside-out design tells me at a glance, without the need to unwind it, that I reached 12,724. I think it was my idea to separately color the digits: blue for thousands (and tens of thousands), red for hundreds, blue again for tens, and green for ones. The only exception was when a digit other than the ones changed: in that case, I wrote all succeeding digits in the same color as that of the changing digit. This novel coloring scheme kept things interesting, though it probably slowed me down, what with all the pencil changing. I can see now, however, that I had discovered a short cut: I wrote a full column of an unchanging digit before switching pencils to write the next column.

When we moved to Morristown, summer of 1974, I attended a new school, Peck. (Naturally, Nana started calling me "Peck's Bad Boy," after the scamp from the popular books of her childhood.) There, I took to drawing maps.

If you think about it, maps are mathematical objects – collections of polygons, symbols, and scales. Though I enjoyed copying political maps on tracing paper, I particularly enjoyed a project in which we were asked to map a fictional place. I truly went to town, summoning reality *ex nihilo*, sketching street grids and shading business districts that I overlaid with crosshatched railroad tracks and wavy blue rivers. Colored pencils – optional for number rolls – were essential for maps. Though I had a big box, it seemed I only needed to use my favorites. For Europe, these were blue, orange, yellow, and green. I never stopped to wonder why that might be.

Soon, a milestone on the road to artificial intelligence was reached. On June 21, 1976, my last day of fourth grade, two mathematicians at the University of Illinois at Urbana-Champaign (HAL's birthplace in *2001: A Space Odyssey*), announced a proof of the venerable four-color problem, proving that *all* maps can be colored with just four colors. The result strengthened an earlier proof from 1890 that no more than five were required. Reducing it to four had taken mathematicians the better part of a century.

What's more, the mathematicians, Kenneth Appel and Wolfgang Haken, had a most unlikely collaborator – a computer. Their proof was, in fact, the first *computer-assisted* proof, meaning that it relied upon the speed and accuracy of a computer to laboriously check steps that they could not check themselves. The human ingenuity behind the approach was the realization that only a particular set of 1,936 maps need be checked: the mathematicians then set the computer loose on this set. After a thousand hours of computation, it had verified that none of the special maps needed more than four colors. Q.E.D. – or as Thomas Dolby sang in one song, "*Quod erat demonstrandum, baby!*"

Most mathematicians applauded this ingenious solution of a notoriously intractable problem, but a few were aghast and others uneasy that a computer had validated part of the proof. After all, what if there was a flaw in the code, or a bug in the processor? (These things happen.) In time, however, the mathematical community became more comfortable, as have we all, with the idea of relying on technology to supplement our brainpower.

Something was gained in learning that a map of Europe, Earth or any world that a child dreams up is colorable with just four colors, but something was lost, too. Mathematicians must now concede that in some respects, computers can "see" further than they can, and that future progress in math may only be possible by standing on the "shoulders" of machines. (How awkward it is to describe our relationship with computers. I'm using quotes everywhere.) And though this problem has been solved, are we any closer to *understanding* the solution? As a child, I pondered challenging questions by pressing the rubber eraser of a pencil against my lower lip, or a ball of rubber cement against the tip of my tongue: their scent and taste helped me think. Computers need no such stimuli, but neither can their answers offer comparable enlightenment.

I "solved" Tic-Tac-Toe on my own, with a pencil, on the day that I could be sure I would never lose again. Mathematicians say a game is solved once we possess a playbook listing the optimal next move for every situation, so that by following those moves we are guaranteed to win (or at least not lose, depending on the game).

Connect Four was another, more interesting, game that I played with siblings and friends. Red and Black take turns dropping checkers in one of seven columns, with pieces landing atop other pieces dropped previously in the same column. The goal is to place four pieces of your color in a row, column, or diagonal. In 1988, while I was sending faxes for AT&T, a computer program solved Connect Four. It demonstrated that, with optimal play, the first player can force a win.

Checkers was another childhood favorite, as far beyond Connect Four in terms of complexity as Connect Four was beyond Tic-Tac-Toe. In 2007, while Carol and I looked for happiness in the town where I'd grown up, checkers succumbed to the computer as well. A specially programmed computer can no longer lose at checkers. (Optimal play by both sides guarantees a draw.)

Not all games are solvable. Chess, for example, and Go, the ancient Japanese board game, have more positions than atoms in the universe, so no complete playbook can be compiled. But that doesn't stop computers from defeating the best humans, even if the computers play "imperfectly." In 1997, Garry Kasparov, the world chess champion, was decimated by Deep Blue, a computer program. That was just two years after I'd seen Kasparov with my own eyes defeat his rival Anatoly Karpov in a championship match in a Manhattan auditorium. Kasparov had vanquished Karpov with nerves of steel, but against an electronic opponent, it was Kasparov who came unglued: his renown, sufficient to unnerve grandmasters, was of no avail against an opponent without emotion. Today, it is accepted that humans cannot defeat the best chess programs. So if you can't beat them, join them – today's grandmasters rely extensively on computer analysis to prep for matches against other humans.

And in 2011, Carol and I, then living in Manhattan, watched a computer named Watson defeat the world's best Jeopardy players. This was as impressive a milestone as winning the world chess championship, for the domain had shifted to areas of expertise long regarded as the exclusive province of humanity: general knowledge of the arts, the humanities, and the idiosyncrasies of the English language. (Though I suspect it may yet be a while before computers have the sense of humor displayed by Ken Jennings when he riffed on a meme by writing on his Final Jeopardy card, "I, for one, welcome our new computer overlords.")

When I was born, experts felt that these milestones lay far in the far future. To think, they've all been surpassed in my lifetime! I feel like my grandmother, who lived to see a brand-new world wrought by radio and television.

Proposition 2 (Benford's Law): *The first digit of a randomly selected number is more likely to be low than high.*

Statement of Problem
      Measure something. It could be the population of a town, the length of a river, or the distance of a star from Earth. Now examine the first digit. It has a roughly 30% chance of being "1," 15% of being "2," and so on until "9," which has just a 5% chance.

Interpretation
      Technology doesn't always make us smarter.

Proof

While I enjoyed *Encyclopedia Brown* adventures and *Hardy Boys* mysteries, I also checked out math books from the library. Most were beyond my ken, so all I got from them was the *sound* of logic, as infants in cribs, when they hear conversation, absorb the sound of syntax. Some books, though, were elementary enough to grant me a foothold, and from them I learned of logarithms and number bases.

Meanwhile, at garage sales, yard sales, thrift stores, and consignment shops, Nana bought me slide rules for next to nothing. They were worthless, having been obsolesced by the electronic calculator, but I don't think Nana knew. Perhaps she thought scientists still used them, or perhaps she continued to associate them, via old movies, with science. Maybe she thought that different slide rules perform different calculations (they generally don't), or more likely, as with all those copies of *Sergeant Pepper's Lonely Hearts Club Band*, she'd simply forgotten she had bought me so many.

Whatever her reason, it was thanks to my grandmother that I owned a dozen of those mechanical calculators with finely-scaled middle bars, transparent sliders, magnifiers, and hairlines that aligned the scales as finely as desired. Some came in their original cardboard boxes, with tightly-wedged instruction books printed in tiny fonts on onionskin paper. I didn't have the patience to unfold and decipher that origami, but had I done so I would have been granted the arcane skill of estimating, in the time-honored way, products, quotients, roots, powers, and logarithms.

By the time my math homework required the calculation of logarithms, the electronic calculator was widespread. Mom bought our first family calculator for the princely sum of a hundred dollars, when dollars were dollars, but that was just for her business use. My friend Dave had one, too. He was proud of its ability to accept inputs in "reverse Polish notation" and his proficiency at entering them; when he did so, he would turn the calculator away so that you couldn't see which keys he was pressing. In this way, electronic calculating devices first entered our homes.

It is a general principle that the first uses of a new technology are the most trivial. The first thing a new computer owner tries are the games; and when I got my own calculator, I used it to work through the pages of a riddle book that a classmate had lent me. Each page stated a riddle, then laid out a calculation; after performing the specified operations, one flipped the calculator upside down to read the answer. For example, an upside down 0.7734 yielded "hELL.O."

In eighth grade, I learned something new about logarithms. On a shelf of the Livingston Mall branch of Walden Books, I found a book called *A Number for Your Thoughts*. I asked Mom if she would buy it for me for Christmas; again, by buying me a book, she furthered a career. In the chapter entitled "The Baffling Law of Benford" I learned the following:

Scientists sometimes needed to calculate logarithms to a greater precision than slide rules could manage, so they consulted a large paper directory. (Picture something the size and shape of an automotive parts manual.) In 1881, an astronomer named Simon Newcomb noticed that the early pages of these directories – in particular, the pages with numbers beginning with one – had the most wear. Mathematical progress being fitful, this observation lay forgotten for fifty years. But in 1931, Frank Benford, a physicist, formulated the law that partially explained Newcomb's observation. (And when he did so, Benford's Law became the latest example of Stigler's Law, which says that no scientific law is named after its discoverer.)

My favorite high school subjects were math and English. Given that my first two books introduced me to letters and digits, big surprise! My favorite childhood tale, *The Phantom Tollbooth*, whisked me to the twin towns where I most wanted to live, Digitopolis and Dictionopolis. Of the two, I favored math. The main reason was that in math, or so I believed, perfection was attainable. Each time I opened a new math textbook's pages scented with vanilla and almond, I thought of the iced numeral cookies of Digitopolis. I would trace my index finger across the still crisp corners of the pages, and seek enlightenment – I would turn to the first assertion and read it, word by word, phrase by phrase, staying with it until I had mastered it. Then to the next. In math, a subject that builds on itself, one can do that.

At Montclair State, I went back to math. For one class project, I used a Markov process approximation to calculate the most frequently visited property in the board game Monopoly. (It's Illinois Avenue.) For another project, I recalled what I'd read as a boy of the counterintuitive phenomenon that is Benford's Law, and in particular one explanation for it – organic growth, the source of so many quantities found in nature, which Man eventually measures. If, as Jerry Lee Lewis once sang, there's a whole lot of doubling going on, there ought to be a trace of it in the first digit distribution of measurements. It occurred to me that I could check this rather easily.

I walked down to the computer lab, sat at a terminal, and wrote a quick BASIC program to calculate the powers of two: 1, 2, 4, 8, 16.... Then I tracked the first digits, which turned out to have a distribution much like Benford's, with ones significantly more common than nines. Essentially, I'd just shown that organic growth could account for the law.

Revisiting this memory today, I'm humbled in the way that the surviving Apollo astronauts must be each time they pick up a cellphone. This calculation can now be performed in a minute on any desktop computer, no programming needed. Excel can count far higher than that old computer ever could – to two raised to the $1,024^{th}$ power!

There is another explanation of Benford's Law. The 30% - 15% - ... - 5% Benford distribution is the only distribution that is *scale-invariant*. That is, if you start with a large set of measurements whose first digits are distributed in accordance with Bedford's distribution, and multiply them by a constant factor, the distribution does not change. That's important, because it says that it's irrelevant what units you use to measure distance: meters or feet, miles or light years. This, for me, is the most compelling argument for Benford's distribution.

Finally, a law of my own: the number of mysterious eighth-grade phenomena that are now straightforward is equal to the number of straightforward eighth-grade phenomena that are now mysterious. Let's call it Baldan's Law, as discovered by the Beatles: *"The love you take is equal to the love you make."*

Proposition 3 (The Bolzano-Weierstrass Theorem): Every bounded sequence has a convergent subsequence.

Statement of Problem

Given an infinite sequence of numbers with no number too small or too large, one can find an infinite subset which, when viewed as a sequence in its own right, approaches a particular number.

Interpretation
　　If you don't stray too far, you'll hit on something.

Proof
　　Each summer, the National Science Foundation, a federal agency that supports research and education in the sciences and mathematics, sponsors Research Experiences for Undergraduates (REU), programs designed to give college undergraduates a taste of graduate work.
　　In 1992, an REU program took place in my hometown of Madison, on the campus of Drew University. The sponsor was David Housman, a math professor whose research interest was in the specialized field of cooperative game theory. (A pioneer of this field, John Nash, was made famous by the biography and movie, *A Beautiful Mind.*) I was one of six students chosen to attend, as was Carol, who eventually became my partner not only in math but in life.
　　Had it not been for Dr. Stevens, the Montclair State teacher who brought the REU program to my attention and encouraged me to attend, I would not have gone. As usual, when confronted with something new, I was reluctant. But I took it as a favorable omen that the course would take place in Madison, on a campus I knew well from the one week that I had spent there as an undergraduate student and – more meaningfully – from my many youthful visits to the student center game room. Even if the six-week program went badly, I wouldn't be homesick. I wouldn't even have to sleep on campus.
　　A month before the program began, Dr. Housman mailed out a stack of research papers in a manila envelope: our personal introduction to cooperative game theory. He also included a list of students' names and addresses, which I admit was the page that I studied most closely. I was one of three guys and three gals, all from the Eastern United States, from Charlotte to Boston.
　　Over the next few weeks, as the weather warmed, I repeatedly read those papers on my family's glassed-in porch overlooking Crestview Avenue. That was never a comfortable room; my family rarely used it. Its southern exposure admitted too much sun, and its dusty windows of louvered glass, which creaked upon opening, badly needed a wash. Near an antique coffee grinder whose bottom drawer contained a trace of musty, tasteless grounds, two bowl-shaped bamboo chairs were the only places to sit. It was hard to know where to position oneself in them

to avoid slumping. I would inadvertently scrape them on the Moroccan red tile floor while struggling to make myself comfortable, usually at a thorny point in the logic.

On Sunday, June 28, after dawdling all day, I drove to Professor Housman's for a cookout. He lived on Loantaka Way in a starter condo that must have been small for his growing family of four. I parked in the lot and found the driveway where everyone had gathered.

The professor was shorter and younger than I'd imagined, with sandy brown hair and a matching mustache. He greeted me warmly, shaking my hand before returning to the grill. Nearby, my future colleagues milled about, talking. They had arrived much earlier than I, not only to get the lay of the land but to claim the most comfortable rooms of our campus lodging, an old white house near the east entrance that we called La Casa Hispanica, after the sign out front, which indicated that it was the meeting place of the Spanish Club. It had no air conditioning, so the students had taken, in order of arrival, the cooler first and second floor rooms, leaving me with an oppressively warm garret beneath an eave, in which a former resident had affixed to the ceiling glow-in-the-dark stars and moons, a wishful bit of hothouse thinking.

At the foot of the driveway, I introduced myself to Mary Dana and Carol. I could instantly tell that they were already friends. Mary Dana was petite and blonde, with a Southern accent that, had I been more experienced, I could have traced to Charlotte, just as a barbecue aficionado can identify North Carolina from its vinegary sauce. And Mary Dana was no Southern belle – she was a firecracker! As the only extrovert among introverts, she would be our catalyst, the one who planned cookouts and field trips. Despite flirting with me, she would also play Cupid to Carol and me that summer, once she'd taken our temperatures and judged them conducive to a reaction.

> *She will put you together*
> *With someone or other*
> *And see what transpires*
>   - John Howard, "Deborah Fletcher"

I offered my hand to each of these two young ladies, who having noted my age on the attendee information sheet, had endowed me with the mysterious qualities of an "older man." Mary Dana was amused that I looked and acted younger than she'd expected.

"Hi Mary, nice to meet you," I said.

She opened her eyes wide in what I hoped was mock umbrage:

"My name is Mary *Dana*. How would me to call you Jah?"

I stammered a quick apology, admitting to an ignorance of the grand tradition of compound Southern names.

Then I turned to Carol, who wore contact lenses, though I didn't yet know that. I admired her long, straight, dark hair and longer, straighter, deep purple T-shirt that stretched to her knees. That morning, Carol had driven from Pennsylvania in her clunker of a Reliant K, next to which I'd parked. She was relieved to see that her next six weeks would be spent among students not unlike herself – easygoing, unpretentious, a little geeky.

The other "geeks" were Darren, Luz, and Roger.

Darren, a Moravian College student, was the most avid carnivore I've ever met. He nearly salivated over David's grilling burgers, and was equally enthusiastic the following weekend at my house, when Dad hosted another cookout for us all.

Luz attended Rutgers. She became an American citizen that summer, so of course Mary Dana organized a celebration: atop the faded, Tara-like grand staircase of La Casa Hispanica, she draped a congratulatory banner that she had designed for the new American. Luz responded in turn with a box of pastries from a Portuguese bakery in her neighborhood, in Newark's Ironbound section.

Roger was a Harvard man. Blessedly "Type B" for an Ivy Leaguer, he unraveled math problems in his head while playing frisbee and hacky sack. The rest of us considered him a stone cold genius, and he would be the only one among us to attempt the proof of a major result that summer. Though we didn't understand his conjecture, it certainly excited Dr. Housman; until the following fall, that is, when the professor found a minor flaw in his reasoning that invalidated the proof. (Roger had assumed the existence of a particular object whose existence could not be verified. But haven't we all?)

I trained my sights on Mary Dana and Carol. They were both pretty, but I especially took to Carol's dark hair and easygoing nature. As a test, I bought each a stuffed animal from the FAO Schwartz store at the

Short Hills Mall – a gray elephant for Mary Dana, and a blue triceratops for Carol. Mary Dana was dismayed by her gift; she was sensitive to the extra weight that she was carrying that summer, which she attributed to the Pill. But Carol loved the triceratops, which reminded her of a song she sang as a child:

> *Triceratops has three long horns*
> *A beak like a parrot, and a frill where its neck is*
> *Triceratops has four big legs, and a tail in the back*
>   - "The Triceratops Song" from *Our Dinosaur Friends*

But she was too shy to sing it. Not yet knowing me well, or my taste for fanciful music, she felt it would be the better part of discretion to keep it to herself, and stay simple and sweet.

We three had another thing in common – relationships of long standing. Not that they were ironclad.... Mary Dana's boyfriend was a regular Rush Limbaugh listener, which she considered a strike against him. Carol was seeing a good guy, but his dispositions toward small-town life and stay-at-home wives would likely prove problematic down the road.

> *I want to see Paris, insane on the Seine*
> *I want to do that bull run thing in Spain*
> *I want to go to England, and walk down Penny Lane*
> *Half a pint in Ireland may wash away my pain*
>   - E, "Nowheresville"

And I was with Colleen, whom I invited one day to La Casa Hispanica to see the house and meet my new friends. She liked Carol, but was wary of Mary Dana's clothes and attitude, which she called "froofy."

Returning to day one: after dinner we convened in Professor Housman's tiny living room, sitting where we could, some of us cross-legged on the carpet. Our advisor introduced himself, described his research interests, and then mentioned that he had selected each of us from over one hundred applicants. As we gave each other congratulatory nods, I recalled the idea that may have ensured my admittance to this august group – my proof of the Bolzano-Weierstrass Theorem.

I was taking Real Analysis with Dr. Parzynski, who taught from his own textbook. I often stopped by his office, where he worked to the sound of a jazz station that scared away most undergraduates, though not me. One day, I arrived with what I believed to be a simpler proof of a theorem than the one that he had outlined in his text, one that didn't require certain other propositions that he had used to set up his proof. In mathspeak, Dr. Parzynski had set up "machinery" to prove a theorem that didn't require it. I believed I had a proof from first principles, and was eager to hear his reaction.

The proof had come to me while watching the World Series at Nana's house. Earlier that evening, she had cooked up one of her more elaborate productions: six or more dishes, starch on top of starch – egg noodles, mashed potatoes, dumplings, breaded and fried chicken cutlets, and more. Ella plated each at the stove, then walked them across the kitchen one by one, burning her fingers along the way.

Stuffed, I retired to the even more stuffed living room couch with its busy floral pattern and sewn-in buttons. Paul Erdös, the eminent mathematician, famously defined mathematicians as machines that turned coffee into theorems, but I ran on carbohydrates. I turned on the television. The Twins and Braves were playing in that year's Series, but the game wasn't particularly compelling, so I started thinking about the Bolzano-Weierstrass Theorem. It seemed to me – I can't exactly say why – that it had to have a simpler proof.

Why not select a subsequence, term by term, always choosing the next number to be larger than the previous? If you can do that infinitely many times, then the resulting increasing sequence, bounded above by hypothesis, must be convergent – and you're done. If on the other hand you can't do that, then take the last number you reached before getting stuck and begin a *new* subsequence with that number. Starting with the next term in the original sequence, repeat the above process. You either get an increasing, bounded subsequence (so you're done), or you get stalled again. Take the stopping point as the second number of the new subsequence. Now – this is key – it must be smaller than the first number. Proceed infinitely many times; by that time you have either constructed an increasing bounded subsequence or a decreasing bounded subsequence. Either way, there is a convergent subsequence, and the theorem is proved.

It had to be right! I toasted my luck with a soggy Entenmann's coffee cake donut as Scott Erickson struck out another Brave.

Back in his office, Dr. Parzynski was noncommittal:

"Sequences are tricky. They can exhibit all kinds of crazy behavior. Let me think about it."

To me, the proof seemed sound. And several days later, Dr. Parzynski came around, pronouncing it correct in a decidedly off-hand manner. He had verified it, so he said, via "another line of reasoning." I got no pat on the back, but neither was my teacher annoyed that I'd found a simpler proof than the one he had published. I was proud enough of my proof, however, to outline it in my application to Dr. Housman, and later in my application to Miami University's graduate math program. At Miami, I even got the nickname "John Bolzano" – but not for the proof, for the similarity of our last names.

Proposition 4 (Fermat's Last Theorem): If a, b, and c are positive whole numbers, and n>2, there are no solutions to the equation $a^n = b^n + c^n$.

Statement of Problem

Elementary algebra is the study of equations. When n=2 in the equation above, we have the beloved Pythagorean Formula (again, by Stigler's Law, not discovered by Pythagoras), which is solved by infinitely many triangles with integer lengths. However, if n is greater than 2 in the equation above, there are *no* solutions.

Interpretation

There are an infinity of ways to turn a crazy obsession into one's life's work.

Proof

In high school, I suffered from math overconfidence. Princeton cured that. There, I took just one math class, fall of freshman year, an advanced placement course in Linear Algebra with Dr. Gunning. Tall, round-faced, and nearly bald, he smiled a lot, either due to his students' incomprehension or at his own for having to teach us. I think he had a sense of humor, though I didn't understand the jokes he sprinkled in lectures that he delivered in a tweedy British accent. In retrospect, I'm sure I wasn't the only student who was lost; back then, I assumed I was.

Math textbooks are like clothing stores – the sparer they are, the more they'll cost you. A clothes horse intuitively knows that a shop where a few dresses hang without price tags at widely spaced intervals will be expensive. A graduate math student learns that math texts with few pages, diagrams, or numbers will be taxing.

Every afternoon, I palmed my slim black linear algebra textbook and walked across campus. On the way I sometimes saw Dr. Bowen, our University President, lost in thought, following his own world line, on the way to the athletic fields to watch freshman football practice. (On account of his wizened face and distracted manner, behind his back we Princetonians called him "Bilbo Baggins.") I was also headed toward those fields to fulfill my duties as a volunteer football "manager," a job consisting mainly of carrying sacks of footballs to and from the clubhouse. On the sidelines, I stood near the other managers (two gawky girls hoping to meet football players) and a young, mustachioed trainer who was there to treat injuries. But those were rare in practice, so he and I would pass the time making wagers. Once he bet me that I couldn't throw a football as high as the arc light directly above us. I grabbed a football and made the throw of my life, a tight spiral directly upward about twenty yards that came within inches of striking the light, thereby losing the bet but winning his respect and the relief of having narrowly avoiding disaster.

During practice, I'd stare at the pages of my Linear Algebra text, which were covered in arcane propositions. In that class, the hardest I'd yet to encounter, I got a B- – a joke as difficult to fathom as anything Dr. Gunning had uttered all semester. I'd learned next to nothing.

Math classes met in Fine Hall, the skyscraper looming above campus. (Okay, it had thirteen floors. On our horizontal campus, it was a landmark.) My classmates may have been aware of the legendary talent assembled in Fine's cluttered shoebox offices, but I was oblivious. I certainly had no clue that the tall, thin redhead with the prematurely receding hairline whom I occasionally passed in the hall was Andrew Wiles, then thirty-one and new on staff.

Wiles' proof of math's most famous conjecture, Fermat's Last Theorem, has been retold so often as to qualify as a modern legend. (Interested readers should consult the highly enjoyable *Fermat's*

Enigma, by Simon Singh.) When Wiles first encountered Fermat's "theorem" (technically not a theorem since it had yet to be proven), he was ten. He immediately vowed to prove it, but soon he realized that the necessary tools were beyond his grasp. So he locked the problem in the back of his mind for twenty years while he matured into a gifted young mathematician.

In 1986, Wiles returned to Fermat. (By then, I no longer went to Fine Hall. Determined to not repeat my Linear Algebra disaster, I changed my major to English and kept on the more picturesque, central part of campus.) Recent results in the field of algebra, particularly the arcane backwater of elliptic curves, had given Wiles hope that the problem might actually be tractable, so he went for broke: he would devote himself to it for as long as it took. He worked in secret for seven years, confiding only in his wife, publishing a few minor results to keep tenure. Even that much was dangerous, because Fermat's Last Theorem was considered the Holy Grail of crackpots, too difficult to merit the attention of any but the most obsessed. That kind of reputation was the last thing a tenured young professor needed.

In June of 1993, the month I graduated with a bachelor's degree in math from Montclair State, Wiles unveiled his proof to the world. Not only did the mathematical world take notice, but so did the general public; it even made the front page of the *New York Times*. For a brief while, Wiles was that rarest of things, a math celebrity.

Meanwhile, I was off to grad school.

Proposition 5: 2.9999999... equals 3

Statement of Problem
Fractions can be represented as repeating decimals. But whole numbers can, too. This fact trips up many math students when they first see it. After all, math is supposed to be an exact science and 2.999... (repeating forever) is obviously just shy of three, and close only counts in horseshoes, not math....

Interpretation
Disregard appearances. Always refer to first principles.
Proof

Having enjoyed three years of math classes at Montclair State, I considered graduate school. But I was wary of committing to a doctoral degree. A bachelor's had taken me nine years – a doctorate might take me twenty! A master's, on the other hand, should take only two.

When I shared this idea with Dr. Stevens, he offered some advice. He told me to be wary of schools with strong doctoral programs, where master's students get lost in the shuffle. Following his advice perhaps a bit too literally, I ruled out any university offering a doctorate in math.

Late one Friday, I received a call on the Madison "teen line." I'd fallen asleep, so I was groggy as I listened to a pitch from a recruiter at the University of North Carolina at Chapel Hill. I politely declined. I'd already decided against that math powerhouse; besides, why would I attend a school that wanted me to stay up late Friday nights? Anyway, the school I was targeting was Miami University, the public state college that I'd seen the previous summer with my REU group.

There, our capstone talks had been given at the annual meeting of the local chapter of Pi Mu Epsilon, the mathematical honor society. Miami was located in the small, staid, four-square town of Oxford, Ohio, an hour from Cincinnati and ten hours from Madison, New Jersey. Dr. Housman hired a rental van for what proved to be a memorable trip.

Our instructor drove most of the miles there. At one point, I sat in back between Mary Dana and Carol, which was rather pleasant. Mary Dana draped a light blanket over us for warmth, and then tried to take more than her fair share of the back seat, which pushed me against Carol. I didn't mind.

On the return trip, Mary Dana scheduled the middle-of-the-night shift for Carol and me. We piloted the van while the others in back got shut-eye. As Carol drove, I did my best to keep talking so that we'd stay awake, but fatigue made it hard to generate conversation. Carol solved the problem by producing a cassette.

What a mix! I still have it, and jokingly mention it from time to time in conversation with Carol. She had received it as a gift from a college acquaintance, a photography major who fancied himself a music connoisseur as well, as evidenced by his name for it: *Welcome the Angry Men of the Socio-Political Sexual Revolution.*

I was dubious. Side A had been named *The Revolution Will Not Be Televised*; side B, *Consider Yourself Warned!!* It was too dark in the cabin to read song titles, so I had no chance to brace myself for the onslaught of punk I was about to hear: Faith No More, Fugazi, the Dead Kennedys, and more. The cassette clicked, then music hurtled loudly from the speakers. There was a stirring in back.

"Turn it down!" Carol shrieked.

To be fair, the mix wasn't completely bad. It even included a few bands I knew and liked; these happened to be the ones that Carol did, too. But in the not-so-humble opinion of someone who had been making mixes for a decade, this was the work of an amateur. Most tellingly, there was no continuity: the tape even had a song by the singing sisters, the Roches. Their rendition of Handel's Hallelujah Chorus sounded like nothing else on the mix. Little did Carol and I suspect that one day in the far future, we would marry and live in the same apartment building as one of the Roches.

Oxford had eateries that included an ersatz Chinese restaurant, a dodgy British pub, and several bland pizzerias. But we weren't there to gormandize (or surf, as I later said to folks who didn't know where Miami was; perhaps I should have said instead that I attended Oxford); we were there to present research. I was nervous about mine, because my progress had been fitful. I had foundered, in particular, in an attempt to write a computer program to enumerate all possible four-player "simple games." In short, I was trying to answer the question: in how many ways can four people form coalitions? Only now, decades later, do I recognize the bearing the problem had on our six-person real-life social situation that summer. Carol, Mary Dana, and I were a coalition of three (per Darren, we were the "cool people," the only time I've ever belonged to that category), and the others were singletons.

My program tallied 180 four-player simple games. I knew the right answer was 182, from a paper published decades earlier by one of the giants of cooperative game theory, Lloyd Shapley. (Incidentally, we'd met Shapley earlier that summer at a conference in Stony Brook, New York. Later that day, the girls and I limped home by subway and train after my Ford Tempo was incapacitated by a pothole at the entrance to the Queens Midtown Tunnel.) Where were those last two games, I wondered? If I couldn't count the number of four-player games, I had no hope of finding a general method to count games of five players, six players, or more. Dr. Housman, who was more than generous with his time, checked my work and found one I'd missed. Where was the other?

At a conference that fall, Dr. Housman ran into Shapley again and asked him.

"Oh, the published result was wrong."

To quote Charlie Brown: "Aargh!"

Then again, had I known the correct result that summer, I might have made more progress with my research – and less with Carol.

***

A year later, now enrolled at Miami, I led a two-car caravan to Ohio. Dad and Nana followed in Nana's blue Delta 88, to which Clay and I had installed a junkyard hitch, one that could precariously pull a small trailer. Inside the car and trailer were "a few things" that Nana hoped would make my new home cozy.

She was disappointed when she saw my apartment at the edge of town near the crossing where hundred-car freight trains trundled by at night, to the accompaniment of high-pitched whistles. To save money, I'd rented a so-called "first floor" unit that was actually half underground. The little light that penetrated the living room and bedroom windows allowed only a glimpse of legs coming and going.

Still, Nana did her best. She set up, on either side of a sofa, a matching pair of tall, bell-shaped glass bowls; once she was gone, I filled them with salt water taffy that I'd purchased the previous weekend in Long Beach Island. One I filled with candies in pink and yellow wrappers, the other with candies wrapped blue and green. Soon after, my new colleague Keith stopped in to check out my digs. Sitting on the sofa, he turned alternately to the coordinated vases of taffy, then took in the apartment's general tidiness.

"Are you sure you're not married?" he asked.

At Miami, I took Real Analysis with a Dr. Burke, a long-tenured teacher. He was tan, angular, laconic, and every bit a country gentleman. When not teaching, he generally ruminated over math problems in his office while new age music played.

So the world goes round and round
With all you ever knew

They say the sky high above
Is Caribbean blue
 - Enya, "Caribbean Blue"

One time in class, Dr. Burke mentioned in passing that 2.999... equals 3. Old hat to me, but news to my classmates Lew and David. After class, the three of us returned to our student offices at the back of Bachelor Hall's second floor, where we presided over our own sparsely-attended office hours (so goes the cycle of life!) in linoleum-tiled rooms overlooking the first hole of the frisbee golf course, a favorite destination of ours. Thumping his notebook on his desk, David unwrapped a stick of Doublemint – paper first, then foil – then whirled toward Lew and me.

"How is 2.9 repeating the same as 3? Prove it."

My unrehearsed answer burst forth:

"If they aren't the same, name a number between them."

Enlightenment swept across David's face.

"Ah....! Very tricky!"

Not in the slightest. It was just the simplest explanation that came to mind. Sometimes I can cut to the heart of things.

Proposition 6 (Gödel's Incompleteness Theorem): Any consistent, logical system powerful enough to include arithmetic contains true propositions which cannot be proven.

Statement of Problem

Modern math is logic-based. In fact, it's nothing but a logical system. A few axioms are assumed true without proof and, from these, one can prove any proposition true or false. Or so it was thought.

Then, in 1931, Kurt Gödel, a spare, bespectacled twenty-five-year-old student at the University of Vienna, dropped a bombshell concerning the limits of knowledge that changed the mindset not only of mathematicians but of philosophers. That was the year he proved the first of several "incompleteness" theorems with which his name shall forever be linked.

Interpretation

Some things will forever remain beyond our reach.
Proof
Andrew Wiles and I crossed paths, but that is almost certainly not true of me and Kurt Gödel. He died in 1978, having lived for decades in the town where I would one day attend college; but my family didn't go to Princeton when I was young, even though it wasn't far.

But who can say for sure? I recall an invention I dreamt up one summer when a child: a device taking as input the name of anyone you chose and outputting the exact time and place you and that person were nearest, before meeting for the first time. Back then, I'd have quizzed it about girls I liked; now I would ask it about Gödel. I'm afraid that the answer will forever be undecidable.

The earliest Princeton trip I recall was the rainy Sunday that I asked Dad to take me to the Princeton Record Exchange, a music store I'd heard of. Mom needed a mini-vacation from us kids, so Dad agreed to drive us. We fought over the radio until we found *American Top Forty*: a memory that lets me peg the date as June 27, 1982, due to the top three songs: "Ebony and Ivory" (Paul McCartney and Stevie Wonder), "Don't You Want Me" (the Human League), and "Rosanna" (Toto). During the show the host, Casey Kasem, mentioned that a member of the Human League had previously been an electrician, which came in handy when he later took up synthesizer. Dad simply shook his head at the absurdity of modern pop music.

It was a dreary day. Rain fall in droves all the way to Princeton, and I left the store disappointed. I'd yet to learn the difference between a college record shop and a mall record store: the former is stocked, almost exclusively, with obscure titles for which I'd yet to develop an appreciation. (I bought only one record, a 45 rpm single of the Bay City Rollers' "I Only Want to Be With You.")

Even had our visit taken place years earlier, perhaps during the height of the disco craze (a craze the Princeton Record Exchange never experienced), seeing Gödel on the street would have been unlikely. That's because for the second half of his life, Gödel was a wraith, a timorous hypochondriac who fasted for fear of poison, and was rarely seen anywhere but his office at the Institute for Advanced Study, the scientific Shangri-La located two miles outside of town. He is more centrally located now: his final resting place is Princeton Cemetery, just two blocks off the main drag, Nassau Street.

> *Around Nassau town we did roam*
> *Well, I feel so broke up, I want to go home*
>   - The Beach Boys, "Sloop John B"

Gödel lies there among notables like computer scientist Alonzo Church, statistician John Tukey, game theorist John von Neumann, and physicist Eugene Wigner.

At Miami University with Lew and David, I'd taken Mathematical Logic, taught by a Professor Gass. One goal of the course, beyond an introduction to the "calculus" of logic, was to guide us toward an understanding of Gödel's incompleteness theorems. (Readers who don't wish to enroll in graduate school can consult Douglas Hofstadter's *Gödel, Escher, Bach: An Eternal Golden Braid*, perhaps the most entertaining math book ever written.)

My classmate Lew was our graduate class' hardest worker. Of solid Midwestern stock, square-jawed, broad-shouldered, he was born to a farm family that lived just across the Indiana state line, beyond the diner in the tiny town of College Corner with its excellent meatloaf that he and I would treat ourselves to on Friday nights. Each harvest, Lew delivered pumpkins to market; in November, he helped his elder brother set up, in the family's roadside farmstand, a model train set that turned figure eights. The two brothers cared for their mother, who had been widowed early; and during our time at Miami, Lew married his dark-haired sweetheart, Jane, an elementary school teacher. All this and mathematics too! I couldn't have managed it. Lew had apparently been strengthened by the religious college he'd attended, despite its lacking a strong math program. He was now well on the way to becoming a tenured university professor.

In contrast, David was the only surfer dude I've ever known. He would likely have been an actual surfer at a West coast school, but he had gone instead to Lake Superior State, a small college in Sault Ste. Marie, Michigan, where any waves that exist are washed away at the junction of Lake Superior, Lake Nicolet and Lake Huron. At that time, Lake Superior State was known for its dominance of collegiate hockey, which was one of David's obsessions; in his Bachelor Hall office, he kept a hockey stick beside his frisbee golf discs and rollerblades. (One day he pressed me to try the latter, and I nearly killed myself on the slippery linoleum.)

David's dark hair cascaded in waves to his shoulders, breaking some of his own students' hearts. Nothing phased him: not work, nor the demands of his students, teachers, or girlfriends. And he didn't get worked up about politics. Though just five years apart in age, I now see he was a member of a younger generation. I was Generation X and he was a proto-Millennial, a social joiner who disliked divisive issues.

Miami was a teaching school: each instructor, from the longest-tenured professor to the lowliest graduate assistant, was expected to educate. Lew, David, and I were three different types of teacher. David befriended his students, who warmed to his slacker attitude. Lew taught earnestly, patiently, and fairly – qualities that served him well later as a professor. As for me, my well of empathy ran dry in three semesters. I wearied of students staring out the window while I enthused over interesting problems; God only knows the looks I got while I wrote on the blackboard. I gave up teaching just in time; had I stuck with it, "Will this be on the test?" might have been the epitaph on my gravestone. By my final semester, I had minimized the energy that I spent on teaching so that I could concentrate on my own studies.

Back to Mathematical Logic. Limitations have always intrigued me; maybe that's why I was never a world beater. I can't understand people who flatly refuse to consider the possibility of failure; in a perverse way, that trait strikes me as a singular failure of imagination. I'm particularly intrigued by limits on aspiration. I don't mean Princeton Cemetery; I just mean that life's deepest lessons involve limits. You can't live forever. You can't change others. And you can't inspire a love of mathematics, no matter how good your teaching, in psychology students who are taking precalculus just to satisfy a requirement.

Knowledge has limits. Some of my favorite math theorems quantify these limits. Proposition Four earlier in this chapter asserts that there are *no* solutions to a particular class of equations. That's a negative result, but a result nonetheless. Gödel's Theorem runs deeper. It reveals a truth that no mathematician would have believed in 1900: there exist theorems that can *never* be proven true or false. To the uninitiated, this might sounds like defeatism. Even early twentieth century mathematicians were horrified by this implication. But I was born in a later age, when it had become clearer that human ingenuity was playing itself out. I find Gödel's result not only intuitively plausible, but comforting.

Proposition 7 (Euclid's Parallel Postulate): Non-parallel lines intersect.

Statement of Problem

Two thousand years ago, Euclid founded geometry. He posited five axioms (or postulates) to be true. Every high school geometry student learns them today. They are:

1. Every pair of points defines a line segment
2. Every line segment can be infinitely extended to a line
3. Every point and radius define a circle
4. All right angles are equal
5. Any pair of lines intersecting a third line at non-right angles (so the lines aren't parallel) eventually intersect.

Interpretation

We'll all meet again, maybe.

Proof

Euclid's fifth postulate always troubled mathematicians. It didn't seem self-evident like the other four: if two lines are slightly inclined toward one another, will they eventually meet if extended far enough? Hard to say. And since geometry's purpose is to model the spatial relationships of the universe we live in, it seemed dangerous to assume too much.

Mathematicians initially hoped to prove the parallel postulate from the other four axioms, thereby avoiding a leap of faith. By the 1800s, they realized there were three paths open to them. The first was to simply accept the fifth postulate, which results in Euclidean geometry, the geometry of a flat surface. Or they could replace the fifth postulate with the assumption that *no* lines are parallel, that all lines eventually meet. That's elliptic geometry. Finally, they could replace the fifth postulate with an assumption that one can draw *infinitely many* parallel lines through a point not on a line – that's hyperbolic geometry. All three of these geometries are logically consistent, and one of them actually describes our universe.

But as a student of limits, I knew I had reached mine. I was glad that I had not signed on for the additional years that a doctoral degree would have entailed. No more teaching. No more summers subleasing apartments to students who trashed them. And no more cramming for exams: as my last semester neared its end and the Osage orange trees on the frisbee golf course deposited their gnarly green charges onto the turf like bocce balls, we grads were so harried by the prospect of our approaching oral exams that we no longer had time to play a round. I knew then that it was time to "pack my bag" – though not without first accomplishing what may be my all-time greatest sporting achievement.

David held the nine-hole course record of 25. (I can verify this now by checking the red spiral ring notebook in which we recorded our scores.) On the Saturday before orals, I was in Bachelor Hall looking for a golfing partner. The only one around was Jonathan, whom I convinced to put aside the books.

That day, I was lights out. I had distance and impeccable touch. I scored a hole-in-one on the fifth, a hole we'd all thought impregnable – over two hundred feet from the tee to a basket that could not be seen around a dogleg of tall trees. I wound up, sailed the frisbee around the treetops, and waited. Ten seconds later, faintly but clearly, I heard the clanging sound of rattling chains. Jonathan just stared, mouth agape.

It was my final shot that sealed the deal. I needed a par on the ninth to beat David's record, but my frisbee lay in a thicket of trees and shrubs about twenty feet from the hole. My only hope was to heave it as hard as possible through the brush with pinpoint accuracy: it wasn't even clear that there was a path to the hole. I took a couple of minutes to size up the angles... then stepped away to measure it again. All the while, Jonathan watched wide-eyed, saying nothing. I got back in the sticks to line up the shot, then wound up and let go. A couple of twigs broke, but the disc sailed in. Jonathan was flabbergasted. Slowly, emphasizing each word, he said:

"You are a beast. I've never seen such concentration."

Yes, but could I muster it for my upcoming test?

The oral examinations took place in a windowless, first-floor classroom in Bachelor Hall. After being asked to open wide (that's a joke), I was told to take a piece of chalk and stand at the blackboard. Nervously, I faced my three examiners, whom I had hand-picked from the math faculty. They finished talking shop. One got up to close the hall door, and we began.

The first question wasn't bad. But follow-up questions about real analysis, complex analysis, and abstract algebra that were designed to probe the depth of my two years of study had me waffling, fumbling, and backtracking. "Can there exist a function that is everywhere continuous and nowhere analytic?" I was asked. Who knows? I lost count of the leading questions meant to untrack me and guide me toward any sort of meaningful analysis. Gradually I realized that, despite my efforts, I knew next to nothing. It was humbling. If this was meant as a rite of passage, to spur me on to a doctorate, it had quite the opposite effect.

After an hour, I was dismissed. From the other side of the closed door that now separated me from my instructors, I looked down the long inner hall to the departmental office that had been dark since the end of semester. What were my teachers discussing? Perhaps an upcoming cookout; maybe they were just letting me sweat a bit for tradition's sake. Or maybe I hadn't passed. I wasn't sure what that would entail, though my summer was wide open and my lease ran through August. In the dark hall, with the air conditioning extinguished, I could practically feel the summer heat throb through the glass panes that separated me from the outer corridor looking onto the courtyard.

To pass time, I began to read bulletin board flyers advertising long-past deadlines: enrollment dates for summer programs, invitations to talks by visiting professors that had been delivered and then forgotten. Having exhausted this reading material, I reasoned it would not hurt to take a walk in the fine, fair, late-morning air of early summer.

Paper Lion came to mind. That was George Plimpton's account of the summer of 1963, when he crashed the Detroit Lions training camp to try out for quarterback, so that he could write about the experience. Of course, he failed miserably. Finally, on the day he left training camp, as his now-former teammates struggled under the heat of the noonday sun and the yoke of coaches pushing them to the breaking point, he walked past a tennis court on which two young ladies dabbled at tennis. He revisits this scene in the book's final paragraph:

> *And then, oddly, something came to mind which was unexpected. I found myself thinking not of the obvious or pleasurable aspects of my stay with the Lions.... Instead, I seemed to hear the odd sound I remembered from my last day with the team when I walked up from the practice field – the long bleat from the players being whistled together by*

> *the coaches, almost one of sorrow – and once again I seemed to see the girls with their racquets on the tennis court, the sound catching them in lovely poses of arrest, the bells of hair turning at their shoulders as they stopped their play to turn and listen, peering at the pines, their head tilted for the sounds drifting up from the practice field beyond.*

That's how I felt. It was also how I would feel years later, after my career at a Jersey City financial firm. What I best remember now of those years are not the actual work I did, but rather the waterfront walks from the train station to my office – the symmetrical row of bollards near the light rail tracks; the mauve sunrises couched in morning mist, nestled like tissue paper in the crevices of the Manhattan skyline; the smell of the blueberry muffin I would buy at the café next door to work. Likewise, long after I have forgotten how to integrate a Cauchy curve, I will remember the scent of cut grass on the frisbee golf course and the clanking sound of the chains after an on-target toss.

I could not have walked far, but I can't be sure, my mind having wandered. Returning to Bachelor's interior hall, I nearly collided with one of my professors:

"John, where were you? We've been looking for you!"

I started to say something in my defense, but he interrupted me with the news that I had passed. I had my master's degree.

I was among the first of my class to hear those words. Others would present themselves to their own committees, get the good news, and then chart trajectories through life. With the exception of Lew, I never saw any of them again. (Or should I say, not yet? It may depend on the shape of the universe.) I assume that many, particularly the statisticians, went into industry. Others may have gone into academia. David may have become a snowboarder.

But here's the interesting part. Physicists still don't know the shape of our universe. I'm not being facetious, not entirely; you can read about the strides being made toward answering that question in Janna Levin's memoir, *How the Universe Got Its Spots*. As she explains, while quantum physics does a great job of explaining the microscopic world, we still don't know the shape of things over vast stretches of space and time. Is our universe Euclidean, elliptic or hyperbolic? We don't even know whether it's finite or infinite.

One interesting possibility is finite and elliptic. If that's the case, then one day our paths through the universe will curve back on themselves, and we'll meet again.

Proposition 8 (The Monty Hall Problem): If you are on "Let's Make a Deal," when Monty Hall asks if you want to switch doors, do so.

Statement of Problem

At the end of *Let's Make a Deal*, the long-running TV game show, plaid-clad Monty Hall offered contestants a choice of three curtains, or what I'll call doors. One concealed the grand prize, perhaps a vacation or car; behind the others were booby prizes, such as a pet goat.

Once the contestant selected a door, Monty would reveal a booby prize behind a *different* door. With two doors remaining, he would then turn to the contestant and ask, "Would you like to switch from your original choice?"

Interpretation

Never be afraid to change your mind.

Proof

I packed my Tempo with everything that had survived Ohio and began my long drive home with little thought to my future. As I sat beside boxes of peanut butter buckeyes, a Ohio delicacy, from Young's Dairy and United Dairy Farmers, I rolled my car windows down to an early summer morning and turned the radio to the left end of the dial. Soon I was flying past farms to the sound of an accordion-fueled jig called "Sadness Grows," by a Vancouver band that was new to me, Spirit of the West. The song was infectious, and I wasn't sad; rather, I was happy to be coming home. I supposed I would resume my previous life and go back to temp work, which at least offered flexibility. Life would soon offer other options.

In the back of my mind, I contemplated the actuarial field, where many mathematicians found homes, or so I'd heard. By the following spring, I had my first professional job, as an actuary. Three years later, I moved to a better job at Chubb, an insurer based in Warren, New Jersey.

At Chubb, I was an actuarial assistant, or junior actuary. Some friends and family referred to me as an "actuarial," which is an adjective, not a noun, but I let it slide. For these folks I composed a brief "elevator speech" to explain what an actuary does. ("Measures risk" is the shortest possible description.) My Aunt Ro called one day to tell me how proud she was when, during the course of her regular late-night reading, she had encountered the word "actuary" and knew what it meant!

"What book were you reading?" I asked.

Something by Grisham, she said. Yes, that's how many people first hear about actuaries, in the context of crooked insurance companies.

Like my peers, I studied for the ten actuarial exams, the field's well-established path to accreditation. I'd always enjoyed studying for tests. My workday consisted mostly of preparing personal automobile rate filings, the documents filed by insurance companies with state insurance departments to justify their rate changes. Actuaries crunch numbers, determine new rates, measure the impact of the change on an insurance company's book of business, and fill out paperwork. After doing filings for several small states, I was promoted to working on a rate increase for New York.

I assume a statute of limitations will protect me if I admit, twenty years on, that Chubb considered New York to be its "cash cow." The company was very profitable among well-to-do New Yorkers willing to pay premium rates for the Chubb brand. It went without saying that actuaries didn't screw up New York rate filings – but I did. I'm not sure how I did it, even today. All I remember is that after the filing was submitted, I found a calculation error (it may not even have been mine) and brought it to the attention of my manager, Greg.

Greg was the most easygoing manager I've ever worked for. He participated in our weekly ultimate frisbee games, during which I huffed and puffed to keep pace with my peers, ten years younger than I. Even before he was transferred to Bermuda to handle Chubb's reinsurance unit, Greg was tailor-made for shorts. But when he heard what I had to say, he just frowned.

The next day Greg invited me to *his* manager's office, where we were joined by two senior underwriters. My grand-manager explained that I *would* be kept aboard, because it was my first such mistake, but that my error *would* cost Chubb money, and that it was serious enough to be grounds for dismissal. I listened in silence, but not without a little cynicism: if I didn't know what I had done wrong, and no one was going to bother to explain it to me, then I wouldn't get worked up about it. And as I said, the error may not even have been my own. Perhaps this meeting with the underwriters was just a bit of theater intended to demonstrate that we actuaries meant business, that we had an appreciation for the business side of things and weren't just the numbers wonks they made out to be. (How can you tell an extroverted actuary? When he speaks, he looks at the *other person*'s shoes.)

When our department moved to Whitehouse Station, I followed. I considered renting a room in the West Jersey wilds from an elderly woman to whom I'd spoken once on the phone, but then decided to buy a house. My coworker Steve, one of the few actuaries slower than I was on the ultimate frisbee field, advised against it: other than Chubb, he pointed out, there were no insurers in the area, so I would in effect be indenturing myself to my employer to meet my mortgage. But I threw caution to the wind and bought a place beyond the ridge on Route 78 that was so treacherous in winter, its blasted rock outcroppings veined with stalactites the size of semitrailers.

My four-bedroom Colonial was in Stewartsville, a crossroads just this side of the Delaware River. It was even further from the world I'd grown up in than the city-sized truck stop a few miles east, which sold New Jersey's cheapest gas and a hundred kinds of jerky. I'm sure my new neighbors didn't know what to make of the single young man who'd bought the large home at the end of their cul-de-sac; to them, I was the odd fish who appeared outside only to jump on the trampoline that I'd placed by the septic tank, or run the electric lawnmower at the end of its hundred feet of extension cord, or walk to the end of my driveway to confirm that I wasn't playing my stereo too loudly. (With a whole house to myself, I tended to play it loudly enough to obliterate the roar of the interstate truck traffic distantly visible through gaps in the trees.)

In time I advanced, and began participating in the process of interviewing job candidates. Actuaries tend to interview their own: on a typical day, a job applicant would run a gauntlet of actuaries, each of whom had a favorite way to judge a prospect's worth. Each of us had our pet questions, nothing overly hard or requiring specialized knowledge, to gauge how an applicant thinks on his or her feet. Fred, for instance, would ask, "How many basketballs do you think would fit in this room?"

or "How many rivets would you estimate there are in a jet airplane?" I'm glad that I wasn't asked those questions; they sounded more suitable for engineers.

I do remember the questions that I was asked when I interviewed. Over lunch at a local restaurant, my grand-manager asked me who Alan Greenspan was. That was easy. Then he asked:

"Which equal-mean distribution, binomial or Poisson, has a larger variance?"

"Well, I would guess Poisson. Should I work it out?"

"Sure."

I did, realized my initial guess was wrong, and changed my answer. So when I got the job, I attributed it to my ability to think on my feet – and a willingness to change my mind.

My own pet question was the "Monty Hall Problem," a puzzle that had its fifteen minutes of fame when Marilyn vos Savant posed it in her column in *Parade* magazine on September 9, 1990. *Parade* was, and is, a little semi-glossy "magazine" that, when I was growing up, appeared like clockwork each Sunday on our doorstep, inside the Sunday *Newark Star-Ledger*. It contained recipes, coupons, and advice columns. As a young teen, I'd give it a quick look and occasionally grab it by mistake when I absconded with the Sears and Macy's flyers that pictured girls a few years older than I, wearing cotton underwear.

In 1986, vos Savant debuted her *Parade* column, "Ask Marilyn." Her capsule bio said she was *The Guinness Book of World Records* holder of the world's highest IQ, 228. (Never mind the fact that the IQ scale was designed to max out at 170.) Vos Savant occasionally posed logic puzzles. The week after she correctly wrote about the Monty Hall problem, and correctly concluded that the contestant should always switch doors, she was inundated with letters not only from armchair mathematicians but from academics who claimed she had erred. But she hadn't. They had.

One day I interviewed Dorrie, an actuarial candidate, and posed the Monty Hall problem to her. Her eyebrows arched. Her initial reaction was the same as that of most people: it shouldn't matter which decision you make – stick or switch. But she didn't want to commit right away, so she asked me to repeat the question, which I did. Finally, she grimaced and said, with a shake of her head:

"No, it shouldn't matter which door."

I explained why it did. And it isn't hard to see when viewed in the right way:

When you first choose a door, there is a one-out-of-three chance that you correctly guessed the location of the grand prize. In that case, switching doors is a bad move, and you will get a booby prize. But in the event that you did *not* guess correctly at first, switching doors means you win! (Remember, Monty has already revealed the location of one booby prize.) To summarize, switching is bad one-third of the time, and good two-thirds of the time – so you should always switch. It's actually like life. Rarely do you find the prize on the first try. It pays to stay flexible.

A few weeks later, I received a letter at work from Dorrie, whom we'd hired despite my being on the fence about her. She wrote of her plans to relocate – and then took me to task for asking her the Monty Hall question, which she didn't consider to be fair game. At the least, she said, I could have posed it differently. I thought about it, but wasn't sure how else I could have asked it.

Then again, maybe Dorrie had a point. I later read that Paul Erdös – one of the world's leading experts on probability theory, the one who characterized mathematicians as machines running on coffee – had refused to accept the answer to the Monty Hall problem for a full week until a Bell Labs colleague patiently explained the solution to him.

***

There's my mathematical life in eight propositions. As is typical with survey courses, I've just scratched the surface; with regard to the mathematics involved, there are many books to which I could refer the interested reader.

I'm no longer a practicing mathematician, but I still keep up with the discipline, in a recreation way. I may no longer have the fortitude to plow through a textbook, but I enjoy learning that it takes at least twenty-one differently-sized squares to construct a larger square, or that it's more likely to win at bingo on a row than on a column, or that the smallest possible number of non-empty Sudoku squares is seventeen. (That last assertion is still a conjecture.)

But my favorite results remain those that place limits on our knowledge. In this chapter alone, those include Gödel's Incompleteness Theorem, our inability to prove the four-color theorem without computers, and our continued ignorance of the shape of our universe.

I humbly submit that the most interesting objects to contemplate are those that we'll never know.

Correlation and Causation

A short digression on the difference between correlation and causation, two concepts covered in introductory statistics courses.

Causation is familiar from physics: A causes B, or B causes A.

Correlation is trickier: A and B happen together. A may have caused B. B may have caused A. An unknown C may have caused both. Or, more likely, a *lot* of things, not all of which can be known, make A and B usually happen together. If the correlation is strong enough, A and B may appear to be causally related, even when they aren't.

Finally, A and B may have happened together by pure chance.

These distinctions may not seem important, but for many years they were my job.

***

I didn't consider a career until I was thirty. I didn't see the point. Between stints at school and temporary jobs (mailroom guy, word processor, administrative assistant), I'd managed fine.

At twenty-four, I felt it was time to finish college. I transferred to Montclair State and changed majors. At my new school, unlike at Princeton, many professors liked to teach. I stuck to them and avoided the rest. Since, by and large, the student body wasn't particularly motivated, I had the teachers' attention. I availed myself of their office hours, and they viewed my visits as breaks from the grind.

In computer science class, I discovered a gift for programming, one good enough to make a living. But I decided against a comp sci major because I was drawn to "pure" mathematics, the kind difficult to find a use for in real life, unless you are a teacher.

I enrolled in Montclair State's teacher certification program. My first semester, I was asked to intern for three days at a New Jersey high school to observe a working teacher. I chose to work with Mrs. Boepple, my one-time calculus teacher. She said she'd be happy to supervise.

It certainly felt odd sitting in my old front-row desk next to the door of the C Hall classroom where I had once taken calculus. I had to reorient myself, to see class from a teacher's point of view. The first day, Mrs. Boepple had me take her quiz on permutations and combinations.

Given that I hadn't seen the material in a while, I was satisfied with my 95. On top of my paper, Mrs. Boepple wrote in red ink, "Welcome back, John!"

> *Welcome back*
> *Your dreams were your ticket out*
> *Welcome back to that same old place*
> *That you laughed about*
> — John Sebastian, "Welcome Back"

More disorienting was a trip to the teacher's lounge. As a student, I had never looked inside the room at the foot of B Hall whose door nearly always remained shut. I shouldn't have been surprised to see how small it was: long-imagined places, like places from one's past, always seem small. The lounge was crowded with teachers on free period. Sitting on a small sofa near a mini fridge was my former physics teacher, Mr. Bucher. He said hi, and we made small talk. Other faces struggled to place mine, and I got some distrustful looks, as though I were a spy. I felt like the actor in *Gosford Park* who admits to have been living "below stairs" to study the servants up close, in preparation for a future role.

But I soon realized that I liked mathematics too much to sacrifice the time and credits needed for a teacher's certification. So I became a straight math major and kicked thoughts of a career further down the road.

It wasn't until after graduate school that I thought of an actuarial career, even though my sixth-grade teacher had forecast that I would one day be an actuary. (I'd forgotten that fact; it was my childhood friend Clay who reminded me.) Dr. Stevens, my principal advisor at Montclair State, thought the idea was sound. The actuarial exams, he said, despite their reputation for difficulty, were certainly easier than the ones I had been taking in college.

Still, it took another year of work as a temporary office worker to convince me to make the leap. Maybe it was just an odometer click: I was turning thirty. I signed up for the first actuarial exam, which was on calculus, so it would be a breeze; then I would apply for a job. Mom and Dad were happy to see me try something new, but I didn't play up its significance, in case it didn't pan out.

At age 30, I still had a lingering romantic notion about eastern Pennsylvania, so I eschewed nearby test sites and took my first exam at Lehigh University. On the morning of test day, I tidied the piles of practice tests on my parents' kitchen table, got in the car, and put on the new album by Brian Wilson, the soundtrack to something new.

> *Orange crate art was a place to start*
> *Orange crate art was a world apart*
>   Brian Wilson and Van Dyke Parks, "Orange Crate Art"

I arrived several hours early. Having no plan, I went to the library to pass time. I was done studying, so I went to the literature stacks and found a wonderful biography of Proust by George Painter (for more on that, turn to Side A for the chapter "Monsieur Proust"). I was so immersed in its maps and text that I nearly lost all sense of time, which would have been appropriate, if inconvenient. But I returned to the present and aced the exam.

With a master's degree and an actuarial exam to my credit, I was ready to find a job. One sunny morning, I walked to the reference area at the Madison Public Library and found a thick binder that listed, by industry, employers of scientists and mathematicians. Paging to insurance, I jotted down the names and addresses of ten companies that might hire entry-level actuaries. Back at home, I printed out form letters, placed them in envelopes, affixed stamps, and walked them to the post office. Then I awaited results. (How quaint all of this seems today, with everything so automated, virtual, and impersonal!)

One company responded: Insurance Services Office, located in the Seven World Trade Center building. They invited me to an interview.

On the big day, I boarded a train for Hoboken, then took PATH to the World Trade Center, where in a sea of humanity I ascended those interminable, never-to-be-forgotten escalators. I threaded a path through the pedestrian mall, exited the side doors to Vesey Street, and climbed two half-flights of stairs to enter a ribbed glass tube that carried me across traffic and into ISO's lobby. (In an inspired turn of irreverence, Jim Callahan, a future coworker, dubbed this entrance "The Hamster Tube.") I took an elevator to the twenty-first floor, where an HR representative ushered me into a windowless room slightly larger than a broom closet, then placed before me the multiple-choice test given to all applicants for quantitative jobs, leaving me to it.

It wasn't hard; I even identified a trick question that I'd wrongly answered on my first pass through the test. I smiled at the wording that had been designed to mislead. The final question required the most thought:

"Why do you want to work at Insurance Services Office?"

With loads of time at my disposal after blitzing the multiple-choice questions, I sat back to think. I then composed a two-page essay – an ode, a paean, a veritable love letter – to Manhattan, the town where I suddenly knew I wanted to work for the rest of my life. HR had probably never seen its like, unless they still had Walt Whitman's application on file.

I got an offer. It was a little paltry for someone with a master's degree working in Manhattan, but it was larger than any salary I had ever seen, so I said yes. This money soon came in handy when Dad died and I gave Mom my paychecks (net of essentials: books, records, sweets, my monthly train pass) to pay the property taxes on our house, which had become an albatross and which Mom would soon put on the market. It felt good to help out, and Mom eventually paid me back, with interest.

I enjoyed work, and passed the actuarial exams one by one. With each came a raise. I was one of many actuaries-in-training at ISO, a company with a reputation as an industry proving ground. Most of my cohort would leave for positions of increased responsibility elsewhere, but others like my managers would stay at ISO for their entire careers. Anyone with a flair for the routine, a willingness to follow procedures that had been codified decades earlier, an affinity for numbers, and an eye for detail, could make it at ISO. I was handed a few challenging projects, but eventually grew bored. After two years, ready for a break, I asked my manager Mike for a leave of absence.

Mike was the lifelong upward striver I would never be, working long hours every day, sometimes well into evening. Unlike ISO's officers and top executives, he did not live in a well-heeled suburban enclave but in hard-boiled Manhattan, which was a perfect match for his personality. (I just recalled a strange encounter one Saturday, when I was shopping in the City. From afar I saw Mike approach, and loudly called his name. He didn't hear me. I called again – more loudly, despite my proximity

– still nothing. On the third try, I shouted. The inveterate New Yorker continued staring straight ahead, impassive, never making eye contact, completely ignoring me as he passed.)

Mike was a chronic smoker. Only meetings and cigarettes took him away from his desk, and then only meetings after he started chewing Nicorette, which only made him more irritable. The day he was named Assistant Vice President, I approached him as he spoke with Jason, his consulting econometrician. Mike told Jason a joke I didn't quite catch about doing anything to climb "that greasy pole," and Jason laughed. To be sociable I joined in, which made Mike think I'd overheard their entire conversation. He eyed me closely, then smiled warily. I vowed to never again laugh at a joke that I didn't understand.

So when I walked into Mike's office to tell him I needed a leave of absence, he was surprised. Casting about for an excuse, I told him that I needed exercise: long work days, commute included, had me putting on weight. As was usual with Mike, he suspended his disbelief while I talked, took another piece of gum, and formulated a measured response. Then he offered a bit of advice I'm glad I did not take: he said that returning to the corporate world after walking away from it was very difficult.

But I was young, so I knew better. Life's principal characteristic is intermittence. Feelings come and go. Situations recur. Decisions can be unmade.

I moved to Maine, where I lived on a temp's wages. Months later I returned to New Jersey and got engaged. In need of a full-time job again, I met with Mike, who'd forgotten his advice of a few months earlier. He made an offer, but I instead chose Chubb, where the money and commute were better. I married. Two years later, I was separated, waiting eighteen months for a no-fault divorce. Then I bought my house in the woods, in Stewartsville.

I began seeing Carol, whom at that point of my life I had known for ten years. It dawned on me that she understood me better than my first wife ever had. At first, we saw each other only occasionally, but one day she called to say that she had broken her wrist while roller skating at the Roxy, a Manhattan nightclub. I drove to the City to feed her two cats, because Carol couldn't open their cans of food. Watching me work the can opener, she reevaluated my potential as a husband.

Carol visited my home in the sticks, bringing her cats, her right arm in a cast. The cats spent the night hiding from the resident mouse, a visitor I'd captured repeatedly in a counterweighted trap that I would bait with peanut butter and release again in the woods. Like Politburo officials reviewing a military parade from a raised dais, the cats regarded me warily from the highest available perch, a terraced nook near the top of the brick fireplace. We humans slept on the floor, on blankets, with Carol's arm hanging heavily at her side while she slept.

One Sunday soon after, I dropped Carol off at the Chatham train station so she could catch the return train. She called me that night in tears; she missed me. So I sold my house, she broke her lease, and we moved to Hoboken, to an apartment high above the train tracks. It was now too far to commute to Chubb, so I quit. ISO rehired me as a pricing actuary in their personal automobile department.

Quick quiz. Was all of this the work of correlation or causation? Did A cause B cause C cause D, or were these events independent? Were they all the results of unverifiable personality traits X and Y? Or am I simply rephrasing the eternal question of free will versus predestination? A purely causal universe implies the latter, which most people would reject. But a purely correlative universe, in which all is contingent, is no more satisfying. Are we the sum total of our genes? Do our characters determine our lives, or can they be changed? And is the world too big for any of this to matter?

***

The years passed. I advanced steadily, on schedule, the ISO way.

Then one morning, Beth, an extroverted, attractive, and highly regarded senior manager who was a few years older than I, invited me to her manager Kevin's corner office. Beth lived near Bruce Springsteen's house, and had often seen "The Boss" in concert. Had we been closer in age and pay grade, I might well have developed a crush on her.

I took a modest chair along the back wall of Kevin's office, and Beth sat beside me. She announced that she would like to put me in charge of a new division of four that would build "predictive models" for ISO's insurance lines. She had chosen me because I had demonstrated an interest and ability in my work with statistical models. (It is true that I had independently volunteered to study their potential use in my current department's pricing analyses.)

As I listened, my head swam with responses. I knew "yes" was the desired one, but as usual when confronted with something new, my heart said, "No, no, no!" And since, on the whole, my heart has served me well, I left the door open: I said that it was an interesting idea, and that I'd speak with Carol and get back. Beth seemed a bit surprised at my hesitation, but was otherwise satisfied.

The next day I said yes, even though I was still wavering. Never having managed before, I was unsure of my people skills.

On the third day, as I entered a large conference room to attend a department-wide meeting, I saw Kevin in the audience, an unoccupied folding chair beside him. I sat down and told him in a low voice that I may have changed my mind. He betrayed no surprise, which in turn surprised me. I later learned that imperturbability – the quality of never appearing surprised – is an essential characteristic of a senior executive.

That afternoon, my manager Pat stopped by my desk and invited me to his office. He asked me to sit down. Then he offered his advice, which was to never turn down a promotion.

After getting Carol up to speed that evening, she said:

"Might as well give it a go."

***

For the next seven years, I managed a team that worked with the ratemaking units at ISO to advise clients how to price their traditional insurance products: personal automobile, commercial automobile, homeowners, general liability, and commercial property. Many clients had abandoned ISO's traditional pricing recommendations to build their own predictive models; now we would turn the tables with the benefit of our proprietary industry data. We would build new models and sell them to our clients, particularly small insurers who lacked the data or actuarial expertise to do it themselves. In effect, we would level the playing field, enabling small companies to set their rates more accurately so that they could compete with behemoths like State Farm, Allstate, Progressive, and Geico. And possibly, by raising the industry bar, we would win back the large insurers as well.

I led an interesting team. Fred, the senior member, was ten years older than I. A physicist by training, he had a long face, a dark, scraggly beard, square eyeglasses, and a German sense of humor. He could program in languages that I'd never even heard of and possessed a thorough knowledge of statistics, a field in which he was essentially self-taught, having learned it from textbooks that he had acquired piecemeal through the years, which now lined the bookshelves of his office.

Fred didn't mind reporting to me despite my lack of experience, provided he had his own office. Beth pulled strings to make that happen, finding one for him on another floor. When I needed a break, I'd walk down the several floors to Fred's office, where I would find him humming, muttering, and crosschecking his handwritten notes against his monitor, which he stared at nearsightedly. Soon he'd ask me to take a seat and joke that I, too, would one day need glasses; in the meantime, he admired my willingness to wear contacts. (I've never worn contacts, and for a reason I don't understand, I never corrected Fred of his misunderstanding.) On the rare occasions that Fred wasn't in his office, I would wait a few minutes and idly remove textbooks from his shelves. After opening them to random pages and reading a line or two, I would return them, none the wiser.

Fred had joined my team because he often missed deadlines. His previous team, having tired of his fastidiousness (or thoroughness), was happy to have him reassigned. Fortunately for us both, my team did research so we rarely had deadlines, or even well-defined deliverables. Fred could continue working at a slow, methodical pace, and I could let him.

Over time, the other positions on our team were filled by a series of promising young actuaries who shared two characteristics: a horror of ISO's typical routine, and an eagerness to add predictive modeling, that hot new actuarial skill, to their resumes, thus increasing their marketability. Within ISO, whenever there was an opening in my unit, it marketed itself. I would just sit back and wait for the next fresh-faced actuary, a star in another department, to appear in my doorway and ask if I had a moment to talk. And I'd say to myself, "Here comes another!"

I gave little guidance to junior team members. I would suggest statistical models, programming procedures, and software packages to investigate, then set them loose. Being young, smart, and eager to shine, they did fine. Then the day would come: for a second time, they would unexpectedly appear in my doorway, requesting a moment to talk. This time, they would close my door and tell me that they were moving to a position of greater responsibility (and pay) at another company. And I would say to myself, "There goes another!"

But while working for me they were a delight, rarely presenting me with the personnel issues that impacted other managers. Secretly, I wished I was one of them: with my energy taken up by managerial tasks – meetings, presentations, budget forecasts – I no longer found time to learn the analytic techniques mastered by my team. At the same time, ISO, in an attempt to become leaner, reorganized several times. We managers were assigned to discuss a book called *Our Iceberg Is Melting*, a business fable about a tribe of Antarctic penguins who blithely ignore climate change until the day that a freethinking penguin leads them to a new iceberg. It was cute.

***

Over time, statistical models grew more sophisticated. We actuaries kept up with the latest developments at twice-annual meetings in the usual cities, the ones that love to host conferences: Chicago, Las Vegas, Orlando. There, we made the acquaintance of exotic models that had never graced the pages of *Vogue*. (I got a couple of calls from women who'd seen my name on LinkedIn and assumed that I, like them, directed a modeling agency.) We learned the ins and outs of neural networks, lasso and ridge regressions, support vector machines, geospatial smoothers, and Markov Chain Monte Carlo models.

The main drawback of most if not all of these models was our inability to explain them – not just to laypeople but to our own actuaries, actuaries at client firms, and the insurance regulators who would decide whether to approve them for industry use. Why, they asked, did model A assign rate B to insurance applicant C? It was hard to say. Not for nothing were these models called "black boxes."

Not only had models evolved, so had the data: the age of "Big Data" had arrived. More information was known (or wrongly assumed known) about individual insurance risks than had ever been assumed to be knowable. Insurance companies linked their claims and underwriting databases to data that they bought or otherwise acquired from third parties of every stripe: utilities, marketers, social networks, rideshare companies, federal and state governments, and others.

When data had been scarce, all insurers knew of policyholders was what was written on application forms. Consequently, few variables were actually used to underwrite and price insurance: an auto insurance applicant who specified age, garaging address, vehicle, and policy limits was close to being quoted a final price.

Now it seemed that every variable not legally proscribed (such as race) was up for grabs. In a privacy-free world, the data is there. To take just one of a thousand examples, how about occupation? Some insurers now price on it. If teachers have more accidents than actuaries, why not charge them more?

Well, I can think of many reasons why not, but the main *statistical* reason goes back to causation and correlation. Maybe causation is at work: perhaps teachers, all else being equal, drive more dangerously than actuaries. But *all else being equal* is a treacherous phrase. All else is never equal, and even if it were, we would never know. Teasing out the statistical effect of occupation from a thousand other differences between insurance applicants is very difficult. Predictive models – those big, dumb, complex calculators – are oblivious to such considerations; they run through a thousand iterations of complex equations that obscure an underlying logic that can never be fully understood, and finally output a surcharge for teachers. Is it correct? Hard to say. It depends on the model, and the other variables considered for inclusion.

Equations aside, why would teachers be more dangerous drivers than actuaries? More likely than not, for reasons other than their actual jobs. I mean, why should what one does between the hours of 9 a.m. and 5 p.m. – short of working underground in a mine, which might affect one's vision, perhaps – affect rush hour driving skills? Occupation as a model variable is unfair because it captures the effect of *something other than occupation*. It's almost like rating someone based on the color of their skin, which isn't allowed.

Perhaps teachers live in more urban areas, where accidents are more common. Perhaps, earning less money, they drive older, more accident-prone cars. Or maybe actuaries work more often at home, or favor public transportation, or make use of flex time, and so are on the road less often during peak hours.

Now include hundreds of other variables in a model. Democrat or Republican? Facebook or Instagram? Depending on the type of model and the variables at one's disposal, models will ascribe different portions of the higher accident rate of teachers to their occupation, thus producing different answers for the "teacher surcharge." But you'll never know which answer is "most" accurate, or get at *why* teachers deserve a surcharge at all. Models calculate, but they don't explain.

Automobile accidents are not physical laws. You can't explain them by appealing to one or a few causes, like gravity or magnetism. They're mostly random, fluke events. And to the degree that causation is at work, it cannot be determined from finite and imperfect insurance data. There isn't enough data in the world to determine what factors are truly fundamental, or what their true effects are.

Yet, statisticians and actuaries frequently adopt "kitchen sink" approaches: they take all available variables, however unreasonable they appear at first glance, toss them in models, and see which ones "stick." Then they calculate the model's improved accuracy over the current rating plan. This step, so crucial, is often ignored, or botched, because it requires finesse and a fair amount of additional "holdout" data, data not used to build the model. Nor is the calculation simple. This problem, the question of model comparison or "lift," occupied much of my time.

***

Stepping back again....

Complex models have hidden costs. *Should* teachers be charged more for insurance, even if, on average, they have more accidents than actuaries? Shouldn't we instead give them a break? Aren't they already paying their debt to society by teaching?

Society, or the government representing it, must decide whether occupation is a socially acceptable rating variable. It shouldn't be left to individual insurance companies, because a single company is powerless to effect change. If teachers are truly worse risks than actuaries, an altruistic insurer taking the "high road," pricing teachers and actuaries equally, will lose money: teachers will buy their policies, pushing that company's costs higher, and actuaries will flock to other insurers. The net effect for the company in question is a loss; and for the industry, a little more profit at the expense of teachers.

This arms race – more data, faster computers, more complex black boxes – is a waste. It benefits large insurers who can spend on data, statisticians and actuaries, but not the public at large. I confess to having had socialistic thoughts: replacing the competitive insurance marketplace with a single-payer system, and allowing just a handful of allowable, societally acceptable variables. No more data mining. No more big data. Of course, that would mean fewer jobs for actuaries, so I would in effect be legislating myself out of a job.

Meanwhile, automobile insurers are testing variables that seem to have little to do with driving cars. Anything conceivably linkable to an individual, or the neighborhood in which he or she lives, is fair game:

- Credit history. Number of cards? Amount owed? Defaults?
- Commute. Highways or local roads? Proximity to airports, schools, laundromats? How many left-hand turns?
- Driving style. Rapid accelerations? Hard braking and cornering? Late night driving?
- Home. Rent or own? Second home? Gated community?
- Education. High school, college, graduate school?
- Vehicle upkeep. Recent repairs? Regular oil changes?
- Social media. Which platforms? How well-connected?
- Marketing. Income bracket? Magazine subscriptions?

Insurers with data could build models having *thousands* of rating variables that might squeeze out a slightly higher profit margin *in aggregate* while returning laughable results for particular individuals due to bizarre rating factors. (Surcharges for red cars, and surcharges for moonroofs... unless you have both, in which case you get a *discount*? Sure, if that's what the model says!) Insurers might be tempted to price based on one's favorite baseball team, if it ekes out a few more dollars, regardless of whether it's fair to Mets fans. The temptation is there. For large insurance companies, a fraction of one percent saved in future claims payments represents millions of dollars to the bottom line.

***

At actuarial conferences, I encountered a new type of model called price optimization models. To me, they seemed unethical.

All actuarial students memorize the following:

> *A rate is reasonable and not excessive, inadequate, or unfairly discriminatory if it is an actuarially sound estimate of the expected value of all future costs associated with an individual risk transfer.*

What do these words mean? Among other things, they mean that equally risky individuals should be charged equal prices, enough to cover the costs of issuing policies and paying future claims, with a reasonable provision for profit. But price optimization models turn this principle on its head: they use personal information about the insurance applicant to predict how price sensitive he or she is. Applicants who are likely to care less about money can be charged more, netting additional profit.

I can't see how this squares with the words italicized above, much less fairness in general. Then again, how different was this from the contractor who notices the elegant detail of your porch and charges you more to paint the exterior of your house? (Or, as another example, the scene in *Paper Moon* when young Tatum O'Neal sizes up the elegance of a widow's living room and instantly quotes a much higher price for the Bible that her scheming, obituary-combing father is selling?) For that matter, how different are price optimization models from my experience at Chubb, when New York State insurance policies were priced to keep in such a way as to keep the golden goose alive?

The difference is one of degree. We're programming computers to be unfair in the same way that humans have been unfair for centuries. Actually, since computers will eventually do everything better than we can, they will be more unfair. To borrow a phrase from philosophy and a concept from science fiction, what should be computers' "categorical imperative"? To make a buck whenever one can be made? If computers enable ultraefficient unfairness, should insurance companies take advantage of it? Perhaps a non-insurance analogy is in order. Should the ruling political party be allowed to use computers to optimally gerrymander, thus ensuring their continued reelection?

If tomorrow's world is to be run by computers, we should at least program them to be fair. To do so, we need to exercise ethical judgment. (And if people cannot be trusted to exercise ethical judgment, then we should regulate it.) Ethics are the one thing humans still do better than computers.

***

Two more reorganizations, and I had a new boss, Glenn. He was educated in Germany, and had taught economics at a South American university before moving to the United States. His knowledge of the actuarial profession was incomplete, so he quizzed me on occasion about talks that I had heard, and given, at actuarial conferences.

Glenn and I didn't completely agree on the role that actuaries should play within an insurance organization. He felt they should be business first. In contrast, I felt that as mathematicians and technicians, actuaries ought to operate on a higher, more objective plane.

He was amused by our profession's continued debate over price optimization models. "You actuaries!" he would say. "When I booked my last flight, the airline changed my fare three times before I check out! How is that fair?" He challenged our preoccupation with "fairness."

I had counterarguments. People don't have to fly, but they need insurance; actuarial statements of principles (including the passage I quoted earlier) were at odds with price optimization models; and the actuarial profession, unlike many professions, is self-regulated, and so must police itself more diligently.

But I was never put to the test. ISO, not being an insurer, didn't sell policies directly to consumers, and so price optimization models were never high on our list of projects. Not that my managers didn't float the idea of advising insurers how to build their own price optimization models. But it wasn't in our wheelhouse: to build them would require more personal data than we could easily acquire or maintain.

Putting aside price optimization models, my team encountered issues with other model variables. The junior actuaries working for me were eager to build the best models they could, and to try any data they could lay their hands on, but they also understood the complications.

Meetings with the Government Relations Department, which vetted our models before we submitted them to regulators, brought these issues into the open. The following conversation is hypothetical, but serves to illustrate the problem.

In our models for Homeowners policies, we used variables not commonly employed by the industry. Let's keep it simple. Suppose we determined separate rating factors for swimming pools, basements, and detached garages. We would then be invited by Government Relations to a meeting to develop "stories" that they could use to explain these new factors to regulators.

"Okay, swimming pools. A surcharge. Why?"

We'd look around the table at each other, those of us who had built the models and those of us who couldn't tell a regressor from a protractor, and try to hammer out an explanation.

"Um, which model is this?"

"Liability."

"Oh, that's easy – swimming pools are dangerous."

"No, wait, it's the wind model."

"Oh. Let's see. It must be the deck furniture. It blows around and damages the house."

"But it says here it's a discount, not a surcharge."

"Oh, right." Another look around the table. Hands on foreheads, thinking.

"Maybe folks with swimming pools are better risks, being more careful about putting away their outdoor furniture?"

"But how does that explain a discount for basements? Wouldn't they hurt themselves carrying the furniture down the stairs?"

"It's not a discount. It's a surcharge. The discount is for detached garages, where there are no steps to navigate."

I would come to dread these meetings. Lord knows we tried, but eventually we'd throw up our hands. The only reason we could really offer for a surcharge or discount was: *that's what the model says.* Why does the model say that? *Because that's what the data says.* In the final analysis, we were working with black boxes. When Government Relations didn't like a certain surcharge or discount, we would remove the variable from the model to see if and how any of the other variables' factors changed, and whether the revised model was as effective and powerful as the original one. More often than not, we were left with a weaker model that was no easier to explain than the one we had started with.

Another proposal to cross my desk raised my eyebrows. It was a model for "smart" homes, ones having sophisticated security systems, with sensors and cameras throughout the house. They would enable us to collect variables such as the percentage of time that windows are left open, or the number of times the front doorbell is rung, or the number of loads of laundry getting done, or how late homeowners stayed up at night. A bit Orwellian, hmm? I paused to wonder about the difficulty of disentangling all the statistical effects, and then about the privacy implications - in that order.

Actuaries are problem solvers. Most of those with whom I have worked were keen to explore a brave new world of data and analytics. But as I tend to do, I pondered limits. I wondered about the possibility of actuaries being replaced by (to borrow a term I heard at a professional conference) "actuaries in a box," that is, automated statistical algorithms. Before that happens, would regulators step in to save us from ourselves, mandating the use of simpler, more explainable models? One way or another, I wondered how my profession would look in the future. Like others in our accelerating world, would it change beyond recognition?

But the change I came to desire was not so much one suggested by ethics, as by restlessness. Programming and analytics were young persons' games: I was ready to begin another phase of life.

Still on the Line

If you were anywhere near a radio in the late '60s or early '70s - in a kitchen, maybe, or living room, car, shopping mall or elevator - you heard the music of Jimmy Webb. You probably just didn't know it.

His songs weren't the sort to start revolutions and, often as not, were sung by artists consigned to that new ghetto of the record business called "mood music" or "easy listening." But however smooth and sedate they were on the surface, however lush their strings, those songs had depth. Besides, Jimmy Webb didn't care what you thought, because he wasn't talking to you. He was addressing his great lost love, Suzy.

For example, in "Worst That Could Happen," the monster hit for Johnny Maestro and the Brooklyn Bridge that still gets played on oldies stations, a tremulous tenor voice begins:

Girl, I heard you're getting married....

Jimmy Webb originally wrote that song for The Fifth Dimension, a song I knew from a greatest hits compilation, one of Dad's eight-track tapes. But it was another Jimmy Webb song on that tape, the soaring "Up, Up and Away," that I most loved as a child as we criss-crossed the country during summer vacations.

When we were in the motorhome, we would sing about towns:

Gary, Indiana, Gary, Indiana,
Not Louisiana, Paris, France, New York, or Rome, but
Gary, Indiana, my home sweet home
    - The Music Man, "Gary, Indiana"

or listen to songs about towns:

Let's go to Luckenbach, Texas
With Willie and Waylon and the boys
This successful life we're livin'
Got us feuding like the Hatfields and McCoys
    - Waylon Jennings, "Luckenbach, Texas"

Or we'd play Dad's eight-tracks. "Worst that Could Happen" wasn't in Dad's collection, because it wasn't a hit for The Fifth Dimension. To be honest, I can't imagine it being sung by Marilyn McCoo. Not that her voice couldn't handle it, but I can't figure it sung by a woman: it's so obviously a song of unrequited love from a man to the woman who got away. Jimmy wrote it for Suzy.

> *Baby, if he really loves you more than me*
> *Maybe it's the best thing for you*
> *But it's the worst that could happen to me*

To my taste, the Brooklyn Bridge's arrangement is too overdone, too polished, too produced. But when the trumpets conclude the last chorus by quoting Mendelssohn's wedding march, and at the word "worst" a lone horn lands a punch to the gut, it makes its point.

Another Webb song that could be charged with melodrama is "MacArthur Park," the seven-minute epic that Richard Harris, the Irish actor, took to the top of the pops in 1967. (Donna Summer duplicated the feat ten years later.) It is most famous for the lines:

> *Someone left the cake out in the rain*
> *I don't think that I can take it*
> *Because it took so long to bake it*
> *And I'll never have that recipe again*

But its most revealing lyrics are:

> *I recall the yellow cotton dress*
> *Foaming like a wave*
> *On the ground around your knees*

That was Suzy's dress. She wore it to her office job at Aetna Life Insurance Company in Los Angeles, where she and a girlfriend worked. They took bag lunches to nearby MacArthur Park. But one day, Suzy accepted a lunch invitation from a former high school classmate, Jimmy, now a struggling songwriter who lived nearby. That lunch must have made an impression on him, because he later immortalized it in song:

> *The birds, like tender babies in your hands,*
> *And the old men playing checkers by the trees*

Finally, he predicts:

> *After all the loves of my life, you'll still be the one*

    Dad liked "MacArthur Park." He had that one on eight-track, too. (Of course, I mean Richard Harris' rendition. Dad didn't like disco or subsequent styles of music.) Though a fan of "MacArthur Park," "Worst That Could Happen" and "Up, Up and Away," I'll bet Dad didn't know that all three songs were penned by one young man from Oklahoma. Because Dad wasn't hip to the latest crop of songwriters, not that there was anything wrong with that. Even Frank Sinatra, whose music Dad loved, wrongly attributed the Beatles' "Something" (a ballad that Sinatra classified as a "perennial" and Dad called an "evergreen") to Lennon and McCartney, rather than George Harrison. But it was Harrison, not John Lennon or Paul McCartney, who was sick with lust for Patty Boyd, the woman who inspired "Something" and who was later the muse for Eric Clapton's smoldering "Layla."

    I listened while Dad piloted the motorhome (and the dashboard stereo) and Mom served as combination co-pilot/stewardess, arranging atop a fold-out table between the driver and passenger seats a cutting board laden with Triscuits, pork rinds, and Cracker Barrel cheese. (Mom and Dad were back on the protein-heavy Atkins Diet.) I perched in the aisle, helping myself to snacks and seeing Dad occasionally turn my way, offering a grand view of his right sideburn. Then he'd introduce another favorite song with his catchphrase, "And then I wrote...."

    That was a big one, up there with "one swell foop." Dad filled the inevitable downtime on cross-country trips with those phrases and games. For instance, there was our ongoing game of Kong, in which Dad tried to trick us into saying "king." For example, he might innocently ask Frankie and me:

    "Who's your favorite Met?"

    We'd name their slugger, Dave Kingman, and he'd answer:

    "KONG!"

    And thump us playfully on the head.

Or, "What's Mom's favorite supermarket?"
"Kings."
"KONG!"
Or he would retell one of several jokes we never tired of hearing, like the one about the dog that could speak, but only words sounding like "woof." The punch line was that when the dog is asked his opinion of the greatest ballplayer ever, he answers "Ruth," but on second thought changes his mind and says:

"Hank Aaron?"

Then there was the one about the immigrant knowing only one phrase in English, "hommina cheese sandwich." Everyday he orders the same lunch at the same diner, for twenty years. Then one day they run out of ham – so he orders something else. Analyzing that joke strictly syntactically, it's identical to the one about the talking dog!

Or Dad would try a pun:
"The other day I was outside, and it began to snew."
"What's snew?"
"Oh, nothing. What's new with you?"

Eventually we would return to the radio, or the eight-track. Dad curated our music until we were old enough to develop our own tastes. And when he particularly liked a song, he would introduce it by saying, "And then I wrote...." Cole Porter wrote songs on the piano, but Dad wrote them on eight-track.

I suppose Dad wasn't entirely joking. He just happened to be as possessive of his songs as, one day, I would be of mine. And to be honest, "Macarthur Park" wasn't in his pantheon, like Sinatra's "Summer Wind." "Summer Wind" was Dad's song the way "Strawberry Fields Forever" would later be mine: I might as well have written it, since it spoke for me so well. I think "MacArthur Park" was a little too much of an art song, a little too highfalutin', too much like the "younger generation" for Dad to embrace. But how different was it, really, from the classicism of "Summer Wind"?

Like painted kites, those days and nights, they went flyin' by
The world was new beneath a blue umbrella sky

MacArthur Park is melting in the dark
All the sweet green icing flowing down

***

Once, I wrote my own "MacArthur Park." It was horrible.

Mr. Russo, my junior year high school English teacher, annually organized a student art exhibition called "Literature and the American Experience," for which each student was tasked with creating an artifact illuminating a classic American literary work that we'd read in class. I chose *The Grapes of Wrath*. Satirical as always, I designed a board game called "La Lucha" that looked and played like Monopoly, but which I had modified to reflect the experience of migrant farm workers. Precious little hotel building happened; you were lucky to keep out of jail. (Or maybe in it, since so many bad things happened outside.)

Considering me a writer of some ability, Mr. Russo assigned me the task of composing a foreword for the exhibition brochure. This would be distributed to attendees: visiting English classes stopping by during school hours and anyone – students, teachers, parents – who was interested enough to drop by after school.

I labored over that foreword like Joyce over *Ulysses*. To what avail? It would mainly be seen by classmates. Yet I spent hours dredging my soul, looking for an approach to my subject. I reworked it into a state of maximum incomprehensibility one Saturday evening on my grandmother's rolltop desk, and then again the following afternoon on my aunt's back patio, between dips in her swimming pool. I finally chose not to write of Steinbeck, the class struggle, or the American Experience, but something altogether more psychedelic. I'd write a sort of coded love letter. For I was in thrall to a girl in that class; she would read the foreword, and I would write something worthy of a muse, knocking it out of the park.

Athletes have mantras. They tell themselves, "Keep your head in the game" and "Stay within yourself." I'd heard those phrases on baseball diamonds, but didn't think to apply them here; instead, I wrote a long, meandering, vocabulary-addled disquisition about nothing at all, incorporating every odd and arresting image that presented itself to my mind's eye, and closing with the most recent: the astral aura beneath the surface of my aunt's swimming pool that was in fact the blurred halos of light produced by the glow of the recessed lights beneath the blue, chlorinated waves far above.

We were milling about the classroom, putting the final touches on the exhibition, the day before its grand opening. Two classmates, Malcolm and Russell, were huddled together, reading my foreword, laughing. Russell turned to me and asked:

"What were you on when you wrote this?"

I shrugged, forcing a laugh. What else could I do? I couldn't pronounce her name. And it hadn't yet occurred to me to compare my work to "MacArthur Park."

Mr. Russo disliked it, but in the crush of a hundred other tasks, he let my foreword go to press. He probably wished he'd assigned it to a more sensible writer. On the other hand, as a child of the 1960s, perhaps he appreciated the psychedelia.

And then I wrote....

***

Jimmy Webb wrote several hits for Glen Campbell, who recently died of Alzheimer's disease at the age of eighty-one. Glen was huge in the early 1970s when he hosted his own variety show, *The Glen Campbell Goodtime Hour*, back when television and radio programmers had not yet abandoned hope of reaching every demographic. He frequented the pop and country charts for years, selling forty-five million records. Not bad for a sharecropper's son.

Glen's greatest hits collection was also in heavy rotation on our motorhome eight-track. My younger sister Robbie loved duetting with Dad on "Rhinestone Cowboy." Another hit on that tape, one that had barely scraped the top thirty, was a song called "Where's the Playground, Susie?" Dad would sing its simple chorus to my sister, his little "Peanut":

Where's the playground, Susie
If I decide to let you go and play around?

Jimmy Webb was writing to Suzy again, this time skipping the pseudonym. It wasn't the catchiest song on the tape, but I liked its chorus. Since Dad sang it with Robbie, I thought it was a song from an adult to a young girl, like Gilbert O'Sullivan's "Clair," another radio hit of about that time. But Jimmy was still singing to his high school love:

The end has come and found us here

> *With our toys scattered all around us here*
> *The puzzle that we never found an answer for*
> *Still asks us, darlin', just what all the games are for*

Jimmy and Suzy were went out briefly in high school. To frame the relationship in early adulthood was either wish fulfillment on the part of Jimmy, or a thought exercise. Either way he was asking, why are relationships so complicated?

"Where's the Playground, Susie" came out during the culture wars of 1969, which could explain its lackluster performance on the charts. Alongside hippie anthems like "Hair," "Aquarius" (by the Fifth Dimension, no less!) and "Good Morning Starshine," it must have sounded positively baroque. The Beatles piled on with "Get Back," a song about JoJo and Loretta, societal misfits hitting the road, having amorous adventures, and pursuing "California grass." Baby boomers hitchhiked, explored alternative lifestyles, and joined communes. Couples tested the waters of open relationships: the word "swinger" entered the lexicon. Paul Mazursky's film debut, *Bob & Carol & Ted & Alice*, whose promotional poster notoriously showed the four principal actors in bed, was a surprise comedy hit. Even Mike Kekich and Fritz Peterson, two members of those pinstriped squares, the New York Yankees, traded families!

Back in our motorhome, it was inconceivable that Mom and Dad harbored similar thoughts. The same was almost certainly true of Glen Campbell's middle-America fans, who would have heard "Where's the Playground, Susie" as just another well-crafted countrypolitan song without suspecting what it was about, who had written it, or why.

It was "Wichita Lineman," though, that became Jimmy Webb's trademark Glen Campbell hit. Depending on the day of the week, it might be my favorite song ever. I'm not alone in feeling that way. One critic proclaimed it "the first existential country song," while another wrote, "It's one of those rare songs that seems to exist in a world of its own – not just timeless but ultimately outside of modern music."

But it has an origin story. One day, Jimmy found himself motoring along a desolate Oklahoma highway. As his odometer ticked off miles, he watched a line of telephone poles receding to a vanishing point.

As he later recalled:

I was driving along... just blinking and trying to stay awake, and all of a sudden there was somebody on top of one those telephone poles, that one there has a guy on it, and he had one of those little telephones hooked into the wires. For some reason, the starkness of the image stayed with me like a photograph. I never forgot it.

He later asked himself, when sitting at his piano: what was that repairman saying, and to whom was he speaking? Being the product of Webb's imagination, "Wichita Lineman" had to be about Suzy. (Glen later confirmed it was.)

I can hear you singing in the wire
I can hear you through the whine
And the Wichita lineman is still on the line

Time stops for three minutes and eight seconds. Campbell's subtle and expressive vocal is pitch perfect, as is the arrangement by the famed Los Angeles session musicians known as "The Wrecking Crew." As a child hearing the song, I was carried to high and lonesome plains I'd hardly seen. (My family's only foray through the Oklahoma panhandle was when I was seven years old.)

Later, when I had my own Suzy, this song reminded me of her. I recall a day in my parents' bedroom. I'd cluttered the floor with my record collection, making yet another mix tape on my father's Radio Shack stereo (I'd yet to acquire my own high-end system) when Dad walked in. Suddenly I blurted out that I looked forward to the day when I was old like him, and no longer plagued by thoughts of women. He laughed and said:

"John, it doesn't work that way!"

***

Last summer, I took my seat in the Robert Shackleton Playhouse in Cape May with a hundred other fans as we waited for Jimmy Webb to appear. (Carol was out of town, so I was on my own.) The stage was appropriately crowded with 1960s-1970s vintage furniture and bric-a-brac, which every other night that week was the backdrop for Neil

Simon's *Chapter Two*. Among the mid-century modern furnishings – geometric wood bookshelves stocked with period best-sellers (from my seat I could recognize the spine of Michener's *Hawaii*), primitivist Chagall-style paintings, and spherical lights suspended like Japanese paper globes – sat a grand piano. Its lid was propped open to project unamplified sound clearly to the back row of the theater.

A few minutes late, Mr. Webb walked onstage, natty in his glossy velvet suit and deep purple button-down shirt. He took a seat on the piano bench and waited a moment to acknowledge the adulation of his awestruck audience, most of whom had known him for decades, at least through music. He looked young for seventy-one, a little jowly perhaps, but still had a thick head of hair. He even had sideburns like Dad once had, a nod to a hippie past that his close friend Glen Campbell, an establishment type, never stopped kidding him about. His right sideburn, the one facing us as he sat at the piano, reminded me of the one I saw on Dad's face when he drove the motorhome. I could swear that it trailed down his face in the exact outline of the state of California.

For the next two hours, Webb played songs and told tales of his life. He began with his strict Oklahoma upbringing by his father, a Baptist farmer and war veteran. He recalled the prayer that he offered to God when he was fourteen, on the day he first heard Campbell's angelic falsetto on his transistor radio; he was driving the family tractor when "Turn Around, Look at Me" came on. When it was over, he told himself that one day he would write a song for Glen. He told of his family's move to California, and his gut-wrenching decision to remain when his father moved them back to Oklahoma after his mother's death. And he described a blossoming career that led to friendships with luminaries like Bob Dylan, Leonard Cohen, and Waylon Jennings.

He never mentioned Suzy. I know, because I was listening for her name. But I heard nothing, unless I missed something subtle.

After many songs and stories, Jimmy Webb closed with his two best known songs, "Wichita Lineman" and "MacArthur Park." Each was wonderful in its way, but "Wichita Lineman" was a revelation.

Having heard the song for fifty years, beginning with those long-ago plays on Dad's eight-track, the last thing I expected to hear on this evening was the song in a new light, but I did, thanks to the way that Mr. Webb phrased the closing line:

And the Wichita lineman is still on the line

I'd always heard it as an expression of resignation – that after all this time, the telephone repair lineman was still working at his lonely day job in the middle of nowhere, with his only companions being a long line of telephone poles.

But now I understood it to mean that he was still *listening in* on the line, still listening for *that voice* in the wire, trying to pick up a signal. And once Mr. Webb dispatched the lapidary lyric in two quick verses (he was laboring on a third when Glen told him on the phone not to bother; he'd already recorded the song – what would a third verse have said?), he embarked on a long instrumental coda that gradually climbed the keyboard to the piano's highest register, where it nearly ran out of keys (it reached the highest note) before culminating in a series of tapped, staccato notes like the dots and dashes of Morse code. I don't know Morse: was Jimmy typing Suzy's name? Taps diminished in volume as he shifted his weight on the bench, directing all his attention to the keyboard with the focus of one lost in thought, as though listening for a harmony. He lowered his right ear to the keys as the tapping grew so quiet that the audience strained to hear whether he was, in fact, still playing the piano. Only when his hands came to a rest did we know that he was done, and only then did it feel right to applaud.

***

You may be wondering: who is Suzy?

After leaving Aetna, Suzy Horton became a dancer. She worked at a few casinos in Lake Tahoe, where she met her first husband. Their wedding was the one that Jimmy Webb memorialized in "Worst That Could Happen." That marriage didn't last: it was the Seventies, after all.

Suzy later married Bobby Ronstadt, cousin of the famous Linda, becoming Suzy Horton Ronstadt. Their first date, oddly, was a Linda Ronstadt concert during which Linda performed several Jimmy Webb songs. After the show, Suzy and Bobby got to talking about Jimmy. It didn't take long for Bobby to realize that his future wife was the famous songwriter's muse. He asked her:

"How could you not see what this guy's got for you?"

She said simply, "Well, I liked his songs."

Following the Northridge earthquake, Bobby and Suzy moved to Tucson, where Suzy became a songwriter in her own "write." She even penned a few answer songs to songs that Jimmy had written for her. She concludes:

> Jimmy's songs have followed me my whole life, and we are still friends to this day. Jimmy has a lovely wife, and I have a wonderful husband. They have both had to deal with our histories. I mean no disrespect to anyone but I have to say, I have loved Jimmy for fifty years and I always will.

Dream Seven

The last of seven dreams I had while writing this book.

I am in an apartment building's large, sunlit atrium, looking through plate glass windows and a revolving door to the street outside. I'm late for class, the only one I'm taking this semester, which meets on Mondays at Montclair State. I consider calling Colleen to say I'll be late, but then I remember that cell phones don't yet exist. My SUV is parked outside, but a fierce rain, nearly horizontal, pelts the sidewalk which the sun, somehow, still illuminates. Rather than wait for the storm to pass, I walk down a concourse and exit through another door, where the sun is shining and it is dry.

I'm hungry, so I stop at an outdoor bazaar, at a candy booth owned by an immigrant from India. The booth is momentarily empty, but then the proprietor appears with his young son. I want to give him my business, but his store carries nothing that tempts me. There are exotic sweets with strange flavors, and unappetizing American candies such as Tootsie Rolls as large as logs.

But I would feel awkward simply moving on, so I engage the man in conversation. He describes the Parisian suburb we're in, whose name I recognize as the site of recent civil strife. He complains that Paris is not at all what Americans take it to be; directors like Woody Allen and writers like Adam Gopnik misrepresent it as a quaint haunt for ex-pats. He particularly complains about Gopnik, who though he once lived in Paris, portrays the city as too safe, painting it with words like Peter Mayle paints Provence, or Thomas Kinkade paints everywhere.

I thank him and head for my car. Along the way I see with new eyes. The sidewalks are teeming with interesting people, men and women of all ages and nationalities. There are children, but mostly old folks of every stripe, some with head scarves and others with dark, thick beards, the sort of people one doesn't see in Hollywood movies. And suddenly I realize that I am either about to see, or appear in, a new film by Wes Anderson.

Mr. Anderson has directed a few of my favorite films. He paints characters with broad strokes; his heroes and heroines range from geeky kids to young men from the Subcontinent to crusty old Midwestern barbers to young women with audaciously asymmetric tattoos. His films are an acquired taste; few of my friends get him. But I wasn't about to miss his new one.

It is set beneath and within the tallest tree in the world, a giant oak (I recognized it by its bark) that makes the redwoods look like scrub. As the movie unfolds, its extent is gradually revealed via a continual upwards camera pan, with detours down its more voluminous branches. Most of the film's characters stay on solid ground, but the more intrepid climb. Bill Murray, who appears in all Mr. Anderson's movies, plays a reluctant hero: finding himself in the tree, he realizes that he is as stuck as a cat, and that the only way out is to keep climbing. It isn't hard, because there are benches every so often, as in a giant tree fort. I watch as Murray and other characters ascend; simultaneously, thanks to the magic of point-of-view camera, I see the secrets that await them in the uppermost branches.

As the camera climbs, I see platforms, catwalks, hanging rope bridges, and structures that paradoxically gain in bulk and complexity with altitude. The treehouse miraculously does not collapse under its own weight. Its byways and pathways offer settings for new scenes, new characters living on high, and excuses for the sort of showboating camera shots that Anderson adores, which leap vertiginously into the sky like carnival swings. Off one platform, a pirate ship made completely of wire races along a rollercoaster track, then soars into the void. It isn't powered by anything that I can see, a Rube Goldberg device and perpetual motion machine in one.

I can see that Anderson's new film owes a debt to the most recent Richard Powers novel, *The Overstory*, about an apocalyptic environmental battle between California tree huggers and the corporations determined to log the last redwood stands. That book portrays the redwoods as unimaginably rich ecosystems, dense beyond understanding, populated by vegetal beings with a sentience far exceeding ours. But the tree in my dream is even taller and more complex than the redwoods, an incredibly complex stage set of filmmaking bravado.

This can't be a Hollywood film, because it lacks a hero. The climbers? The tree? Moviemaking itself? And yet it has a compelling plotline: Man has overbuilt Nature; will Nature still support Man?

Near the crown is a mammoth structure – no mere treehouse, it's as large as a hotel. One climber, an audacious young woman, has made it this far. She hurriedly searches the rooms for someone, or something. She rifles through furniture drawers. The camera turns corners scarily as it follows from her perspective.

Suddenly everything changes. On-screen, a close-up of the title page of a book, like the title card of a silent film, appears with the text:

Arbeitscher 38
Book 38

The film that I'm watching is no longer about a tree, but about a man's search for the writer of a fairytale about a tree. And I am split in two: I'm the protagonist, and at the same time watching him.

I'm astonished to learn that the fairytale writer is still alive, living at such and such a place on Earth, at such and such a latitude and longitude that I could visit should I choose. I don't. Doing so would rob the world of its majesty, just as a view of the treetop would rob the film of its mystery. Contacting the writer of the fairytale would be tantamount to attaining the crown, which would make me complicit in turning one of the last remote places on Earth (Everest, Antarctica, the Marianas Trench) into *terra cognita*.

***

I wake up. I write down the details of this dream, then reconsider the strange words indented above. They feel like an address. I check online as the coffee brews. They are not an address: "arbeit" is the German word for work, or labor. I know no German, and have no idea where these words came from.

Bonus Tracks

Preface
by the author's brother, Dan

My brother John, who's twelve years older than I am, but really belongs to another era, tends to link songs with places and times that he heard them. His name for these lucky conjunctions is "place-songs."

Well, I know about place-songs! Take this one:

I know the rent is in arrears
The dog has not been fed in years
It's even worse than it appears
But it's alright

That's the Grateful Dead's "Touch of Grey," from 1987. It came to my attention five years later via my friend Dave, Madison High School's resident Deadhead, during the long summer following eighth grade.

I was in my room. In an age before WiFi, I was struggling to set up an old stereo receiver, the kind with speaker wires. I stuck two of the wire ends in holes behind the speakers, wrapping the others around the receiver's metal posts. Maddeningly, the wires lacked color-coded plugs. I lamely tried to thread the connections, but when I placed the album *In the Dark* into the tray of my first-ever CD player (a recent gift), I got zilch.

In stepped Dad. He snipped the wires' butchered ends, stripped an inch or two of fresh sheathing, twisted the exposed copper in a tight spiral, inserted the newly pointy ends into the speakers, and – eureka! – to my delight, the stanza above boomed aloud. But Dad's face now wore a scowl. He looked at the stereo, then at me, and in a voice dripping with snark, asked *"What is this?"* I told him with some embarrassment. He didn't speak; he didn't need to. The look of disgust on his face said it all.

John says that Dad couldn't have known the first thing about the Dead. But, looking back, I'd say his expression said he did. Enough to frown on the idea of his son being a fan of drug-fueled, hippie crap.

By way of contrast, a completely different look lit up Dad's face whenever he heard another hit of that era, "What's Up?" by 4 Non Blondes. Each time he heard it on the radio or on my stereo, he'd proudly announce the band's name. I thought his was an odd and arbitrary liking, but I was glad we both liked a contemporary tune. Recently, I added it to my repertoire at gigs and open mics, and far above the cloud of cotton wadding over my head, I can sense Dad getting a kick out of it. When I strum the initial chords and sing, "Hey-ey-ey-eyyy!", I still hear him calling out "4 Non Blondes!" I seriously doubt my Grateful Dead covers are getting a similar reaction.

Rest easy, Dad. More than drugs, music moves me. Literally. For example, "Drive" by the Cars – you know, the song with the video where Ric Ocasek walks on water. In a stronger, more vivid way than the mere recollection of facts, certain songs make me remember *feelings*, if that's possible. And not just what my feelings were, but how I physically *felt*. When I hear "Drive," I not only remember my Aunt Ro's kitchen as it was when I was a child, but how I felt when I was in it, among family. The feeling is so genuine that I refuse to listen to that song, save for once in a great while. I bottle it up like a potion, afraid that each sip, no matter how carefully rationed, will be my last, and that when the bottle runs dry the feeling will evaporate, like it did for young Moonlight Graham when he stepped across the threshold of infield dirt and emerged on the gravel path as Dr. Graham in *Field of Dreams*.

The strange thing is this: I don't remember hearing "Drive" in my aunt's kitchen. But for some reason that song, that room, and that time of life live in the same room in my mind, permanent neighbors.

The Beach Boys, "Good Vibrations" (1966)

Author's note: "Bonus tracks" appear by release date (year in parentheses). I formed memories of them in a different order.

My high school peers considered the Beach Boys a joke. They weren't played anymore on rock and roll radio; they were strictly on the "oldies" station, unlike their contemporaries The Beatles, The Kinks, The Rolling Stones, and so forth. To us they were the crew cut, striped-shirt hucksters of a "California lifestyle" of surfing and hotrodding -- activities they'd given up twenty years earlier, if indeed they'd ever done them at all. They occasionally played shows at beaches and amusement parks, usually without their founder and principal songwriter, Brian Wilson. And they trotted out their oldies once a year for the Capitol Fourth fireworks show on the National Mall. (Except for 1983, when Secretary of the Interior James Watt vetoed them because, for him, they still represented the counterculture. Nancy Reagan later apologized on behalf of the White House.)

Time has been kind to Brian Wilson. After years of a debilitating mental illness, he reentered the world in the '90s, completed his legendary *Smile* album in 2004 (if I were to choose the single most unlikely event in rock history, that would be it), and still tours today. His reputation has not only been rehabilitated; his songs are now part of the songwriting "canon." Just yesterday, in fact, I got an e-mail announcing an upcoming appearance, with ticket prices from $79-$149. The promotional copy begins: "He's been called the Gershwin of his generation...."

Of course, as a high schooler, I took issue with my peers about almost everything. So I disagreed with them about the Beach Boys, too. A classmate of mine, a gal, said she'd heard that serious American musicians viewed the Beach Boys much as British musicians viewed the Kinks, a completely overrated band. But I thought they were amazing. The precise dawning of this realization is clear in my memory.

It was ninth grade. I walked into the room that would later be my mother's home office but was then the TV room, and over to the family hi-fi, a receiver/phonograph combo used only by me to play records and listen to the radio. Accordingly, I kept it tuned to WNBC-AM, my favorite pop station.

I turned it on. Instantly, I was pummeled by a wave that induced stomachache and vertigo – the good kinds, I mean, which you get on rollercoasters. Utterly unlike any pop music I knew, what I heard had to have been played on ethereal instruments, ones without names. (I still can't name them. I had to look up "Electro-Theremin.")

Though it lasted twenty seconds, it seemed like forever. Or, as the name of the Beach Boys' greatest hits album would have it, one "endless summer." Then it segued into a song I knew well, "Good Vibrations."

What had befuddled me was the song's middle section. What a subversive trick Brian Wilson had pulled on the American public! James Watt was right: it was as if the Soviets had snuck a coded message into one of the 1960s biggest hits. But the song which Brian Wilson said was about "cosmic vibrations" was pure Brian: he'd composed an avant-garde piece with tack piano, jaw harp, sleigh bells, and yes, an Electro-Theremin. The weirdness begins as the song's feel-good "vibes" reach their peak. Then, as they threaten to dissolve forever, we return to the chorus big time. Brilliant.

I practically ran to the phone to call my music buddy, Dave.

"Okay, this is what you should do," I said. "Put 'Good Vibrations' on right in the middle, and listen. You won't believe how weird it is!"

The Monkees – *"Listen to the Band"* (1969)

In the beginning there were my parents' singles and albums. Then, one hot summer day of 1976, thanks to a TV commercial, we knew we needed our own.

As always, Frank, my younger brother, figured it out first. After repeated viewings of a direct response ad during daytime reruns of *The Monkees*, he sent one of Mom's checks to an outfit called Laurie House, a low-budget mail order company. And sure enough, one eternity (six-to-eight weeks) later, he received a package in the mail.

It was a double "gatefold" album. With hindsight, today I see the telltale signs of corner-cutting. The packaging was so cheap it had no liner notes – there wasn't even a track listing! But we didn't care; we played it nonstop. We listened in the TV room, the former garage that Dad had made into our playroom. We arranged kitchen chairs in a circle, as if to play musical chairs, and Frank or I would drape Side A over the spindle of Mom's old record player, the one with the built-in speakers. Soon the first song would blare forth, and we'd tear round the chairs like a train run amok, miming the pull of steam whistles as Micky Dolenz sang:

> *Take the last train to Clarksville*
> *I will meet you at the station*

And for two full sides, the hits kept coming – "Daydream Believer," "I'm a Believer," and others – until we were too bushed to move.

But there were four sides. I didn't know it then, but many of the songs on sides three and four had not appeared on any earlier Monkees' greatest hits collection. When I was alone and in a more contemplative mood, I listened to them too. What I heard delighted me: the music turned dreamlike and confusing, the lyrics harder to parse. The vocals on "Tapioca Tundra" and "D.W. Washburn" were loaded with studio effects and sounded otherworldly; "Porpoise Song" was strangely sad. Then there was "Listen to the Band."

That was a Mike Nesmith tune. Mike was the tall Monkee. From the sitcom, I knew he was the deadpan guy who wore a stocking cap. As a composer, his songs sounded more "country" than his bandmates' pop. He was actually the Monkee who wrote the most songs, the group's most accomplished musician.

In the 1960s, that was considered a low bar. The Monkees were a breech birth, delivered by talent agents on a deadline. TV execs wanted a telegenic American band to rival the Beatles, so they conducted a nationwide search, piecing together a band that the nascent rock press called "The Pre-Fab Four." My uncle Mike, then a precocious eleven-year-old, latched onto this criticism, and held the Monkees' parentage against them. But by the time I heard them, the rock press had forgotten them, and I could listen without prejudice to all their songs – fast and slow, written by others and by themselves. After hitting the charts several times with professionally-written songs, the Monkees fought their label to get their own compositions on subsequent albums. Listen to the band, indeed.

The song begins with twangy guitar:

Hey, hey, mercy woman
Plays a song and no one listens

Then as it nears the chorus, it veers into hopped-up soul thanks to a squadron of close-miked horns that fairly leapt from Mom's old stereo speakers, seven years later. After that brief release, the song digresses into a semi-classical interlude (making this the first-ever country/rock/soul/classical composition?), taking its sweet time to circle back to the melody. After a while, distant muffled drums sound far down in the mix, triggering the horns again, and finally the cathartic return to the chorus.

"Listen to the Band" taught me that pop songs needn't be direct or succinct. To be hits, maybe. But not every song aspires to the top of the pops; there were many modes of being, some more esoteric than others. To use a metaphor that would not have occurred to me then, Mike Nesmith's tune was the sonic equivalent of a great wine: unfolding slowly, getting to where it's going only after a good many digressions.

Jim Croce – "Cat's in the Cradle" (1974)

I surely knew it when I was young, this song with the curious title and nursery-rhyme chorus. It was all over the radio, after all. But it was only during that transition to adulthood that we called "junior high" (our teachers called it "hell") that I really heard it for the first time.

At the west end of a rectilinear, stone block building, one old enough to have once been the town high school, a large room let in the sun. Most of its windows faced south or west, which, as pioneers and desperadoes knew, was a good way to escape. In that room, every day for one quarter of the year, we had music class under the direction of Mr. Latto.

Mr. Latto was heavily built, stout but not obese, with a white beard. He looked like he sang opera. He certainly played it: per state regulations, he played all kinds of music, even ones he didn't like. There was even a segment on modern pop, which was when my classmates' ears would prick up and shake off the torpor of warm afternoons.

One day our class was postponed for several minutes so that our Vice Principal, Ms. Vanella, could talk morality. In particular, she noted a trend that had come to her attention (as though to protect the guilty, she said she'd "read about it"): see-through jeans. I listened, wondering how one might see through denim. Ms. Vanella tried reason on us, never raising her voice or becoming animated. But she made it abundantly clear that no girl who wore such things was doing herself any favors.

I was glad when she left, so Mr. Latto could play more music. He walked slowly to the front of the classroom and introduced the next piece; then he pressed a button on the professional-grade cassette deck residing on a shelf up front, and we heard "Cat's in the Cradle."

I'm pretty sure most of my classmates knew it. Gone were the previous units' difficult tribal rhythms and classical polyphony – just a simple acoustic guitar. I let down my guard and let my mind wander, but eventually fell into the trap that the song had set, and began listening closely. That's when I heard everything I'd never heard before.

Ten seconds in, before the lyric, alongside the acoustic, I heard a sitar, an oboe, chimes, and a bowed instrument. But if one listens closely, words are everywhere, even in instrumental passages: the sitar represented time immemorial, unchanging human nature through the generations; the chimes announced that the song we were about to hear was a fable; the oboe and strings, tugging another way, said it was not.

Then the heartbreak began.

Art affects us by foreshortening time. It can represent a lifetime in minutes; only then do we hear time's awful heartbeat. Harry Chapin's lyric said that life is not endless, regardless of the rubella and diphtheria shots we received in the gym each spring. The opening verse relates a boy's birth and first steps; the second, his learning baseball; the third, his college graduation. His father observes all this, but isn't really present. Then, after retirement, when he wants to get to know his son, he learns that his son has grown up like him: too busy to make time for family.

My Dad wasn't like that. He took us places, no matter how busy the restaurant business. So, against all odds, this song found a hole in my heart that I never knew was there.

I was swept up by an unaccustomed feeling. Before I knew it, I realized I was about to cry, right in the middle of a roomful of classmates listening idly to a familiar song that seemingly caused them no distress. Panicked, I knew I had to stop the tears, but how? Was it like a nosebleed – should I raise my head? Should I lower it to the desk? Whatever I did, it worked. Those tears, emissaries of my soul, were detained at the border.

Perhaps I should have let them go. Not since then has a song almost made me cry; it would be nice to know how that feels. Crying might have opened up avenues. I've always had trouble with emotion, even when portrayed in art, so I might have learned something.

On the other hand, I would have been a fool.

I remember a college lecture about Diderot's *Rameau's Nephew*; the speaker quoted a critic who said, "If this book doesn't make you cry, you aren't alive."

Maybe the tears don't have to fall.

The Boomtown Rats - "I Don't Like Mondays" (1980)

One hot, sticky day of late spring, I sat behind the wheel of my father's faded blue Dodge pickup with its rusted flatbed, dodgy breaks, and tailgate that didn't close, jumped two speed bumps as I neared the front doors of Madison High School, where I'd gone to pick up my sister from an after-school club. It must have been spring of senior year.

By then, "I Don't Like Mondays" was five years old. It was born on January 29, 1979, when Bob Geldof, lead singer of the Irish rock band The Boomtown Rats, was giving an interview at Georgia State University's campus radio station. During a break, the studio's teletype machine began to rattle, then spit out a developing story about a sixteen-year-old girl who had decided to shoot up an elementary school playground. When apprehended, she merely said, "I don't like Mondays. This livens up the day."

I wore a checked linen shirt too warm for the sun; sweat beaded under my armpits and pooled on my chest. The truck's air conditioner didn't work, so I had rolled the windows down and tuned the radio to WNEW. The song had just started to play as I pulled up in front of the school entrance; with the piano's dramatic initial cascade of notes and chords, I felt an instant flush of recognition.

This recognition was not just the return of an old friend, a song I'd often played on my copy of the Boomtown Rats' album *The Fine Art of Surfacing*. It was also sympathy with the girl in the song:

> *The silicon chip inside her head*
> *Gets switched to overload*
> *And nobody's gonna go to school today*
> *She's gonna make them stay at home*

Like her, I was an outsider; unlike my siblings, who participated in after-school activities and socialized easily with classmates outside the confines of school, my social circle was small. Like the girl, I wanted the world to know that this was the way I liked it (and that I had good taste in music, to boot), so I raised the volume in the hope that someone I knew, perhaps a music buff (like Kevin, who'd be wrapping up baseball practice), or a pretty girl (leaving a meeting of the school newspaper or yearbook club) might notice me in my unusual choice of wheels, a vehicle that my English teacher had dubbed the "John Steinbeck pickup," listening to a gorgeous song with odd, antisocial lyrics. Through it, I proclaimed my otherness, my tendency to buck trends, to ride against herd, like the outcast in Don McLean's "American Pie":

> *I was a lonely teenage broncin' buck*
> *With a pink carnation and a pickup truck*

I wanted in, but on my terms. Meanwhile, the sun vaporized the windshield, scorching my fingers on the fraying vinyl of the steering wheel, which slowly unraveled. I sidled to the curb to wait for Robbie, and listened to the lyric:

> *Sweet sixteen ain't that peachy keen*
> *Now it ain't so neat to admit defeat*

Sometimes things look good until they suddenly, inexplicably, go wrong. High school was nearing an end, four years of work concluding successfully. I'd soon be heading to college; my family assumed I'd have fun there. Dad even made an uncharacteristic joke: that if I should get in bed with someone, I should be sure it had a partition.

I ought to have been happy, but was not. Maybe it was just body chemistry. Perhaps, like the girl in the song, I had a silicon brain.

Cliff Richard – "Dreaming" (1980)

Such a breezy song. So breezy, in fact, that after it peaked in the top twenty, I was the only person who remembered it. Breezy enough for a summer's evening on a yacht, or a windswept autumn day in a parked car with the radio on. But by an accident of programming, for me it always forecasts snow.

On junior high snowy winter mornings, our kitchen radio was tuned to 1250 WMTR, one of the last community AM radio stations that believed it could be all things to everyone. It gave folks the information they needed before work, interspersing golden oldies and a few current hits that weren't too wild. I'd guess, based on their frequent repetition, that the station's music library contained about ten of the latter – no doubt all the budget allowed for. These included the two recent smashes by sixties pop veteran Cliff Richard: "We Don't Talk Anymore" and this one. Anyway, on a snowy day, we kids would hover near one or the other of the two kitchen radios -- the squat radio/cassette player on the countertop under the microwave, or the tall one on the counter by the two wall telephones – and listen to school closings.

Life was real then, as in "real time." Time-shifting had yet to be invented: if you weren't there to receive the phone call from school secretaries working their way through telephone trees, then the only way to know if school was canceled was to listen to interminable listings on the radio. It might take half an hour, or longer. The morning DJ, instead of doing his usual spiel pitching auto dealerships, would announce the names of schools and towns in the order that they had been phoned in. There was no time to run to the bathroom, because there was no order to the closings. You had to stay tuned, in the moment, glued to the radio. Madison Junior High might follow the Happy Camper Day School of Far Hills, or St. Basil's Regional Prep in Glen Gardner (delayed opening, 10 a.m.), or not. There was no online search, no fast forward, no shortcut. You listened as the snowflakes slowly accumulated on the kitchen windowsill, slowly forming patterns on the glass.

And when the announcer needed a drink of water or a nip of something warmer, he cued up a prerecorded spot for Kenvil Power Motors, the school closings sponsor. This was a small outfit on Route 46, way out by Hackettstown, that I discovered quite by chance years later, one day when driving around. When I saw its sign, it might as well have said "Source of the Nile," so mythical a place it had in my imagination. I offered a silent prayer for all the snow it had made possible.

Occasionally, to break the monopoly and monotony of words, the announcer played a song. He would never introduce it; nor, when it was over, would he back-announce it, so it wandered lonely as a cloud - or a snowflake. And on snowy mornings this song was, often as not, "Dreaming":

> *Never letting chances pass me by*
> *I'm gonna dream you right into my life*

And now I see that's precisely what I was doing while I listened to the radio – dreaming – elbow on countertop, waiting for a complete stranger to say the name of my school, bundled in a vest coat and winter hat, hoping that the day would be mine to spend as I saw fit, an entire sunlit day stretching far into the future (once I'd cleared a path to the driveway). These are life's best moments, when time offers a plenitude of options, filling your day with possibilities that dwindle as you pursue them.

Steve Winwood, "While You See a Chance" (1981)

My brother's room after dark, maybe eight p.m. No one is in; I can see through the doorway from the hall. It feels like winter, so it must have been... let's see... this song debuted on the pop charts in February, so winter is right. It may have been cold and dark outside, but within a warm pocket of sound my mood is far from despondent. It's strangely charged, as if I were a glass rod and this song a silk cloth, like in that physics experiment; or as if the hall carpet were supersaturated with static. No static on FM, though: the station comes in loud and clear on Frank's cool, gray, stainless steel receiver, unlike my matte black one in every way. Against the glow of its lime green backlight, I see a hairline indicator like that of a slide rule indicating the station Frank was listening to when he left the room.

It's the new song by Stevie Winwood, if I may invoke the name by which he was known when he wasn't much older than I am now, before he turned into a star. He was once in a band called Traffic; I know because Nana bought me one of their albums, *John Barleycorn Must Die*, at a garage sale. I listened to it once or twice, but for me its most memorable aspect was its big gatefold cover designed like a needlepoint sampler on coarse cloth. Traffic was an important '70s band, in an era when rock aspired to art, before punk, power pop and new wave cured it of a terminal case of seriousness. I had no use for Traffic.

But this song was different. It begins with an organ solo, longer than the one that fit on the single. Rock radio luxuriated then in grand gestures, before marketers made it toe the line for the audience's benefit. This was Winwood's first foray into pop, long before he settled into a personal runout groove of assembly-line overproductions like "Higher Love" and "Back in the High Life."

The first verse did not exactly sound like a statement of purpose from someone reaching for the brass ring:

> *Stand up on a clear blue morning,*
> *Until you see*
> *What can be alone on a cold day dawning*
> *Are you still free? Can you be?*

Funny thing is, I always heard those first two words as "strung out." For the era, that would have been a blatant drug reference, though not one I would have recognized. I wish those *had* been the words; they would have better fit the mood of the song. Having heard advertisements for this album on my favorite AM pop radio station (Mr. Winwood's promotion machine kicking into gear), I knew the album was *Arc of a Diver*. Every arc, even those ending in water, has a nadir, and this sounded like music for life's lowest low, a soundtrack to a hungover Sunday morning:

When there's no one left to leave you
Even you don't quite believe you
That's when nothing can deceive you

And yet, despite all lyrical indications to the contrary, the fifteen-year-old that I was then would tense upon hearing this song, as if ready to spring from the diving board of life. I would hear in its Hammond organ a hope: that life's knife-edge would cut the right way, severing any remaining complications between me and romance (the lyric ends with "find romance") without one drop of blood being drawn.

The Police, "Every Little Thing She Does Is Magic" (1981)

I heard this song in my washed-out gray T-shirt and elasticized maroon shorts behind the thick blue line that marked the perimeter of the junior high school gym's basketball court. Class had yet to begin. My classmate Phil was reading morning announcements over the public address system; it projected his words, spoken in the school office, to a nearby loudspeaker. After announcements, Phil played this song, which sounded pretty good despite the low fidelity. Somehow he must have gotten permission to play it; was it a dedication from one classmate to another? It *was* a quintessential teenage love song:

> *I resolve to call her up a thousand times a day*
> *But my silent fears have gripped me*
> *Long before I reach the phone*

Absorbed by the music, I was not focused on the girl to my right, who also sat behind the blue line in baggy tee and shorts. She was a year older, an eighth grader whom I did not know. (Throughout my school years, I rarely noticed kids in grades other than my own.) Suddenly, to my surprise, I realized she was speaking to me as if she knew me:

"Hey, I saw you on the news last night!"

Suddenly she was more interesting than the song.

I had indeed been on the evening news. I'd been looking forward to it, but it had taken a long time because I kept getting bumped by breaking news. By the time I made it, my two minutes of fame hardly seemed worth it. Truthfully, they embarrassed me.

My cousin Donna worked for John Stossel, consumer advocate on the *CBS Evening News*. She'd heard that two clean-cut kids were needed for an interview with Barry Halper, New Jersey's foremost baseball card collector. It was hoped (I didn't know this) that the kids would gawk and coo as Halper opened up vaults of expensive, vintage trading cards, perpetually shielded from sunlight in the recesses of huge cabinets that slid frictionlessly from the walls of wood-paneled rooms.

Frank and I may have been the first siblings in the world to see them up close. Frank was duly gobsmacked as Halper displayed his collection to the rolling camera; his eyes were big as saucers. I was also impressed, but felt I should pull my weight and ask respectful questions about how he had procured his collection, and so forth. As it turned out, when the piece finally aired, my incisive questions were left on the cutting-room floor. Frank's interjections made the cut, and I looked like a victim of stage fright. It was all very disappointing.

Still, this girl was enthusiastic:

"Yeah, I saw you with the cards. Very cool! Congrats!"

I smiled sheepishly, blushing a little. I wanted to say, "Well, yeah, but I actually said more than they showed on TV." But I mainly wanted to thank her. Before I could, though, I had to ask... "what was that last word, again?

"Congrats!"

And that was the first time I ever heard the abbreviation for "congratulations." It really caught me off-guard. Not only did it take me an instant to register its meaning (so I must have seemed a bit vacant, as I was on television), but I was befuddled by the realization that this girl, whoever she was, was way cooler than I would ever be, because she so naturally used words like "congrats." She was the kind of girl Sting might have been singing about, since she had contrived to transform an unwieldy five-syllable word into something quick, pithy and cool. I was forever doomed to be the kid tripping on the telephone, or the television. To this day, whenever I hear this song, or the word "congrats," I think of that girl whose name I will never know.

N.B. Of all the place-songs in this chapter, this is the only one I know to be flawed. I graduated eighth grade in 1980, and this song came out in 1981, so I couldn't have heard it in junior high school. Mea culpa – or, as I was later cool enough to say, "My bad!"

Rick Springfield, "Jessie's Girl" (1981)

The first time I heard what I now consider to be the definitive song of 1981, I was riding shotgun alongside my cousin Lynn. As driver, she controlled the car radio, which she had tuned to an FM station that was new to me. I listened passively, because I was still a boy, a neophyte to the pleasures of FM radio, a kid who didn't know his ear from his tympanic membrane. But something twitched when I first heard this song's insistent opening riff, one announcing to the world that something was about to happen.

Not only was I ignorant of song and station, but I didn't know the singer. I couldn't have picked out Dr. Noah Drake (a regular on *General Hospital*, one of my grandmother's favorite soaps) from a police lineup. Nor did I know that the man playing him had been trying to make a go of the music biz for a decade. (He had managed one fluke hit many years earlier, in a completely different style.) Nor did I know that "Jessie's Girl" would one day be considered a quintessential "new wave" song. Beyond its obvious theme of jealousy, I didn't even understand its lyrics. For one thing, Jessie sounded like a girl's name; for another, I didn't understand the line, *"I wanna tell her that I love her, but the point is probably moot."* What is "moot," I wondered? (I still don't know: does it mean "debatable" or "irrelevant"?)

What I knew was that the song sounded great. But what did Lynnie (as I called her) think? She was in her twenties, so she might have a completely different take on it, more worldly-wise. Did she see through Springfield's swagger and bravado, instantly recognizing it as a pose, or did she like it as much I?

Later I'd wonder whether "Rick Springfield" was a role, like "Noah Drake." Were the song's jealousy and lust sourced from real life? New wave was always stigmatized as not being heartfelt. People said it was rife with style, and had zero authenticity. Rick Springfield would later have many hits, but to my mind none of them rang true like this one – it was supposedly based on an actual friend, is that why? One of Springfield's minor (justifiably forgotten) later hits was "Bruce," in which he complained that he was always being confused with Bruce Springsteen. Fat chance. The confusion must have begun and ended with their names because, musically, they didn't sound at all alike. And while Springsteen's authenticity has been charted on the level of Woody Guthrie's and Pete Seeger's, Springfield's has long been consigned to the discount bin of a fast fashion store.

I don't buy it. A great song is a great song. It doesn't matter if it's "heartfelt." As if one could ever know what is in a man's heart.

I was quiet as we pulled out from a gas station and continued to Spring Lake, the posh Jersey Shore town where Lynnie's parents, my Aunt Ro and Uncle George, rented a summer house. It was a large square monolith furnished in white, with an elevator at its core. An elevator! It was like living in an office building. Very cool.

That summer, I paid a couple of visits to Spring Lake, but what I mainly remember is "Jessie's Girl." At the beach house, I mostly stayed indoors, spending time on its vacant top floor, a kind of attic whose small windows overlooked a street leading to the beach, through which I daydreamed about the young women walking by in swimming suits. They thought the world of Rick Springfield, and not at all about me. Now that's jealousy.

Joan Jett, "I Love Rock n' Roll" (1981)

In the 1970s, few women rocked.

Top of mind, I only come up with Linda Ronstadt and Suzi Quatro. Ronstadt got regular airplay in the US, but Quatro was better known as "Leather Tuscadero," Fonzie's badass girlfriend/biker chick on *Happy Days*.

That's what made this song by Joan Jett so novel when it raced to the top of the pops in the summer of 1981, hanging around for seven uncomfortably hot weeks. It was loud, obnoxious, provocative, and sung by a woman.

I wasn't a particular fan; I liked my pop a little more subtle. But I could not deny that the song was catchy, or that the singer had charisma. And she could wail. For once in a hard rock song, the guitar wasn't some sort of phallic stand-in.

I was fifteen, and my family was making its annual trek across America to see my mother's West coast relatives. One night in the heartland, we stopped the motorhome at a campground for its nightly fix of water, sewer, and electric, and I decided to accompany my younger brother and sister to a camp "social," some sort of youth jamboree at the clubhouse. There was a jukebox, and it played loudly. At some point, someone punched the buttons that triggered a song I already knew so well from its first notes:

> *I saw him dancin' there by the record machine*
> *I knew he musta been about seventeen*

I secretly wanted a girlfriend like that, one who'd just take me by the hand and help me overcome my inhibitions. But I sat, a wallflower on a bench, jukebox to my right, letting the bass roll me.

But to my surprise, a girl did indeed sit down beside me, even though I was neither acting cool nor (God forbid) dancing, as the lyrics suggested. She said "hey." Then she offered me a cigarette.

It was the second time that I'd ever been offered a drag, and the first since I was a boy. My parents would not have been pleased! I politely declined her offer, which frankly scared me to death. It was a bit fast, wasn't it? So I returned to the relative safety of Joan Jett's music, and soon the girl was gone.

Foreigner, "Waiting For a Girl Like You" (1981)

You must understand that this is *not* the sort of song I ordinarily like. It's slow, ploddingly so. It's unapologetically romantic. It's a *power ballad*, for chrissake.

It begins with an eternal piano note that seems to be desperate to resolve to a chord, to find a mate:

So long, I've been looking too hard
I've been waiting too long

That chord, I know now, was played by the one and only Thomas Dolby, on hire to Foreigner that day. I had yet to learn his name, but I sure did when he hit the charts in 1982 with the synth funk "She Blinded Me With Science." *That* was my kind of song: a bit daft, mostly unserious, and quite unromantic. (Too many pop songs in 1981 were heartfelt; had it been the other way, with satire setting the charts afire, I might have been a romantic instead.)

But for one night – Thanksgiving Day, 1981 – this ballad, just a month old, quite improbably became *my* song.

My parents, feeling that our holiday celebration had hit a rut, or perhaps just wanting to test drive our new motorhome, decided that we would spend Thanksgiving at a South Jersey campground, perhaps the only one not yet closed for the season. Their best friends, the Alofs, would also bring their young kids, in their own motorhome.

The weather was seasonable for late fall, sunny and cool. We parked our outsized vehicles side-by-side, far from anyone else. That afternoon, we played a makeshift game of wiffleball near our campsite as the mothers prepared dinner; I also watched some pro football on the little black-and-white TV perched by our motorhome door. My Lions convincingly won the first game of the doubleheader, but in the nightcap the Cowboys edged the Bears, 10-9, despite a record-breaking performance by Walter Payton.

At some point, Mom and Dad had a fight. It led to Dad's eating dinner by himself in the motorhome, a sandwich constructed from the only food that hadn't made it outside with the rest of us to the campfire where we took our feast.

My parents made up later that night. But I escaped from the forced togetherness and went for a walk in the dark. From our encampment, I espied a structure not quite a football field away, shadowed against the dusk. As I left the proximity of our fire, I was glad to have donned my zip-up jacket, as the air had turned cool.

I neared the structure. It was large and round, all stone, with a long bench around its perimeter. Two steps led up and in; at its center was a raised platform, some sort of stage. But before I had even gotten that far, I was aware of *that song*. It floated in the air; its source must be nearby. And then I saw it – a boombox leaning against the stage. I saw no soul nearby. This song, which I should have viscerally hated, suddenly seemed perfect for this still night. It was a miracle – who'd left this radio here for my benefit?

I looked again, and saw no one: that is, not until I noticed two human forms in the gloaming, at the far end of the gazebo. They were slumped against the ledge, quite still, sitting in repose, near one another. And then I made out the tips of two lit cigarettes faintly glowing the same tint of orange that always embellished the coils of the motorhome's cigarette lighter just before Dad touched it to his cigarette. A couple of teens smoking, probably. Probably also getting away from families. It must be their radio.

Mid-step, I pivoted on my toes and turned back, returning the teens to dreams then in progress.

> *It's more than touch or a word can say*
> *Only in dreams could it be this way*

Delirious/In a Big Country (1983)

I wish I could describe autumn. I could say, "my favorite time of year," but that would mean nothing to you. Or I could have you listen to these songs, but that, too, would work just for me. You had to be there.

In 1983, for a moment, we had a shore house. I don't know the whole story, but Dad made an arrangement with our next-door neighbor, Mr. Artiglere, an old-school Italian with whom I was not on speaking terms, and not just because we used the fence at his property line as our wiffleball bench. Soon, in Manahawkin, near the overpass to Long Beach Island, we had an old house, nothing fancy. It abutted a canal that wound through a waterfront development, and it came with a small powerboat.

It was autumn. Autumn, not fall. Fall is generic, a disease we're susceptible to, but "autumn," my favorite word, is a parade of soft vowels alighting on a leaf pile. I have a vague memory, more powerful for its vagueness, of a childhood afternoon spent with Mom and Dad while they looked at houses. We saw one on a large lot, far back from the road, surrounded by hardwood trees that had shed nearly all their leaves, which a chilly wind had swept into piles against a stone wall. I don't think I've ever felt more content than at that moment. The feeling returns each time that memory does.

Years later, our shore house felt like that. Imagine the same sort of late-season weather, overcast, borderline cold. We arrive at the front door late on Friday, the light already failing. Dad struggles with the front door – none of the keys seem to fit – but it finally opens. We enter a dirty, unheated, screened-in porch: an inauspicious start. But I immediately see the hi-fi on a wall shelf. Later that night, as the family gathers around a television inside the house proper, I fiddle with the radio tuner until it picks up a nearby pop station playing Prince's "Delirious."

Singing falsetto, Prince plays a cheesy, squeaky synthesizer line that hopefully will not be the last thing I remember on my deathbed. I knew the song – it was in the top forty – but it sounded utterly out of place on a quiet Friday night at the end of the world, like a transmission from a long-extinct alien civilization.

For a rocker like Prince, "Delirious" was kind of "bubblegum." Then again, his taste was eclectic, open to everything. (In fact, he was currently at work on a foray into pop psychedelia, *Around the World in a Day*.) I've always liked bubblegum – the catchy pop of the '60s and '70s, like the Archies' "Sugar, Sugar" and the Bay City Rollers' "Saturday Night," which made love sound sweet. But it was just too strange hearing "Delirious" on a Friday night in a place everyone knew was nowhere. I turned it off.

The following day, a sunny Saturday, we went for a ride. First we drove to the island, which was nearly deserted. We stopped at a small grocery store; I stayed in the car and listened to the radio. Then we returned to the mainland and stopped at a big indoor flea market full of booths. At one, I was beguiled by rack after rack of 45-rpm records; and because prices were minimal, I bought old singles by unknown bands, like the Pastel Six's "Cinnamon Cinder" and a tune called "The Grooviest Girl in the World." I didn't hear them until I got home to my record player, but they would not disappoint.

Back at our new house, we began sprucing up. I raked leaves out front while listening to Kasey Kasem count down the top forty, as I would have done at home. Peaking at #17 was "In a Big Country," by the Scottish band Big Country. It was their American debut, and I was hooked by the fanfare of guitars introducing the song – they sounded like bagpipes! (At the time, I thought they *were* bagpipes.)

> *I've never seen you look like this without a reason*
> *Another promise fallen through*
> *Another season passes by you*

I listened and thought of a girl who might as well have been at the other end of the earth. The song lyrics, the leaves I raked, said that another season had passed without my having made an imprint in her mind. I lay in a nearby hammock and listened on.

The Voice/All Out of Love/Our House/Come Dancing (1981-83)

I heard many of the hits of my high school years from three seats behind Joan, the driver of Madison school bus #4.

Mornings, Mike claimed the window seat beside me. Afternoons, I got the window because Mike presumably had better places to be than a bus. Long before I had to, I was the commuter with the seat up front, removed from the rowdy element in back and the gauntlet of the narrow aisle. I should have been elsewhere, participating in extracurriculars or at least walking with friends, but I was on the bus *again*.

The radio was my companion. It often played the songs listed above. Others, too. "The Voice" was the comeback hit by the Moody Blues; it proved they'd mastered the latest crop of synthesizers. I heard Pat St. John played it one morning on WPLJ as our bus rocketed down Garfield Avenue, the apogee of its long orbit to school. I listened blissfully to its long middle section (which, I later learned to my disappointment, was greatly edited on the 45). The synths swooped like my heart as I thought of certain girls; I wouldn't be surprised to learn there was a key change there somewhere.

A word about music choice. Joan and Margaret (Fridays, bus #1) preferred pop to rock (which was not yet today's "classic rock"). But, if petitioned, or if they were simply feeling charitable, they'd flip the dial from AM to FM and tune in WPLJ or WNEW. Sometimes this required the persuasion of an upperclass alpha male; one would slide across the seat behind the driver (the one reserved for alphas) as gracefully as Gene Kelly; then he'd reach for the tuner knob, flicking it with a quick motion of the wrist. Our drivers didn't always fall for their charm, however, and turned it right back to light pop.

Pop and rock – I liked 'em both. The first hit by Australian balladeers Air Supply, "All Out of Love," drew me in with a melody that wandered, step by step, to and from the tonic. I didn't mind its sappy lyrics; just as some girls' faces are worth looking at, even when one doesn't know what lies behind them, some songs are worth hearing solely for their melodies.

As for the final two songs above, they will forever be linked together in my mind. "Our House" and "Come Dancing" were in the top ten simultaneously during the spring and summer of 1983, and they offered similarly sentimental looks at youth.

The Kinks' song, which hearkens back to the austerity of 1950s London, begins:

> *They put a parking lot up on a piece of land*
> *Where the supermarket used to stand*
> *Before that they put up a bowling alley*
> *On the site that used to be the local palais* (i.e., dance hall)

Let's see... this means that the singer is *already* at three removes from the past he is eulogizing. The British angle makes it harder to relate to the song's details, but I could still catch the humor in a sister's dalliance with a local bloke who never quite gets what he hopes for when he takes her out on dates.

Madness were younger than the Kinks, but (of course) still older than me. So they also spent their childhoods in an age of stay-at-home mothers:

> *Father gets up late for work*
> *Mother has to iron his shirt*
> *Then she sends the kids to school*

What I particularly liked about this song (so much so that I mined it for my yearbook quote; a girl classmate – which one? – complimented me on my choice) was the wistfulness behind its hijinks. Already, as a high school junior, I fretted over my imminent departure for college. So I related to the pathos of a song about leaving home, leavened though it was by an arrangement punctuated by trumpet blasts, hinting at the chaos of a large household. (And Madness *was* a septet.) Running underneath it all was a line of lyric so insidiously woven into the chorus that I could never quite make it out. That is, not until the day when I purchased the twelve-inch "extended" version of the song at the Short Hills Mall and placed it on my home turntable: in that remix, the line is finally isolated: *something tells you that you have to move away from it.* But I didn't yet know that, riding on the bus.

Always Something There to Remind Me (1983)/ That Old Black Magic (1959)

Saturday afternoon, driving past the high school in my orange Beetle. I'm with my pals John and David and, as always, we have the radio on. We're listening to a new song climbing the charts, the debut by the British duo Naked Eyes. I like its synthesizer arrangement (strange keyboards had invaded America) and off-key melody that sounded like a row of water glasses randomly filled, struck by the bowl of a dessert spoon. Perhaps it was the best man at a wedding vainly trying to hush the crowd.

Dave: I walk along the city streets you used to walk along with me.
John: And every step I take reminds me of just how we used to be.
I guess I was listening to the radio, not to my friends.

The song was older than me. Written by Burt Bacharach for Dionne Warwick, Dusty Springfield had made it her own, and turned it into a hit. I liked Naked Eyes' take because it was so *ironic*. The mechanized drums and electronic keyboards ratcheted down the melodrama, boosted the kitsch, and twisted the emotion. It was like a troubadour in cap and bells; the singer didn't seem to mean what he was saying. I could hear him wink offstage.

I habitually made light of feelings, and liked music that did the same. I had gone on record (so to speak) with my dislike of songs that wore their naked little hearts on their sleeves (e.g. Billy Joel); I liked lyrics to take more adventurous and oblique approaches, undercutting pathos and expressing ambivalence toward love.

It was for this reason that music fans with long memories hated the Naked Eyes cover. My tenth-grade history teacher, Mr. Chemerka, who revered the original, despised it. A writer for regional arts newspaper *EC Rocker* who'd actually met David Lee Roth and gotten him to pose in tube socks in our school colors, Chemerka had cred among my peers. I, on the other hand, was just another know-it-all. So Chemerka could dismiss Naked Eyes, the "New Romantic" duo with teased hair and Korg keyboards who minced in melodies made famous by rock royalty. And I kept my admiration under my hat, not even sharing it with my car mates.

This generational clash brings to mind another classic song, "That Old Black Magic." Written by Harold Arlen in 1942, it was a hit for Louie Prima in 1959 when he enlisted wide-eyed ingénue Keely Smith to join him in a duet. Keely went for it, unleashing five minutes of sheer craziness in the studio while her chaperoning mother was in the ladies' room. I loved the song, but didn't yet know a key fact: it was a send-up of an earlier ballad.

Prima features in the food flick *Big Night*. In one scene, a mousy middle-aged florist describes Prima's sound to someone who has never heard it, calling it "raucous." That's a good word for Prima's take on "That Old Black Magic," which he transforms into a manic parody of the thrills and chills of romantic love. Saxophones trace neon rollercoaster arabesques: *"That same old tingle that I feel inside/When that elevator starts its ride."*

In our kitchen, Dad played a cassette mix of music he'd recorded off WPAT, the easy-listening station. (Recording off the radio was a short-lived hobby of his.) Frank Sinatra's languid take on "That Old Black Magic" started. Unfamiliar with it, I waited for the tempo to accelerate, but it never did. Knowing only Prima's version, I grew impatient; then I complained to Dad (and Mom, who'd joined us in the room):

"This is way too slow! It sounds ridiculous. It should be faster."

To me it was lugubrious, practically a parody. Of course, I now know it was Prima's version that was the parody. Mom and Dad, who usually left my music opinions alone, rushed to Sinatra's defense:

"It's just different, John. Calling it 'ridiculous' is wrong."

I shrugged. I realized that for Mom and Dad, "That Old Black Magic" would always be a slow love song.

Craning my head to the left, to the driver's side window open to a summer day, I realize that I'd missed the entrance to the high school drive.

Lindsey Buckingham – "I Want You" (1983)

Aunt Ro asked me to drive her Cadillac to my house so that Dad's personal mechanic could have a look at it. It seems that almost as soon as I'd gotten my driver's license, I'd been driving for my aunt: this was nothing new. Whenever her regular drivers were busy, I would chauffeur her – as far as Manhattan, if necessary – to doctor's visits and on errands.

So, having spent an evening of conversation with my grandmother and my aunt in my aunt's well-lit faux country Essex Fells kitchen, it was fairly late on a Friday night when I got behind the wheel of an unfamiliar car. I was alone, and gloriously free to listen to music as loudly as I liked. And I had a cassette with me: a dub that I'd made of Lindsey Buckingham's new album, *Go Insane*.

It took me a while to play it. Easing myself into the leather driver's seat of my aunt's pale white Coupe de Ville, I went through its controls. Compared to my Beetle, it was night and day! The power seats purred when I pushed the buttons that actuated their motors; I maneuvered the seat, the seat back, and the headrest until I practically lay in luxury's lap. Next it was time to adjust the air conditioning – something else my car lacked – until it was properly frigid, stopping the summer night's sweltering heat at the border of the power windows. Not until I reached the Livingston Mall was I ready to insert the cassette.

Lindsey Buckingham may have been one-fourth of one of the world's biggest bands, Fleetwood Mac, but he was never shy about flying his freak flag. In 1979, in the wake of the band's hugely successful *Rumours*, he masterminded one of the strangest top ten hits ever in "Tusk," a bit of pop dada backed by the University of Southern California's marching band. So it shouldn't have been a surprise that his new solo album would, on one hand, pay tribute to one of rock's great iconoclasts, Brian Wilson, who had spent years in bed, and on the other dive deep into his songwriting id.

"I Want You" is track one. It begins with the clanging bell of an old-fashioned alarm clock. It blared from the speaker directly in front of me, then panned slowly to the far end of the car's wide-bodied cabin. Thus began an oddly syncopated rhythm, with a male voice singing in two channels, slightly out of phase, inducing nausea (the good kind).

But despite the hermetic feel of the recording – lockstep, inelastic, as sealed off from the living, breathing world outside the recording studio as the frigid air of the conveyance I was piloting through a hot suburban night – the music sounded glorious, practically symphonic. I had never heard such fidelity in a car; I was cocooned at two removes from the world. I told myself that I really needed to upgrade my home stereo, so it would sound as good as the one in this car.

It was July, 1984, the summer I abandoned pop in search of more interesting songcraft. Had my aunt, father, or siblings heard this song, they would have been nonplussed. I listened to the words: were they about emotions, or stereo recording?

> *I'm the spartan splasher*
> *Defensive man of steel*
> *If the right one don't get you*
> *The left one will*

Later that summer, I played "I Want You" for my friends in my parents' rec room. It was the first song of a "Name That Tune" contest: the goal was to identify the artist. No one could. Nor could anyone fathom what drew me to the song. But for me, it was a perfect two-car collision of pop and art, idealism and realism, joy and disappointment, conformity and eclecticism. It mirrored my internal state as I steeled myself to attend college that fall. I was of two minds about leaving home: my left channel urged me on, my right channel shouted it down. Together they made a glorious racket.

At least I appreciated what Lindsey Buckingham was attempting. In this respect, I was superior to Stevie Nicks, Buckingham's former lover and still-current bandmate, about whom he had written the song in an effort to get over their breakup. "I Want You" didn't mean that to me, but a great song serves many interpretations.

China Crisis – "Working With Fire and Steel" (1983)

An unusual "place-song" in that I didn't hear it at the moment it became one. But Dad did, and it was his reaction I remember.

I've already said how Dad had lost track of pop music by the mid-1970s. By the time I was in high school, entire movements had flowered and faded – disco, punk, yacht rock – without Dad's noticing. New wave was long in the tooth, and I was now drawn to something called "indie rock." Thus I came to own an album by a British band (quite incongruously) named China Crisis. Their first album was so interesting that even Walter Becker of Steely Dan took note; he got himself in the producer's chair for the next one. The band straddled the line between pop, art, and the new electric sounds, without abandoning melody.

Unfortunately, I couldn't reproduce their sound in my bedroom. For want of money (it'd take the earnings of my first full-time job to swing it), I'd yet to upgrade my home stereo. As for my car, my cassette deck sounded cheap, but my pal Clay, a technical wizard and true star, had connected it to an after-market amplifier that significantly boosted its volume. Finally, I could hear 10cc over a 350cc engine. The cassette deck's "sweet spot" was rock with a melodic (not overdriven) bass: the Climax Blues Band's "Couldn't Get It Right" was – at least in my car – the greatest song in the world. Electronic keys, in contrast, didn't fare well. And it didn't help that vibrating beneath each of my vinyl-to-cassette "dubs" (recorded on my brother's stereo when he wasn't around), was a very audible hum: feedback from a loose wire.

One day, Dad needed to use my car. (His was at the mechanic's, a not uncommon occurrence.) I happily lent him my keys, but as soon as he pulled out of the drive, I realized that he would hear China Crisis as soon as he turned the ignition. I wondered what he might think.

China Crisis were artsy, stoic, self-conscious, a little avant-garde. And it wasn't easy figuring out what they were on about. Their album *Working With Fire and Steel* had songs about the class struggle, civil rights, and other weighty topics, but the lyrics sometimes seemed like children's rhymes. The title song went:

> *I could never keep a beat*
> *Too busy in my paradise*

Put a crocodile in high office
And something out of place inside

And there's one f-word. It's blurted in an off-hand way, and is rather hard to hear, but I sensed its presence. I wouldn't know for sure until the arrival of the Internet.

I pictured Dad as the '50s gentleman in suit and tie thoughtfully considering a Jackson Pollock in that famous Norman Rockwell painting, driving down our street trying to make sense of this song, . It was unlike any he'd have known from decades of listening to the radio.

Each generation confounds its predecessors. The old folks ask, "This is art?" Or, "This is what the kids do today?

The answer, of course, lies in institutional and scientific change: new social bonds, new technologies, new economic ties. If any or all of these change, so must music. If the old guard wants to keep their stranglehold on the hit parade, they'd better be good stewards of the world, ensuring its continued and unchanging health. Good luck.

Dad returned from his errand and handed me my keys. He looked me in the eyes a moment:

"John, is everything okay?"

Sure, I said. Everything's swell. Why did he ask?

He didn't say. But I'm sure it was China Crisis. Thanks to them, he'd seen a side of me he didn't know was there.

David Bowie – "Let's Dance" (1983)

I didn't know it then, but I grew up during a transitional time in pop music. With MTV's debut in 1981, image challenged sound for pop supremacy. At first I was hooked by the pairing of sight and sound; in Nana's living room I'd record hours of "videos" (promotional music videos) off MTV (her cable system had MTV; Madison's didn't yet), onto VHS cassettes to watch at home with my music buddies.

And for a while, *Friday Night Videos* was appointment viewing. The one-hour NBC show was a new video showcase. Each week, it would culminate in a vote (via land line!) to determine whether the reigning favorite would retain its crown or lose it to a hot newcomer.

So it shouldn't be surprising that when my family visited Grandpa Hines in Washington State in April, 1983, I tuned in (three hours early) to *Friday Night Videos*. Frank and Robbie eagerly joined me. And while we were getting brainwashed, Mom, Dad, and Grandpa sat in the kitchen and talked. The subject they skirted was my Nana Edie, who had passed away four years earlier. I wondered how my grandfather could continue to live in a house full of memories of her. Now it was just him, his German shepherd Duke, and his copies of *Ring*, the boxing monthly; and once in a while a visit from his children and grandchildren.

After the fun video of a then-current favorite of mine, the Human League's "Fascination," we were treated to that week's featured video, promoting David Bowie's latest hit, "Let's Dance." The sound of Bowie, that pop chameleon, trying on Nile Rodgers' production shoes for size, was as incongruous in the audio sphere as was, in the video, the image of a pair of ruby red dancing shoes in a desert hacienda.

In youth, one emotion quickly follows another. All you need is a new outfit, or song, or style (if you're David Bowie). The night before, there'd been a network airing of *West Side Story*. I'd seen it, but still watched with interest. Then, too, the adults talked in the kitchen; but my siblings played elsewhere, not so interested in old show tunes. During the bridal shop scene, Grandpa made light of Maria's solo, "I Feel Pretty," singing a line or two to make me laugh.

That night or the next, after *Friday Night Videos*, I retired for the night to the foldout sofa (which Nana Edie had always called a "davenport") in the traditional living room of chintz furniture that no one ever used It was unseasonably cool, but Grandpa wasn't running the heat. I had just one thin blanket; regardless, I was warm, uncomfortably so. In fact, I was burning up. I couldn't understand why, but there did seem to be a nearby source of radiant heat. I rose from the sofa to seek it out, but the further I got from the mattress, the colder it felt. As an experiment, when I returned to the sofa I removed my blanket – still warm. I wondered whether something supernatural was at work, perhaps a sign from my dead grandmother. I adopted that explanation, however unlikely it may have been, and offered a silent prayer for her. I vowed not to share this impression with anyone, and haven't until now.

The Jacksons and Mick Jagger – "State of Shock" (1984)

Like a virus, this tune compromised my defenses. It infiltrated my ears, and then my nervous system. I was exposed to it several times during its incubation phase, but not since. I'm now immune.

This is not a good song. Its only significance – and then only to me – is that I vividly recall the last time I heard it.

Michael Jackson was at the stage of life when one collects rock stars. First he acquired Paul McCartney, with whom he co-wrote and performed the insipid ballad "The Girl is Mine." (McCartney balked at Jackson's proposed refrain, *the doggone girl is mine*, but Jackson convinced him it had the right "feel." Michael was right, but it still irks me that he had the temerity to explain songwriting to *Paul McCartney*.) Soon, with the mountains of cash he'd earned from *Thriller*, Jackson bought the Beatles' songwriting catalog at auction.

Having bagged a Beatle, Michael set his sights on Rolling Stone Mick Jagger. He co-wrote this song with him, if that's the right term for one long, abrasive, mind-numbing riff. It's the sort of thing that used to work for the Stones, but here it sounds like Michael is crashing a party. (Then again, I always preferred the Beatles to the Stones.)

The night before high school graduation, my orange VW Beetle climbed a Madison hill, easing to a stop outside a white Colonial home with stone facing. The windows were ablaze, the front porch lit. To quote a then-recent Stones' hit, I was waiting on a friend. I sat there in my first car, which Dad bought for a pittance because it was unreliable, unsafe, and smelled of gasoline. (I occasionally pushed it downhill to start the engine; the hill might come in handy.) The girl I was waiting on was one I'd thought about often, but this was the first time we'd see each other outside of school. I'd requested this interview, and she'd granted it out of pure kindness; she knew I was set to deliver the salutatorian speech the next afternoon, and probably figured I was nervous. I was, but more so about seeing her.

I didn't have to wait more than a few seconds; she must have been waiting on me. The front door opened, then the screen, and there she was in the doorway. Light streamed from inside and the porch light dimmed momentarily, as the backlighting illuminated her hair. Before she closed the door, she turned stage left (her right) to call out a quick goodbye, to her parents I imagined. I figured she was telling them that she would be back soon.

She dashed to the car in her "sailor suit." I'd seen her in it at school once or twice – it was a style then – a white, knee-length dress with a big collar, and a cornflower blue sash cinched at the waist. She reached for the passenger door handle while I sat at the wheel, not having thought to get out and open the door for her. I sensed a momentary hesitation, a squeamishness, before she settled into the passenger seat. She probably didn't want to sully her dress; perhaps it was the gasoline smell. The contrast between my beater and the elegant girl stepping into it was extreme. I'd never thought of myself as being from the wrong side of the tracks, but at that moment I was a grease monkey. I should have fetched her with a four-horse equipage, but all I had was old German engineering with scarcely more power.

After our quick hellos, she asked where we were going. I hadn't planned anything, so I said we'd just drive around. I executed a sharp U-turn, pointing the car downhill in case it stalled. From force of habit, I turned on the radio to an FM station I listened to.

"State of Shock" blared forth. Not quite the mood I wanted to set! My companion grimaced. She knew the song, and didn't like it at all. That was all I needed to know – I turned it off, and haven't heard it since.

She did like Michael Jackson's music. I recall a day in study hall, in the cafeteria, when she and a gal pal sat with me. They talked about drama class, and the musical they were rehearsing. At one point, her friend mentioned that during the performance, she would be lifted aloft by a handsome boy in our class – evidently one of drama's perks. Then they talked about Jackson's then-current hit, "P.Y.T. (Pretty Young Thing)," which they both liked. Even I had to admit it was catchy, thanks to the wizardry of the producer, Quincy Jones.

But on the whole, I didn't like Jackson. He was no "King of Pop" to me. And as for "State of Shock," my friend was definitely right. After I extinguished the radio, we talked a long while about everything under the stars except music.

R.E.M. – "Camera" (1985)

To truly appreciate something, encounter it anew.

In my mid-twenties I knew a gal, a junior manager at a financial firm who was working her first post-college job. To make ends meet, she lived with another gal, a musician, with whom she'd gone to school. Like many twenty-somethings taking dead aim at life, they hoped to live near the cultural opportunities of the City, so they rented an apartment in a gritty blue-collar enclave.

Meanwhile, I lived in amber. My peers, like the young of most species, fanned out and begin new lives, but I stayed put and marked time, listening to music and developing memories that have persisted like photographs. I lived in suburbia with my parents, a world away from my friends' new apartment, though it was just a forty-five minute drive. Exactly forty-five: I know because one day, leaving my parents' driveway, I popped in a recording of Rachmaninoff's Third Symphony, which neatly fit on one side of a C90 cassette.

As its final A minor chord resounded, I parked the car and spotted a former classmate and mutual friend. We walked together to the entrance of the apartment building, where the musician buzzed us in. On the threshold, I told the musician about my drive, and how long it had taken, and she confirmed that Rachmaninoff's Third Symphony was indeed forty-five minutes long. She knew, because she was a harpist.

We spent the afternoon and evening in conversation while the sun slowly subtended the living room windows. In a bulky stand near one wall, the harp dominated the room. I rose at one point to take the measure of its bulk, and the complex arrangement of its varicolored strings, but mostly I sat with my friends on the sofa. Joss sticks, the kind that mask the smell of marijuana, perfumed the air, but (at least during my stay) no weed was smoked. The gals spoke of work, poking fun at their bosses, levelling some mirth at one whose name, inappropriately enough, was "Dick." The whole time, the harpist played albums on a stereo, cuing a new one as soon as the preceding one ended.

One album attracted my particular attention. I didn't notice it at first because the harpist and I were engaged in music talk. I mentioned the punk band Hüsker Dü (in Norwegian, it means "do you remember"), who had just released an album that I liked, one less cacophonous than their earlier efforts. The harpist said her erstwhile college roommate sometimes played a Hüsker Dü song inspired by the real-life stalking and murder of a waitress in Minnesota. The song was "Diane"; that was her name, too. I said I didn't know the song, as I didn't like the band's early music, which was played at breakneck speed without much regard for melody. The harpist, smiling, said that whenever the lead singer of the song snarled her name, he did it in a drawn-out wail, making it sound like "dying." What a gruesome thought! And how strange that she should relate this story with a smile. These young gals had thicker skins than I.

A new song began, a ballad. It kept halting, as if the band were in the process of learning it. It slowly moved to the foreground of my attention. Actually, it must have been there a while, lying in wait like Diane's stalker, because when the chorus returned, I realized I was anticipating it. I had unconsciously absorbed its lyrics:

> *From the inside room, when the front room greeting*
> *Becomes your special book*
> *It was simple then*
> *When the party lulls, if we fall by the side*
> *Will you be remembered? Will she be remembered?*

It perfectly described the scene I was in: rooms, friends, books, music, memory.

The conversation dwindled. Either the party had lost steam, or I was the problem, my mind being elsewhere. All I could think was that I knew this song from somewhere... where? I couldn't even place the band. I wanted to ask the harpist, but she'd left the room. I asked her roommate, who didn't know; she helpfully offered to ask the harpist when she returned.

The song spoke of the inevitability of being an outsider, even among friends. But it was consolatory.

When the harpist returned, she told me we were listening to side B of *Reckoning*, R.E.M.'s second album. The song was "Camera."

I owned that album. In fact, I'd listened to it several times, but never had it registered like on that day. I grew quiet. Soon my friends walked me to my car, and I drove home lost in thought.

XTC – "Dear God" (1986)

Having persuaded the administration of Princeton University that a one-year leave of absence was in the best interest of all concerned (I barely recall the interview with the Dean of my residential college, so I must have been nervous), I was free to enjoy the summer of 1986 in a sundappled haze of well-being.

Sundays were the exception. That was the day that my former high school mates would assemble for a game of softball at the Shunpike Avenue fields. But that summer, each Sunday at about noon, rain would sweep in; an hour later, the infield would be a quagmire and the outfield a swamp. Even if anyone showed up, any softball we would have used, even one fresh from a box purchased at Alfred's Sport Shop, would have had a short lifespan. Yet another game was canceled.

But one Sunday, the sun stayed true. The grapevine was activated, and we had players galore. Some were former upperclassmen, whom I hadn't seen since days when I would dart through their shadows in high school hallways, shuddering as the temperature dropped precipitously. Many still lived locally, having found jobs with fathers, uncles, and cousins at gas stations and family businesses. We had enough players to field eight defensive positions a side, leaving just right field vacant (hence an automatic out).

That day, we played for hours. Guys returned frequently to the ice chests full of Rolling Rock and Bud, but I abstained to stay sharp. With time, players reaction times' dropped; bottles lined the infield, and at bats took longer. At one point I stroked a ball to deep centerfield: I tore round the bases like a madman to complete a home run (needlessly, for the outfielders had long since given up on the ball). And all afternoon, a boombox sat between third and short, where infield dirt met outfield grass. It played WNEW-FM, pure classic rock – Skynyrd, Zeppelin, the Doobies, and so forth. I paid little heed, focused on the game.

A girl began to sing. She sounded no older than ten. Her whiny, sing-song voice was accompanied only by acoustic guitar:

> Dear God, hope you got the letter and
> I pray you can make it better down here
> I don't mean a big reduction in the price of beer

How fitting, given the overindulgence all around me!

That wasn't the first time I'd heard "Dear God," which had been released a few weeks earlier, but it was the first time I'd heard it in its entirety. And hearing it from the shortstop position of our softball field was as incongruous as hearing my name on Yankee Stadium's public address system, announced by the stentorian voice of Bob Shepherd. With this song playing, I wondered how anyone could focus on the game. And so yet again I was made aware of the wide gulf between my perception of music and that of others. I was probably the only player marveling at a song not about those classic rock's trinity – cars, weed, girls – but rather God's ontology:

> *Did you make disease and the diamond blue?*
> *Did you make mankind after we made you?*

This song bothered me a long while. I'd skip it when listening to *Skylarking*, the album on which it appears, or at least I'd skip its final verse, which is accompanied by a strident rhythm and lyrics that seemed to me to be overly dismissive of the possibility of God's existence in a world full of evil. It sounded like the curdled anger of an atheist, not the humanist I knew songwriter Andy Partridge to be from his other compositions. It was certainly out of place on an album that otherwise, as Partridge said in interviews, was like "a summer's day baked into a cake." It made sense to me that the band had originally pegged the track as a B-side; it got on the album only after radio stations began receiving requests for it. In a sense, this song was the threatening weather that didn't fit the idyllic summer of '86.

And I was the canary in the (diamond) coalmine; no one but me heard this song's warning. They played and drank, and the next rock classic blared forth. But other canaries in other coalmines did: Partridge got bags of hate mail; record stores boycotted the album; and a troubled Binghamton, New York high school student made the news after holding a faculty member at knife-point until his school played "Dear God" over its PA.

All of which left Partridge aghast. In later interviews, he admitted that doing justice to such a weighty topic in a three-minute pop song was well-nigh impossible. That day, I was the only one to notice how he had fallen short of the mark.

The Smithereens, "Behind a Wall of Sleep" (1986)

Life's greatest disappointment? The inability to understand a moment's importance. If we could appreciate events as they unfolded, wouldn't *that* be the life?

I didn't date as a teen (if I had, this book would be quite different), but I was asked from time to time. One day, on the way to class in D Hall, a girl proposed a double date at the Florham Park Roller Rink; and twice I was asked to "Sadie Hawkins" dances. I always said no, utilizing a series of rationalizations that can be traced to a common ancestor, fear. Fear of entanglement; fear of losing my ego, fear of giving myself away.

But one girl in my class was unfazed by my intransigence. More interested in me as a pal than as a boyfriend, she worked hard to strike up a friendship. We had music in common; and once as we walked down E Hall she said she liked the way I sighed. Only from her could I bear such a remark with equanimity. We went out casually a couple of times, with others, and she always kept me under her wing so I wouldn't feel awkward. I owed her much, though of course I didn't appreciate it then.

We kept in touch after graduation. At the Madison Theater, we saw *Out of Africa*, the autobiographical Isak Dinesen love story starring Robert Redford and Meryl Streep. Afterwards, I told her that though I'd found the movie pleasant (actually, too long), I couldn't fathom the characters' motivations. She looked at me oddly, taken aback by my lack of empathy. My friend finished college, and then went overseas.

When she returned to the U.S., she even tried – again, something I see only in retrospect – to set me up with a friend. The three of us went driving one night, my friend at the wheel, me in the passenger seat, her friend in back. While the gals chatted, I absentmindedly flipped on the radio: it was playing the Traveling Wilburies' "Handle With Care," a recent hit. My friend didn't recognize it.

"What is this?" she asked.

The gal in back was amused. "The Traveling Wilburies!"

"Who's that?" my friend asked.

"You don't know the Traveling Wilburies? George Harrison, Bob Dylan, Roy Orbison, and...." She hesitated.

"Jeff Lynne!" I chimed in.

"Yeah, Jeff Lynne!"

Now it was my friend's turn to be amused. Not only had she missed that big hit, but she didn't know that that particular constellation of talent had ever formed from the stardust of rock 'n roll. Apparently the band's renown had not followed them overseas.

We later drove to the Nautilus Diner for something sweet. At a table in the large, well-lit dining room to the right of the entrance, the gals ordered calorie-laden desserts, the kind I normally crave. But for some reason that night I was a contrarian, and stuck to a small ice cream parfait. My friend shook her head. Why the diet? *Mangia!*

The summer of 1990, my friend invited me to the New England house she lived in with other grad students. I accepted, not thinking what I might be committing to, happy to have several hours in a car during which I could share cassette recordings of recent discoveries. Among these was an album by a New Jersey band, The Smithereens. When I mentioned their name, a flash of recognition lit up my friend's face: she'd met one of the band members! That is, she had a girlfriend upon whose couch the musician in question would crash, and on one visit to her friend's place, the musician groggily walked into the room wearing only his underpants, coffee cup in hand. I laughed, somewhat embarrassed, and cued up more music. (I can always cue up more music.) I played The Smithereens' "Behind the Wall of Sleep," a propulsive rocker with a strong bass accompaniment.

The song was from the band's major-label debut, *Especially For You*, which I'd bought on impulse at a Los Angeles record store, knowing nothing else about the band. It turned out to be one of my great blind discoveries. It's a song about romantic obsession:

> *She had hair like Jeannie Shrimpton back in 1965*
> *She had legs that never ended, I was halfway paralyzed*

Then it continues:

> *She held a bass guitar and she was playing in a band*
> *And she stood just like Bill Wyman, now I am her biggest fan*

At this point, my friend, listening in the passenger seat while I drove, turned and asked, "who's Bill Wyman?"

"You don't know?" I was incredulous. "The bass player for the Rolling Stones."

"Oh," she smiled. "Right."

She was a musician. She'd played in a band. And she had seen way more concerts than I had. Was she putting me on?

Once at our destination, she showed me around. The last of her housemates was clearing out for summer vacation, so we would have the place to ourselves. I noticed that the housemate had left behind, against the base of a bedroom wall, a large framed black-and-white photo of two female nudes in some sort of yoga position. Very artsy, I thought.

I stayed for the weekend. Naturally, I checked out the local radio stations. There was a radio on the living room mantelpiece that I tuned to a modern rock station that played lots of interesting new stuff: on it I discovered Jellyfish, a band that would become a favorite. Their song "The King Is Half Undressed," is what enables me to pinpoint the time as the summer of 1990. I thought the song quite cool, but my friend thought it was juvenile.

We saw the sights. At an outdoor farmer's market, we gathered ingredients for a homecooked dinner, which we ate, incongruously, at a table that could have seated ten. It was the only piece of furniture in a hundred-year-old formal dining room that was empty now that her housemates had gone. At this point, things took a turn for the worse: I made a lame joke that my friend took exception to. (In retrospect, she was right to get upset; it was a reflexive, chauvinistic remark.) To cool her anger, she got on a long phone call with a friend. Bored, I went to the room where I would sleep. I was exhausted, and before I knew it, I was asleep atop the still-made bed, fully dressed, my head on the pillow that my friend had jokingly promised I could "have my way with."

When I awoke, the light was on. My friend stood in the doorway in a robin's-egg-blue nightgown that trailed to her bare feet. She was the woman (I was going to write "girl," but she taught me in high school that after graduation, females were "women," not "girls," no matter what rock lyrics said) whom I never properly thanked for her friendship. I owed her an apology.

But I was tired. I told her so, and asked if she would mind turning off the light. Then I ducked back behind the wall of sleep.

Bruce Springsteen, "Tunnel of Love" (1987)

My favorite Bruce song, though it lacks the crunch of "Hungry Heart," the hook of "Glory Days," and the propulsion of "Born to Run." It sets a mood, though, with a memorable set of lyrics.

It all takes place at an amusement park:

Fat man sitting on a little stool
Takes the money from my hand
While his eyes take a walk all over you
Hands me the ticket, smiles, and whispers "good luck"

One Saturday, home from college, I drove to the Livingston Mall to buy the 45-rpm single. Not the album: I wasn't a Springsteen fanatic. In fact, I've never owned a Springsteen album; for me, he's one of those artists who shoots off the occasional dazzler, a firecracker crystallizing all his best qualities. At the mall I saw his album stacked several deep in bins and end-of-aisle displays, but I found the cover art off-putting: the aging (he seemed old then than he does now) rock star facing the camera, uncomfortable in a bolo tie, dark jacket, and white shirt buttoned to the neck, next to a convertible on a deserted beach. It seemed like a pose. I much preferred the 45 sleeve with its cartoony collage of five-cent ticket stubs and postcards touting the thrilling time offered by the tunnel of love.

The River, Springsteen's breakout album, came out in 1980. I was only dimly aware of it. Having no older siblings and being too young for "Born to Run," I had only AM radio to rely upon, and it had not yet jumped all over "Hungry Heart." I was at home with my parents, who had invited their friends, the Alofs, to dinner. Afterwards, while I helped wash the dishes, Mr. Alofs mentioned Springsteen's name. He told Mom and Dad that "The Boss" was going to be huge.

The Alofs weren't rockers. The husband, a jewelry salesman, looked every bit the complacent and well-fed Dutch burgher. His wife was very thin, with a permanent tan. Perhaps they'd seen a cover story of Springsteen in *Time* or *Newsweek* while they waited in a supermarket checkout aisle. Springsteen was getting great press; renowned critic Jon

Landau had written that he'd "seen the future of rock and roll, and its name is Bruce Springsteen." So be it.

But to me, Springsteen is an Easter Island statue, an icon gaining in stature with time precisely because no one quite understands it. He's the property of the generation before mine, the cool kids who were into rock before I was. And though he technically resides in my birth state of New Jersey, it's a part I don't know well, a mythic land of highways and horse farms. I wouldn't be surprised to learn, a thousand years from now when the Garden State is underwater, that Springsteen will have become a saint. Even now he's credited with miracles, saving lives at hours-long revivals at which he feeds hungry crowds fishes and loaves.

At my final job, I reported to a woman ten years my senior. She and some of her peers lived near Bruce, and revered him. These were unsentimental, no-nonsense women. But they had grown up in central New Jersey at a time when no one believed that a vintage rocker could come from that terroir. He and they had ripened together, and they had developed a taste for the skinny punk kid from Freehold who'd grown up a latchkey child to become a legend. He was the stray dog who'd won best in show, the one who preached salvation through sex in "Prove It All Night," the one who in "Born to Run" told Wendy to:

Wrap your legs 'round these velvet rims
And strap your hands 'cross my engines

Sure, "tunnel of love" was a sex metaphor. But that's just part of it, Bruce was saying now in 1987:

And you've got to learn to live with what you can't rise above
If you want to ride on down through this tunnel of love

That is, everything that matters comes later.

Jill Sobule – *"Lucy at the Gym" (1997, 2000)*

Having hitched my horses to the family wagon, I set off on a seventy-mile trek to buy two months of supplies at the nearest bulk dry goods provisioner.

That is, I was making the bimonthly Costco run, an hour each way from our backwater burg. This time I was on my own, so it was like old times: I boosted the car stereo to a level that would have made my wife fear for my hearing.

At one point, the shuffle dialed up "Lucy at the Gym." And as soon as I heard its initial strums, a jolt of electricity coursed through me. Taking my eyes from the road to examine what was happening, I watched my arms and legs pop with goosebumps. Large ones, too, no mere pinpricks! I wondered at my fifty-five-year-old body – how could it call forth such a response? Goosebumps are a definitive proof of the power of music.

Even more so is music's hold on the memory.

A Sunday night in 1997. I was thirty-one, in bed in my childhood bedroom. My father had passed away a year earlier. I was listening in pajamas to Vin Scelsa's *Idiots' Delight*, the last free-form program on New York City's commercial dial, which played on my old clock radio.

I'd rearranged the room since Dad's death. The bed now faced away from the windows, oriented opposite to all the years before. (The word "orient" calls forth an odd memory of a time when Mom was working a crossword. She was stuck on the clue "bright": Dad suggested "orient." Mom didn't buy it, but Dad insisted. She looked it up and he was right, something Dad never let her forget.)

The clock radio that had been on Dad's homemade built-in bookshelves now sat by my bed, on a little end table. Was Dad's death the fulcrum by which I measured time? Would it always be B.D. and A.D.? Perhaps I'd rearranged my room to memorialize this division; perhaps I'd lost the patience to cross the room to turn off the radio.

Vin's guest was Jill Sobule. I owned two of her albums; she was in the studio to promote her latest, *Happy Town*. One of its songs, "When My Ship Comes In," was an upbeat number in the style of Ramsey Lewis. After Vin played the studio recording, Jill explained how, during the recording, her kid brother, who was part of the group doing backing vocals, had so much fun singing a vulgarity in place of the word "ship" that she kept breaking up laughing.

Jill then picked up her acoustic to play a new song, one she'd just written but had yet to record. She cleared her throat, then began. The song was the one I was listening to now in the car, one that could make time stand still and generate goosebumps.

It concerned something that to my knowledge had never before been set to song – an anorexic young woman's compulsion to exercise. It's told from the point of view of the singer. Whenever she hits the gym (which isn't often), she sees Lucy pedaling furiously, watching the clock, getting up only to weigh herself.

In the final verse, the singer realizes that, this time, Lucy isn't there. She immediately suspects the worst, that Lucy has met her maker. And she pictures Lucy being shown around a gleaming, new, heavenly gym where:

> *Everyone is beautiful and thin*
> *And no one has any sins*
> *And life can begin*

Jill finished singing, strumming a last few chords. After a long, audible silence, Vin offered an insufficient compliment: "You certainly find interesting topics to write about." But I was floored.

***

We met twenty-five years later. Jill was headlining a singer-songwriter workshop in my new hometown, far from the centers of culture where she usually played. As part of the closing ceremonies, she played a general admission show in the ballroom of my town's signature hotel.

Afterward, while Jill posed for photos on the temporary stage from which she had performed, I saw something that seemed to happen in slow motion: the photographer, having chosen the rear stage curtain as a backdrop, had Jill stand by it; she shifted her weight to it; then she nearly crashed through the curtain, which had no support. Only the quickwittedness of the festival organizer, who stuck out his arm and caught her, saved her a precipitous fall.

She took a moment to regain her composure, then stepped down from the stage to greet the fans who had queued up to say hello.

When I got to the head of the line, I threw caution to the wind. I launched right into the memory of that night long ago when I heard her play on the radio in my lonely room. And unlike (I fancied) her reactions to other fans, she seemed to take particular note of what I said.

"Yes, I remember!" she said, screwing up her eyes. "That must have been... let's see... 1997?"

I nodded, then helped her to place some supporting details. When I reminded her of her kid brother's antics, she laughed. We then shook hands and went on with life.

***

Such brief yet vital connections happen whenever and wherever music plays – even if only in one's head. To adopt another metaphor, music is a lighthouse: it orients us in time, demarcates the past, and fixes the shoals of shadowy memory.

Music is also a link to others. I have little in common with Jill Sobule, a professional artist/activist whose only hit was about kissing a girl. But one day she went to the gym, made an observation, and embedded it in a song that has never stopped resonating with me.

Like my brother said, songs are miracles. They remind you not only where you were when you heard them, but what you were thinking, and also *how you felt*. That is the magic of song – it transports you through time.

You have reached the end of Side B.
To listen to Side A, please turn over the book.

Lightning Source LLC
Chambersburg PA
CBHW021927290426
44108CB00012B/749